THE ONE YEAR®
WOMEN
IN CHRISTIAN
HISTORY
devotional

THE ONE YEAR®
WOMEN
IN CHRISTIAN
HISTORY
devotional

Daily Inspirations from God's Work in the Lives of Women

RANDY PETERSEN
ROBIN SHREEVES

Tyndale House Publishers, Inc.
Carol Stream, Illinois

Visit Tyndale online at www.tyndale.com.

TYNDALE, Tyndale's quill logo, The One Year, and One Year are registered trademarks of Tyndale House Publishers, Inc. The One Year logo is a trademark of Tyndale House Publishers, Inc.

The One Year Women in Christian History Devotional: Daily Inspirations from God's Work in the Lives of Women

Designed by Jennifer Phelps

Citations for portions of text taken from other sources appear at the end of the book and are noted by devotional date and the last words of the quoted material.

Printed in the United States of America

ISBN 978-1-4143-6934-1

20   19   18   17   16   15   14
7   6   5   4   3   2   1

CONTENTS

FEBRUARY 2, 3, 4: Monica
FEBRUARY 5: Motherhood
FEBRUARY 6: Anthusa
FEBRUARY 7: Macrina
FEBRUARY 8: Olympias
FEBRUARY 9: Marcella
FEBRUARY 10: Galla Placidia
FEBRUARY 11: Clotilde

WOMEN OF THE MEDIEVAL CHURCH
FEBRUARY 12: Heloise
FEBRUARY 13: Bertha of Kent
FEBRUARY 14: Love Letters
FEBRUARY 15, 16: Hilda of Whitby & Caedmon
FEBRUARY 17, 18: Hrosvitha
FEBRUARY 19: Empress Theodora
FEBRUARY 20: Kassia
FEBRUARY 21: Clare of Assisi
FEBRUARY 22: Caring
FEBRUARY 23: Radegunde
FEBRUARY 24: Margaret of Scotland
FEBRUARY 25: Marie de France
FEBRUARY 26: Hildegard of Bingen
FEBRUARY 27: Eleanor of Aquitaine
FEBRUARY 28: Gertrude
MARCH 1: Devotion
MARCH 2, 3: Julian of Norwich
MARCH 4: Marjery Kempe
MARCH 5: Marjery Kempe & Julian of Norwich
MARCH 6, 7, 8: Catherine of Siena
MARCH 9: Blanche of Castile
MARCH 10: Angela Merici
MARCH 11: Christine de Pizan
MARCH 12, 13: Joan of Arc
MARCH 14: Catherine of Genoa
MARCH 15: Women in the Pre-Reformation Movements
MARCH 16: Marguerite Porete
MARCH 17: Brigid
MARCH 18: Bridget of Sweden

WOMEN IN JESUS' MINISTRY
MARCH 19: Mary of Bethany
MARCH 20: Martha
MARCH 21: The Syrophoenician Woman
MARCH 22: Salome

MARCH 23: Joanna

MARCH 24: The Woman with a Bleeding Problem

MARCH 25: The Woman at the Well

MARCH 26: The Woman who Anointed Jesus' Feet

MARCH 27: Pilate's Wife

MARCH 28: Female Disciples

MARCH 29: The Woman Caught in Adultery

MARCH 30: Women in Jesus' Parables

MARCH 31: The Widow of Nain

APRIL 1: On the Value Jesus Placed on Women

APRIL 2: Peter's Mother-in-Law

APRIL 3: Veronica

APRIL 4: Mary the Mother of Mark

APRIL 5, 6, 7: Mary Magdalene

APRIL 8, 9, 10, 11, 12, 13: Jesus' Mother, Mary

APRIL 14: On the Importance of Women at Jesus' Tomb

WOMEN OF THE REFORMATION ERA

APRIL 15: Idelette Calvin

APRIL 16, 17, 18: Teresa of Avila

APRIL 19, 20, 21: Katharina von Bora

APRIL 22: God's Green Earth

APRIL 23: Marguerite of Navarre

APRIL 24, 25: Jeanne d'Albret

APRIL 26: Elizabeth Barton

APRIL 27: Anne Boleyn

APRIL 28: Lady Jane Grey

APRIL 29, 30: Queen Elizabeth I

MAY 1: Argula von Grumbach

MAY 2: Anne Askew

MAY 3: Katharina Zell

MAY 4: Mary Queen of Scots

MAY 5: Keepers of the Faith

MAY 6: Jacqueline-Marie-Angélique Arnauld

MAY 7: Marguerite Marie Alacoque

MAY 8: Queen Anne

MAY 9, 10, 11: Susanna Wesley

MAY 12: Anne Hutchinson

MAY 13: Mary Dyer

MAY 14, 15, 16: Madame Guyon

MAY 17: Katharina von Schlegel

MAY 18: Mary Fisher

MAY 19, 20: Anne Bradstreet

MAY 21: "Mary" Bunyan

MAY 22: Elizabeth Bunyan

MAY 23: Elizabeth Hooten
MAY 24: Margaret Fell
MAY 25: Juana Inés de la Cruz

WOMEN OF THE ENLIGHTENMENT ERA

MAY 26, 27: Sarah Edwards
MAY 28: Hannah More
MAY 29: Barbara Heck
MAY 30: Lady Selina Hastings
MAY 31: Women Preachers in New Denominations
JUNE 1: Bathsheba Kingsley
JUNE 2: Sarah Osborn
JUNE 3: Mary Rowlandson
JUNE 4: Phyllis Wheatley
JUNE 5: Hannah Adams
JUNE 6: Elizabeth Ka'ahumanu
JUNE 7: Anne Dutton
JUNE 8: Sarah Crosby
JUNE 9: Elizabeth Ann Seton
JUNE 10: Isabella Graham
JUNE 11: Ann Lee

WOMEN OF THE MISSIONARY ERA

JUNE 12, 13: Ann Judson
JUNE 14: Betsy Ross
JUNE 15: Henriette Odin Feller
JUNE 16, 17, 18: Elizabeth Fry
JUNE 19: Dorothy Carey
JUNE 20: Ellen G. White
JUNE 21, 22: Susan & Anna Warner
JUNE 23: Phoebe Palmer
JUNE 24, 25, 26: Emily Dickinson
JUNE 27: Hannah Whitall Smith
JUNE 28: Ella Wheeler Wilcox
JUNE 29: Jane Borthwick
JUNE 30: The Poetic Voice
JULY 1, 2, 3: Fanny Crosby
JULY 4: Julia Ward Howe
JULY 5: Harriet Beecher Stowe
JULY 6: Elizabeth Payson Prentiss
JULY 7, 8: Catherine Booth
JULY 9: Evangeline Booth
JULY 10: Angelina Grimke
JULY 11: Elizabeth Blackwell
JULY 12: Eliza Shirley

JULY 13: Jarena Lee

JULY 14, 15, 16: Frances Ridley Havergal

JULY 17: Frances Willard

JULY 18: Sojourner Truth

JULY 19: Sarah Adams

JULY 20: Mary Lyon

JULY 21: Mary Ann Paton

JULY 22: Anna Shaw

JULY 23, 24: Lottie Moon

JULY 25: Abigail Roberts

JULY 26: Josephine Butler

JULY 27: Harriet Winslow

JULY 28: Nancy Gove Cram

JULY 29: Antoinette Louise Brown Blackwell

JULY 30: Harriet Newell

JULY 31: Women and the Missionary Impulse of the 1800s

LESSONS FROM HYMNS PENNED BY WOMEN

AUGUST 1: Cecil Alexander, "Jesus Calls Us"

AUGUST 2: Carolina Sandell Berg, "Day by Day"

AUGUST 3: Margaret Clarkson, "So Send I You"

AUGUST 4: Charlotte Elliott, "Just As I Am"

AUGUST 5: Annie Flint, "He Giveth More Grace"

AUGUST 6: Melody Green, "There Is a Redeemer"

AUGUST 7: Eliza Hewitt, "When We All Get to Heaven"

AUGUST 8: Lydia Baxter, "The Gate Ajar for Me"

AUGUST 9: Carrie Breck, "Face to Face"

AUGUST 10: Darlene Zschech, "Shout to the Lord"

AUGUST 11: Elizabeth Clephene, "The Ninety and Nine"

AUGUST 12: Eleanor Farjeon, "Morning Has Broken"

AUGUST 13: Gloria Gaither, "Because He Lives"

AUGUST 14: Dora Greenwell, "I Am Not Skilled to Understand"

AUGUST 15: Elvina Hall, "Jesus Paid It All"

AUGUST 16: Clara H. Scott, "Open My Eyes, That I May See"

AUGUST 17: Annie Hawks, "I Need Thee Every Hour"

AUGUST 18: Katherine Hankey, "Tell Me the Old, Old Story"

AUGUST 19: Julia H. Johnston, "Grace Greater Than Our Sin"

AUGUST 20: Helen Howarth Lemmel, "Turn Your Eyes upon Jesus"

AUGUST 21: Twila Paris, "We Will Glorify"

AUGUST 22: Civilla D. Martin, "God Will Take Care of You"

AUGUST 23: Audrey Mieir, "His Name Is Wonderful"

AUGUST 24: Rhea Miller, "I'd Rather Have Jesus"

AUGUST 25: Carol Owens, "Freely, Freely"

AUGUST 26: Adelaide Addison Pollard, "Have Thine Own Way"

AUGUST 27: Leila Naylor Morris, "Let Jesus Come into Your Heart"

AUGUST 28: Priscilla Owens, "We Have an Anchor"
AUGUST 29: Louisa Stead, "'Tis So Sweet to Trust in Jesus"
AUGUST 30: Mary Artemisia Lathbury, "Break Thou the Bread of Life"
AUGUST 31: Kate B. Wilkinson, "May the Mind of Christ My Savior"

WOMEN OF THE MODERN ERA (1900–1970)
SEPTEMBER 1: Jessie Ames
SEPTEMBER 2: Dorothy Day
SEPTEMBER 3, 4, 5: Gladys Aylward
SEPTEMBER 6: Aimee Semple McPherson
SEPTEMBER 7: Isabella Lilias Trotter
SEPTEMBER 8, 9: Ida Scudder
SEPTEMBER 10: Evelyn Brand
SEPTEMBER 11: Lisa Beamer
SEPTEMBER 12, 13: Amy Carmichael
SEPTEMBER 14: Carrie Judd Montgomery
SEPTEMBER 15: Mary McLeod Bethune
SEPTEMBER 16: Kathleen Kenyon
SEPTEMBER 17: Corrie ten Boom
SEPTEMBER 18: Mildred Cable, Evangeline French, & Francesca French
SEPTEMBER 19: Agnes Ozman
SEPTEMBER 20: Lettie Cowman
SEPTEMBER 21: Coretta Scott King
SEPTEMBER 22: Ethel Waters
SEPTEMBER 23: Rosa Parks
SEPTEMBER 24: Grace Noll Crowell
SEPTEMBER 25: Katharine Drexel
SEPTEMBER 26: Katharine Bushnell
SEPTEMBER 27: Henrietta Mears
SEPTEMBER 28: Betty Stam
SEPTEMBER 29: Duk Ji Choi
SEPTEMBER 30: The Changing Face of Church Leadership
OCTOBER 1, 2, 3: Mother Teresa
OCTOBER 4: Ruth Bell Graham
OCTOBER 5: Joni Eareckson Tada

WRITERS' CORNER
OCTOBER 6: Elisabeth Elliott
OCTOBER 7: Elizabeth O'Connor
OCTOBER 8: Laura Ingalls Wilder
OCTOBER 9: Louisa May Alcott
OCTOBER 10: Catherine Marshall
OCTOBER 11: Evelyn Underhill
OCTOBER 12: Madeleine L'Engle
OCTOBER 13: Simone Weil

OCTOBER 14: Dorothy Sayers
OCTOBER 15: Flannery O'Connor
OCTOBER 16: Gracia Burnham
OCTOBER 17: Modern Young Women of Faith
OCTOBER 18: Martha Williamson & Roman Downey

ASSORTED LESSONS FROM WOMEN THROUGHOUT HISTORY
OCTOBER 19: Mathilda Wrede
OCTOBER 20: Clara Swain
OCTOBER 21: Catharine Beecher
OCTOBER 22: Rebecca Cox Jackson
OCTOBER 23: Mary Slessor
OCTOBER 24: Mechthild of Magdeburg
OCTOBER 25: Faltonia Proba
OCTOBER 26: Mahalia Jackson
OCTOBER 27: Edith Schaeffer
OCTOBER 28: Anne of Bohemia
OCTOBER 29: Phoebe P. Knapp
OCTOBER 30: Augusta Pulcheria
OCTOBER 31: Women of the Reformation
NOVEMBER 1: The Extraordinary Ministry of Ordinary Women
NOVEMBER 2: Georgia Harkness
NOVEMBER 3: Maggie Kuhn
NOVEMBER 4: Thérèse of Lisieux
NOVEMBER 5: Helen Kim
NOVEMBER 6: Bernadette Soubirous
NOVEMBER 7: Genevieve
NOVEMBER 8: Patricia St. John
NOVEMBER 9: Marie B. Woodworth-Etter
NOVEMBER 10: Eva Burrows
NOVEMBER 11: Florence Nightingale
NOVEMBER 12: Pandita Ramabai
NOVEMBER 13: Eudokia of Heliopolis
NOVEMBER 14: Olympia Brown
NOVEMBER 15: Lucy Peabody & Helen Barrett Montgomery

WOMEN WE'RE THANKFUL FOR
NOVEMBER 16: Queen Victoria
NOVEMBER 17: Egeria
NOVEMBER 18: Rebecca Protten
NOVEMBER 19: Gertrude Chambers
NOVEMBER 20: Polly Newton
NOVEMBER 21: Eva von Tiele-Winckler
NOVEMBER 22: Anne Piggot
NOVEMBER 23: Lucy Farrow

INTRODUCTION

The news of Jesus' resurrection came first to women. And women were in the room at Pentecost—leading Peter to quote the prophetic word that "your sons *and daughters* will prophesy." Historians tell us that the caring ministry of women helped the early church grow, even as it was being persecuted. "What women these Christians have!" exclaimed one fourth-century pagan.

Ever since, at the key junctures of Christian history, women have been there—teaching, healing, writing, praying, nurturing, inspiring, and so on. They have shared their unique gifts with the church, sometimes overcoming great obstacles to do so. This book is a celebration of their work, an examination of their faith, and a challenge to all readers.

One caution: while going through this book, you might find yourself saying, "What's *she* doing in here?" We may have included women associated with groups or causes you disagree with, or some women you have a low opinion of. You might even doubt whether they're really Christian.

In putting together this book, we've tried to identify women who have been *significant* in Christian history. They're not perfect, and in some cases they might not even be exemplary. But we hope that our devotional writing will at least make you think, and maybe inspire you to commit yourself to God in a new way—whether following the examples of these historical women or avoiding their errors.

Let's face it. Over the centuries there have been major disagreements among Christians over the accepted role of women. Please do not see this book as an attempt to sway you to one side or the other. We simply offer you the stories of women who have made a difference in the church and in the world, and we invite you to consider how God has worked in them and through them.

And then consider how God wants to work in and through *you.*

Randy Petersen
Robin Shreeves

ON THE MOVE

Priscilla

ACTS 18; ROMANS 16:3; 1 CORINTHIANS 16:19; 2 TIMOTHY 4:19

Moving through the New Testament, you can't get far without meeting Priscilla and her husband, Aquila. They're mentioned in Acts 18 and in three different epistles. Even more amazing, we find them in three different cities. They meet Paul in Corinth. In Ephesus, they counsel the great preacher Apollos. And when Paul writes his letter to the Romans, they're already there, hosting a church in their home.

It all proves tantalizing for a biblical detective, putting together the clues to assemble a dossier on this power couple. First, we note that they are always mentioned in tandem. Whatever they did, they did together. Then we consider their names. Priscilla ("ancient") is a noble Roman family name, and Aquila ("eagle") has ties to the Roman army. We could surmise that they had some family money, and that would explain how they had a house in Rome large enough for a church. It might also suggest that they *owned* the tent-making business that temporarily employed Paul. But that's all guesswork.

We know they were forced to leave Rome when Emperor Claudius expelled the Jews in AD 49. They resettled in Corinth, and that's probably where they became Christians. They went with Paul to Ephesus, but then it seems they went back to Rome for a time.

Travel was rather easy in the first-century Roman Empire. Roads built by the Roman army were often paved, and seas were patrolled by the Roman navy, discouraging pirates. And remember that Priscilla and Aquila made tents, something bought by travelers. It would make sense for them to travel wherever the market was good. But they seemed to be guided by a different economy: Where could they do the most good for God's Kingdom? Sometimes they needed to be at Paul's side, supporting his ministry, and sometimes they needed to nurture believers in other locations.

How many times in your life have you moved? The logistics of relocating can be stressful, but this biblical couple reminds us that God can use us wherever we go. You might think that a job or a school or a family commitment has brought you to your current home, but there's a higher purpose here. God has work for you to do.

Work for the peace and prosperity of the city where I sent you.

JEREMIAH 29:7

TEACHING THE TEACHER

Priscilla

ACTS 18; ROMANS 16:3; 1 CORINTHIANS 16:19; 2 TIMOTHY 4:19

One of the curious details about Priscilla and Aquila is that she's usually named first. In a patriarchal culture, it was unusual for a woman to get top billing. Several theories have arisen to explain it. Was she better known among the Christians? Was he a later, reluctant convert? Or does this reflect that her social standing—from a patrician family of Rome—exceeded his?

At the very least, it would indicate that Priscilla was just as involved in ministry as her husband was, and perhaps more so. And that reveals an interesting dynamic in Ephesus when this couple confronted the preacher Apollos.

He was a star, "an eloquent speaker who knew the Scriptures well." Apollos came from Alexandria, a center of Jewish scholarship. "He taught others about Jesus with an enthusiastic spirit and with accuracy" (Acts 18:24-25). We know he later went to Corinth, where a number of people preferred his preaching to Paul's. He had a gift, and he used it effectively.

But there was a problem. Apollos "knew only about John's baptism" (Acts 18:25). Apparently he preached fervently about repentance, social justice, and Jesus the prophesied Messiah. Perhaps he even preached about the atoning sacrifice of Christ. But the idea of the Holy Spirit indwelling believers—this was new to him. When it came to the thought of resurrection power filling the lives of Christians, well, he wasn't there yet.

Imagine the sheer gall it would take for Priscilla and Aquila to sidle up to this renowned preacher and say, "Nice sermon, but you're missing something." Yet that is what they did. Apparently their approach was winsome enough to be accepted. Many men in that era (and ours) would find it difficult to be corrected by a woman, but perhaps Priscilla and Aquila together found a gentle way to address the issue. Apollos listened to them, and he became an even more dynamic preacher.

Should you correct every theological error you encounter? Maybe not. But can you find winsome ways to engage others in conversation about what's true? When people are presenting a partial gospel, can you gently fill in what's missing?

Paul challenges us to "speak the truth in love" (Ephesians 4:15). Clearly Priscilla and Aquila got that message.

---

*When Priscilla and Aquila heard him preaching boldly in the synagogue,
they took him aside and explained the way of God even more accurately.*

ACTS 18:26

JESUS IN THE HOUSE

Priscilla

ACTS 18; ROMANS 16:3; 1 CORINTHIANS 16:19; 2 TIMOTHY 4:19

In this age of megachurches, we often forget that the church started in people's houses. Oh, the day of Pentecost erupted with preaching to crowds, but soon afterward the converts were meeting in homes (see Acts 2:46). Throughout Acts and the Epistles, we find evidence of "house churches." There was the occasional lecture hall, but generally Christians met in rather small groups. Remember that Jesus said he would be present "where two or three gather in my name" (Matthew 18:20, NIV).

In major cities of the Roman Empire, many workers would live in tenements or shacks, but noble families would have more spacious homes. Typically the entrance to such a house would lead to an open atrium, which would be ideal for group gatherings, holding thirty, fifty, even a hundred people. The early church had a mix of socioeconomic classes: slaves, workers, public officials, and patricians. Those with bigger homes would host church meetings.

Priscilla and Aquila probably had money, whether inherited from their noble families or earned from their tent-making business. In any case, we find them hosting house churches in at least two locations—Rome and Ephesus—and maybe also in Corinth. Imagine how important this would have been for the early church—to have a home in a new community, a place to meet, a foothold.

Wealth is dangerous. Jesus often warned against trusting in money, but he also challenged us to be good stewards of what we have. This stewardship was modeled by Priscilla and Aquila, who used their substantial resources for the good of the church—supporting missionaries, hosting churches, and establishing good relationships all around.

What resources do you have, and how are you using them for God's purposes? Can you use your home for a prayer group? Could you open up a spare room for a traveling missionary? Can you use your business connections to create flexible earning opportunities for Christian ministers (as Priscilla and Aquila may have done for Paul)? Could you consider moving to a new location to start a church there (as Priscilla and Aquila did)?

Don't feel bad about what you have. Use it!

Give my greetings to Priscilla and Aquila, my co-workers in the ministry of Christ Jesus. . . . Also give my greetings to the church that meets in their home.

ROMANS 16:3, 5

STAND BY ME

Phoebe

ROMANS 16:1-2

Paul had just completed his masterwork, the Epistle to the Romans. This was as clear a statement of his theology as he could offer, rich with references to the Jewish Scriptures but showing a new way: grace rather than works, the life of God's Spirit rather than a law-addled death. And who would carry this precious cargo to the church in Rome?

Phoebe.

Paul needed someone he could trust, someone respectable enough to be well received in Rome, perhaps someone with the resources to make that journey safely. Phoebe fit the bill, according to the two verses about her that Paul added at the end of the letter.

She lived in Cenchrea, a harbor town just east of Corinth, where Paul was at the time, so the transfer of the document would be easy. Paul called her a "deacon" of the church there (Romans 16:1). This word can be a generic reference to any servant, but it took on an official meaning in the early church that it still has today. So it's possible that Paul was just saying she served that church, but he might have been using this as an official term, presenting the Romans with her résumé. In any case, she was "worthy of honor" (verse 2).

Another fascinating word describing Phoebe in Romans 16:2 is often translated "helper." In Greek, it's *prostatis*, literally "one who stands in front." This is the only time the word is used in the New Testament, but elsewhere it means "defender" or even "president." It's likely that Paul was referring to her as a supporter or patroness of his work. She "stood by him" during his ministry, or even "stood in front of him" to defend against criticism.

Where do you stand? Do you stand beside your church leaders, supporting their ministry—or do you take every opportunity to criticize? Do you stand by those people who are struggling in their faith, helping them to grow—or do you judge them? Do you stand in front of your family and friends, defending them from destructive forces—or do you sit idly by?

Maybe you could be a Phoebe.

Welcome her in the Lord as one who is worthy of honor among God's people. Help her in whatever she needs, for she has been helpful to many, and especially to me.

ROMANS 16:2

CLOTHING TIME

Dorcas

ACTS 9:36-42

Has a funeral ever surprised you? Some people live lives of such quiet devotion that no one knows how special they are—until they're gone. Then everyone steps up to tell how helpful the dearly departed soul was. "Wow," you say, as one person after another gets up to talk, "I never knew."

The funeral of Dorcas was something like that. A Christian from the town of Joppa on Israel's coast, "she was always doing kind things for others and helping the poor" (Acts 9:36). When she died, her friends sent for the apostle Peter, who was ministering in a nearby town.

When he came to the viewing, it must have been a surreal sight. The poor widows of the town had flocked to the funeral, and they had brought clothing Dorcas had made for them, which they showed Peter. These were their testaments to the goodness of this woman.

Caring for widows and orphans is an important part of Jewish tradition. In that culture, losing a husband usually meant losing one's income, and so the generous people of the community had to pick up the slack. But Dorcas had done more than merely give alms. She had created items of clothing, very personal gifts, for these needy ones. She wasn't just throwing money at the problem; she was using her creativity to get involved with people. No wonder they showed up at her wake.

Wake turns out to be a good word for it, because Peter prayed for a miracle and got one. After sending the mourners out of the room, he said, "Get up, Tabitha," using her Hebrew name. She sat up. Then he took her out to greet those who were weeping over her death.

How can you use your creative gifts to help others? Of course, creativity means more than singing or painting. It might mean sewing seams or running meetings or tending children or managing budgets. God has dished out all sorts of abilities that we use to build our own homes and careers. But every gift he gives needs to be re-gifted. We receive his love and are to freely share it with others, especially those in need. Dorcas understood this, and as a result, she touched many lives.

The room was filled with widows who were weeping and showing him the coats and other clothes Dorcas had made for them.

ACTS 9:39

CREATIVITY

God created. What he created is so awesome that it actually speaks to us and reveals God's existence. "The heavens proclaim the glory of God," says the psalmist (19:1). Millions of stars in the sky, the roaring ocean, birds flying in perfect formation above our heads, even the lone dandelion in the middle of a green lawn all reveal something about God to those who take a moment to look and listen.

We, too, are creative because we are made in God's image. Creative expression has always been a way for God's people to share what they know about him. Words, written by Christians through the centuries and shared with others, have helped to fuel imaginations and bring a deeper understanding of who God is.

In the 1400s, when women were routinely treated as second-class citizens, Christine de Pizan used her poetry to explore the unique traits of women as created by God. Her writings brought light to an important societal issue: the status of women, which was less than God would have it be. Christine's writing influenced her generation.

Many of the familiar hymns of the church were written by women who wanted to express their faith through words and music. When Charlotte Elliott realized that she could come to God without having to fix a few things about herself first, she wrote "Just As I Am," a hymn that a hundred years later became a much-beloved altar call song at evangelistic meetings.

The immense power of love that conquers evil is a central theme of Madeleine L'Engle's, *A Wrinkle in Time*. This twentieth-century adolescent novel has been teaching youth and adults alike about the power of love for more than fifty years and continues to be at the top of YA reading lists—ensuring that its message will be spread for generations to come.

On January 6, many Christians celebrate the magi's visit to the Christ child, often with an explosion of creativity—skits and songs in Holland, practical jokes in England, music and creative cookery in many other traditions. So if you have a poem, song, story, dance, or tweet inside you, offer it up to the Lord. The Creator of your creativity will love it.

God created human beings in his own image. In the image of God
he created them; male and female he created them.

GENESIS 1:27

MOTHERS KNOW BEST

Eunice and Lois

2 TIMOTHY 1:5

When they healed a lame man, Paul and Barnabas blew the circuits of the people of the backcountry town of Lystra. *Who were these wonder workers?* There was a local legend about two gods coming through in disguise, so when Paul and Barnabas displayed divine power, they were hailed as these gods. Paul had to be Hermes, the messenger, while Barnabas was assumed to be Zeus (see Acts 14:8-20).

When the apostles finally delivered their message about Jesus the Messiah, many received it in faith—including a Jewish woman named Eunice and her mother, Lois. When Paul came back to Lystra a few years later, he connected with Eunice's son, Timothy, who was probably a teenager at this point. Paul eventually took Timothy with him as an assistant (see Acts 16:1-5).

Timothy's father was a Gentile, and he doesn't seem to be a factor in this story. Was Eunice, then, a single mom? Maybe, or maybe her husband just wanted nothing to do with her religion. In either case, it would have been a challenge—eased, no doubt, by Lois's presence.

More than a decade later, Paul wrote two epistles to Timothy, by then a young pastor in Ephesus. The apostle commends Timothy's faith, which "first filled your grandmother Lois and your mother, Eunice" (2 Timothy 1:5). Later Paul notes that Timothy had "been taught the holy Scriptures from childhood" (2 Timothy 3:15). But there was more than just Bible knowledge here. The next verses discuss how Scripture helps and equips us. Elsewhere in the same letter, Paul urges his protégé to be the kind of Christian who "correctly handles the word of truth" (2 Timothy 2:15, NIV). It seems that Timothy wasn't just drilled in the facts of Scripture; he was bathed in its truth.

Many parents make Bible education an important part of their children's lives. That's great. But we can learn something deeper from Timothy's mother and grandmother. To begin with, they themselves were filled with the faith that they passed on to this boy. It was a reality in their lives, and it became a reality in Timothy's life. That made the Scriptures more than words on a page; they were a passageway to a powerful relationship with Christ.

You have been taught the holy Scriptures from childhood, and they have given you the wisdom to receive the salvation that comes by trusting in Christ Jesus.

2 TIMOTHY 3:15

KNOCK KNOCK KNOCKING

Rhoda

ACTS 12:1-17

It's one of the funniest stories in the Bible, featuring a seemingly scatterbrained servant girl in what you might call a "situation comedy." Her name was Rhoda.

Christians were living in a tense time. While the church was growing, there was also greater persecution. James had been executed. Peter was arrested and imprisoned, awaiting the same fate. The believers met at a home in Jerusalem to pray for him.

The home belonged to Mary, the mother of Mark and thus a relative of Barnabas, as we know from Colossians 4:10. It seems she was an affluent widow originally from Cyprus, and she might have brought Rhoda from there. (There is also some speculation that the Last Supper was held in her home.)

Under high security the night before his trial, Peter felt his chains fall off. The guards were fast asleep. An angel led him out to the streets of the city. From there, Peter found his way to Mary's house and knocked at the outer gate. Enter Rhoda. Answering this middle-of-the-night knock, she was so excited to see Peter that she ran to tell the others . . . and left him out front, still knocking. Inside, the other Christians wouldn't believe her. "You're out of your mind!" they said, but she stuck to her story. Then they heard more knocking and went to see for themselves.

It was not the first time that a Christian was called crazy for delivering good news, nor would it be the last. When the women came back from the empty tomb talking about resurrection, it "sounded like nonsense" to the disciples, before Peter and John raced to the tomb to check it out (Luke 24:11). The apostle Paul, who was also called crazy, wrote that God has "used our foolish preaching to save those who believe" (1 Corinthians 1:21).

Rhoda is an early example of a courageous truth teller. She witnessed an answer to prayer and she said so, even though it was far fetched. The history of the Christian church is populated with truth tellers like this, whose simple insistence prompts others to see for themselves. We still need such truth tellers today.

This foolish plan of God is wiser than the wisest of human plans, and God's weakness is stronger than the greatest of human strength.

1 CORINTHIANS 1:25

AFRICAN QUEEN

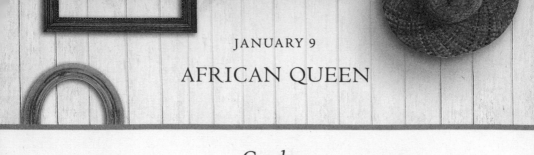

Candace

ACTS 8:26-39

Ethiopia isn't very far from the Middle East, but many ancient folks considered it the end of the earth. There were legends about fierce female warriors who lived south of Egypt's civilized society. And while the Romans conquered the Mediterranean basin, bringing a certain unity to lands from Algeria to Arabia, the Ethiopians remained outside their control, wild and free.

That makes the New Testament story of the Ethiopian eunuch especially interesting (see Acts 8:26-39). This man was the official treasurer in the court of Candace, queen of Ethiopia. Well, *Candace* (or *Kandake*) was actually a title rather than a name, something like *Pharaoh* in Egypt. The eunuch served the Kandake of Ethiopia, whose proper name was probably Amantitere.

But what was this Ethiopian doing in Jerusalem, and why did he have a scroll of the Hebrew Scriptures? More important, what happened when he got back home, after Philip baptized him?

Judaism has a long history in Ethiopia, possibly dating back to the Queen of Sheba. There's a dubious legend that Solomon fathered a child she bore, thus creating a strain of Jewish royal blood in Africa. More likely, Jews just migrated there during times of war or famine. The eunuch was probably a Jew himself, returning from a pilgrimage to Jerusalem. We might wonder if he had bought his Scripture scroll there and was taking it back to a Jewish community in Ethiopia. Otherwise, it would be strange to travel with such a rare and precious item.

According to tradition, the newly baptized eunuch returned home and evangelized many Ethiopians, including the Kandake. With royal influence, Christianity gained a strong foothold in the area. The warrior-queen had met the Prince of Peace.

In the opening verses of the book of Acts, Jesus tells his disciples that they will be witnesses for him "in Jerusalem, throughout Judea, in Samaria, and to the ends of the earth" (Acts 1:8). For seven chapters, the disciples are holed up in Jerusalem, but chapter 8 explodes outward. A revival occurs in Samaria, Philip meets a traveler on a road in Judea, and this man takes the message back to his queen in a mysterious region known by many as the end of the earth.

We are witnesses of a truth that moves ever outward.

You will be my witnesses, telling people about me everywhere—in Jerusalem, throughout Judea, in Samaria, and to the ends of the earth.

ACTS 1:8

R-E-S-P-E-C-T

Junia

ROMANS 16:7

P aul called her "highly respected among the apostles," but Junia hasn't gotten much respect from translators. To be fair, the Greek name used in Romans 16:7 could be either masculine or feminine, and thus many scholars assume that Paul was praising "Junias," a man. Yet the name is found hundreds of times in other Greek literature, and is always feminine.

The next complication concerns the phrase "among the apostles." Linguistically, this could mean merely that the apostles knew Junia and respected her. An alternate reading would include Junia (and Andronicus, probably her husband) as "apostles" themselves. This would reflect Paul's larger sense of the term *apostle*—not just the original twelve disciples or a small group of leaders, but everyone who carries the gospel to new places.

As Jews who became Christians before Paul did, this couple might have been in Jerusalem at Pentecost, when the church was born. Perhaps they were among the three thousand new believers that day. Then maybe they carried that message back home and started a church. Was that "home church" in Rome, or did they plant churches in different cities (as Paul did)? All we know is that they had been in prison with Paul at one point, possibly in Ephesus, and that they were ministering in Rome when Paul wrote his epistle.

So how important was Junia? In the modern debate about women in church leadership, she could be hailed as a female apostle or dismissed as only one of numerous women working faithfully for the church. But let's be careful about dismissing. Whether she herself was considered an apostle or not, she was still "highly respected" for the work she did.

Any debate about Christian leadership must be shaped by the upside-down nature of our faith. The humble are exalted. We follow a Master who washed feet. We lead by serving. So we could guess that Junia was not trying to win respect. She was just serving the Lord, going where he called, sharing his truth—even if that meant being thrown into prison. Christian leadership is not about fame or acclaim or titles. Humble service is what earns the lasting respect of all those who follow Christ—not just in the first century, but now as well.

Greet Andronicus and Junia, my fellow Jews, who were in prison with me. They are highly respected among the apostles and became followers of Christ before I did.

ROMANS 16:7

CAREER MOVE

Lydia

ACTS 16:11-40

S he was in sales, and business was good. No, we don't have Lydia's profit-loss statement, but all the signs are there. She came from Thyatira, a city in Asia Minor known for its purple dye. Throughout the Roman Empire, purple fabric was a luxury item, and Lydia was part of that industry. But when we meet her in Acts 16, she's in Philippi, Macedonia, far from her hometown. Was she a field rep for the purple-dye industry, opening up the European market for her Thyatira-based company? Or was she an independent merchant, taking advantage of the latest fashion trends to build her own career? We can assume she was doing pretty well, since she owned a house in Philippi large enough to host visitors.

Lydia is described as a "God worshiper" (or God fearer), the term for a Gentile who attended Jewish services. Perhaps she had connected with the synagogue back home in Thyatira, and now, in Philippi, she had sought out others who would also pray to the God of the Jews.

As Paul shared his insights about Jesus the Messiah, Lydia was apparently the first to respond. You might say she "opened up the European market" for the gospel, since she's usually considered the first Christian convert on that continent. Paul and his associates—Silas, Luke, and Timothy—were invited to stay at her home, giving them a base of operations during their stay in Philippi.

That's all we know about this businesswoman—just a few verses in Acts 16. But we know a lot more about the church she started. After Paul preached that day, Lydia *was* the Philippian church. A short while later, a jailer and his family would trust in Christ, and perhaps a former fortune-teller, but how many others joined this church in the short time Paul and his team were there? Yet, a decade later, Paul would write a joy-filled epistle to this group.

Do you think Lydia might have applied her business acumen to the growing of a new church? When God gets ahold of our lives, he changes us, but he also uses our talents and experience in a whole new way.

You have been my partners in spreading the Good News about
Christ from the time you first heard it until now.

PHILIPPIANS 1:5

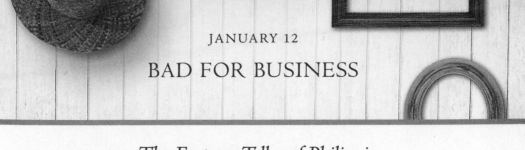

BAD FOR BUSINESS

The Fortune-Teller of Philippi

ACTS 16:16-24

Human trafficking is a shameful blight on the modern world, but there's nothing new about it. Paul and Silas encountered it in Philippi, and they responded with the power of God.

A young woman was enslaved by men and forced to tell fortunes. Clearly her slavery was spiritual as well as physical. She was demon possessed, and her handlers were using her supernatural powers to make money. The Greek text actually calls her demon a "python spirit." Such snakes were associated with magical powers and Greek gods (especially Apollo). Perhaps she even used a snake as part of her act.

It's interesting that she (or her demon) was the aggressor with Paul and Silas. They were just going to the river to pray, but she followed them, shouting that they were "servants of the Most High God" (Acts 16:17). This behavior went on for days until Paul took action, ordering the demon to leave her.

There's some light wordplay in Luke's telling of this story. In verse 18, we learn that the demon "went out" of her; in verse 19, her handlers realize that their profits just "went out" as well. The same word in Greek is used to describe both situations, and that makes sense. They were making money on her misery. Her healing was bad for their business.

We never hear about this slave girl again. Paul and Silas were taken to court, beaten, and thrown in jail, but what happened to her? Was she released from her slavery, now that she was no longer profitable? Did she become part of the church that later received Paul's epistle? Did she take it to heart when she heard, "I am certain that God, who began the good work within you, will continue his work until it is finally finished on the day when Christ Jesus returns" (Philippians 1:6)?

Look around and you'll see lots of people enslaved in various ways: spiritually, mentally, and physically. We may be called to offer them freedom, wholeness, and help in the name of Jesus Christ, but it's seldom easy. And there are some folks who won't like what Jesus does. For those who make a practice of using and abusing people, Jesus is bad for business.

She followed Paul and the rest of us, shouting, "These men are servants of the Most High God, and they have come to tell you how to be saved."

ACTS 16:17

TEAMMATES

Euodia and Syntyche
PHILIPPIANS 4:2-3

A cynic might say that Christian history is all about church fights. In the first few centuries, disputes over various heresies shaped Christian theology. Later, church splits made big news—the East-West Schism, the Protestant Reformation, the Methodist movement, Pentecostalism, etc. In each case, there have been faithful people on both sides, each side believing that the other was terribly wrong.

We see a glimpse of this in Paul's letter to the Philippians. Two women were disagreeing. We know nothing about the details of this tiff, but it was important enough for Paul to mention. We don't even know who Euodia and Syntyche were, apart from what Paul tells us. They had worked side by side with Paul in spreading the gospel, but now they were working against each other.

From clues in Acts 16, we might guess that these women were hosting or leading house churches. It's even possible that one of these women was also known as Lydia, the woman who had opened her home to the apostles on their initial visit.

Now Paul urges them to "Settle your disagreement"—literally to "be of the same mind" (Philippians 4:2). Was the dispute personal, procedural, or doctrinal? We know of other church rifts based on a Jew-Gentile division, or on policies regarding holidays or what food could be eaten, but these themes don't appear in Philippians. What does appear is the beautiful hymn to the humility of Christ in chapter 2. There, the people are urged to "be of the same mind" and to share the mind of Christ. Perhaps the Euodia-Syntyche dispute was merely a matter of "complaining and arguing" between two people who liked to get their own way (Philippians 2:14).

Note that Paul does not take sides, nor does he criticize the character of either woman. Instead, he affirms them for their past efforts. He also asks for some mediation from his "true partner" (Philippians 4:3). The Greek word he uses is *syzygus*, which could be a name, but it also means "teammate," a fellow ox pulling a plow. This could be Timothy or Epaphroditus, both mentioned already in this epistle—or it could refer to the whole church. All of us can step up and bring peace to contentious situations, affirming the contenders but also calling them to abandon their pride and to agree to pull together in the Lord's work.

Please, because you belong to the Lord, settle your disagreement.
PHILIPPIANS 4:2

OVERCOMING EXPECTATIONS

Women ran from Jesus' empty tomb with a tale of resurrection. Sadly, "the story sounded like nonsense to the men" (Luke 24:11). We learn two important things there: (1) that men don't always take women seriously, and (2) that God does. Throughout history, God has entrusted important work to women, though they've often had to fight against cultural expectations to carry it out.

Consider Perpetua, a young noblewoman, and Felicitas, her maid. Both faced brutal death before a cheering crowd. Their heroism in that arena inspired many Christians in the difficult years that followed. There were well-known male leaders of the church in that time—Origen, Tertullian, Irenaeus—but these two women captured imaginations as no one else could. No one expected them to make the ultimate sacrifice. Perpetua's own father begged her to back down—surely people would understand her family commitments—but she remained true to her faith . . . and paid the price.

Our history is full of queens and ladies who were expected merely to look pretty, bear heirs, and wave to the people. In numerous cases, these women overstepped those perceived boundaries, using their wealth and power to do good, building the church or helping the poor.

Plenty of commoners made uncommon contributions too. Joan of Arc was a poor teenager who sensed God's call and led an army—unheard of for a young girl! Phillis Wheatley was sold as a slave in colonial America but learned to read and write, becoming an influential Christian poet. An Albanian nun devoted her life to the "poorest of the poor" in Calcutta and became the world changer we know as Mother Teresa.

At a certain point, however, we run into the paradox of Christian history: *real Christians don't seek fame, just service.* That means there are vast numbers of faithful servants—women and men alike—whose names will never appear in history books, despite the great things they did.

One of them is our friend Peggy Parker, who passed away in 2010. Chances are, you've never heard of her, because she quietly served as a pastor of small Methodist churches; the devoted mother of a special-needs child; and an encourager of pretty much everyone who crossed her path . . . including us. She never cared much about people's expectations; she had work to do.

And so do we.

I can do everything through Christ, who gives me strength.

PHILIPPIANS 4:13

ON THE SPOT

Deacons Arrested by Pliny

AD 112

The governor had a problem. He didn't want to be a tyrant—and yet he had an illegal cult meeting in his district—*the Christians*. Should he crack down on this group? He wrote to the emperor for official guidance.

The police were getting lots of tips about secret Christian meetings. Some tips were just gossip, but others proved true. Officials had arrested two women who were called "deacons," apparently with some sort of responsibilities in this forbidden sect. Under torture, these women added to Governor Pliny's developing knowledge of the church.

"On a certain day they get together before dawn," he wrote to Emperor Trajan, "to offer hymns to Christ as God, and to take vows together—not to commit crimes but to *abstain* from theft, adultery, and cheating. Then they gather again to eat, and it's just ordinary, harmless food." Reading between the lines, we might understand Pliny's plight. *These are good people! Why are we arresting them?* That attitude was supported by the emperor's response—basically, "Don't bother the Christians if they don't bother you."

Consider these two anonymous women. We might assume they were simply doing their jobs when they were nabbed. Were they planning the next meeting or just cleaning up after the last one? Perhaps they were sticking around to pray with someone who proved to be a snitch. In any case, they were suddenly "on the spot," interrogated by the governor's henchmen.

Were there any secrets they needed to withhold under torture? Maybe. But it is the nature of Christianity to share freely with others, so we might guess that these women eagerly told their captors all about their weekly meetings. *We are so excited about Jesus that we can't stay away! Why don't you join us next week?*

Nowadays it's easy for Christians to feel embattled, fighting for our rights as believers, but we don't get that attitude from these two deacons. It seems that their winsome response to interrogation confirmed the good feeling that the governor (and emperor) already had about Christianity—and it might have given their fellow Christians some breathing room.

---

*In the same way, the women [wives of deacons or women who
serve as deacons] are to be worthy of respect, not malicious
talkers but temperate and trustworthy in everything.*

1 TIMOTHY 3:11, NIV

JANUARY 16

WHAT I AM

Perpetua
CA. 180–203

Perpetua was a young Christian noblewoman in Carthage around the year 200. The authorities were demanding that everyone show their loyalty by offering a sacrifice to the "divine" spirit of the Roman emperor. Devout Christians refused to do this—Jesus was their only Lord. Though she had recently given birth, Perpetua refused to sacrifice, and she was arrested.

Her father visited her in prison and begged her to recant. *Didn't she realize that Christians were being hauled off to the city arena to face wild animals or gladiators in front of bloodthirsty mobs? Wouldn't she consider her little baby or her aging papa and save herself?*

"Look at this vase," she told him, "or that pitcher. Can it be called by any other name than what it is?"

"No," he responded.

"Then I can't say I'm anything other than what I am, a Christian."

Despite the pleas of her father and brother, she stood trial before the governor and refused to perform the sacrifice. "Are you a Christian?" he asked point-blank.

"Yes, I am."

Sentenced to face the beasts in the arena, she was still "in high spirits," as observers reported. She understood this as her calling—to die for Christ. Her own diary of her arrest, imprisonment, trial, and preparation for martyrdom was widely distributed among the early Christians, inspiring many to remain faithful in tough times. (It is one of the earliest Christian documents we have written by a woman.) Of course it was another writer who added a vivid account of her death. Despite official attempts to shame and humiliate her, Perpetua stood strong to the end, even guiding the sword of a trembling gladiator to her throat.

Perpetua might ask each of us, "What are you? A Christian? A faithful servant? One who is called to honor Christ with your life—in your work, in your relationships, in your worship? If that is truly what you are, why would you let any obstacle stop you?" We often feel pressure to hide our faith from others, to deny that we know Jesus, but how can we say we're anything other than what we are: followers of Jesus?

It is no longer I who live, but Christ lives in me.

GALATIANS 2:20

INSIDE STORY

Felicitas

CA. 180–203

In the early years, some Roman critics attacked Christianity as a low-class religion, welcoming slaves and women along with noblemen. "Guilty as charged," responded the Christians, who continued to treat slaves and slave owners as equals despite the objections of snooty scribes.

So when some Christians were rounded up in Carthage around AD 200 for failing to offer a sacrifice in honor of the emperor's divine spirit, the group included both the upper-class Perpetua (see yesterday's entry) and her slave, Felicitas.

The slave girl had a problem: she was eight months pregnant. Since the Romans had a law against executing pregnant women, she worried that she might lose the opportunity to die along with her friends. Two days before their scheduled execution, the imprisoned believers prayed about this—and immediately Felicitas felt labor pains. The premature birth was difficult, but she successfully bore a daughter, who was then given to a Christian friend.

An assistant guard snidely commented on her painful delivery. "You think this is bad? Wait till you're tossed to the beasts. Should have thought of that before you refused to sacrifice."

The slave girl responded with dignity: "My current pain I suffer alone. But then, someone else will be inside me, and he will suffer for me, just as I'll be suffering for him."

Felicitas rejoiced that she could go with her friends into martyrdom, and she knew that Jesus would be with them—*inside* them—as they suffered. Yes, their experience in the arena was brutal, facing wild beasts and then gladiators, but these believers helped each other. The slave stood side by side with her mistress, and at that moment class and wealth were irrelevant. All that mattered was their devotion to Jesus.

Suffering can be a lonely ordeal, in the third century or the twenty-first. But Felicitas grasped a secret that helped her get through it, as it can help us today. Jesus suffers our sorrow with us, and he brings us ultimate joy.

My old self has been crucified with Christ. It is no longer I who live,
but Christ lives in me. So I live in this earthly body by trusting in
the Son of God, who loved me and gave himself for me.

GALATIANS 2:20

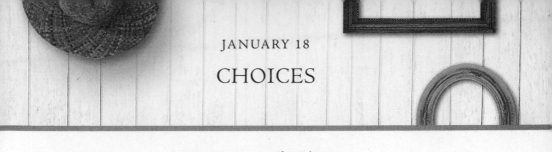

CHOICES

Perpetua and Felicitas

———— D. 203 ————

Perpetua and Felicitas were commanded to pay homage to the Roman emperor by offering a sacrifice to his "divine" spirit. As devout Christians, they clearly understood this as idolatry.

Both had good reasons to stay alive. Perpetua's father begged her to reconsider, for his sake and for her infant son. With her upper-class estate, she could possibly provide funds and meeting space for the church for years to come. Felicitas had just given birth to a daughter. Didn't she have an obligation to stay and nurture that little girl?

Many of us today would take a practical approach: compromise now on this little sacrifice in order to accomplish a greater good later. We do this in many ways in the routines of our lives. We pay homage to the gods of our age—money, celebrity, technology, pleasure—sometimes ignoring the spiritual issues involved. You might take a higher-paying job, even though it would limit your church involvement. You might chat with a friend about tabloid headlines rather than truly listening to her needs. Every day we make choices about what altar we're going to sacrifice upon.

For Perpetua and Felicitas, the choice was clear, as it was for hundreds of other early church martyrs. They worshiped *Jesus*—not the emperor, not the empire, not personal comfort, not even their own families—and they felt privileged to suffer for him. The ancient account calls their date in the arena "their victory day." They strode into the stadium "joyfully as though they were going to heaven." It describes Perpetua "with a glowing face and a calm step, God's beloved, the bride of Christ, putting down everyone's stare by her own intense gaze." Perpetua and Felicitas were confident they had made the right choice.

Consider this: long before TV or Internet, how could you get a message across to thousands of people at once? By acting it out in a stadium. These faithful women demonstrated their eternal love for Christ in a painful but effective way. And their sacrifice helped to win an empire.

Don't be surprised at the fiery trials you are going through, as if something strange were happening to you. Instead, be very glad—for these trials make you partners with Christ in his suffering, so that you will have the wonderful joy of seeing his glory when it is revealed to all the world.

1 PETER 4:12-13

TEST THE SPIRITS

Maximilla

D. 179

The verdict is still out on Maximilla. She and her colleague Priscilla were either courageous prophets or dangerous heretics. They belonged to a Christian sect that emerged in the late 100s in Phrygia (part of modern-day Turkey). The group became known as Montanists (after Montanus, their founder), but they called themselves "spiritual" Christians, setting themselves apart from other "carnal" Christians.

You could imagine that this wouldn't go over well with all those other Christians. Always mindful of Christ's return, the Montanists mandated a strict lifestyle. They also believed that the Holy Spirit was still giving messages through prophets—such as Maximilla and Priscilla.

The established church felt threatened, and many Christian leaders harshly criticized this movement. Hippolytus asserted that the Montanists were deceived by these two so-called prophetesses, exalting them above the apostles. While he acknowledged that the Montanists agreed with the established church on the main points of faith, he was uneasy with their "novelties"—including females in leadership and their diet of radishes. Some had problems with the fact that Maximilla and Priscilla had left their husbands. Other critics accepted that the group was experiencing supernatural power but assumed it was demonic. Two bishops tried to exorcise the prophetesses.

Maximilla seems to have been the most vocal of the Montanist leaders. She is reported to have said, "The Lord sent me as a devotee, revealer, and interpreter of this promise and covenant. I was compelled, willing or unwilling, to learn the knowledge of God." Rejected by official church leaders, she complained, "I am driven from the sheep like a wolf. I am not a wolf. I am Word and Spirit and Power." She predicted that, after her death, the end would come for the Christian church. That didn't quite happen. She died in 179.

So what are we to make of this woman? What can we learn from her? Christian historians still disagree on her legacy, so we're not going to solve that matter on these pages. Our challenge, however, is always to "test the spirits," as John told us (1 John 4:1, NIV). Turn away from those voices that do not express the truth and grace and love of Jesus. Open up to those that do.

Do not believe everyone who claims to speak by the Spirit.
You must test them to see if the spirit they have comes from
God. For there are many false prophets in the world.

1 JOHN 4:1

SOCIAL RESPONSIBILITY

It's never been so easy to figure out where your friends stand on social issues. Just log on to Facebook on any given day, and you'll find any and every cause being championed by your friends—often causes that are in opposition to each other.

Even your Christian friends may have differing views on what social responsibility involves. Take environmentalism, for instance. Some may see it as focusing on "Mother Earth" and taking attention away from God, while others may seek to honor and obey the Creator by finding renewable energy sources and conserving open space.

Women have always been involved in social-responsibility issues, and often their faith has been a driving force.

The Bible tells of Joanna, who was a financial supporter of Jesus' ministry (see Luke 8:2-3). Long before she fully realized who Jesus was, she personally saw the importance of what Jesus could do for people when he cured her ailments. She took on the responsibility of funding Jesus and his apostles so they could help others as they had helped her.

Ida Scudder was an American doctor who became a medical missionary to India around the year 1900, fighting against the diseases that many of the women there contracted. She realized that she couldn't do it by herself, and so she founded a medical school for girls (which later went coed) to ensure that future generations would have medical care.

Then there's Jessie Ames, who organized women to speak out against racism in the South in the 1930s. Through their efforts, big changes were made.

Jesus had a lot to say about social responsibility. Even more important, he was the best example of a socially responsible person we have. He fed the hungry, healed the sick, looked beyond a person's nationality or race, practiced nonviolence, and literally gave himself to save the world.

A debate has raged for some time: Is it more important to help people or to preach the gospel to them? The service-filled lives of countless women and men in Christian history make it clear how shortsighted that question is. We honor Christ by helping those he helped. And we help people by sharing Christ with them. We must never ignore people's spiritual needs, but neither should we downplay their physical needs. Jesus calls us to minister to both.

The godly care about the rights of the poor; the wicked don't care at all.

PROVERBS 29:7

WHERE THE ACTION IS

Flavia Domitilla

CA. 65–100

Three generations of Roman women bore the name Flavia Domitilla. Domitilla the Older was married to Vespasian, a general who became emperor in AD 69 after a four-way struggle for control of Rome. She had two sons, Titus and Domitian (who both became emperors), and a daughter, Domitilla the Younger, who gave birth to our third Flavia Domitilla, who became a saint. For twenty-seven years, these women were wives, sisters, daughters, and nieces of the most powerful men in Rome. This was where the action was.

As you might have figured out, Saint Flavia Domitilla was a Christian. This was a problem once her uncle, Emperor Domitian (81–96), began aggressively promoting the classic worship of the god Jupiter. Still, legend has it, Flavia Domitilla used her estate to hide Christians, host worship services, and provide sacred burial.

As one story goes, Uncle Domitian hatched a plan to kill all Christians and Jews. He just needed a senate vote to confirm it. But Domitilla helped her husband, then serving as Rome's consul, to make a courageous choice, giving up his office in order to delay that vote. It worked. The murderous plan was put on hold as the senate went about electing a new consul, but apparently both Domitilla and her husband were revealed as Christians—he was killed; she was exiled to a volcanic island.

Imagine growing up in the epicenter of imperial power, participating in political intrigue, and then suddenly being exiled. Was she grateful for the peace and quiet, or did she long to make more of a difference? Where do you find yourself these days—where the action is, or where it isn't? Are you struggling to stay true to Christ amid tough challenges, or are you wondering if there are any challenges left for you?

About that same time, another Christian was exiled to another remote island. The apostle John used his downtime to listen to Jesus, and he wrote the book of Revelation to help believers deal with Domitian's reign. That seemed to be the secret of Saint Flavia Domitilla: whether in excitement or exile, keep listening to Jesus.

[I am] your partner in suffering and in God's Kingdom and in the patient endurance to which Jesus calls us. I was exiled . . . for preaching the word of God and for my testimony about Jesus.

REVELATION 1:9

MUSIC MAIDEN

Cecilia

SECOND OR THIRD CENTURY

What will you be known for? Is there some trait, some activity, some contribution that future generations will remember about you? In the case of a Roman girl named Cecilia, it was singing. She became a patron saint of music in the Catholic church and beyond.

Despite a rich tradition surrounding her, there's very little we actually know for sure about Cecilia. She lived in the second century . . . or the third. She was martyred in Rome . . . or maybe Sicily. Her death is commemorated on September 16 . . . or August 11 . . . or maybe November 22.

A fanciful story about her circulated during the fifth century. It involved the arranged marriage of Cecilia to a pagan named Valerian, who soon became a Christian, along with his brother. The two brothers were arrested and killed for their faith. Before Cecilia could be arrested, she arranged for her house to be used for Christian worship in the years to come. Authorities tried to kill her in various ways, but she hung on for three days—during which time she was preaching to visitors . . . and singing.

How much is fact and how much is fancy? It's hard to say. But the music is one morsel of this legend that has stuck. It was said that Cecilia heard heavenly music when she married Valerian—perhaps a foretaste of the groom's conversion? And her deathbed crooning inspired the faithful, not only then and there, but throughout the centuries. Raphael painted her, Chaucer wrote about her, and Handel hailed her in music. Some say Paul Simon's pop song "Cecilia" invokes this saint as his muse.

So . . . what will you be known for? All the money you've earned or the people you've touched? The house you live in or how you use it to show hospitality? Your power in the neighborhood or your love for your neighbors?

Or maybe, like Cecilia, you'll be remembered for the songs in your heart and the praises on your lips.

I will hold my head high above my enemies who surround me. At his sanctuary I will offer sacrifices with shouts of joy, singing and praising the LORD with music.

PSALM 27:6

LIGHT THE DARKNESS

Nino

FOURTH CENTURY

She was a stranger in a strange land, and yet her quiet devotion won a nation to Christ. Her name was Nino, and while many legends have circulated about her, we'll try to stick to the basic story.

It was the AD 320s, in the kingdom then known as Iberia, now part of Georgia, tucked between Turkey and Russia. A very early historical document calls Nino a "captive woman," a slave transported from somewhere in the Roman Empire to this outlying land. Her life of virtue and prayer gained the attention of the Iberians, and she explained that she worshiped Christ. This was a god they had never heard of.

A desperate mother sought a cure for her sick baby, and Nino prayed for healing. When the child was cured, word went out through the nation. Soon the queen, who had a serious illness, visited Nino and was healed. The king was overjoyed and wanted to pay this wonder-working slave, but the queen wisely explained that the only way to reward Nino was to worship Christ, her God.

The king refused at first, but shortly afterward, he was out hunting when a strange darkness enveloped him. As the ancient historian explains it, "Suddenly his spirit, tormented by despair of being rescued, was lit up by a thought: 'If indeed that Christ whom the Captive had preached to his Wife was God, then let Him now deliver him from this darkness, that he too might forsake all other gods to worship Him.'" Before he could even utter that thought, "the light of day was restored to the world."

He kept his vow, learning the way of Christ from Nino and leading the whole nation into faith. He even contacted Constantine, emperor of the newly Christianized Roman Empire, asking him to send a bishop and priests. And all this because of one woman who lived out her faith in less-than-ideal circumstances.

Influence is a curious thing. It's hard to know when you'll have an impact on others. When you show a simple kindness? When you pray for your neighbors or coworkers? When you humbly but courageously speak up about your faith? Nino did all these things, and God used her efforts mightily.

Live clean, innocent lives as children of God, shining like bright lights in a world full of crooked and perverse people.

PHILIPPIANS 2:15

ADVENTURE STORY

The Story of Thecla

SECOND CENTURY

It might be considered the first Christian romance novel. *The Acts of Paul and Thecla* recounts the adventures of a young woman who follows the apostle Paul through Asia Minor. It is clearly fiction, but its astonishingly early date (about AD 160) leaves some scholars wondering if it contains a germ of historical truth. For instance, it gives a vivid description of Paul (medium size, balding, crooked legs, bulbous knees, large eyes, brows that meet, a protruding nose) that might reflect an ancient eyewitness account, since it was written less than a century after Paul's death.

As the story goes, Thecla was sitting at her window in Iconium when she heard Paul preaching in a nearby house. Transfixed by his message, she committed herself to faith and to lifelong virginity—which was a problem for her fiancé, who arranged to have Paul arrested. Thecla sneaked out to visit Paul in prison, and upon his release, she followed him as he carried the gospel to other towns.

She herself was later imprisoned for refusing the advances of a nobleman, and she was condemned to face wild beasts in the arena . . . except one lioness took a liking to her and fought off the other beasts. In another account, Thecla plunged into a pond with vicious sea lions to baptize herself, and the sea lions were miraculously killed.

Whether she really existed or not, Thecla serves as an example of an independent but faithful woman. This "runaway bride" stared down violence and humiliation in order to devote her life fully to God. Her story reminds us a bit of Daniel and friends—saved from lions and from almost-certain death, she took the opportunity to preach about Jesus as "a refuge to the tempest-tossed, a solace to the afflicted," and the women of the town cheered her release, saying, "There is one God, the God of Thecla."

Maybe your life is an adventure too. Okay, so you're not jumping in a pool with ravenous sea lions, but you do have issues. Miracles are still wrought by the God of Thecla and Paul—sometimes the precious miracles of everyday life, and sometimes immense miracles beyond our wildest fantasies.

He rescues and saves his people; he performs miraculous signs and wonders in the heavens and on earth. He has rescued Daniel from the power of the lions.

DANIEL 6:27

SMALL WONDER

Blandina

D. 177

Things turned very ugly very fast for the Christians in Lyon. The year was AD 177. Bishop Irenaeus had been well respected, and the church had been tolerated—but suddenly there was open hostility. Christians were banned from the public markets. Some were arrested on trumped-up charges. Mobs protested against them.

Some of this was based on ignorance. Christianity was seen as a perverted sect, guilty of incest, child sacrifice, and cannibalism—since they preached "brotherly love" and partook of the "body and blood of the Son." Enemies spread vicious rumors, and the mob believed them. So did the Roman officials, who tried and condemned many Christians.

The imprisoned Christians also fell victim to budget cuts. Gladiator games were getting expensive. It was much cheaper to send convicted criminals (in this case, Christians) into the arena against the wild beasts.

Among these Christian "criminals" was a slave girl named Blandina, who amazed everyone with her endurance, even wearing out her torturers. By one report, they were "weary and exhausted. They themselves admitted that they were beaten, that there was nothing further they could do to her, and they were surprised that she was still breathing for her entire body was broken and torn." She simply would not deny her faith in Jesus.

Even in the arena she prayed fervently and confidently, and the animals wouldn't touch her . . . on the first day. They had to take her back to the prison, where she greatly inspired the other believers, "tiny, weak, and insignificant as she was," according to one ancient writer. She finally succumbed on another day in the arena, where she was attacked by a bull.

Consider this: we know nothing about Blandina's life. Surely she had friends, a family, daily tasks, and perhaps some responsibility in her church fellowship. But we don't know any of that. We know only how well she handled suffering.

When you go through difficult times, it's easy to feel "tiny, weak, and insignificant," but maybe that's when you'll have the greatest influence. Like Blandina, you can inspire others with the tenacity of your faith.

Even when we are weighed down with troubles, it is for your comfort and salvation! For when we ourselves are comforted, we will certainly comfort you. Then you can patiently endure the same things we suffer.

2 CORINTHIANS 1:6

THREE SISTERS

Agape, Chionia, Irene

D. ABOUT 310

In the first decade of the 300s, Emperor Diocletian launched a last vicious attack against Christianity, trying to rid the empire of this pesky menace once and for all. Christians had endured several periods of persecution in the previous two-and-a-half centuries, but this was the worst yet.

In the middle of all this were three sisters from the town of Thessalonica—Agape, Chionia, and Irene. (The first and third were named for the Christian virtues of love and peace. *Chionia* is the Greek word for "snowy.") As often happens with ancient saints, there are several legends about them, but all depict a trio of devout young women.

As the story goes, they refused to participate in sacrificing to the pagan gods of Rome, and this got them in trouble with the authorities. One other problem was that they possessed illegal Christian books. (This was before the church had officially gathered the New Testament, so these "sacred texts" probably included the gospels and the letters of Paul, as well as more recent instruction.) When the sisters refused to sacrifice, eat the sacrificial food, or give up their books, the first two women were burned to death. In a perverse punishment, Irene, who had committed her virginity to God, was sent to a brothel, but she died before she could be defiled. (There are different stories of how this happened, but it's generally seen as God's protection of her purity.)

Nowadays there are many Christian books, including this one, that aren't worth dying for. But what about the Bible itself? Would you risk your life just to own a copy of God's Word? Would you risk your reputation to carry it to work? Would you risk a relationship to quote a potentially helpful verse to a friend?

These three sisters knew that the Scriptures were not just a badge to wear or a flag to wave, but a line of connection to God. These writings kept them focused on the one person who was worth living and dying for. They can do the same for us.

The word of God is alive and powerful. It is sharper than the sharpest two-edged sword, cutting between soul and spirit, between joint and marrow. It exposes our innermost thoughts and desires.

HEBREWS 4:12

ON THE MARTYRDOM OF WOMEN

It's remarkable how many of the early church's martyrs were women. This is surprising on two counts. First, for most of Christian history, men have held the key roles in church leadership, so you might expect women to be overlooked in the writing of that history. In fact, some modern historians complain that this is indeed the case. But it doesn't seem to be true with martyrdom. For every Polycarp there's a Perpetua.

A second surprise has to do with Roman sensibilities. Compared with the Greek civilization that preceded it, Roman culture had a relatively high view of the value of women. If you trace the intrigues of the first-century imperial court, you find a number of prominent women wielding power. They were still the power *behind* the throne, but they held considerable sway. It was the power of matrons that held together the noble households of Rome.

So why were so many Christian women arrested and tortured for their faith? Why were they killed in public in the most humiliating ways? You would think that Roman gentility would go easy on the women. Not so.

We must not underestimate the simple bloodlust and mob mania of the Roman persecutors, but there are other factors as well. Women were prominent in the early church, both in numbers and in power. Slaves and working-class people of both genders were coming to Christianity, but also a number of noblewomen. We get a few examples of that in the book of Acts, and it continues through history. The Roman historian Tacitus told of a judge's wife, Pomponia Graecina, who was accused of "foreign superstition" and handed over to her husband for trial. She was most likely a convert to Christianity.

Maybe the Romans felt threatened by this "liberation movement"—for slaves, for workers, for women. Maybe they thought the persecution of women would specifically discourage other women from converting.

If so, it backfired. The crowds in the arenas saw women of great strength and courage standing up for their faith against the most horrendous terrors. Perpetua, Blandina, and many others spoke out about their faith and acted it out in dramatic ways. In so doing, they became powerful examples for all Christ followers to come.

Women who claim to be devoted to God should make themselves attractive by the good things they do.

1 TIMOTHY 2:10

CINDERELLA STORY

Helena

CA. 248–CA. 327

A s we piece together the story of Helena, it begins to sound like a fairy tale—until it goes horribly wrong. She was a commoner who wed a prince. Ancient sources call her a "stablemaid," and the "prince" was Constantius, a general with hopes of becoming Rome's emperor. One legend says Helena and Constantius were wearing matching bracelets when they met—a sign that this was a match made in heaven. She bore him a son, Constantine.

But then the love story sours. When Constantine was still a teenager, his father dumped Helena for a new wife who aided his political ambitions. Was this the end for Helena? Hardly. Her son was still being groomed for greatness, so she stayed near him in the court of Emperor Diocletian as he rose through the ranks. There she had a front-row seat to one of the most amazing religious turnarounds in history.

For two and a half centuries, the Roman Empire had persecuted Christians. In fact, Emperor Diocletian was conducting the toughest persecution yet. But when he died, there was a power struggle involving several other generals and Constantine, who had succeeded his dying father. Before an important battle, Constantine saw a vision of Jesus predicting victory. This led to his conversion, and as he consolidated his power and became emperor, he made Christianity the official religion of Rome. Within a mere fifteen years, Christians had gone from prisons to palaces.

And Helena herself was finally a queen. Constantine publicly honored his mother in many ways, perhaps trying to make up for his father's rejection. It's not clear when exactly she became a Christian, but she apparently did, since later in life she took a special interest in the Holy Land, finding biblical sites and rebuilding churches.

How does the arc of your life compare with Helena's? Have you seen some dramatic ups and downs too? Is your story a fairy tale or a horror flick—or both? Whether you're a queen or a stablemaid, a lovesick teen or a single mom, God has plans for you, and these plans will not be thwarted.

"I know the plans I have for you," says the LORD. "They are plans for good and not for disaster, to give you a future and a hope."

JEREMIAH 29:11

THE EXPLORER

Helena

CA. 248–CA. 327

The Holy Land had been under Roman rule for nearly four centuries, but the Roman authorities didn't care much about the events that made it holy. Several Jewish rebellions had sprung up there before being crushed by Rome's military might. And then there was this Jesus movement that had started there—but it had been persecuted by Rome almost from its beginning.

Yet now things were different. The new emperor, Constantine, was a Christian, and he made Christianity the official religion of the realm. His mother, Helena, held unusual power for a queen mum, and she took on the challenge of restoring the holy sites of Christianity. This meant travel and research and some excavation, an impressive pursuit for a woman reportedly in her seventies.

The results were also impressive: the building of churches at the site of Jesus' birth in Bethlehem, resurrection in Jerusalem, and elsewhere. She's also credited with finding holy artifacts, including pieces of the cross. All sorts of legends surround her regarding the magical power of this "true cross." (Apparently there were many fake pieces, but supposedly only the pieces of the true cross could heal people.)

If you have difficulty with this, good. The second commandment forbids the worship of any "graven image" (Exodus 20:4, KJV). God knew that we humans like to trust in material things, and indeed many religions throughout history have granted divine power to temples and statues and other things. But history shows that Christians aren't immune from this temptation either. We can applaud Helena's efforts to honor the origins of Christianity, but we must remember that God alone deserves our worship, not the sites and trinkets of our faith.

Modern-day believers might take a challenge from this as well. What do we consider holy? The church building, or the worship that goes on there? The leather-bound Bible on the shelf, or the words inside it? The way things have always been done, or the way God wants us to serve him today?

You must not have any other god but me. You must not make for yourself an idol of any kind or an image of anything in the heavens or on the earth or in the sea. You must not bow down to them or worship them, for I, the LORD your God, am a jealous God who will not tolerate your affection for any other gods.

EXODUS 20:3-5

MARRIAGE

The Bible contains very few examples of good marriages. Go ahead: try to come up with a list of five. With Adam's blaming, Sarah's jealousy, Rebekah's scheming, Jacob's favoritism, and so on, we don't find many pairings worth emulating. Okay, Priscilla and Aquila show up, but we have precious little information about them—other than the fact that they were *together*. Whether hosting a church, working with Paul, or tutoring Apollos, they were a team. But the data on other biblical marriages is either negative or nonexistent.

We find more of the same as we scan church history. Many prominent Christians were unmarried, and many others had spouses who were anonymous or nearly so. Yet here and there we find marriages where both partners are known to history. What can we learn from them?

These marriages seem to come in two varieties. Some follow the teamwork model, as presented by Priscilla and Aquila. Consider Ann and Adoniram Judson, among the first American missionaries sent overseas. They pioneered mission work in Burma and inspired many missionary couples to follow. A generation later, Catherine Booth was clearly a teammate of her husband, William, in founding the Salvation Army. Both of the Booths preached and led meetings. They also worked together in organizing the sort of relief efforts that the organization is still known for.

Other wives have attained fame for their strong and unique support of their famous husbands. Katharina von Bora, a former nun, married the reformer Martin Luther. Their marriage itself was a Protestant strike against Catholic tradition, but Katie was no trophy wife. Matching Martin's fiery temperament, she brought some order to his chaotic life. In a different way, Sarah Edwards provided support for her husband, the brilliant scholar-preacher Jonathan Edwards. He drew from her deep faith and wisdom as well as her organizational ability. There are many other wives who surely deserve half the credit for the achievements of their well-known husbands, and yet they remain rather invisible to history.

Shouldn't we consider both of these models "teamwork"? Whether the husband and wife step side by side into ministry, or whether one uses supportive gifts to bolster the other, they are serving God together. In our marriages, then, it's not so important who gets the most attention, but how well God is served.

Again I say, each man must love his wife as he loves himself, and the wife must respect her husband.

EPHESIANS 5:33

SACRIFICES

Paula

347–404

Married young to a wealthy man, Paula enjoyed what her husband's money could provide. She dressed in silk, adorned herself in gold, and was carried from place to place by servants. But when Paula became a Christian, she gave up all the luxuries.

Paula was a widow in her early thirties when she converted. In the following years she used her inherited wealth for the church's needs. But her sacrifice did not end with giving away her wealth—she also turned to a life of deprivation.

She ate only bread and oil and drank only water. It's said she rarely bathed or slept. Eventually she dedicated her life to financially supporting and serving Jerome, a Bible scholar working on a Latin translation of the Bible. To help him, she left her home and her young children.

This raises some challenging questions for us. Was Paula's life of self-imposed deprivation necessary to serve God? Paula must have thought so, and maybe that's how God was leading her, but does he want that for all of us? Most of us would understand giving money to help a ministry, even in substantial amounts, especially if we were left (as Paula was) with a sizable inheritance. But the rest of it, particularly leaving her children, seems a little crazy. Yet Jerome's translation of the Bible was so important, and Paula's support so integral to its completion, that calling her sacrifices crazy might be too harsh.

Sacrifice is an uncomfortable word. God asks all of us to make sacrifices, to give up some of our comforts for him. He might even ask us to do something that seems a little crazy. So the challenge remains: What sort of sacrifice is God calling you to make? Money? Time? Relationships?

You may never know the lasting effects of those sacrifices. Over the ages, the Bible has been carefully translated and passed down through the efforts of many faithful people, and Paula was one of them. Like her, you have no idea what the results of your sacrifice might be, but you know God does.

Don't forget to do good and to share with those in need.
These are the sacrifices that please God.

HEBREWS 13:16

WHAT DO YOU KNOW?

Marcellina

CA. 330–98

It can't be easy to have a smart kid brother. Imagine the family rivalry as the young one takes every opportunity to prove himself smarter than his big sister. Ambrose was indeed a gifted boy, but he owed a great deal of his success to his wise sister, Marcellina. Tradition says that she made a special effort to teach him not to seek power through knowledge, but through virtue.

Their father worked in the government of the Roman Empire, which had just turned Christian under Constantine the Great. How would the once-persecuted church deal with its newfound freedom and power? Everyone was still figuring that out. Already there were major disputes between different types of Christians holding different beliefs about Jesus.

Ambrose excelled in his studies, following his father's footsteps into public service. Perhaps it was Marcellina's influence that helped him establish a reputation for wisdom and patience, not just intelligence. Once, he walked into an angry crowd of Christians fighting over who their next bishop would be. As he tried to make peace, someone shouted, "Ambrose for bishop!" and soon both sides took up the chant.

It was in this role of bishop that Ambrose fulfilled his sister's expectations. He exerted great power over the church—preaching, composing hymns, writing theology, challenging the emperor when necessary, discussing philosophy with those of various viewpoints, even mentoring a young Augustine. He was hailed for his great knowledge, but even more for his integrity and virtue. He could have enjoyed a princely income when he took office, but he refused, choosing to live an ascetic life—except he did make sure to provide for his big sister, Marcellina.

His sister's advice is valuable in any century. Where do you seek power? In your intelligence, your connections, your beauty, your money? Marcellina tells us all to discover our true strength by living the way Jesus taught us, in simplicity, integrity, and love.

While knowledge makes us feel important, it is love that strengthens the church. Anyone who claims to know all the answers doesn't really know very much. But the person who loves God is the one whom God recognizes.

1 CORINTHIANS 8:1-3

PATIENT IN PRAYER

Monica

CA. 331–87

How long should you pray before you just give up? A year or two? A decade? Monica prayed for thirty years that her son would know Jesus, and that miracle slowly came about, making her literally jump for joy.

We're not sure when Monica herself came to faith. Her name has pagan roots, suggesting that her parents were not Christians. She was also married to a non-Christian man, with whom she had at least three children. The oldest was precocious—with a brilliant mind and a nose for trouble. His name: Augustine.

From his boyhood, Augustine inspired many tears and many prayers. In his autobiographical classic, *Confessions*, he wrote about the various sins of his youth—from stealing pears in a neighbor's orchard to having adolescent sexual exploits. But Monica never wrote him off. She kept weeping and praying, which irked him at the time. At one point Augustine told her they would get along fine if she would just give up her faith. She never did.

Sneaking away one night from their home in North Africa, he caught a ship to Rome. There he established political connections and also dabbled in cultic philosophy. Climbing the political ladder, he later landed a job at the emperor's headquarters in Milan.

Meanwhile Monica continued praying for her errant son and for her husband—who became a Christian just months before he died. Eventually she moved to Milan to join Augustine. Her prayers continued, now at close range.

Then one day Augustine had a mystical experience of sorts, hearing a child's singsong voice telling him to read a portion of the Bible, which he did. That text inspired him to finally say yes to God.

When he told his mother, "she leaped for joy victoriously" (he wrote later), thanking God, who had "granted her far more than she had ever asked for in all her desperate, woeful cries."

Patient in prayer, Monica serves as an example for all of us. No matter how long you've been at it, keep praying. The Lord answers our cries in ways we might never expect.

We keep on praying for you, asking our God to enable you to live
a life worthy of his call. May he give you the power to accomplish
all the good things your faith prompts you to do.

2 THESSALONIANS 1:11

THE DREAMER

Monica

CA. 331–87

Perhaps every mother dreams of great things for her children. In Monica's case, the "great thing" was a relationship with Christ, and the "dream" was an actual dream. Concerned for her oldest son, Augustine, as he lived the wild life of a college student, she found comfort in a strange vision.

"She saw herself standing on a sort of wooden measuring stick, and there was a bright young man coming toward her, happy and smiling at her, though she was grieving and bowed down with sorrow," Augustine later wrote. When she explained that she was bemoaning the destruction of Augustine's soul, the visitor pointed to the other side of her. There was Augustine, sitting there. The visitor said, "Where you are, he will also be."

Monica found great comfort in this. Later she shared her ongoing worries about Augustine with a priest, who told her, "It is impossible for the son of these tears to perish." This prophecy also buoyed her up. Somehow her son would come to faith.

After about another decade of praying and waiting, Monica's dream finally came true. At age thirty-two, Augustine became a Christian. Now where she was, spiritually speaking, he also was.

Going back to Bible times, there's a long history of God guiding people through dreams, but it's a tricky business. In his tell-all book, Confessions, Augustine mentions that Monica also had some dreams when she was trying to fix him up with a good wife. "She did, indeed, see certain vain and fantastic things," but he attributed them to her "strong preoccupation." Even Monica had to admit "she could distinguish, by a certain feeling impossible to describe, between [God's] revelations and the dreams of her own soul."

That might serve as a helpful distinction for us, too. God may use our hopes and dreams to comfort us, inspire us, or to remind us of his promises. But sometimes we just dream about things we want, and if we're honest with ourselves, we usually know the difference. In Monica's case, the dreams were tested by her interactions with others. In the first case, a priest confirmed the promise of her dream with his own wisdom. In the second, Augustine confirmed that she was just being a meddling mom.

God speaks again and again,
though people do not recognize it.
He speaks in dreams, in visions of the night.

JOB 33:14-15

PLAYING POLITICS

Monica

CA. 331–87

The Roman Empire had always crackled with political intrigue, but in the 300s there was a powerful new player: Christianity. In a stunning turnaround, this once-persecuted faith became the official religion of the realm. Suddenly it was cool to be a Christian, and for many, faith became just another political ploy.

Augustine was caught up in this turbulent time. Moving to Rome in 383, he connected with some senators who still embraced the old paganism and were plotting a comeback. The next year, he moved to Milan to work for the Christian emperor. He was covering all the bases. Since it was now politically expedient to be a Christian, he claimed to be one. Like many other political opportunists of the time, he was labeled a "catechumen," a Christian in training, but he stopped short of the actual baptism that would confirm genuine faith.

His mother, Monica, had her own political strategy, you might say. She had prayed fervently for her non-Christian husband and for her oldest son, Augustine, as he dabbled in various religions and wild behaviors. Her tactic was durability: she would outlast them. Though her loutish husband was difficult to live with, she stayed with him, combating cruelty with kindness, and eventually he trusted Christ.

Augustine's journey took a bit longer, but she stayed in his life even when he was most rebellious. He knew she was praying for him when he went off to study in Carthage and sowed some wild oats, and later when he ran off to Rome to pursue his dreams.

Whatever disappointment she felt, it didn't break their relationship. She kept loving him. When he became an "expedient" Christian, she didn't buy it but kept praying for an authentic commitment. After moving to Milan, Monica connected her son with her priest, the brilliant Bishop Ambrose, one of the few whose intellect could match Augustine's. And then she waited for God to work.

If politics is all lies and manipulation, then count Monica out. But if it's a matter of choosing the wisest ways to affect others positively, then she played it perfectly. Scripture urges us to practice such wisdom, wooing others with love and grace.

Live wisely among those who are not believers, and make the most of every opportunity. Let your conversation be gracious and attractive so that you will have the right response for everyone.

COLOSSIANS 4:5-6

MOTHERHOOD

Many women will say that becoming a mother changed their understanding of God in various ways—like their knowledge of the concept of unconditional love. For many parents—mothers and fathers alike—only when they experienced the unconditional love they had for their children were they able to grasp how deeply God loves them, no matter what.

This book has stories of many mothers.

One of these mothers is the prayer warrior Clotilde, who influenced her husband, a pagan king, when she prayed for the healing of their ill sons. Eventually, when he was in need, this king prayed to "Clotilde's God" and became a Christian, leading many to conversion.

There's also Louisa Stead, a mother who was left to care for her daughter alone after her husband died trying to save someone else's child. She endured poverty and at times had no food to feed her daughter. Out of her experiences came a hopeful poem that turned into the beloved hymn "'Tis So Sweet to Trust in Jesus."

Monica tirelessly prayed for the conversion of her son Augustine. Susanna Wesley dutifully taught the Scriptures to her sons, John and Charles. And, of course, there's Mary, the mother of Jesus, whose willingness to become a mother under scandalous circumstances changed, well, just about everything.

One thing all these mothers have in common is that they looked to God for hope when times were tough. They trusted that he would help them. They influenced others around them—husbands, children, family, and friends—with their comfort, their faith, their prayers, and their examples.

The care and comfort that mothers can give is often a glimpse of the care and comfort that God always gives. When you're in need of comfort, think of how your mother (or someone who was a mother figure to you, like a grandparent, a neighbor, a friend's mom, a teacher) offered you comfort. Know that God offers that type of comfort too.

This also gives us an angle on an age-old question: Why doesn't God always give us what we ask for? Well, good moms don't give their kids ice cream every time they scream for it. In the same way, God doesn't always fix things the way we hope he will, but he does provide what's best for us.

This is what the LORD says: . . . "I will comfort you
. . . as a mother comforts her child."

ISAIAH 66:12-13

TEACHING BY EXAMPLE

Anthusa

CA. 347–407

Children learn many things from their parents—some from their words, but more from their actions.

Relationships were important to Anthusa, and she taught this to her son and daughter. Her husband died when the children were young, and as a woman of class and substance, she easily could have married again—but instead she chose to focus on her children. As a result, her son, John, grew up with a broad education, a thorough knowledge of the law, the arts, and the politics of the newly Christianized Roman Empire of the mid-300s.

He also grew up with a deep faith of his own. In fact, John was planning to enter a monastery, but his mother asked him to wait. "Do not make me a widow a second time," she said. "Wait at least till I die. . . . When you have buried me and joined my ashes with those of your father, nothing will then prevent you from retiring into monastic life. But as long as I breathe, support me by your presence."

She wasn't trying to keep him from following God's leading, but she knew relationships were important. For the time being, he would serve the Lord by remaining with her. Later he did enter the monastic life, so extremely that it damaged his health. Then, returning to public life, he became a powerful church leader and a popular preacher, earning the nickname Golden Mouth, or *Chrysostom*.

At one point he used his speaking and relational skills to quell a violent tax revolt in Antioch. Later, in a turbulent power shift, he was pressed into service as bishop of Constantinople. With a reputation for upholding justice, he fought abuses of power in the priesthood and even the imperial court. Though he got in trouble for criticizing those in authority, John won widespread respect for a life of integrity and a commitment to solid relationships—things he had learned from his mother.

What are you teaching your children, or anyone who look up to you? Are you teaching them to treasure good relationships over life's conveniences? Are they learning to live lives of integrity—not only from your words, but also from your example?

Keep putting into practice all you learned and received from me—everything you heard from me and saw me doing. Then the God of peace will be with you.

PHILIPPIANS 4:9

LIVING LARGE AND DYING WELL

Macrina

330–79

Her brother called her "Macrina the Great." Of all the nicknames that brothers give sisters, that's a pretty good one, and it shows the sense of love and honor within this extraordinary family. Macrina had not just one, but three famous brothers, and all credited her with a great deal of their success.

After centuries of persecution, the 300s brought freedom and power to the church. One key issue was deciding what Christians believed. The church needed leaders who could preach and teach and write good theology. Basil of Caesarea, Gregory of Nyssa, and to a lesser degree, Peter of Sebaste stepped up to do just that—with the help of their brilliant sister, Macrina.

Theirs was an affluent family from the region of Cappadocia in Asia Minor. Macrina grew up with a thorough religious education (unusual for a girl), memorizing huge portions of Scripture and cheerfully following a regimen of hourly prayers. Her beauty, wisdom, and heritage attracted many suitors, and she became engaged to one. But he died before the wedding, and Macrina then decided to devote her life fully to God. Staying on the family estate, she cared for her parents and siblings, living simply.

Holiness became her focus. She started a community of like-minded women who stepped out of their worldly pursuits in order to connect with God more fully. (The monastic movement was quite new and especially rare for women.) From her inheritance, she funded a hospital. All the while, she encouraged her brothers to refuse the trappings of church power and to remain humble.

You might say that Macrina the Great "lived large"—not in the extravagance of her wealth but in the commitment of her heart. As a result, her influence was huge—on her family and on her world. And when it came time to die, she did that well too, in the arms of her brother Gregory, who recorded her final prayer: "You have granted me that the end of this life should be the beginning of true life. . . O eternal God, . . . whom my soul has loved with all its might . . . lead me to the place of refreshment, where is the water of peace."

Living large and dying well. That's Macrina's story, and perhaps our own.

To me, living means living for Christ, and dying is even better.

PHILIPPIANS 1:21

TREASURE TROVE

Olympias

368–408

Poor little rich girl. That was the status of Olympias, born near Constantinople in 368. Her wealthy parents died when she was young, leaving her an inheritance that drew the interest of suitors far and wide. Even Emperor Theodosius got involved, arranging for her to marry one of his administrators, just so her fortune wouldn't get into the wrong hands. Then her husband died, and the suitors returned.

Apparently Olympias was tired of it all. Still only about twenty years old, she announced that she would not marry again but would serve the Lord.

This did not sit well with the emperor. It was hard to criticize her decision publicly, but leadership was still about money and power, and Theodosius wanted Olympias's money under his power. So he took it. Well, he placed it in a trust for her, under his control until she turned thirty.

The young woman wrote him a thank-you note. He had lifted this financial burden from her. She only asked one small favor: Could he give that money to the church and to the poor?

The cagey emperor had been outplayed. How could he deny this public, pious request? He decided to give the money back to Olympias, and he watched as she disposed of it, helping the poor, the sick, and widows and orphans like herself. She even bought hundreds of slaves and set them free.

This young woman understood something that many Christians don't: the only treasure that matters is in heaven. It's not wrong to have money, but it's a burden. Olympias experienced this early in life. She was widely wooed, but it was for her fortune, not for her heart. She decided to invest her heart *and* her fortune in the things that truly matter to God.

Where are you investing your heart and your fortune?

Teach those who are rich in this world not to be proud and not to trust in their money, which is so unreliable. Their trust should be in God, who richly gives us all we need for our enjoyment. Tell them to use their money to do good. They should be rich in good works and generous to those in need, always being ready to share with others. By doing this they will be storing up their treasure as a good foundation for the future so that they may experience true life.

1 TIMOTHY 6:17-19

OPEN HEART, OPEN HOME

Marcella

325–410

The New Testament gives us the vivid picture of the church as a body. We are feet and hands, eyes and ears, each part with a different specialty. In one passage, Paul has fun with the idea, imagining how absurd it would be for ears to sulk about not being able to see. Every part of the body—the human body *or* the church body—is important, and the different parts work together for the good of all and ultimately for God's glory.

We see that played out in the story of Marcella, a well-to-do Christian widow at the turn of the fifth century. Her gift, we might surmise, was hospitality. After her wealthy husband died, she gave up her high fashion and wore a simple brown dress, without makeup or an elaborate hairstyle. What's more, she gathered other Christian women who did the same thing. Her home became the headquarters for this "brown dress society" as they worshiped the Lord and served others. She is credited with founding the first convent in the Western church.

Marcella also employed her gift of hospitality with the scholar Jerome. When the pope gave Jerome the task of translating the Scriptures from their original Hebrew and Greek into Latin, it was Marcella who gave him a place to work. Jerome used his gifts of scholarship and language to produce a translation that the church relied on for a millennium and a half. But he was just one part of the body, as was Marcella with her hospitality (and Paula with her own support of the project—see January 31). Jerome was known for a fiery temper, and he made some enemies, but Marcella helped to keep that in check. So again we see different gifts working together.

How has God gifted you? Are you a scholar, a teacher, a helper, an administrator, or, like Marcella, a happy host? How does God knit your abilities together with those of others to accomplish his purposes? Celebrate that today.

The human body has many parts, but the many parts make
up one whole body. So it is with the body of Christ.

1 CORINTHIANS 12:12

SURVIVOR

Galla Placidia

392–450

The story of Galla Placidia reads like an adventure novel—except it might seem too far fetched. Born a princess in the late 300s, daughter of the great Roman emperor Theodosius I, she was raised in the family of his top general and eventually got engaged to the general's son. Education, wealth, prestige—you might say she had it all.

But after the death of Theodosius, power fell to Placidia's jealous half-brothers. In the struggle that followed, Placidia lost both her fiancé and the general who raised her. The chaos created an opportunity for the Gothic forces perched on the borders. Around the time of the infamous "sack of Rome" in 410, Placidia was kidnapped by the invaders. History doesn't give us many details, but a few years later, she married the Gothic warlord Ataulf.

Was she simply a trophy wife for this leader, or was there genuine love here? Had she turned her back on her Roman family, or did she just see an opportunity to cast her lot with the winners? Whatever her inner struggle was, her life got worse. Ataulf was assassinated, his heirs were murdered, and Placidia was sorely mistreated.

As a bargaining chip in a peace treaty, she returned to Rome, where she was forced into a marriage to another top general, who later became emperor and then died of an illness. Continuing political struggles in the 420s led to a situation where Placidia essentially ruled as empress in the name of her four-year-old son.

Despite her many ups and downs, Placidia was a survivor—and for about two decades she was the most powerful woman in the empire, probably the world. She exerted her power not only in the political affairs of Rome, but also in church matters. Christianity was struggling with the identity of Jesus. Some emphasized the humanity of Christ; others his divinity. Placidia took a middle position—that Jesus was "truly God and truly man"—a position that would be confirmed in the Council of Chalcedon in 452. Without Placidia, that council might not have happened.

Maybe your life feels like an adventure novel too. How can you follow your dreams when you're struggling to survive? As Placidia well knew, the God-man Jesus promises strength in those struggles.

Here on earth you will have many trials and sorrows.
But take heart, because I have overcome the world.

JOHN 16:33

PRAYER WARRIOR

Clotilde

475–545

Europe was a muddled, befuddled land at the end of the fifth century. The central power of Rome had faded, and various warlords were struggling for power. Tribes were emigrating from Asia and settling in, often by force. Religiously, many had adopted an Arian form of Christianity (holding that Jesus was not fully God) and some still followed old pagan gods and rituals.

Clotilde was born in 475 in what we now know as France. Her father was the provincial king of Burgundy, but his kingdom was falling apart. In 492 she was given in marriage to Clovis, king of the pagan, war-loving Franks, a tribe that had just conquered the northern territory of Gaul.

We don't know a lot about Clotilde except this: she was a devout Christian, and she prayed a lot. Surely she prayed when her first son became ill and died, shortly after his baptism. When her second son also became sick, she certainly prayed again. This boy recovered. Clovis was observing all of this. Was he learning that prayer is more than a magic charm, that it's a conversation with a caring God? And what did he think of the fact that his wife was praying for *him*, for his conversion?

In 496 Clovis went into battle against a rival tribe and saw quickly that he was greatly outnumbered. He needed a miracle to avoid a tragic loss . . . and perhaps his own death. So he prayed to "Clotilde's God," promising that he would be baptized as a Christian if God granted him a victory in this battle.

So it happened. The battle was won, and Clovis was baptized, along with about three thousand followers. Say what you will about the mass conversion, but this series of events essentially made France officially Christian for centuries to come, and that influence extended throughout Europe. A woman prayed, and look what happened!

One recurring image in medieval art is Clotilde in her royal robes with an angel nearby, often holding a shield. And Clotilde is praying.

What kind of "prayer warrior" are you? Have your prayers won victories in the lives of those you love? Have they helped to deepen the relationships God has with you or with others? Keep praying. God still works miracles.

Never stop praying.

1 THESSALONIANS 5:17

STAR-CROSSED LOVERS

Heloise

CA. 1100–64

Before Romeo and Juliet, there were Abelard and Heloise. Their story occurred in the early 1100s, and it captivated the romantic imagination of the late Middle Ages. It was a tale of scandalous passion, tragic turns, and brutal violence. But where Shakespeare's fictional characters, penned more than four centuries later, hurtled toward a tragic death, Abelard and Heloise found a new kind of life.

Both were brilliant. Heloise was raised by her uncle, who provided her with the best education possible. Even in her teens, her intelligence and academic insight were widely known. Peter Abelard was a leading philosopher in Paris, known for edgy thinking, sometimes accused of heresy. Perhaps it was inevitable that these two great minds would connect. Abelard was hired as a live-in teacher for the young Heloise.

And somewhere in the midst of their lessons, they fell madly in love, carrying on a torrid affair. She became pregnant. He apologized to her uncle and asked for Heloise's hand in marriage. They had a secret wedding, fearing that Abelard's career might be damaged if people knew he had married a student (who, by the way, was twenty years younger). But when Heloise was sent to stay in a convent for a while, the men of her family mistakenly thought that Abelard had abandoned her. They attacked him in his bed one night and mutilated him. (Let's just say he wouldn't be fathering any more children.)

Their romance was over. Abelard became a monk, Heloise a nun. Years later they began writing letters to each other. This correspondence, later published and distributed widely, sort of processed their relationship, reexamining it in hindsight with appropriate longing and regret. Yet it also contains theology, philosophy, and the highly educated musings of two very smart believers.

How many Christians today are still mulling over some past relationship—regretting their own mistakes or pining after someone who "got away"? Often these feelings keep us from fully enjoying the life God has given us. Let the past be past, and live today for the Lord.

I want you to know, my dear brothers and sisters, that everything that has happened to me here has helped to spread the Good News.

PHILIPPIANS 1:12

THE QUIET QUEEN

Bertha of Kent

539–612

If you are reading this Christian book in English, you owe a great deal to Bertha. She wasn't a preacher or a writer or an organizer—she just lived a life of faith that affected everyone around her, and it eventually changed the course of a nation.

A French princess who had learned Christianity in her family, probably from a devout grandmother, Bertha was given in marriage to the Saxon king, Aethelbert of Kent. Although he was not a Christian, it might have been part of the prenuptial agreement that he would allow his new queen to practice her Christian faith. In fact, when she moved to Kent, she brought along a priest, who set up services in Canterbury, in an old Christian mausoleum from Roman times.

It was the end of the sixth century, and Europe was a hodgepodge of religion and culture. Roman influence had ebbed, and various Germanic tribes with an assortment of pagan beliefs controlled the region. In 596, Pope Gregory sent a missions team to England, which was welcomed warmly by Bertha and her priest—and also by King Aethelbert, who had gained a positive impression of Christianity from his wife. The team set up in the Canterbury church and began evangelizing the territory. Five years later, the king himself was baptized, and many of his people with him. The Christian faith had a foothold in England that it would never lose (and in fact, that church in Canterbury continues to worship Christ to the present day).

Bertha's quiet testimony had won her nation to Christ. Even the pope recognized her contribution, writing to her, "Your good deeds are known in various places. . . . Just as the expression of your Christianity has brought us great joy, may there be joy in heaven over the work you have yet to do."

What effect are you having on your society—your family, your neighbors, your coworkers, maybe even your online friends? Can your quiet love and devotion draw them ever closer to the Savior?

Let your good deeds shine out for all to see, so that
everyone will praise your heavenly Father.

MATTHEW 5:16

LOVE LETTERS

Ever since Jacob fell in love with Rachel's face and figure, the mere glimpse of one's beloved has made men go weak in the knees and caused women's hearts to flutter.

Our focus on women in Christian history reveals lots of arranged marriages in which women used their status to do good things, widows used their inheritance for charity, or other women denied marriage altogether to devote themselves fully to God's work. But as history progresses, we begin to see something else—wives who become partners in ministry with their husbands.

This is lovely, but it's Valentine's Day! Where are the flowers, the kisses, the love letters, the sweet nothings whispered in the ear?

Thank God for John Newton. Here was a man of wild passions who sinned boldly and repented well. He fell hard for Polly when he visited her family as a teenager. ("When I first loved you," he wrote later, "I dreamed of you night after night for near three months.") Over the following years, as he tried to make a career as a sailor, a naval officer, and eventually the captain of a slave ship, he kept pining for sweet Polly. (In fact, more than once, his efforts to visit her sabotaged his career success.) When he finally popped the question, she said no. He tried again and again. When she finally accepted, "I sat stupid and speechless for some minutes. . . . My heart was so full . . . that I knew not how to get a word out."

A month later they were married—and he kept writing to her. "I arose before the sun to pray and give thanks for you." "I find some new cause of endearment in you, every day."

John Newton is best known for writing the hymn "Amazing Grace," coming from a deep sense of gratitude for God's love. Yet he also left a legacy of love letters to his wife, deeply grateful for *her* love. "Perhaps we may not be rich—no matter. We are rich in love."

Today, no matter what our circumstances, we can be grateful both for God's amazing love and for the human love he has allowed us to enjoy.

You have captured my heart,
my treasure, my bride.
You hold it hostage with one glance of your eyes.
SONG OF SONGS 4:9

MOTHER, MAY I?

Hilda of Whitby
614–80

She stood for peace, nurtured faith, and supported the arts. At a critical time in Britain's history, Hilda became a spiritual mother to many—even though her own family life had been less than ideal.

In the political intrigue of the day, Hilda's father was poisoned when she was just an infant. She was raised in the court of King Edwin of Northumbria, her uncle. In 627, Edwin converted to Christianity, and his whole court was baptized—including thirteen-year-old Hilda. But then Edwin died in battle a few years later.

We don't know much else about Hilda's life until she was thirty-three, when she became a nun. Ten years later she was put in charge of a double monastery in Whitby, where men and women lived separately but worshiped together. This became a center for Celtic Christianity, and Hilda's reputation as a spiritual leader grew. "Because of her outstanding devotion and grace," wrote the contemporary historian Bede, "all that knew her called her mother."

Christianity was growing in Britain, but there were two distinct strains of it. The old Roman church had mostly been driven out by pagan tribes in the 400s and only recently restored by Pope Gregory's outreach (and Bertha's influence) in 596. But there was an even older tradition of Celtic Christianity that had never left the British Isles, but burrowed in monasteries, mostly in the north. Now both were expanding— the Roman church with its order and organization and the Celtic church with its vibrant spirituality—and there were some conflicts. One key issue, believe it or not, was the date of Easter. In 664, church leaders decided to hold a peace conference of sorts. The site: Hilda's monastery at Whitby. We can only assume that Hilda's maternal presence assured both sides of a fair hearing. As a result, the Synod of Whitby stands as a crucial unifying moment in the history of the British church.

Sometimes the biggest influence you can have is not in what you say or do, but merely in who you are. Once you gain the trust and admiration of others, you can bring them together in amazing ways. Have you seen this happen in your world?

God blesses those who work for peace, for they will be called the children of God.

MATTHEW 5:9

THE PRODUCER

Hilda and Caedmon
SEVENTH CENTURY

Throughout history, great artists have always needed supporters—people to recognize their talent and give them opportunities, to encourage them and even fund their work. Hilda of Whitby was someone like that, and her support was seen most significantly in the work of an unlikely songster named Caedmon.

He was a common laborer, tending the livestock at a farm near the monastery that Hilda managed. As the story goes, he was at a banquet one night when everyone got to singing, and he left in a funk because he had nothing to sing. But that night he had a vision in which a mysterious stranger ordered him to sing a new song "of the beginning of creation." Caedmon composed it in his sleep and sang it the next day to his foreman—who decided the song was worthy of Hilda's attention.

Apparently Hilda gathered a group to listen to Caedmon, "and they all determined that God had granted him heavenly grace," writes the historian Bede. "They would then explain a passage of sacred history or doctrine, asking him to put it into verse if he could. Agreeing to this, he left and returned the next morning, giving them the assigned passage in beautiful verse form."

Caedmon's gift was recognized by Hilda, and she invited him to join the monastery. There he continued to write original Bible-based songs, establishing a reputation that continues today as one of the first Old English poets. "He tried to draw people away from the love of sin and arouse in them a commitment to good deeds and perseverance," Bede writes.

Hilda's role in Caedmon's career was not unusual for her. Respected by princes and peasants alike, she mentored five different men who became bishops in the region. You might call her the "Barnabas" of Old England, encouraging others to develop their own ministries, just as Barnabas did for Paul and others. We need more like her today.

So, do you know anyone who, like Caedmon, has a hidden talent and a dream? Perhaps you can offer encouragement, not only to use that talent, but to use it in the service of the Lord.

Barnabas brought him to the apostles and told them how Saul had seen the Lord on the way to Damascus and how the Lord had spoken to Saul.

ACTS 9:27

STRONG VOICE

Hroswitha

935–1002

S ome people think Europe was a cultural wasteland in the years 500 to 1400—that medieval folk muddled through life with little education or art. That's not entirely true. There were still a few blazing beacons in these "dark ages"—people like the German nun Hroswitha. (Sometimes her name is spelled Rosvitha, Hrotsvit, or other variants; if you pronounce it "gross-feet," you're pretty close.)

Living in the Abbey of Gandersheim in the late 900s, Hroswitha had opportunity to study and write. It seems she was of noble birth, which would have entitled her to a strong education in her youth, and she entered the abbey as a "canoness," a status that provided a great deal of freedom for personal projects. Overseeing the abbey was a young woman named Gerberg, sister of Holy Roman Emperor Otto I, a great patron of the arts.

A gifted writer, Hroswitha took full advantage of these opportunities. She wrote narrative poems on biblical themes, histories of Otto's exploits, and plays in the Roman style. She found a pun in her own name, which sounds like the Saxon for "strong voice," and she used that strong voice in various ways. The range of her ability—prose, poetry, and drama—is remarkable, as is the sophistication of her work. Hroswitha is hailed as Germany's first female "literary" writer, but her work would stand in comparison with that of any man of the time, and for several centuries thereafter.

Why did she write? "I was eager that the talent given me by Heaven should not grow rusty from neglect, and remain silent in my heart from apathy, but under the hammer of assiduous devotion should sound a chord of divine praise," she wrote in the preface to one collection of poems. "If I have achieved nothing else, this alone should make my work of some value." Well aware of the public criticism she might receive, she urged readers to evaluate honestly, and if they found anything good, to "give the credit to God."

What artistic talents might you have? Are they "growing rusty from neglect" or "remaining silent from apathy"? If you explored those abilities, hammering out some offering of design, poetry, communication, or music, could you "sound a chord of divine praise"?

Beautiful words stir my heart.
I will recite a lovely poem about the king,
for my tongue is like the pen of a skillful poet.

PSALM 45:1

DRAMATIC LICENSE

Hroswitha

935–1002

The art of theater has been overshadowed in recent years by film, TV, and now Internet, but the original "moving pictures" happened on stage—and the history of theater provides great insight into the development of humanity. But theater history has a thousand-year hole in it, one that's filled only by the German nun Hroswitha.

The Greeks basically invented the theater art form, some four hundred years before Christ. As with many other things, the Romans borrowed from the Greeks—and the area they excelled in was comedy. Playwrights Plautus and Terence perfected the farce, with its bawdy, street-level antics. These plays were rife with dirty jokes, so it's no surprise that, when Christians took over the empire, theater was discouraged and sometimes outlawed.

Fast-forward to the late 900s, to a convent in Germany, where Hroswitha reads the plays of Terence and says, "I want to do that too." But where Terence's plays were irreverent, Hroswitha's would be worshipful. Terence's plays were mostly mindless fun; Hroswitha's would embed practical philosophy. Terence used female characters as sexual pawns; Hroswitha would create strong women faced with important choices. Terence joked about fornication; Hroswitha would mock the fornicators and exalt chastity.

In Hroswitha's play *Dulcitius*, a Roman commander pressures a Christian virgin into sex—but he becomes miraculously (and comically) confused and ends up wooing kitchen pots instead. This is high farce, but it also upholds Christian commitment. In *Gallicanus*, a young woman is saved from an arranged marriage when her would-be husband converts and honors her vow of chastity. We wonder if this is close to the playwright's own story. Presumably from a noble family, she would have had suitors, but she chose to serve Christ rather than a husband, and in the convent, she found freedom to worship the Lord and practice her art.

The Bible weaves two themes together: liberation and servanthood. Hroswitha understood that, oddly enough, the two are linked. You find true freedom in serving the Lord—whether you are serving him in and through your marriage, or whether your unmarried life allows you to serve him with single-minded devotion.

You will know the truth, and the truth will set you free.

JOHN 8:32

SAINT AND SINNER

Empress Theodora

500–48

Theodora, the sixth-century Byzantine empress, was either the star of an inspiring rags-to-riches story or a conniving manipulator who slept and cheated her way to the top. Either way, she's on a short list of the most powerful women of all time.

The early details of her life are not in dispute. As a teenager, she worked as an actress at a time when most actresses were also prostitutes. She became the mistress of a provincial governor in North Africa but left him when he became abusive. Wending her way through the empire, she landed in Constantinople, the capital, starting a wholesome new life as a wool spinner. Was it just a happy coincidence that she worked near the palace, drawing the attention of Justinian, the emperor-to-be? He fell hard for her and wedded her—after repealing the law that kept government officials from marrying actresses.

As emperor, Justinian faced numerous challenges, and Theodora was right there beside him—sometimes ahead of him. When riots broke out in the capital in 532, Justinian prepared to flee the city, but Theodora urged him to stay and fight. In a bloodbath, the riots were quelled. The couple made some new enemies, but they kept their power.

The church at the time was badly divided over the nature of Jesus Christ. Some emphasized his single, divine nature, and others followed the Nicene concept that he is fully God and fully man. Here Theodora disagreed with her husband, taking the one-nature position, and occasionally subverting her husband's actions. Some modern scholars think this public disagreement kept a degree of peace in the empire because both parties were being heard.

Amid all the game playing and manipulation, it appears that Justinian and Theodora really loved each other. They certainly *needed* each other—and after she died, he was never the same.

How will history remember you? Saint or sinner, or both mashed together? It may not matter what the masses think; what effect are you having on those closest to you, those who know the true you?

"Christ Jesus came into the world to save sinners"—and I am the worst of them all. But God had mercy on me so that Christ Jesus could use me as a prime example of his great patience with even the worst sinners.

1 TIMOTHY 1:15-16

TIME FOR SPEAKING

Kassia

810–65

She was about to be crowned the winner in a beauty pageant. Well, strictly speaking it was a "bride show," in which the emperor would hand a golden apple to the fairest of them all—and then marry her. Perhaps it was the Eden-like apple that caused Emperor Theophilos to tease the quick-witted Kassia with the line "From woman have come the worse things."

She instantly retorted, "And from woman the better."

Her quick tongue was biblically accurate—Mary's child trumps Eve's sin—but it cost Kassia the queendom. Theophilos thought better of having such a witty wife and married someone else.

The next we know of Kassia, it's the year 843, more than a decade later, and she's the abbess of a convent she founded in Constantinople. Was she brooding over her lost chance at power and glory? Hardly. She was making a name for herself as a writer. Her hymns began to be used in the church. Nearly fifty of them still exist today, and about thirty are commonly used in Eastern Orthodox churches.

Besides hymns, she was also known for a collection of short sayings, including this one: "I hate silence when it is time for speaking." That seemed to characterize her—not only in that "bride show," but as an outspoken proponent of artful worship. She withstood forcible efforts of the emperor (yes, that same guy) to destroy the religious icons churches were using in their services.

Her strong voice is still heard in "The Hymn of Kassiani," regularly chanted during Holy Week in Orthodox churches. A song of the sinful woman who anointed Jesus' feet, it is a lifeline for sinful women today who long for God's compassion.

Sensing Thy divinity, O Lord, a woman of many sins
takes it upon herself to become a myrrh-bearer,
And in deep mourning brings before Thee fragrant oil
in anticipation of Thy burial; crying:
"Woe to me! . . .
Do not ignore Thy handmaiden,
O Thou whose mercy is endless."

"I tell you, her sins—and they are many—have been forgiven, so she
has shown me much love. But a person who is forgiven little shows only
little love." Then Jesus said to the woman, "Your sins are forgiven."

LUKE 7:47-48

RICH LITTLE POOR GIRL

Clare of Assisi
1194–1253

The things you own—do they really own you? Could you give away all that you have, even if you wanted to? You *need* your house, your car, your smartphone. You may talk about simplifying your life, but it's very hard to do.

That's exactly what a girl named Clare discovered in the 1200s. Brought up in a well-to-do Christian family, she heard a sermon by Francis of Assisi and decided to devote herself to his rule of poverty. She ran away from home to join the monastery, taking her vow of poverty on March 20, 1212.

Her family wasn't happy. They sent a squad of knights to bring her back, but Clare stood firm. She would not enjoy her family's wealth. She would not be married off to a rich nobleman. She was wholly committed to Christ now. She had already shorn her hair.

Clare's dream was to start a new order for women, following the same restrictions that Francis had set up for men: no personal property, no community property, dependence on alms. She actually began to win over her family, and her sisters and mother eventually joined her, but her next obstacle came from the church. Leaders liked the idea of a new order of nuns, but the Franciscan rule was a bit much. They kept trying to force Clare's nuns into less austere systems, which she respectfully resisted. When Pope Gregory IX offered to forgive her for any personal poverty-vow breaking she needed to do, she replied, "Holy Father, I crave absolution for my sins, but I desire not to be absolved from the obligation of following Jesus Christ."

The pope soon reversed his position, but when he died, Clare had to win over a new pope . . . and she did. The day before her death, Pope Innocent IV officially approved what became known as the Rule of Saint Clare—the commitment observed by a growing number of nuns known as Poor Clares. There are about twenty thousand of them around the world today.

As a teenager, Clare chose to let nothing get in the way of her relationship with Jesus. It was difficult, but she stuck with that commitment.

What gets in the way of your relationship with Jesus? What are you going to do about it?

[Jesus said,] "Go and sell all your possessions and give the money to the poor, and you will have treasure in heaven. Then come, follow me."

MARK 10:21

CARING

For two and a half centuries, the greatest empire on earth waged a civil war against an unarmed foe . . . and lost. Persecution was brutal, as Roman authorities routinely rounded up Christians and killed many of them. But then, in one of the great surprises of history, the Roman Empire became Christian. How did this happen?

Increasingly, scholars are suggesting that the church used its greatest weapon: *love*. Throughout the empire, Christians quietly became known as people who cared for others—often nursing the sick back to health. This proved especially important as various plagues ravaged parts of the empire. When others feared for their own health, the Christ followers could be counted on to sit with ailing folks, give them food and drink, and pray for them. Women led the way in this ministry of healing and care.

Of course, the caring ministry of women has extended far beyond the early centuries of the church. In the fifteenth century, Catherine of Genoa ran a hospital for poor victims of the plague. She is quoted as saying, "If you want to know how much a person loves God, see how much he loves his neighbor" (an echo of 1 John 4:20). In more modern times, medical pioneers like Elizabeth Blackwell and nurse Florence Nightingale were motivated by Christian compassion. Ida Scudder and Clara Swain are but a few of the hundreds of medical missionaries who have taken their talent for healing throughout the world.

Sometimes we Christians exalt the gifts of preaching and leadership and ignore the equally important gift of caring for people. Not only did Jesus himself carry on a substantial ministry to the sick, but he also said that when *we* help the needy, we are actually serving him (see Matthew 25:40). We certainly care about the spiritual needs of the people we meet, but we must not ignore their physical needs either. The Bible makes no distinction there. Love propels us to help people in any way that we can. So whether you are mopping the brow of a feverish child, driving a neighbor to dialysis, or praying with a friend over a cancer diagnosis, you are showing love to Christ . . . and sharing his love with others.

"Since I began to love," wrote Catherine of Genoa, "love has never forsaken me. It has ever grown to its own fullness within my innermost heart."

We love each other because he loved us first.

1 JOHN 4:19

FRIENDS AND FOES— AND FAMILY

Radegund

520–86

The life of a princess—isn't that what every girl dreams of? If so, you might want to steer your dreams clear of medieval Europe. In that chess game, even queens were pawns.

Radegund was born around 520 to a king of the Germanic land of Thuringia. He was assassinated by his brother, who then adopted Radegund. Her uncle then allied with a Frankish king to kill her *other* uncle, and then double-crossed his ally to take power himself. In retaliation, the uncle was killed, and the twelve-year-old Radegund was made a wife of the new Frankish king—one of six wives, actually. And you thought *your* family was difficult.

In the court of the king, she lived simply and humbly, giving away much of her personal wealth to monasteries and the needy. "There was no hermit who could hide from her munificence," wrote the biographer Fortunatus. But she couldn't hide from the continuing intrigue of high position. When her brother was killed at the king's command, she left the court and became a nun. Later she used her resources to build a double monastery at Poitiers, which developed into a great center of learning.

A number of medieval women forsook high positions to serve in convents, but what's noteworthy about Radegund is the quality of friendships she formed. Two historians of the period—Venantius Fortunatus and Gregory of Tours—were quite close to her. Their records indicate a number of coworkers at the convent who were also her friends. Gregory spoke at her funeral, and the whole congregation of nuns made quite a scene, clamoring, "Lord, spare us this heavy loss. You are taking our light."

How did young Radegund learn about friendship? From her earliest years, she was caught in a whirlpool of backstabbing violence, even in her own family. Yet by the grace of God, she found a new family—people who loved the Lord and shared her commitment to him.

Maybe you've been blessed with a great upbringing. But even if you weren't, just like Radegund, you can find a new family among those who share your faith and love.

Then [Jesus] pointed to his disciples and said, "Look, these are my mother and brothers. Anyone who does the will of my Father in heaven is my brother and sister and mother!"

MATTHEW 12:49-50

TRANSPORTED

Margaret of Scotland

1045–93

I n Scotland there are towns named North Queensferry and South Queensferry. The namesake queen was Margaret of Scotland, and she set up the ferry to help pilgrims cross the Firth of Forth to get to a Benedictine monastery. It seems appropriate that she'd be known for transportation, because she was often on the move.

In 1045 Margaret was born into the English royal family . . . but she was born in Hungary. Her father, known as Edward the Exile, was a potential successor to the British throne, but "potential successors" had a way of dying, so he had been whisked off to Scandinavia, then to Hungary, which had just gone through a religious awakening. As a result, Margaret was brought up in a very pious environment.

When she was about twelve, her family traveled back to England. Though her father soon died, her brother was in line for the throne—but all bets were off when William the Conqueror struck in 1066. Margaret's family fled again, eventually ending up in Scotland. There she married King Malcolm III.

He was a warrior, not especially religious (Shakespeare correctly depicts him as a vengeful opponent of Macbeth). Margaret brought into Scottish life not only her Anglo-Saxon ways and Continental style, but also her deep faith. An ancient biographer tells how she read Bible stories to her husband and urged him to rule justly. Known for charitable works and personal devotion, she welcomed the spiritual disciplines of the Benedictine order into the kingdom. She died in 1093, shortly after learning of the death of her husband and eldest son in battle.

There's an old comic line that says, "Wherever you go, there you are." It was true of Margaret, and it should be true of us. Whether in Hungary, England, or Scotland, Margaret seems to have been fully present, learning the ways of God or sharing them. The ups and downs of our lives may propel us to different places, different jobs, and different relationships, but God is still with us in all of them, and he calls us to serve him wherever we're transported.

You know my thoughts even when I'm far away. You see me when I travel and when I rest at home. . . . I can never get away from your presence!

PSALM 139:2, 3, 7

THE TRANSFORMER

Marie de France

1140–1220

She was probably the most famous writer of her time, but we know next to nothing about her. Her stories and poems were quite popular among the nobles of twelfth-century Europe, yet her biographers have to resort to guesswork. In one poem, she wrote, "My name is Marie and I am from France," and so history knows what to call her.

She had three major works, all very different in character. There's a collection of 103 fables that she translated from English, known as the *Ysopet* (you can hear the name Aesop in that title). Her *Purgatory of St. Patrick*, translated from a Latin original, tells of an Irish knight who visits the underworld à la Orpheus or Dante. But she is best known for her *Lais*, fifteen love poems expressing medieval chivalry.

Her style is sweet and simple, not the overly flowery language you might expect from French romance. As she writes in *Purgatory*:

> I want to disclose
> This writing very carefully
> And to put effort and care into it for the sake of God,
> In order to improve the simple folk.

There is a Christian sensibility to her work, but she's not preachy. She clearly comes from a Christianized culture, but she celebrates folk wisdom and romantic love as well as piety. In fact, her *Lais* were sometimes criticized by church leaders for their treatment of adulterous love affairs. (She didn't promote them, but she didn't always condemn them either.)

Looking over the whole collection of this mysterious writer's work, we can't help but notice that she really didn't create much from scratch. She translated other writings into French, and she recomposed love songs she had heard. Still, she put her unique stamp on everything she covered. She took fables and legends and ballads and transformed them into masterpieces. Her world was better for it.

So, what have you transformed lately? Are you taking the pieces of your life and creating beauty from it—in your relationships, in your art, in your witness? Our God is not only a creator, but a transformer, and he invites us to join him in that task.

Don't copy the behavior and customs of this world, but let God transform you into a new person by changing the way you think. Then you will learn to know God's will for you, which is good and pleasing and perfect.

ROMANS 12:2

VISIONS OF GRANDEUR

Hildegard of Bingen
1098–1179

She was quite possibly the most creative woman ever. Hildegard dazzled twelfth-century Germany with her output—seventy songs, three books of theology, a gospel commentary, a musical play, writings on science and nature, and drawings to dress up those books. She advised popes and bishops, led a convent, took preaching tours, and invented her own language. And it all began with visions—or migraine headaches—that started at age three.

By modern standards, her childhood was odd. Perhaps because of her visions, or because she was their tenth child (a "tithe"), or because they wanted to curry favor with church leaders, her parents committed her upbringing to the church. She was confined in a convent with a holy woman who taught her the basics of faith, as well as reading and writing. It seems her outside contacts were quite limited. Apart from her guardian, who didn't know much beyond the basics, and a visiting monk who taught her music, she was probably alone a lot. Alone to think and draw and compose. Alone with her visions.

In her thirties she became head of the convent, and only in her forties did she begin writing down her visions (after a vision commanded her to do so). And then the creativity that had been incubating for decades poured out of her. Songs and books and hundreds of letters came forth in a grand and unique style. Though women were generally kept from public speaking, Hildegard had four preaching tours of Germany, criticizing church corruption and calling for reform.

Strictly speaking, she was not well educated—and maybe this was part of her appeal. Universities were being founded at this time, and scholars were busy codifying human knowledge. Hildegard was free of all that, free to see God's world in God's light.

Maybe you're uneasy with all this talk of visions. Maybe, like many modern scholars, you assume Hildegard simply suffered migraines. But there's still treasure in her story. Despite her (literally) cloistered childhood, Hildegard was able to enlighten the world with her trust in God, her desire to serve him, and the courage to use her stunning creativity.

No matter where you come from, surely you can do that too.

I will pour out my Spirit upon all people. Your sons and daughters will prophesy.
Your old men will dream dreams, and your young men will see visions.

JOEL 2:28

THE LIONESS

Eleanor of Aquitaine

—————— 1122–1204 ——————

R ich and gorgeous, Eleanor was the greatest catch of the twelfth century—except she refused to be caught. Wife of two kings and mother of three others, she was a lioness stalking her prey. Some historians depict her as a conniving opportunist, but maybe she was just the smartest person in the room.

Her father, a wealthy landowner in France and a duke, died when she was just fifteen, leaving her his title and fortune. She married the crown prince of France, who soon became King Louis VII. They co-led the Second Crusade, which was a disaster. She then divorced Louis on a technicality and married the crown prince of England, who soon became King Henry II. They fought. He imprisoned her. Three of her sons eventually became king but fought one another for that privilege.

You know, just your average, humdrum life.

Her life was epic, the stuff of high drama— and in fact, it has been retold in movies, plays, and novels. But there's one story we should take special note of.

She was still queen of France, and King Louis was waging a war against the pope (which many say she instigated). Eleanor paid a visit to the renowned monk Bernard of Clairvaux, asking him to use his influence to sway the pope on a certain point. She was doing what she always did, pitting power against power.

But Bernard scolded her for her combative attitude. Where was her penitence? Why wasn't she humbling herself before God? Reportedly Eleanor broke down in tears, and Bernard softened his tone: "My child, seek those things which make for peace."

It's unclear whether this was authentic sorrow or just another ploy, but there's a lesson for us. When the world around us is doing battle, when we have to fight for everything we can get, we can sometimes storm into God's presence and try to manipulate him, too. "Do this for me, and I'll do this for you!" As wise Bernard observed, prayer isn't just another negotiation, but a humble peace-seeking.

How will you enter God's presence today?

—————

The tax collector stood at a distance and dared not even lift his eyes to heaven as he prayed. Instead, he beat his chest in sorrow, saying, "O God, be merciful to me, for I am a sinner."

LUKE 18:13

HEARTBEAT

Gertrude

1256–1302

It's hard to get famous for being humble. Yet that's what a thirteenth-century German nun named Gertrude did. History has come to know her as "Gertrude the Great," but she would certainly be embarrassed by that title. She was far more aware of her sinfulness than anyone else was, and she made a special effort to pray for struggling souls.

Probably an orphan, Gertrude joined a Benedictine monastery as a girl. There she showed intelligence and congeniality as she grew. At about age twenty-five, she had a vision—and this set a new course for her life. She eased up on her academic studies to focus on the Bible and theology. Writing in both German and Latin, Gertrude created books of quotations from the saints, translations of Scripture portions, and devotional prayers. The visions continued, and she became a spiritual leader within the monastery and a respected thinker outside the walls.

In one vision, she felt the Lord holding her close, inviting her to listen to his heartbeat. Indeed, that's an apt image for Gertrude's life. Her own heart seemed to beat in rhythm with her Savior's. Her writings indicate an emotional depth of devotion: "O most lovable radiance, when will you satisfy me with yourself? If only I might here perceive the fine rays of your Venus-like beauty for a little while and at least be permitted to anticipate your gentleness for a short time and pleasantly beforehand to taste you, my best share. Ah, turn around now a little so that I may fix my look on you, flower of flowers."

How about you? Have you been hearing the heartbeat of Jesus? We often make spiritual growth a matter of study, and there's plenty to learn about the Lord. But what a difference it makes when we open our hearts to him, as Gertrude did. When we allow ourselves to feel a true spiritual intimacy with him, it will affect every area of our lives.

[Jesus said,] "Look at this woman kneeling here. When I entered your home, you didn't offer me water to wash the dust from my feet, but she has washed them with her tears and wiped them with her hair. . . . I tell you, her sins— and they are many—have been forgiven, so she has shown me much love."

LUKE 7:44, 47

DEVOTION

One trait that marks most of the great women in Christian history is *devotion*. Some have left a legacy of devotional writing that is far more than a matter of gathering pious thoughts to start the day. Women have been pioneers in considering the question, How can we become more thoroughly devoted to God? Throughout the centuries, they have plumbed the depths of Christian love and loyalty.

Devotion generally begins with focus on God: spending time in his presence, getting to know him, and listening to what he has to say. Especially in medieval times, this often became a mystical experience, a spirit-to-Spirit connection. It wasn't just about learning something new about God; it was *knowing* God.

For many women throughout history, those connective moments allowed them to hear God's direction for their lives, which they then pursued with that same loyal, loving devotion.

Angela Merici was so devoted to her call that she said no to a pope. Knowing education was the key to advancement in society, Angela felt called to start schools for girls. She was so good at what she did that the pope asked her to take charge of a group of nuns, but Angela declined, staying devoted to what she believed God called her to—educating young women.

Flash-forward four hundred years or so, and you find American Katharine Bushnell devoted to women who were being forced against their will into prostitution and human trafficking. Though her life was threatened, she leaned upon the promise that Christ would strengthen her. Her devotion and bravery helped to change the laws, and her experience later led her to help similar women in India.

More recently, Dorothy Day's devotion to the poor led her to found a national movement in the 1930s that helped the needy. And many other women have also thrown themselves into causes that God led them into.

It still happens like that today. Devotion to God creates a closeness to him, and when there's a closeness, it's easier to hear him say, "Hey, you have this skill, you have this talent, you have this opportunity to help out with (insert your cause here), and I want you to devote yourself to it."

The LORD says, "I will guide you along the best pathway for
your life. I will advise you and watch over you."

PSALM 32:8

EVERLASTING LOVE

Julian of Norwich
1342–1416

What would people think about you if they had only your writings to go on—your memos, grocery lists, and Facebook posts? Would they be able to piece together your life? Would they know what you were all about?

That's the case with Julian of Norwich. We know next to nothing about her, except from her own writing. Certain clues suggest that she was a woman of noble birth (including the fact that she knew how to write and had time to do so), born in the mid-1300s, and she came from the English town of Norwich. But her unremarkable life changed at the age of thirty-one, when she was deathly ill and had a series of sixteen visions. She immediately wrote them down and spent the rest of her life composing commentaries upon them. The resulting book, *Sixteen Revelations of Divine Love*, stands as a classic of English spirituality.

What was Julian all about? In a word, *love*. In two words, *God's love*. "God is more nearer to us than our own soul," she wrote. Even our own sin cannot pry us away from the Lord's heart. "In falling and in rising we are ever preciously kept in one love. . . . I saw full surely that ere God made us He loved us; which love was never slacked, nor ever shall be. And in this love He hath done all His works; and in this love He hath made all things profitable to us; and in this love our life is everlasting."

This was an important message in the late Middle Ages. You might say that Christianity had "left its first love." The church was largely about power and rules. This idea of God as a loving parent rather than a scowling judge was much needed.

It still is much needed. And that brings us back to the original question: How would people define you? If someone added up your sayings and doings, would they look at your life and say, "This person was all about God's love"?

I have loved you, my people, with an everlasting love.
With unfailing love I have drawn you to myself.

JEREMIAH 31:3

ALL SHALL BE WELL

Julian of Norwich
1342–1416

Do optimists annoy you? Do you get tired of people who try to cheer you up in the most inane ways? "Look at the bright side." "Turn that frown upside down." "It's always darkest before . . ." You get the idea. (Oops—maybe you *are* an optimist; if so, read on.)

The problem is not the joyful attitude itself, but the fact that these cheerleaders usually have little to go on. *So what makes you think this cloud actually has a silver lining?*

A favorite quote from the fourteenth-century mystic Julian of Norwich goes like this: "All shall be well, and all shall be well, and all manner of thing shall be well." At first blush, that would make her the poster child for unfounded optimism, but let's take a deeper look at her writing.

Julian was passionate about the love of God. It was powerful, but it was also what she called "homely"—that is, personal, practical, part of ordinary life. God was a father to her, but also a nurturing mother, holding her tight. And this gives us the reason that "all shall be well." If we are loved relentlessly by the all-powerful God, we can trust him to be there for us in thick and thin. Julian wrote honestly of her own pain, and even of her own sin, but her focus was on the love of God overcoming all of that. "God, of thy goodness, give me thyself, for thou art enough for me."

So if you're an optimist, that's fine. Really. But make it more than just "positive thinking." Mull over the pervasive love of God. Because he loves us, we know that, whether things turn out for the best or the worst, "all manner of thing shall be well."

I am convinced that nothing can ever separate us from God's love. Neither death nor life, neither angels nor demons, neither our fears for today nor our worries about tomorrow—not even the powers of hell can separate us from God's love. No power in the sky above or in the earth below—indeed, nothing in all creation will ever be able to separate us from the love of God that is revealed in Christ Jesus our Lord.

ROMANS 8:38-39

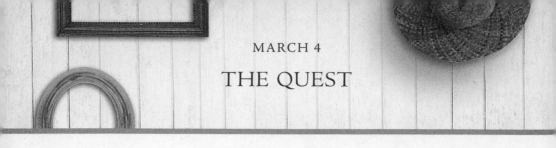

THE QUEST

Margery Kempe

1373–1439

What made her special was that she wasn't. Margery Kempe was not a queen or a princess, not even a highborn lady. She was born into the merchant class. Her father made a good living, and so did her husband. Despite bearing fourteen children, she also started her own home-based business, which eventually failed. She was no scholar; in fact, she probably didn't know how to read or write. Her autobiography was dictated to a scribe. She wasn't a spiritual giant, not a member of any convent or religious order. She was just a working mom with a passion for Jesus.

That passion drove her to make pilgrimages, visiting spiritual leaders and holy sites throughout England and the European mainland. She detailed these encounters in *The Book of Margery Kempe*, generally considered the first autobiography in the English language. Modern scholars appreciate this book, not for its literary merit, but for its glimpse of regular life. (Some question whether all the events in the book really happened, but even as fiction, it's a valuable asset. The history of women in the medieval world is full of nuns and queens because those are the only medieval women we know about—except for the merchant-mother Margery. Through her we learn about town life, rather than convent life or palace life.)

Throughout her book, Margery seems to be searching for something—perhaps for a way that an ordinary person could follow Jesus. She began to question the assumptions of her community—the love of wealth, for instance. Well aware of her own spiritual failings, she was propelled by visions. She hoped these visions were genuine revelations from God, but she wasn't always sure. Some folks in her day thought she was crazy, and some modern scholars agree. But maybe she was just doing things differently.

So what propels you? Are you driven by a desire to provide a good life for yourself and your family? That's great, but how do you define "a good life"? Are you following Jesus' vision or your own? Don't sit there and wish you were a great speaker-author with a hot website and video series. Be you, ordinary you, and follow Jesus.

---

*If any of you wants to be my follower, you must turn from your
selfish ways, take up your cross daily, and follow me.*

LUKE 9:23

WHEN MARGIE MET JULIE

Margery Kempe and Julian of Norwich

1415

Historians love encounters. When they find evidence that one historical figure met another, their wheels start spinning. *What was said? How did each affect the other?*

The Book of Margery Kempe describes such a meeting between the author and Julian of Norwich (the only historical reference to Julian outside her own writings), occurring sometime around 1415. Margery would have been in her forties, a commoner paying visits to various spiritual leaders in England and Rome, learning what she could learn, but also testing out her own Christian experience. Now in her seventies, Lady Julian was living alone in a small room in a church. Margery stayed with her for several days, in "holy dalliance . . . communing in the love of our Lord Jesus Christ."

Try to imagine the dynamics in that room. From their writings, we see Julian as quiet, completely centered in God's love, while Margery was a bundle of energy, self-conscious, desperate to verify her visions. Was there a breathless quality in Margery's plea for advice? Can you hear a sigh from Lady Julian? Perhaps there were many corrections that could have been offered, but the older woman did not rebuke the younger, a fact that Margery took comfort in. It was clear that the Holy Spirit was in Margery's soul, said Julian, but she needed to "measure these experiences according to the worship they accrue to God and the profit to her fellow Christians."

Understand the times. We look back and see two giants of early English writing, but they saw themselves simply as women with visions. Both had critics accusing them of heresy, a charge that could lead to capital punishment in this world and worse woes in the next. So Margery had plenty to worry about, but Julian seemed to be an anchor of calm. "Set all your trust in God," she said, "and fear not the language of the world."

This amazing encounter can instruct men and women in any age. Your experience of Jesus may be misunderstood by those around you. It's always a good idea to test it out with older, wiser believers you respect. Measure your experience by this question: Does it glorify God and help Christians? And then forge ahead, putting all your trust in God.

God has given us his Spirit as proof that we live in him and he in us.

1 JOHN 4:13

BEING HEARD

Catherine of Siena
1347–80

Caterina di Giacomo di Bennicasa, known today as Catherine of Siena, was the twenty-fourth of twenty-five children. Chances are, not all of her siblings survived childhood, but even if she was one of the youngest of eight or nine living siblings, she probably had to fight to be heard. It's no wonder she's known for being outspoken.

As a Dominican nun, Catherine was confident that God was speaking to her and giving her messages to pass on to the pope. In fact, God used her more than once to speak to the powerful men in charge of the Catholic Church.

The fourteenth century saw serious divisions in the church, as the French cardinals took power and moved church headquarters to Avignon. But Catherine told Pope Gregory XI that the Lord wanted him to move back to Rome . . . and he listened to her.

That was not the only time she would tell a pope what she believed to be the truth. Gregory died within a year of returning to Rome. When problems arose with his successor, Urban VI, a rival pope was nominated. Again, Catherine went to the most powerful man in the church to tell him what she believed to be true—God did not want two popes. She seemed fearless.

Speaking an uncomfortable truth to someone powerful, even in the church, is scary. You might feel you don't have the right because you're not as high up as that person. You might fear the consequences or think your message won't be taken seriously.

While Catherine of Siena seemed unafraid, she might have been concerned with these same things. Her truth-telling didn't always achieve the desired results, but she faithfully conveyed what she believed God wanted her listeners to know. When you have to deliver a message you think someone would rather not hear, remember your part is just to speak the truth—in love. No matter what happens next, you've done what's right.

Get the truth and never sell it; also get wisdom, discipline, and good judgment.

PROVERBS 23:23

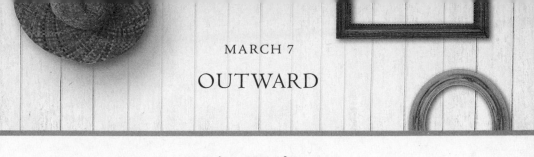

OUTWARD

Catherine of Siena

1347–80

As a child, Catherine developed a survival tactic: "Build a cell inside your mind, from which you can never flee." In that private space, she could sort through her problems and imagine them being solved. Modern psychologists tell us that this is common among abuse victims and other troubled children. In Catherine's case, God met her in that mental retreat. From the age of five or six, she received visions from God, and this relationship developed as she grew. At age sixteen, she was pressured to marry the widower of her older sister, but she refused—partly because the man was a lout, but mostly because she had already pledged herself to Christ.

Later she reached a significant turning point, sensing that Christ was calling her out of her private "cell" and into the wider world. This unleashed a fury of charitable activity. She gave away food and clothing, visited the sick (in this time of plague, there were plenty of them), and spoke out about corruption in society, even among the clergy. Catherine became a prolific letter writer, and her fame as a Christian visionary brought her into the orbits of popes and princes. She had no problem telling them what to do.

Through all this, Catherine seemed to have a strong sense of the *inward life* and the *outward life*. Early on, she learned to retreat within herself and listen for God's voice. Later, she spoke out for God and had a huge impact on the world. "You ought to help [your neighbor] spiritually, with prayer, counseling him with words, and assisting him both spiritually and temporally, according to the need in which he may be," Catherine wrote, adding that the Christian who *doesn't* do this "does himself an injury" because he's not allowing God to show grace through him.

How would you describe your inward life or your outward life? Are they both present, vital, and in balance? Some Christians seem to focus on their personal growth, and there's nothing wrong with that. But do you think God might be calling you out of that protective "cell"? Could he be asking you to engage with your neighbors, to share his love freely and creatively, to have an impact on the wider world?

If we love each other, God lives in us, and his love is brought to full expression in us.

1 JOHN 4:12

THE TREE

Catherine of Siena's Dialogue

—— 1370 ——

In her masterwork, *The Dialogue of Catherine of Siena*, the fourteenth-century visionary Catherine of Siena wrote down a parable God had given her involving a circle of ground, a tree growing in that circle, and an offshoot branching from the tree: "The soul is a tree existing by love, and that it can live by nothing else than love. . . . It is necessary then, that the root of this tree, that is the affection of the soul, should grow in, and issue from the circle of true self-knowledge which is contained in Me."

As the parable expands, the soil with this circle is "the earth of true humility," which "the tree of love feeds itself on." The offshoot branch is described as "true discretion" that "produces fragrant blossoms of virtue." As a result, neighbors are blessed by the fruit and blossoms of the tree.

This proves to be a wonderful image of Catherine's life and work. Her rich inner spirituality sent her roots deep into God's resources. She encountered various types of suffering—physical as well as social—but she found nourishment in her relationship with God. And yet she wasn't just a well-fed tree. She "branched out" in deeds of love for the poor and needy as well as in prophetic messages to the powerful. Her outward actions sprang from her inner connection with God.

How does this parable fit you? Are you planted in good soil? Are you drawing nourishment from your knowledge of God? Are you letting that connection with God blossom forth in good actions that bless others? How does your outward life display the inner reality of your relationship with God? Are you blossoming with the fruit of that relationship, or are you having trouble getting the nourishment you need?

Or is there some other parable that would depict your life? Take some time to talk with God about this. Let him fill your imagination.

I am the vine; you are the branches. Those who remain in me, and I in them, will produce much fruit. For apart from me you can do nothing.

JOHN 15:5

TEACH YOUR CHILDREN WELL

Blanche of Castile

1188–1252

Was Blanche a power grabber, or did she just fill a vacuum? Historians disagree. Her father was the king of Castile, in Spain. Her mother was an English heiress, and several of her uncles ruled England. Blanche was given in marriage to Prince Louis of France. So she was Spanish, English, *and* French. Since there were constant battles among those nations, Blanche was often maneuvering behind the scenes.

When her husband, King Louis VIII, died in 1226, she began to rule the nation on behalf of her twelve-year-old son, Louis IX. And here's where her story takes a Christian turn. Apparently Blanche raised her son right. Amid all the scheming and fighting of thirteenth-century Europe, Louis IX became known as a man of great faith, eventually being declared a saint by the Catholic church. He built chapels, supported Christian art, and arbitrated fair settlements. He credited his mother as the source of his devotion.

What happened here? Did a scheming queen become a trusting mom? We don't know for sure, but there's a clue from 1220, when her husband was still alive and her son was just six. Blanche wrote to the pope with a problem. During the illnesses of some of her children, she had made vows to the Lord, but she had forgotten what she had promised. Perhaps he could consult the Lord and remind her? In response, the pope asked a local minister to assign her some good deeds to do.

Was this a turning point for her? Historians acknowledge that as she became more powerful, she was unusually concerned for the poor, freeing many serfs from debtors' prison. In this highly anti-Semitic culture, she even offered protection to the Jews. Mercy seemed to characterize many of her actions. Were these her ways of keeping a promise to God?

Chances are, you don't have the power Blanche had. But you always have a choice about how to use the power you do have. Will you scheme and maneuver, using the people around you to your best advantage? Or will you seek God's direction, living with mercy, and teaching others to do the same?

Come, my children, and listen to me,
and I will teach you to fear the LORD.

PSALM 34:11

SEE ME

Angela Merici
1474–1540

As a girl, Angela had great hair. Everyone said so. But as she got more serious about God, she didn't want to be seen merely as the girl with the golden locks. So she dyed her hair with soot.

That seems to have been a pattern for Angela's life: seeing things differently, trying to follow God's leading even if it challenged conventional thinking.

Orphaned at age ten, she lost her older sister a few years later, and then her guardian uncle. Yet she seemed to grow closer to God with each trial. At age twenty, with no close family left, she looked outward at her community—and saw girls in great need of education. So she set up a school in her home.

This was Italy at the end of the fifteenth century. The nobility sometimes educated their daughters, and some convents gave nuns training beyond their religious duties, but no one was teaching the town girls. Angela knew that if they ever wanted to be more than a pretty face, they needed education.

The vision expanded to neighboring towns. Angela imagined a whole team of women committed to teaching girls, and she took steps to make it happen. At one point, the pope, impressed with her work, asked her to take charge of an order of nuns who were nurses. Angela was so focused on her educational work that she said no—and a few years later she established a new teaching order, the Company of Saint Ursula (Ursulines).

There's an undocumented story about Angela mysteriously losing her eyesight on a pilgrimage to the Holy Land. She went on anyway, "seeing" the sacred sites with the eyes of faith. On the return trip, her sight came back. The irony is that vision was never a problem for Angela Merici. She saw a need, she saw the value in the girls she taught, and she saw God's footsteps in front of her, leading her forward in ministry.

How's your vision? What has God been showing you? Is there wisdom you need to share with the next generation? Or are there steps to take in your own life to follow God more nearly?

Older women must train the younger women to love their husbands and their
children, to live wisely and be pure, to work in their homes, to do good.

TITUS 2:4-5

POET PROVOCATEUR

Christine de Pizan

1364–1430

A las, God, why did You not let me be born in the world as a man . . . so that I . . . would be as perfect as a man is said to be?"

So wrote poet Christine de Pizan in the early 1400s, satirizing a common view. In a world where women were treated as second-class citizens or worse, she challenged the stereotypes in an intelligent, winsome way.

Her father, a physician and civic leader in Venice, took a position in the court of King Charles V of France, and so Christine grew up amid royal prestige. At age fifteen she married another court official, with whom she had three children. But he died nine years later, and Christine was left to fend for herself—and to provide for her mother and kids. With limited options available, she chose to become a writer, penning hundreds of love ballads personalized for French aristocrats. She is considered Europe's first professional female writer.

But she soon used her fame to call attention to the status of women in society. First she took issue with a popular work that made fun of women. Then she wrote a series of books about "the City of Ladies," describing the valuable contributions of many historical women—wives, mothers, leaders, martyrs. "God formed the body of woman from one of [Adam's] ribs," she wrote, "signifying that she should stand at his side as a companion and never lie at his feet like a slave, and also that he love her as his own flesh."

With biblical arguments, Christine bolstered the confidence of her female readers. "Unless I stray from my faith," she once prayed in print, "I must never doubt that Your infinite wisdom . . . ever created anything which was not good. Did You yourself not create woman in a very special way and . . . give her all those inclinations which it please You for her to have? And how could it be that You could go wrong in anything?"

This woman of faith focused God's truth on an important social issue. May we have the courage to do the same.

"At last!" the man exclaimed. "This one is bone from my bone, and flesh from my flesh!"

GENESIS 2:23

WHAT ARE YOU FIGHTING FOR?

Joan of Arc
1412–31

You probably know some of the story of Joan of Arc. This French teenager donned armor to lead her nation to stunning victories. When the enemy captured her, they falsely convicted her of heresy and burned her at the stake.

It's an inspirational story, but it's not always clear what it should inspire us to do.

Joan, a simple village girl, had religious visions supporting King Charles VII of France, who was being defeated by English armies and by a French faction that disputed his claim to the throne. Her vision-stoked fervor compelled her to seek a meeting with the king, though this was very difficult for a simple village girl. After going through several intermediaries, she finally met the king and spoke of her visions. Then she rallied the French to get behind their king and drive out the English. Wearing custom-made armor and waving a banner (she wasn't fond of weapons), she stormed into battle again and again, leading the troops to a number of surprise victories. Despite being wounded a few times, she succeeded in regaining French territory and seeing Charles officially crowned.

Then it all fell apart. She was captured by the French rebels, who sold her to the English; they conducted a sham heresy trial. (Her biggest crime, it seems, was wearing pants.) Pause a moment to consider that all the parties in this dispute were ostensibly "Christian," which is why her enemies had to twist the church law to subdue her. Years later, she was officially exonerated and even sainted.

But what are we to do with Joan? Consider the power of paying attention to God and following his call. The idea of divine visions might be off-putting to some, but God leads people in all sorts of ways. How is he leading you? Are you paying attention?

And then, what are you willing to risk in order to follow God's call? Don't start making excuses—that you're not smart enough, rich enough, talented enough. Joan was just a country kid, but she was paying attention and following through. What does God want you to fight for, and how will you do that?

We are human, but we don't wage war as humans do. We use God's mighty weapons, not worldly weapons, to knock down the strongholds of human reasoning and to destroy false arguments.

2 CORINTHIANS 10:3-4

THE MAID

Joan of Arc, Told by Christine de Pizan

1429

Living in France during the early 1400s, writer Christine de Pizan sang not only the praises of great women of history but also of a newly emerging heroine: "I know about Esther, Judith, and Deborah, worthy women through whom God restored his oppressed people . . . , but there has been no one through whom he has performed a greater miracle than through the Maid."

She was talking about the "Maid of Orleans," Joan of Arc, the rustic visionary who rose to sudden fame in May 1429, rallying the forces of King Charles VII to break an English siege of the city of Orleans (see March 12).

"She was sent by divine command, guided by God's angel to the king," Christine wrote. "Led before clerks and wise men and was well examined to see whether she spoke the truth."

Christine wrote "The Song of Joan of Arc" on July 31, 1429, while these exploits were still fresh. "Whatever she does, she always has God before her eyes, whom she calls to, serves and prays to in deed and word. . . . Oh, how clear this was at the siege of Orleans where her power first appeared!"

Along with the rest of her country, Christine was amazed by these events. "A young girl of sixteen years (isn't this beyond nature?), to whom arms seem weightless—she seems to have been brought up for this, she is so strong and hardy. And the enemies flee before her, no one can last in front of her. She does this with many eyes looking on and rids France of her enemies, recapturing castles and towns. Never was there such great strength, not in a hundred or a thousand men."

A year later Joan was captured, and a year after that she was executed, but Christine's epic poem freezes this moment of victory in time. "Don't you realize," she implores tepid readers, "that God has a hand in this?"

Look around you. What is God doing in your world? Is he raising up certain people to do his work? Then sing about it.

---

*Miriam the prophet, Aaron's sister, took a tambourine and led
all the women as they played their tambourines and danced. . . .
"Sing to the LORD, for he has triumphed gloriously."*

EXODUS 15:20-21

LOVE BROKE THROUGH

Catherine of Genoa
1447–1510

She had a frustrating childhood and a loveless marriage, but in a flash everything changed for Caterina Fieschi Adorno, commonly known as Catherine of Genoa.

As a child she was very religious, excelling in prayer and penitence. She applied to a convent at age thirteen but was rejected—she was too young. At sixteen she was married off to a Genoese nobleman who proved to be angry, undisciplined, and unfaithful. She withdrew and endured in silence, trying to play the good wife, but deeply disappointed. Ten years passed.

Catherine prayed for the return of her old faith, but that seemed long ago and far away. She visited her sister, who was a nun, and in that convent, knelt to confess her sins. Suddenly she felt her soul pierced by a ray of divine light. She was overwhelmed with a sense of God's love, and that radically altered her life.

This divine love propelled her into the slums of Genoa to help the poor and the ailing (though she admitted that, at first, seeing these illnesses often made her feel ill). A few years later, her husband came around and joined her in ministry. Eventually Catherine became the director of a large hospital in Genoa, while her husband worked in affiliation with a monastic order. When the plague came to town, both were able to help the masses who fell ill.

In the latter years of her life, Catherine wrote and taught about various spiritual subjects—purification of the soul, Christian growth, and God's love. A group of followers recorded her teachings and published them after her death.

Has God's love broken through to you? If so, what has it changed? How do you see your life differently, and how do you *do* your life differently? History is crammed with examples of people trudging along in the religious same-old, when suddenly they are, shall we say, "enlightened." Some divine ray of realization hits the solar panels of their hearts, and they find a new energy. They understand, perhaps for the first time, that God wants more than pious activities from us. He loves us dearly; he wants our hearts.

There is no fear in love. But perfect love drives out fear.

1 JOHN 4:18, NIV

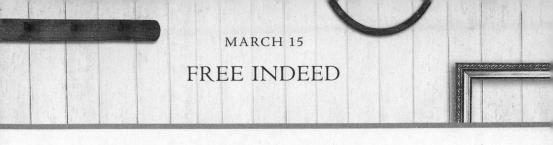

FREE INDEED

Women in the Pre-Reformation Movements

Long before Martin Luther tacked his ninety-five complaints on the church door, launching the Protestant Reformation, others were protesting. The Western church exploded in the 1500s, but the previous centuries had already seen several courageous leaders calling for reform. Groups often formed around these leaders—and these groups had a surprising level of female leadership.

In the 1300s, John Wycliffe riled up English Christians with a strong message against papal authority and the wealth of the church. He began translating the Bible from church Latin to common English. This was revolutionary. If just anyone could read the Scriptures, who needed priests?

Wycliffe's followers were known as Lollards (probably from a Dutch word for mumbling, because they preached in the common tongue). For another century or so, they spread Wycliffe's ideas in the face of persecution. Some critics had a hard time with the idea that Lollard women were speaking out as well as men. One poet chided:

> *Some women . . . though their wit be thin*
> *Will arguments make in Holy Writ!*

It's unclear whether women were actually serving as priests in this movement, but they were learning and sharing Scripture. This is true of several other pre-Reformation movements as well such as the Cathars (Albigensians) and Waldensians of earlier centuries. In the early 1400s in Bohemia, Jan Hus preached a Wycliffe-like message and promoted an even stronger role for women. "Women were made in the image of God and should fear no man," he preached, allowing women to preach, serve on councils, and even fight in battle. (Ironically, Joan of Arc, in a break between her battles, fired off a letter to the Hussites urging them to cease their heretical ways.)

Right or wrong, these movements were preaching *liberation*—freedom from the consolidated power of the priesthood. Central to their teaching was that every human being—male or female—should be able to pray, to read the Bible, to confess sin, to know God, and to talk about God. It's no surprise, then, that even in their restricted culture many women were liberated to serve God according to their gifts.

Our culture is quite different, but you have freedom too. Freedom to know and serve God. How are you using it?

If the Son sets you free, you are truly free.

JOHN 8:36

MISUNDERSTOOD

Marguerite Porete

D. 1310

Sometimes people *want* to misunderstand you, and no amount of explanation will sway them. That seems to have been the case for Marguerite Porete, who was a writer in Belgium in the early 1300s. Her book, *The Mirror of Simple Souls*, is a mystical masterpiece, exploring the love between a "simple soul" and God. It has the feel of the biblical Song of Songs, employing poetic dialogue between a divine lover and the beloved. Written in Old French rather than church Latin, it borrows heavily from the style of court romances. Maybe that was the problem.

From the start, church leaders didn't like it. A local bishop condemned the book, publicly burning it and threatening to excommunicate anyone who read it. In response, Marguerite had the work vetted by three theologians. That didn't improve matters.

The religious elite may have been troubled by the free spirit of her work, by her possible connection with a fringe group, or by the fact that *The Mirror of Simple Souls* was immensely popular. When they called Marguerite to defend it, she refused to answer questions under oath (perhaps fearing they'd trick her into a perjury charge), and this landed her in a Paris prison.

One difficulty was that this book superseded rationality. In Marguerite's view, the reality of God's love goes far beyond any explanation of it. "Truth declares to my heart that I am loved by One alone," she wrote. ". . . It is without return that He has given me His love. *This gift kills my thought* by the delight of His love, which delight lifts me and transforms me." For Marguerite Porete, part of the soul's surrender to God was to stop thinking so much.

In 1310 a church court ruled that fifteen passages of her book were heretical. Since she refused to recant, Marguerite was burned at the stake. Ironically, the book gained popularity after her death, though her name was no longer associated with it. Until the early twentieth century, it was considered an anonymous work.

Sometimes people *want* to misunderstand you, even when you're onto something great. Don't be discouraged. Keep drawing close to God, letting your soul find intimacy with him, no matter what others say.

Love flashes like fire, the brightest kind of flame. Many waters cannot quench love, nor can rivers drown it.

SONG OF SONGS 8:6-7

SLEEPLESS IN KILDARE

Brigid

451–545

Saint Brigid was not given to sleep,
Nor was she intermittent about God's love;
Not merely that she did not buy, she did not seek for
The wealth of this world below. . . .

This ancient poem hails the matron saint of Ireland, Brigid of Kildare. Her history is uncertain—not for lack of information, but because there are so many stories about her, it's hard to discern fact from fancy. It seems she was born in 451 to a pagan chieftain and a Christian slave woman. By one account, Brigid's mother had converted through the ministry of St. Patrick. Other reports indicate a connection between Patrick and Brigid later in her life. "Between Patrick and Brigid, the columns of the Irish, there was so great a friendship of charity that they had but one heart and one mind," says one ancient source. "Through him and through her, Christ performed many miracles."

Various miracles were attributed to Brigid—cleansing a leper (who wasn't sure he wanted cleansing); using her own blood (from a riding accident) to heal a mute child. Even if those are the stuff of legend, this woman still left a remarkable legacy. Brigid was "not given to sleep," in the sense that she got a lot done. She founded the first Irish convent, oversaw an impressive artistic center—known chiefly for its beautifully decorated Bibles—and helped to establish a strong Irish monastic tradition that later re-evangelized Europe.

One story that pops up in various forms involves Brigid and butter. In one telling, an elderly woman appears at the door begging for food. All Brigid has is a dish of butter, which she graciously gives to the woman. She comes back inside to find three dishes of butter miraculously replacing what she had given.

Legends generally grow from kernels of truth. As we sift through the stories, we find a woman with remarkable leadership abilities and a humble heart. She gave her last morsel to a beggar—why? Because "she did not seek for the wealth of this world below." She trusted God to provide for her . . . and he did.

This same God who takes care of me will supply all your needs from
his glorious riches, which have been given to us in Christ Jesus.

PHILIPPIANS 4:19

STAND IN THE PLACE WHERE YOU ARE

Bridget of Sweden
1303–73

Bridget of Sweden kept reinventing herself, meeting each new challenge of her life with creativity and devotion. Her parents were well connected in Swedish society, and so the young Bridget got to meet famous scholars. She also reported seeing divine visions from the age of seven.

But all too soon she transitioned from precocious child to wife and mother. Marrying at age thirteen, she bore eight children who all lived past childhood, an unusual achievement in the fourteenth century. In her late thirties, she and her husband went on a religious pilgrimage, following The Way of St. James in northern Spain, but he took sick on the return trip and died soon afterward. The next stage of her life was benevolent widowhood.

Joining the Order of Saint Francis, she devoted herself to caring for the poor. Then she used her family connections to start a new religious order. Around 1350, with her daughter Catherine and a few others, she visited Rome to get the pope's official endorsement of her new order. One problem: the pope wasn't in Rome at the time. This was a lengthy period of political corruption in which the powerful French king had moved the papacy to Avignon.

Bridget didn't mind waiting. A second purpose of her trip was to improve the moral tone of the age and to oppose the "French captivity" of the church. So she settled in Rome, caring for the poor and speaking about the need for reform. Occasionally she took more pilgrimages, to the Holy Land and elsewhere. In 1367, Pope Urban V, responding to pressure from Bridget and others, returned to Rome for a few years. While there, he did confirm the rule of Bridget's order, which became known as the Bridgettines. Bridget died in 1373, and her daughter Catherine, who later became a saint herself, brought her body back to Sweden.

How have you dealt with life's changes? Have you navigated your way through school, family life, career, and ministry, with maybe a few other stops along the way? Bridget reinvented herself several times, but she kept her focus. She knew that each change offered a new way to serve the Lord.

---

*Let's not get tired of doing what is good. At just the right time
we will reap a harvest of blessing if we don't give up.*

GALATIANS 6:9

ONE THING

Mary of Bethany

LUKE 10:38-42

Have you ever seen a "phone basket" at a party? It's intended as a place to leave your cell phone so you're not tempted to check your texts or Facebook while you're at the event. Sometimes there's a sign that says something like, "Be with the friends who are here." It's just too easy these days to be distracted from a face-to-face conversation by an electronic tug from someone asking about a work project or wondering what you're doing tomorrow night.

Mary would have happily dumped her cell phone in the basket so she could focus on the friends at the party—one Friend in particular. Mary, along with her sister, Martha, and brother, Lazarus, was a friend of Jesus. One night they invited Jesus to dinner, as friends tend to do. It's easy to imagine that even when Jesus was having a simple dinner with some of his friends, he would dominate the conversation. Everything he said was important.

Mary understood that. She sat at Jesus' feet, listening to his words. To sit at the feet of a rabbi like Jesus meant to learn from him as his disciple. Jesus was educating Mary about faith, the same way he taught the twelve disciples he chose to follow him.

Of course, sister Martha, multitasking in the kitchen, became frustrated that Mary was sitting and listening instead of slicing and dicing. When Martha complained, Jesus told her that all her meal preparations were distracting her from the most important thing. Mary had found that "one thing," and he wasn't about to take it away.

The "one thing" was learning from Jesus. Nowadays, we have the Bible to help us learn the things that Jesus taught in person. We can look to Mary as an example of how to treat our Bible-study time—don't allow the other distractions to pull us away.

Leave the cell phone in another room. Shut down the laptop. Focus on the Word. If you bring the things that distract you to your study time, of course you'll be distracted by them. You've got a much better chance of gaining something that "will not be taken away" if you give it your full attention.

There is only one thing worth being concerned about. Mary has discovered it, and it will not be taken away from her.

LUKE 10:42

CHILL

Martha

LUKE 10:38-42

Martha welcomed Jesus and his entourage into her home for dinner with her siblings Lazarus and Mary. Preparations needed to be made, and Martha took on those responsibilities. This distracted her from spending time with Jesus. We don't know what Lazarus was doing, but Mary was sitting at Jesus' feet, listening to his words instead of helping.

Out of frustration, Martha complained, "Lord, doesn't it seem unfair to you that my sister just sits here while I do all the work? Tell her to come and help me" (Luke 10:40).

Jesus gave her a friendly smackdown. "My dear Martha," he said, "you are worried and upset over all these details! There is only one thing worth being concerned about. Mary has discovered it, and it will not be taken away from her" (Luke 10:41-42). In other words, "Chill, friend. Let the housework wait. Join in the most important conversation you can ever have—one with me."

It's easy to get a negative impression of Martha from this story. She seems like the "bad" sister—petty, jealous, and not aware of what is important. But try to look at it differently. Elsewhere the Bible tells us just how well Martha knew Jesus. When Lazarus got sick, both sisters sent for Jesus, trusting in his healing power. Both were upset when Jesus showed up four days after Lazarus died.

But it was Martha to whom Jesus said, "I am the resurrection and the life" (John 11:25). And it was Martha who replied, "I have always believed you are the Messiah, the Son of God, the one who has come into the world from God" (verse 27), one of the strongest statements of faith we find in the gospels. Does that sound like someone who doesn't know what's important in life?

Though Martha was distracted that evening when Jesus came to dinner, there obviously were times when she paid deep, close attention to him. She knew who he was, she must have understood his teaching, but—just like the rest of us—she sometimes found the details of life pulling her focus away from him.

It's comforting to read the simple statement in the gospel: "Jesus loved Martha, Mary, and Lazarus" (John 11:5). He'll give us friendly reminders to spend a little more time with him and a little less time being busy, but he understands.

A dinner was prepared in Jesus' honor. Martha served.

JOHN 12:2

TEACHABLE MOMENT

The Syrophoenician Woman
MATTHEW 14:21-28

Mothers don't take it very well when their children are in desperate need of help and the people who can help them ignore their requests. The Gospel of Matthew tells the story of a mom like that.

It's a strange story. Upon first reading, Jesus' actions seem un-Christlike. This mother says her daughter is suffering because she is possessed by a demon. Although she is not Jewish, she calls Jesus "Son of David." This shows respect for him and his culture, as well as an understanding of who he is. And what does Jesus do? Nothing. He says nothing. He ignores her.

His disciples must have thought he didn't want to be bothered with this non-Jewish woman. They told him to send her away. He replied that he was sent "only to the lost sheep of Israel" (Matthew 15:24, NIV). Did he really mean he wouldn't help her because she wasn't Jewish?

Jewish or not, her daughter needed something only Jesus could give, so she persisted. When she asked again for help, Jesus told her that it wasn't right to "take the children's bread and toss it to the dogs" (Matthew 15:26, NIV). Was he really comparing this woman's child to a dog because she wasn't Jewish? Pretty un-Christlike, right?

What was going on there?

Considering that she needed Jesus' help, the woman then did something very bold. She disagreed with him. She said it was right because "even the dogs eat the crumbs that fall from their master's table" (Matthew 15:27, NIV). Then Jesus commended her great faith and granted her request. Her daughter was healed.

Was Jesus testing her faith? Probably. But perhaps he was doing something more. This might have been what modern moms call a "teachable moment" with his disciples. Jesus created a situation in which this woman had to demonstrate the depth of her faith. This taught the disciples and any other onlookers that Jesus is for everyone. You don't have to have the right religious training or be from the proper socioeconomic class to have faith in Jesus. The moment you have faith, regardless of who you are, you share in what he has done.

Let's stop sending people away for being "not our type," when Jesus sees their faith and welcomes them.

There is no longer Jew or Gentile, slave or free, male and female. For you are all one in Christ Jesus.

GALATIANS 3:28

JUDGMENT SEAT

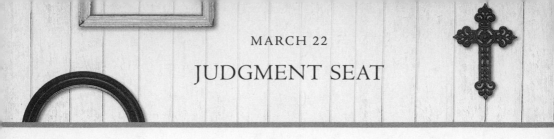

Salome

MATTHEW 20:20-28

Salome had a request for Jesus. "In your Kingdom, please let my two sons sit in places of honor next to you, one on your right and the other on your left" (Matthew 20:21).

Those two sons were James and John, among Jesus' closest disciples. And Mom wasn't doing this behind their backs. They were there, and apparently they were not embarrassed by their mom's request. When Jesus asked if they could "drink the cup" (of suffering) that he would have to drink, James and John told him they could. (See Matthew 20:22, NIV.)

How easy it is to think badly of Salome for this. Was she just a manipulating mother, trying to gain a high position for her sons?

Let's not rush to judgment. This is not all we know of Salome. She was one of Jesus' followers and cared for him when he was in Galilee (see Mark 15:40-41). After his crucifixion, she was with the other women who went to anoint his body and discovered that Jesus' tomb was empty (see Mark 16:1-8). Obviously, Salome herself was a follower of Jesus, and perhaps a friend, too. She was comfortable enough and close enough with Jesus to ask the bold question that she did. And in this case, she and her sons were not reprimanded for their ambition, just challenged to know the full extent of what they were asking. And, as it turned out, James was the first of the Twelve to be killed for following Jesus (see Acts 12:2). According to tradition, John lived the longest but was sent into exile.

It's tempting to judge people on the basis of just one thing that they've done, one encounter with them, or one of their personality traits. Such snap judgments are unfair and unfortunate. We might think badly of Salome's question, but this woman—like anyone—is much more than just one moment in time, one action.

Are there others you might be judging based on a narrow picture of who they are? Perhaps it's time to rethink your conclusions. You wouldn't want someone to judge you based on one bad decision, would you?

Do not judge others, and you will not be judged. For you will be treated as you treat others. The standard you use in judging is the standard by which you will be judged.

MATTHEW 7:1-2

PAYBACK

Joanna

LUKE 8:1-3

Have you ever wondered how Jesus and the twelve disciples paid for things as they traveled? We know Peter and a few others were fishermen before they met Jesus, but they left their nets to follow him . . . apparently giving up their paychecks, too. Matthew the tax collector did the same thing, as presumably the others did.

Noble as that was, they still had to eat and still needed places to sleep as they traveled. With all the walking from town to town, they probably needed new sandals once in a while too. Where did the money come from?

Sometimes they ate and slept in the homes of friends like Mary and Martha. However, there were also people who financially supported Jesus and the disciples, and many of them were women.

Joanna was one of those women. She followed Jesus after he cured her (see Luke 8:2-3). Although we don't know what her specific ailment was, she was dedicated to the one who healed her. She traveled with Jesus and the disciples, along with Mary Magdalene, Susanna, and other women. Luke says these women supported Jesus and the disciples "from their own resources" (verse 3).

Joanna's husband, Chuza, was the manager of King Herod's household, a job that probably came with a lucrative salary. Joanna could have used the money her husband earned to live well, buy fine things, and pamper herself. Instead, she chose to travel simply with Jesus and his other followers, sharing her money with them.

You may know people who have given up higher-paying jobs to do ministry. Can you give something from your own resources to help them make ends meet? This is one way that you, like Joanna and her colleagues, can give back to God. Giving doesn't have to be only in the collection plate on Sunday mornings. Sometimes a specific person, ministry, or mission comes to your attention, and you realize that you have the means and desire to offer some financial support. Joanna chose who and what she supported with her money, and in the same way, you can choose to support the people or ministries that are important to you.

You must each decide in your heart how much to give. And don't give reluctantly or in response to pressure. "For God loves a person who gives cheerfully."

2 CORINTHIANS 9:7

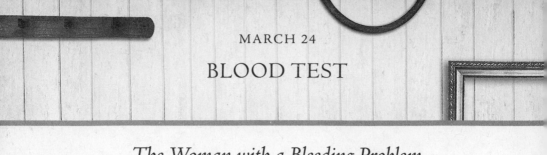

BLOOD TEST

The Woman with a Bleeding Problem

MARK 5:24-34

Cramps. Bloating. Backaches. Headaches. Irritability. Bleeding. Once a month, most women experience these symptoms to varying degrees, and none of them ever look forward to it. Imagine experiencing them every day for twelve years without relief, no matter how many doctors you saw or remedies you tried.

It would be awful, but people would probably be sympathetic and treat you kindly. During Jesus' time, however, Jewish law considered anyone who was menstruating to be unclean, and anyone who touched a woman during that time would become unclean too.

The Gospels tell the story of a woman who touched Jesus in a crowd, believing she would be healed from twelve years of bleeding and suffering. The Bible does not name her, but later church traditions call her Veronica. For twelve years, she probably had been told not to touch anyone or let anyone touch her. Culturally, she would make Jesus unclean by touching him. Despite that, this woman said to herself, "If I can just touch his robe, I will be healed" (Mark 5:28). She was right.

In a crowd where many people were bumping up against Jesus, she not only took the chance of contaminating Jesus when she touched him, but she also took the chance of contaminating others if they accidentally bumped up against her.

Jesus told this woman that her faith had healed her—and nowadays she's usually held up as an example of faith. Her faith is impressive, but so is her courage. She had the courage to risk going against what was culturally acceptable in order to seek after Jesus. She put aside her fear of what other people of faith would say about her, or do to her, because of what they thought she was doing wrong. She knew she needed Jesus and did what she had to do to get to him.

Sometimes you need to do the same. Have the courage to put aside what others are saying so that you can get to Jesus. Flout convention. Break some rules. But have a real experience with Jesus where you can lay your needs before him and let his healing energy flow.

Be strong and courageous! Do not be afraid and do not panic before them. For the LORD your God will personally go ahead of you. He will neither fail you nor abandon you.

DEUTERONOMY 31:6

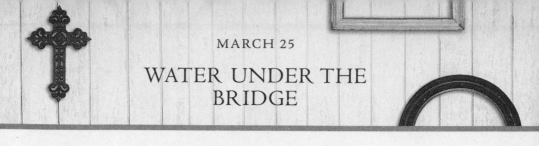

WATER UNDER THE BRIDGE

The Woman at the Well

JOHN 4:1-42

The story is well known. Jesus is alone at a well. A woman has come to draw water, and Jesus asks her for a drink. Today that doesn't seem so scandalous, but in that day, the situation raised several cultural red flags. Jesus was a Jew; the woman was a Samaritan. Jews did not associate with Samaritans, and they particularly would not associate with a Samaritan woman who had been through several husbands and was now living with a man who was not her husband.

Even the woman knew it. The account in John 4 makes it clear that she was surprised Jesus was speaking with her. And yet the conversation that ensued was one of the most important in Jesus' ministry. It's during their back and forth that he calls himself the "living water" (John 4:10). It's here that he talks about worshiping God "in spirit and in truth" (verses 23-24). At the end of this conversation, he declares that he is the Messiah. It is a very important conversation indeed, and one that ends with the woman not only understanding who Jesus is, but also telling her whole town about him.

There are many theological gems here we could pull out and polish up, but let's choose a practical point. Jesus had no problem speaking to someone outside his faith and culture. Many would have chastised him for talking to this woman, but he entered into an intimate conversation with her.

"She's not one of us," some might say. (That seemed to be the attitude of Jesus' disciples when they showed up.) But Jesus didn't care. He spoke to her with kindness, compassion, love, and respect, and the end result was a new understanding—not just for her, but also for her community and for all of us who read the story.

In Jesus' day, there weren't many opportunities for people of different faiths to intermingle, but today those opportunities abound. When those outside the Christian faith enter into relationship with you, will you react with the same kindness that Jesus modeled? Through your words and actions, will they understand who Jesus is?

The time is coming—indeed it's here now—when true worshipers
will worship the Father in spirit and in truth. The Father is
looking for those who will worship him that way.

JOHN 4:23

HEAVEN SCENT

The Woman Who Anointed Jesus' Feet

LUKE 7:36-50

In the Bible there are two accounts of women who pour perfume on Jesus' feet and wipe his feet clean with their hair. These are incredibly intimate moments that we are privileged to get a glimpse of. In one of the accounts, Mary, the sister of Martha and Lazarus, anoints Jesus' feet when he is a guest in her home (see John 12:1-8). In the other account, the woman is unnamed (see Luke 7:36-50).

Jesus was dining at the house of Simon the Pharisee, and an "immoral" woman knelt before him. She allowed her tears to fall onto Jesus' feet; then she wiped his feet clean with her hair. She kissed his feet and poured perfume from an alabaster jar on them.

When the Pharisee questioned how Jesus, if he really was who he said he was, could allow this to happen, Jesus had the chance to explain something that we all need to understand.

The woman, apparently, was considered by others and by herself to be a big sinner. Even Jesus said she had "many sins" (Luke 7:47, NIV). Did she have more sins than the Pharisee? Only God knows. Most likely, she recognized her sins, while the Pharisee was blind to his own. But because she was aware of her sins, was aware of her need for forgiveness, and had faith that Jesus could forgive them, Jesus was able to say confidently to her, "Your sins are forgiven" and "Your faith has saved you; go in peace" (Luke 7:48, 50).

The thing is, everyone sins. When we recognize this and come before Jesus in faith, we can find peace and forgiveness.

Jesus told the Pharisee that a person who is forgiven little shows only little love. Does this mean that you need to run out and commit a whole bunch of sins so they can be forgiven so you can love more? No. We all have plenty of sins to be forgiven already. But when we, like that Pharisee, let personal pride keep us from seeking forgiveness, we miss out on the relationship-deepening pardon God wants to offer us.

I tell you, her sins—and they are many—have been
forgiven, so she has shown me much love.

LUKE 7:47

IMPOSSIBLE DREAM

Pilate's Wife

MATTHEW 27:15-26

Courage. It's tough to summon sometimes. Imagine this scenario: you're the wife of Pontius Pilate, the Roman governor of Judea. Things are incredibly tense in Jerusalem. A man with many followers and even more enemies, Jesus, is being brought to trial before your husband.

The chief priests and the elders of the Jews were jealous of Jesus. They trumped up false charges against him and whipped a crowd into a frenzy against him. As the trial is described in Matthew 27, Pilate completely understood what was happening. Jesus was innocent of the charges. The governor asked the crowd what crime Jesus had committed. They couldn't answer because he had committed no crime. They simply screamed, "Crucify him."

In the middle of this frenzy, Pilate received a message from his wife. She was a Roman citizen and not a Jew. She probably never met Jesus, but it would have been impossible for someone in her position not to have heard of this wonder-worker and the excitement he inspired in his followers. She knew about Jesus, and she dreamed about him.

"Leave that innocent man alone," her message said. "I suffered through a terrible nightmare about him last night" (Matthew 27:19).

That took courage. Would her husband be upset by her meddling? Or what if the message was intercepted by the angry, unreasonable crowd? Still, she knew Jesus was innocent, and she had the courage to speak up. Perhaps because of this message, Pilate looked for a way to let Jesus go: releasing a prisoner for the holiday. But the crowd chose freedom for a common bandit and demanded that Jesus be crucified. Pilate washed his hands and said to the crowd, "I am innocent of this man's blood! The responsibility is yours!" (Matthew 27:24).

Did Pilate's wife take an unnecessary risk? Or should she have pressured her husband even more? The fact is, doing the right thing isn't always going to lead to the desired outcome, but it's still important to do.

By the way, some early church literature suggests that Pilate's wife, named Procula (or possibly Claudia), became a Christian just before or after this.

As Pilate was sitting on the judgment seat, his wife sent him this message: "Leave that innocent man alone. I suffered through a terrible nightmare about him last night."

MATTHEW 27:19

WALKING WITH HIM

Female Disciples

What do you think of when you hear the word *disciple*? Most of us think of the Twelve, those in Jesus' inner circle who followed him and traveled with him day and night. Yet they weren't the only disciples. Some of Jesus' disciples were women.

It's not clear why none of the Twelve were women. Some scholars have sought theological reasons, but the simplest explanation might be mere propriety. With the close quarters Jesus shared with the Twelve, it might have been too scandalous for men and women to be mixed together.

Yet the Gospels indicate that certain women followed Jesus and even traveled with the Twelve at times. Mary Magdalene, Joanna, and Susanna are explicitly mentioned in Luke 8:1-3, along with "many others." A number of these women also were supporting Jesus' ministry financially.

Jesus and his disciples also benefited from the hospitality of certain women, most notably Mary and Martha of Bethany, whose home seems to have served as a base of operations when Jesus visited nearby Jerusalem. You'll remember, though, that these two sisters had a tiff over the fact that Mary "sat at the Lord's feet" while Martha prepared dinner (Luke 10:39). A person who sat at a rabbi's feet was considered a disciple, so Mary was clearly taking on that role. And from her knowledge of Jesus' message, it's likely that Martha was a disciple too.

We shouldn't forget the women who stood beneath the cross as Jesus died and who brought burial spices to the empty tomb. Some of these were relatives, but others, like Mary Magdalene, were followers. Although most of the Twelve scattered, these female disciples were able to brave the Roman threat and show up at these important moments.

Discipleship isn't limited to twelve men who lived two thousand years ago. Many women were disciples too—and still are. A disciple is someone who learns the teachings of a leader and follows them. A disciple of Jesus, male or female, is committed to his truth and his ways. You may not be trudging with him from town to town, but he is certainly walking with you.

Students are not greater than their teacher. But the student
who is fully trained will become like the teacher.

LUKE 6:40

THROWING STONES

The Woman Caught in Adultery

JOHN 8:1-11

The Pharisees, always out to get Jesus, brought a woman to him who had been caught in adultery. What should they do with her? The whole thing had little to do with the woman. It was a trap.

If Jesus said to let her go, he would be going against Mosaic law, which required that she be stoned to death. (Of course, it said that both the woman *and* the man should be stoned, but the Pharisees somehow overlooked that.) If Jesus said to stone her, his message of love and compassion would come into serious question.

Jesus wasn't so easily trapped. Instead of saying, "Stone her" or "Don't stone her," he said these famous words: "Let the one who has never sinned throw the first stone!" (John 8:7). It may have taken the Pharisees a few minutes to let that sink in, but finally they sidled away until it was only Jesus and the woman left.

He asked her if there was anyone still condemning her. No, they were gone. "Neither do I," said Jesus. "Go and sin no more" (John 8:11).

It's good when it's just you and Jesus dealing with your sin. You may have people around you pouncing on every misdeed, but let them walk away. Unless they are sin free, they have no place to judge you. The only one who is sinless, Jesus himself, is giving you a new lease on life.

Many of us, however, keep condemning ourselves. We're good at throwing stones at ourselves. But Jesus makes it clear: he doesn't condemn. He paid the price on the cross for all your sins, and no one, not even you, has the right to punish you. Jesus wants you to move on. Don't continue to dwell on your sin. Step forward into your new life.

By the way, this story poses a quandary for scholars. It probably wasn't part of John's original Gospel—the earliest manuscripts skip it—but it seems to be an authentic story from Jesus' ministry. So we can accept it as "bonus material" in our Bible experience, especially since it affirms a basic biblical theme: the wisdom and compassion of Christ.

If we confess our sins to him, he is faithful and just to forgive us our sins and to cleanse us from all wickedness.

1 JOHN 1:9

MARCH 30

PARABOLIC CURVES

Women in Jesus' Parables

MATTHEW 25:1-13; LUKE 13:20-21; 15:8-10; 18:1-8

Women are not major players in Jesus' parables. They appear in only a handful of the many that he told. But don't let that make you think that women weren't important to Jesus. He wanted people to relate to his parables so they could learn something important. He had to put these truths in contexts they knew.

If Jesus had, for example, told the story of the Prodigal Daughter instead of the Prodigal Son (Luke 15:11-32), people would have been confused. Women did not receive inheritances from fathers and seldom traveled on their own. The message of the parable would have been the same, but those hearing the parable would have missed it.

In crafting his parables, Jesus operated within cultural expectations, so women show up in parables doing rather traditional things. A woman bakes bread with "only a little yeast in three measures of flour," but that yeast gets worked through every part of the dough (see Luke 13:20-21). Bread-baking listeners would understand something deeply true about God's Kingdom. A little bit means a lot. The transformation of the world begins not with big armies, but with a little bit of leaven.

A woman loses a silver coin in her home. She sweeps the floor until she finds it and then calls her neighbors to celebrate with her. "In the same way," Jesus explains, "there is joy in the presence of God's angels when even one sinner repents" (Luke 15:10).

In another parable, a widow nags a judge into a favorable ruling. Unscrupulous businessmen often preyed upon those who had lost their husbands. Though the judge is unscrupulous himself, he is worn out by the widow's appeals—a lesson for us to "always pray and never give up" (Luke 18:1).

In a parable rooted in the marriage customs of the time, Jesus contrasted wise and foolish bridesmaids. The wise ones remained ready—just as we should be ready for Jesus' return (see Matthew 25:1-13).

If Jesus were crafting new parables today, he'd surely include soccer moms, career women, and bridezillas. The truths of God intersect with our experience in real, livable ways. What parable would he tell about you?

[Jesus said,] "I will speak to you in parables. I will explain things hidden since the creation of the world."

MATTHEW 13:35

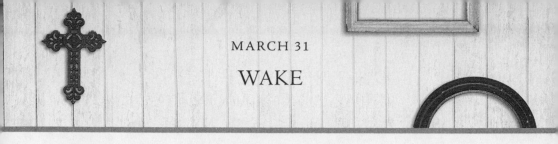

The Widow of Nain

LUKE 7:11-17

The disciples were probably in good moods as they walked at the front of an enthusiastic crowd. Jesus had just healed the servant of a respected Roman officer, and now they were moving on to a new town, Nain . . . and they ran into a funeral procession.

Funerals are usually sad occasions, but this one was particularly sad. A mother had just lost her son, and she was already a widow. With no husband and no son, she had lost all financial support. The life ahead of her looked bleak.

When Jesus saw the widow, "his heart went out to her" (Luke 7:13, NIV). Jesus walked over to her dead son, touched the frame he was being carried on, and said, "Young man, I say to you, get up!" (verse 14, NIV). Of course, the young man got up.

It's interesting that the widow never says a word in the story. She doesn't talk to Jesus or his disciples. She doesn't ask for anything. Still, Jesus has compassion for her. His heart goes out to her, but he doesn't just feel bad for her. He does something about her heartache, even without her asking. Maybe she was too wrapped up in her own grief to even have noticed that Jesus was there. Who knows?

If you look around, there are always opportunities to help people who are having a hard time, even if they haven't asked for help. Sometimes they are so involved with their problems or their heartache that they don't think to ask anyone for help. Sometimes they don't know you have the ability to help them, so they don't ask you specifically.

Like Jesus, you may be able to recognize a need that can be met, even if the person doesn't ask for help. And, like Jesus, you can jump into action and do what you can. No, you can't raise someone from the dead, but you know what skills and abilities you have. Use them to help when it's obvious you can.

If someone has enough money to live well and sees a brother or sister in need but shows no compassion—how can God's love be in that person?

1 JOHN 3:17

ON THE VALUE JESUS PLACED ON WOMEN

Jesus' inner circle may have consisted of men, but he was no woman hater. Throughout his ministry, he interacted with women in respectful, loving ways. He hung out at the home of his friends Mary and Martha. His entourage often included Mary Magdalene, Joanna, Susanna, and other women. When Jesus ministered to women, he honored them as people, in the same way he ministered to men.

In an essay, the brilliant mystery writer and theologian Dorothy Sayers wrote,

Perhaps it is no wonder that the women were first at the Cradle and last at the Cross. They had never known a man like this Man—there never has been such another. A prophet and teacher who never nagged at them, never flattered or coaxed or patronised; who never made arch jokes about them, never treated them either as 'The women, God help us!' or 'The ladies, God bless them!'; who rebuked without querulousness and praised without condescension; who took their questions and arguments seriously; who never mapped out their sphere for them, never urged them to be feminine or jeered at them for being female; who had no axe to grind and no uneasy male dignity to defend; who took them as he found them and was completely unself-conscious.

Sayers's observations about Jesus help to shed light on what Paul wrote in Galatians 3:28: "There is no longer . . . male and female. For you are all one in Christ Jesus." Jesus modeled that truth. Certainly he understood the basic gender differences, but he saw both women and men as people cherished by God.

We pay lip service to that notion in modern times, but we still have trouble looking past the differences. We define things as women's issues and men's issues. We even create Bibles for women and Bibles for men. Perhaps we will always be fighting a battle of the sexes. But that's not what we learn from Jesus.

It's comforting for a woman to know that Jesus values her not because of, or in spite of, the fact that she's a woman. We could say the same thing about men. He values you because you're intrinsically valuable just as you are, male or female, created in God's image—so valuable, in fact, that Jesus gave his life for you.

God created human beings in his own image. In the image of God he created them; male and female he created them.

GENESIS 1:27

DOWNTIME

Peter's Mother-in-Law

MATTHEW 8:14-15; MARK 1:29-31; LUKE 4:38-39

Peter, one of Jesus' closest disciples, had a mother-in-law. Which meant, of course, he had a wife. Surprised? Peter did have a wife, and tradition says she even accompanied him on his missionary journeys after Jesus' death. His wife had a mother, who, not uncustomarily for that time, lived with her daughter and her daughter's husband.

Three of the Gospels mention Peter's mother-in-law (whose name is not given), and they all tell the same story. Jesus had just left the synagogue after preaching with authority and commanding an impure spirit to come out of a man. The spirit obeyed. This amazed the people.

Afterward, Jesus went to Peter's home and found Peter's mother-in-law in bed with a fever. Jesus simply went to her, touched her, and helped her out of bed, and her fever was gone. She went about her day, waiting on Jesus and presumably the others in the home. Later that evening, because of what Jesus had done, many demon-possessed people were brought to him to heal.

We don't know how many hours passed between the time that Peter's mother-in-law was healed and Jesus started driving out demons, but it seems that perhaps for an afternoon, Jesus had some downtime at a friend's house.

Do you ever think of Jesus that way? Hanging at his buddy's house, having a friend's mom wait on him and others, doing the ancient-day equivalent of chilling? Think about it. Jesus took a few hours to get away from the responsibilities of his ministry, enjoy the company of friends, and recharge between exorcisms.

How often do you give yourself time to take a break from your responsibilities and recharge? Your responsibilities might not be as heavy as casting out demons, but people often feel they need to be available to their employers twenty-four hours a day. With today's technology, it's easy to put in several more hours of work once you get home from the job.

If even Jesus needed time to recharge, don't you? If you haven't been carving out some time for yourself to be away from your work responsibilities, how can you start doing that this week?

For everything there is a season, a time for every activity under heaven.

ECCLESIASTES 3:1

THE STUFF OF LEGEND

Veronica

As Jesus was paraded through Jerusalem on the way to his crucifixion, Luke says that a crowd of people followed him. In that crowd, legend says, was a woman named Veronica.

As the story goes, Veronica took pity on Jesus and wiped his dirty, bloody, sweating face with her veil as he struggled on his way. She kept the veil and discovered that the image of Jesus' face was imprinted on the cloth.

Don't look for Veronica's story in the Bible—you won't find it. It's a legend that didn't surface until hundreds of years after Christ's death. There's no evidence that the veil with the image of Christ on it has ever been found or that Veronica ever existed. Some ancient writers connected Veronica with another woman who met Jesus in a crowd—the woman with the issue of blood—but this has no biblical or historical backing.

Yet the story of Veronica has been told for centuries. This gutsy woman who pushed her way through the Roman soldiers to give Jesus a little comfort is memorialized in the stations of the cross that Christians reflect on during Passion Week, and many people look to her story for strength.

If her story actually happened, she was an incredibly brave woman. To be seen as Jesus' supporter at that moment was dangerous—so dangerous, in fact, that one of Jesus' closest friends, Peter, denied even knowing Christ, because he feared for his own life. Maybe the legend of Veronica is made more powerful because of the real story of Peter. She didn't fear for her life, but she showed love and compassion toward Jesus. Her loyalty in the face of danger is something for Christians to admire. Saint Veronica and her veil may be a legend, but we can still be inspired by it. It can be scary to speak up and say you know Christ. You don't know how people will react when you declare your faith in a classroom, the workplace, or even a social situation. But when you're hesitant to associate yourself with Christ, think of Veronica, and push through your fears to identify with the Savior who died for you.

*Pray for me, too. Ask God to give me the right words so
I can boldly explain God's mysterious plan.*

EPHESIANS 6:19

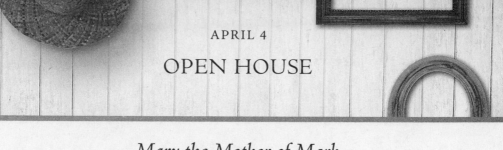

Mary the Mother of Mark

ACTS 12:12

Are all the women in the Gospels named Mary? Not exactly, but there are four distinct (and important) Marys in the story of Jesus, plus two more in the rest of the New Testament. Mary the mother of Mark is mentioned only in Acts 12:12, but once we do a little detective work, we might find her present at the Last Supper.

Let's review. Peter was in prison, probably the Antonia Fortress in Jerusalem. Miraculously freed by angels, he found his way to the home of Mary the mother of Mark, where a number of believers were praying for him. (See our account of Rhoda the maid on January 8.) This brief mention actually tells us a lot about Mary.

As mother of a young man who would soon enter Christian ministry, she was in her thirties or forties. She owned a house big enough for a group to meet in. The house had a gate, which probably meant there was a courtyard and possibly two stories. She had at least one servant. Since there is no husband mentioned, we can guess she was a widow (or that her husband had no connection to Christianity).

Since Mark was related to Barnabas (see Colossians 4:10), so was Mary. We know Barnabas came from Cyprus and owned some land, which he sold, giving the proceeds to the church (see Acts 4:36-37). So it's likely that Mary also came from an affluent Jewish family in Cyprus and now owned a spacious home in Jerusalem, which she used for Christian meetings. That led some ancient Bible scholars to think that Mary's home was the site of the Last Supper. How many other homeowners in Jerusalem would be so supportive of this Galilean preacher?

Whether or not this is true, Mary remains a model of Christian hospitality. This virtue is highly valued in the New Testament and other early Christian writings, leading us to consider how we use our homes for God's purposes. Is your home your private cave, where you and your family retreat from the world to enjoy the fruits of your labors? Or do you find ways to use your domestic resources for ministry? And even if you can't invite people over, can you express hospitality by making people feel "at home" wherever you are?

When God's people are in need, be ready to help them.
Always be eager to practice hospitality.

ROMANS 12:13

LOVE STORY

Mary Magdalene

LUKE 8:1-3

People's imaginations run wild with Mary Magdalene, but the Bible tells us very little about her. Luke introduces her along with a few other female followers of Jesus, and he adds the fact that Jesus cast seven demons out of her (see Luke 8:2). That's the only profile we get. We know she was present at the cross and the tomb, but there's no other background given. Just demons.

Exorcism was actually a substantial part of Jesus' ministry, though modern-minded folks tend to gloss over it. One story from the northeast shore of Galilee involves a man possessed by "many" demons. "Day and night he wandered among the burial caves and in the hills, howling and cutting himself with sharp stones" (Mark 5:5). Demon possession wasn't pretty. It was chaotic and destructive.

So what did Mary of Magdala look like when Jesus first saw her? Was she howling and cutting herself, running around burial caves? Folks keep trying to create a love story between Mary and Jesus, but if this was "love at first sight," it must have been a special kind of love. With the havoc that demons generally cause, Mary must have been a major mess. And why do we need a romance when we have a much, much stronger love at work here?

Jesus looked through the chaos to see a woman in need. He cleared away the spiritual clutter and restored her health. He didn't condemn her for the things the demons had done. He banished them and welcomed her into a new life, following him.

He does the same thing today. Even if you're not afflicted with demons, the power of sin is still destructive. Our lives are filled with regrets over selfish choices, bad behavior, and missed opportunities. We're a mess.

But Jesus peers through our chaotic self-destruction to see someone he needs to redeem. Our problems don't faze him as he speaks his powerful word. We don't have to earn his healing touch; we *can't*. We just receive it. He welcomes us into an exciting relationship with him. Past sins are wiped away. Demons are banished. Bygones are bygones. We can step into a new life with the risen Christ.

Now *that's* a love story.

When we were utterly helpless, Christ came at just the right time and died for us sinners.

ROMANS 5:6

MISTAKEN IDENTITY

Mary Magdalene

JOHN 20:1-18

You've heard the stories. Mary Magdalene was the only female disciple, the former prostitute who repented of her sins and had a romantic crush on Jesus. Some go so far as to say that Jesus married her. The problem is, these stories are fiction. Sometimes they're compelling, entertaining fiction, but there's little historical fact here.

Mary's shameful past involved demon possession, not prostitution. She was listed with several affluent women who sometimes traveled with the disciples and paid for their provisions (Luke 8:2-3). She was *not* the "sinful woman" who anointed Jesus' feet with perfume. The Gospels have no mention of a romantic relationship with Jesus.

The fictionalizing about Mary has been going on for centuries, well before *The Da Vinci Code*. Storytellers have long tried to make her the bride at Cana or the woman caught in adultery. A second-century document dubiously claims to be the "Gospel of Mary," suggesting that she was a better disciple than all the others.

These stories may be clever constructions, and some writers have good intentions. Who can argue with the theme of a fallen woman repenting of her sins? But that's not the real Mary Magdalene. There's enough to learn from her without fudging the facts. We need to let Mary be Mary.

Maybe you have a similar problem. People see you as more of a saint or sinner than you really are. They expect you to play a role—corporate star, supermom, community leader, church pillar—but it all seems like a case of mistaken identity. Does anyone know the true you?

Jesus does.

The Gospel of John gives us a great moment of recognition by the empty tomb. Mary Magdalene is there, in her true role as a faithful disciple of Jesus. She is surely heartbroken over his death and now wondering what happened to his body. Mistaking Jesus for the gardener, she asks for some info. He looks at her, seeing who she really is, and calls her by name. "Mary."

That's all she needs to hear. She knows it's Jesus. "Teacher," she responds.

She is known, and she is loved . . . and so are we.

She turned to leave and saw someone standing there. It was Jesus, but she didn't recognize him. "Dear woman, why are you crying?" Jesus asked her. "Who are you looking for?"

JOHN 20:14-15

BEING THERE

Mary Magdalene

JOHN 20:1-18

When Jesus was arrested, his disciples fled. Peter came back as far as the courtyard to witness Jesus' trial (and deny him). John, who might have had a family connection with the high priest, was the only one of the Twelve at the cross.

But the women who followed Jesus continued to do so, to the cross and to the tomb. Matthew tells us that Mary Magdalene and some other women were "watching from a distance" (27:55-56) as Jesus was crucified. His body was buried by high-ranking sympathizers, but the anointing of the body remained to be done.

That's why Mary Magdalene and other women came to the tomb on Sunday, the first sunup after Sabbath, to honor their departed Lord with a proper burial treatment. Of course you know the Easter story, don't you? The stone out of place, the angels, "He is risen!"

At some point in that flurry of activity, Mary's tears were interrupted by a "gardener," who turned out to be Jesus himself. She must have embraced him in utter joy, because he responded, "Don't cling to me. . . . But go find my brothers" (John 20:17).

Throughout history, debate has raged over the status of Mary Magdalene. Did she have a special place in Jesus' heart? Was she a better disciple than the others? Let's put the arguments aside and focus on a simple fact: she was *there*. This woman claimed her place in the Christian story by being present at the most important events of our faith.

Presence. In our multitasking world, this is a lost art. How often have you tuned out of a conversation? Do you find yourself living on autopilot for minutes, or even hours, at a time? This can happen spiritually, too—and we're not just talking about dozing off during Sunday's sermon (though that could be a problem). Do you spend time in the Lord's presence? Do you pay attention to the things he is doing around you, in you, through you? Do you hear his voice guiding you through life?

Mary's tears kept her from recognizing the risen Christ. But then he spoke her name, and the connection was made. She was present with him, and he with her. Listen carefully now. . . . Is he calling your name?

Remain in me, and I will remain in you.

JOHN 15:4

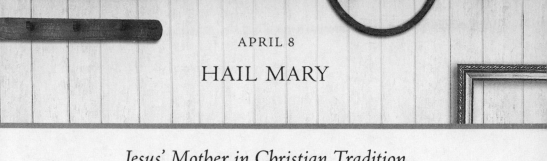

HAIL MARY

Jesus' Mother in Christian Tradition

T he first "Hail Mary" was said by the angel Gabriel, who told this young woman she would give birth to the Messiah (see Luke 1:28). In response to this annunciation, Mary sang a song of praise in which she prophesied, "From now on all generations will call me blessed" (Luke 1:48). That has turned out to be true.

Christians of all stripes honor Mary, the mother of Jesus, but some more than others. While Protestants prefer to stick with the biblical data, Roman Catholics embrace a more elaborate tradition about Mary's history and eternal role, as do Orthodox believers. The Bible declares that Mary was a virgin when she bore Jesus, but Catholics also hold that she is a perpetual virgin, and so the "brothers" of Jesus mentioned in Scripture were really cousins.

The Immaculate Conception and Assumption of Mary are also part of Catholic teaching, maintaining that she herself was miraculously conceived and that her body was "assumed" into heaven. These and other traditions have served to make Mary a sort of "supersaint," nearly on a par with Jesus. Some are quick to say that they "venerate" Mary rather than worshiping her. Such veneration goes way back in history. As early as the second century, writers were speculating on Mary's upbringing, and church councils in the fourth and fifth centuries considered her role in God's plan. As early as the sixth century, debates were raging over the semantics of viewing Mary as the "God bearer" or the "Christ bearer." Orthodox believers still honor Mary as *Theotokos* (God bearer).

Protestants fear idolatry here. In many cultures, religions have male and female deities. Is this just the Christian way of doing the same thing? Does praying to Mary distract from our commitment to Jesus? These are important questions.

Let's come back to our points of agreement. God chose Mary for a special task, and she accepted it with faith and devotion. She is a great example for us in many ways, perhaps mostly for her submission to the will of God. After the angel unfolded God's plan for her, she responded, "I am the Lord's servant. May everything you have said about me come true" (Luke 1:38).

Saying yes to God's wishes. We can all hail that as a worthy attitude.

"Don't be afraid, Mary," the angel told her, "for you have found favor with God!"

LUKE 1:30

LOST AND FOUND

Mary on the Road from Jerusalem

LUKE 2:41-51

A big family is traveling together. There are so many people traveling that it's not noticed when one child isn't with the group when it gets going. The child, while left behind, is capable of taking care of himself. No, this isn't the plot of *Home Alone*. It's a Bible story.

The boy is twelve-year-old Jesus. He had traveled with his family from Nazareth to Jerusalem for Passover. In those days, extended families traveled together. There could have been dozens of relatives and friends in the caravan. When the group started for home, Mary and Joseph assumed that Jesus was somewhere with them. After a day or so, they realized he wasn't, so they returned to Jerusalem.

It took them three days to find Jesus. Imagine their panic while they were searching. When they finally found him, he was sitting in the Temple courts, learning from the teachers and asking questions.

Mary and Joseph were aware their son was the Son of God, even if they didn't fully understand what that meant. When the angel Gabriel told Mary she was going to have a child, he said her son would be given the throne of David, with a Kingdom that would never end. So finding him in the Temple shouldn't have been a surprise, but Mary still scolded her son. "Son, why have you treated us like this? Your father and I have been anxiously searching for you" (Luke 2:48, NIV).

Considering all she knew about Jesus, wasn't Mary overreacting a little bit? (Any parent reading this right now is saying, "Absolutely not!") Mary was acting very human. Even though she knew God had specific plans for her son, she worried. When she couldn't find her son, she might have thought God's plans had been ruined—all because of her own lapse in parenting!

Do you ever worry that God's plans for you have been ruined—and maybe because of something you've done? Don't be so hard on yourself. It's only human to have worries, but as Mary probably learned over and over throughout Jesus' life (and his resurrection), if God wants his plans carried out, nothing, not even our worrying, will get in his way.

"But why did you need to search?" [Jesus] asked. "Didn't
you know that I must be in my Father's house?"

LUKE 2:49

TIME OUT

Mary at the Wedding of Cana

JOHN 2:1-12

Water to wine. It's the first recorded miracle of Jesus. He was attending a wedding with his mother and his disciples. It must have been quite a celebration because the hosts ran out of wine.

Socially, this would have been a disaster for the groom's family, which was responsible for providing the food and drink for the party. In that day, Jewish weddings were a community event, and the festivities lasted for days. It was a badge of honor to be able to provide enough for everyone who chose to celebrate with your family. And it brought personal and social shame if you couldn't.

Mary understood this. When she noticed that the wine had run out, she simply told Jesus, "They have no more wine" (John 2:3).

This is a fascinating exchange. Surely Mary knew her son's potential. If anyone could save the day, he could—but *would* he? Was this an important enough problem for him to fix?

Jesus' response was cryptic. He wondered why she was involving him. "My time has not yet come," he told her (John 2:4). That seems like a no, but Mary wasn't buying it.

She simply went to the servants, pointed to her son, and said, "Do whatever he tells you" (John 2:5). Did she have an inkling that his "time" would be coming any minute now? Apparently it did. Jesus saved the day. He turned jars full of water into jars full of choice wine.

In the process, we learn something valuable about Mary's faith—and our own. Even though there's no evidence that she had ever seen him perform a miracle, Mary knew her son, and she had faith that Jesus could do something amazing about this situation. She brought the need before him and prepared for him to act upon it. It was still his call. He didn't have to change the water into wine. He could have chosen to solve the problem a different way, or not at all.

That's the point of faith. We can't know for sure that God will do something, but we do have knowledge of who he is. We have faith that he'll do something when we ask him for help, even if we don't know what that something will be.

This miraculous sign at Cana in Galilee was the first time Jesus revealed his glory. And his disciples believed in him.

JOHN 2:11

FAMILY TIES

Mary and the Family's Intervention

MARK 3:31-35

Have you ever wondered how long it took Mary to get used to the fact that Jesus was Jesus? Of course, she knew her child would be special from the moment the angel Gabriel told her that she, a virgin, was pregnant. She would bear the "Son of the Most High" (Luke 1:32).

For the first thirty years of Jesus' life, though, it doesn't seem that he was very different from other boys or men. He was probably better behaved or understood Scripture unbelievably well, but the Bible goes silent for most of those years, suggesting that nothing was out of the ordinary. His neighbors just thought of him as "the carpenter's son."

Only when Jesus was baptized by his cousin John around the age of thirty did he begin his public ministry. That's when he started performing miracles and when he gathered a following of disciples.

Even though Mary knew that Jesus was special, it must have taken her a while to get used to the actions of her miracle-performing, crowd-gathering son. In fact, on one occasion early in his ministry, when the crowds gathered around Jesus and his disciples, his family got concerned because he was working right through mealtimes. They tried to take him away from the crowd. "He's out of his mind," they said (Mark 3:21). We're not told whether this intervention succeeded, but a bit later, Jesus was teaching the crowds again when someone brought word, "Your mother and your brothers are outside asking for you" (verse 32). Instead of getting up and going outside immediately, Jesus took a moment to teach.

"Who is my mother? Who are my brothers?" he asked (Mark 3:33). Then he looked at those seated in a circle around him and said, "Look, these are my mother and brothers. Anyone who does God's will is my brother and sister and mother" (verses 34-35).

Jesus was not renouncing his mother and other family members. Instead, he was expanding his family. Anyone could be as close to him as a mother, brother, or sister, as long as he or she desired to do God's will.

Maybe you have a great family, but maybe not. Either way, welcome to Jesus' family. Draw the circle larger, and join with those who seek to please God.

God decided in advance to adopt us into his own family
by bringing us to himself through Jesus Christ.

EPHESIANS 1:5

HORRIFIC

Mary at the Cross

JOHN 19:25-27

It's hard to imagine anything more horrifying for a parent than to watch his or her child, even an adult child, accused and found guilty of crimes he didn't commit, and then beaten, tortured, and ultimately put to death in a humiliating and painful fashion.

It seems impossible that a parent would be able to stand by and watch all that happen, but Mary did. Mary stood by the cross of Jesus. How? How did Mary get through something so horrific? Maybe it was with a little help from her friends.

There were others standing by Mary as she stayed by her son's side. John says Mary's sister, Mary the wife of Clopas, and Mary Magdalene were with her, near the cross. No doubt they all loved Jesus and were devastated by what was happening too, but their presence there must have been a comfort to Mary.

John, who is described in the Bible as "the disciple whom Jesus loved," was there, also (John 13:23, NIV). During his final minutes, when Mary must have been the most beside herself, Jesus spoke to his mother and John.

"Woman, here is your son," he said, referring to John (John 19:26).

Then he gave John a responsibility and honor. "Here is your mother," Jesus told him, indicating that he wanted John to look after Mary when he was gone (John 19:27). After Jesus' crucifixion, John took care of Mary in his home.

Friends and family who loved and cared about Mary stood by her, comforted her, and took care of her when she was facing something that seemed impossible to get through.

Do you have a friend who is going though something very difficult right now? Maybe what she needs is someone to stand by her and comfort her while it's going on. Maybe you can't fix whatever the problem is, but you can be there. Take a look around you. Who could use your love, support, and comfort, a little help from a friend, right now?

All praise to God, the Father of our Lord Jesus Christ. God is our merciful Father and the source of all comfort. He comforts us in all our troubles so that we can comfort others. When they are troubled, we will be able to give them the same comfort God has given us.

2 CORINTHIANS 1:3-4

PRAYPAL

Mary after the Resurrection

ACTS 1:3-14

Picture the scene. Jesus has been resurrected. He appears, off and on over forty days, to his disciples—both the chosen Twelve and other men and women. On the last day—although the disciples didn't know it was the last—he gives them some instructions and then ascends into the clouds.

If you had been there, how long would you have stood, staring off into the sky in amazement? For those who actually were there, it must have been a while, because two angels had to come and tell them to stop staring into the empty sky!

There's a good chance that Jesus' mother Mary was among those staring into that sky. She definitely was with the group when they were all in a room together later. What were they all doing there? Waiting for God to say, "Go!"

The instructions that Jesus gave right before he rose into the heavens were specific. He told his followers that they soon would be baptized with the Holy Spirit. Once that happened, they were to go out, to the ends of the world, and tell others about Jesus.

Jesus' followers knew exactly what they were supposed to do, but they had to wait for one thing, one very important thing, to happen first. They had to wait for the Holy Spirit. When would he show up? Soon.

Soon? How soon? Soon is a relative term. Later that day? Next week? In two months? They didn't know, but they did know one thing they could do while waiting.

Mary and all the others could pray and spend time with God—asking him questions, listening to his answers—until the Holy Spirit came. And that's what they did. "They all met together and were constantly united in prayer."

About ten days later, when the Holy Spirit arrived on the Day of Pentecost, they were ready. They had spent time praying, growing closer to God and each other.

When you have something you're going to do because God has told you to do it, praying about it is an important step. During your prayers, ask questions and listen for answers, so you're ready when the time comes to act.

They all met together and were constantly united in prayer, along with Mary the mother of Jesus, several other women, and the brothers of Jesus.

ACTS 1:14

TOPSY-TURVY

On the Importance of Women at Jesus' Tomb

I f Luke was a marketer, he would have written it differently. A centurion would have confirmed that the tomb was empty, or perhaps the high priest. Instead, his Gospel gives us a group of women seeing angels. Luke even acknowledges the credibility issue: when the women reported it, "the story sounded like nonsense to the men" (Luke 24:11).

The secondary status of women in the ancient world is well known. In some cultures, a woman's testimony wouldn't stand up in court. Men believed men. So this is hardly the way to launch a worldwide religion . . . unless, of course, you're just telling the truth.

Perhaps the greatest testimony to the truth of the Gospel accounts is their utter honesty. These are not puff pieces, telling us only what we want to hear. We get the real picture. Peter often said the wrong thing. Thomas doubted. The other disciples quarreled. And here, at the moment of ultimate victory, in the glow of a resurrection Jesus had predicted, the men refuse to believe the women, because . . . well, maybe just because they're women.

Instead of asking Luke or the other Gospel writers why they wrote it this way, perhaps we should wonder why God made it happen this way. Then, suddenly, we begin to see a pattern. Why was Jesus born to a peasant girl? Why the tiny nation of Israel? Why did he bless the poor and heal the sick? Why did he include children? There is a topsy-turvy quality in all of God's doings. The first shall be last, Jesus said, and in the Resurrection account the supposedly second-class gender is entrusted with the most important news ever: *He is risen!*

The resurrection of Jesus sets us free not only from sin and death, but also from the accumulated injustices of human culture. No group can say to another group, "You don't matter," because Jesus offers new life to all. The Spirit is poured out upon young and old alike, sons and daughters. And so the trail of witnesses extends from the Marys at the tomb to Priscilla, Phoebe, and Lydia, to Perpetua, Marcella, and Mahalia.

Let us all testify boldly to the power of Christ's resurrection in our lives and in our world.

It was Mary Magdalene, Joanna, Mary the mother of James, and several other women who told the apostles what had happened. But the story sounded like nonsense to the men, so they didn't believe it.

LUKE 24:10-11

"THE BEST COMPANION OF MY LIFE"

Idelette Calvin

D. 1549

John Calvin was extremely organized in his theology—and in his love life. Trained as a lawyer, this thinker was one of the giants of the Protestant Reformation, but he was not a "people person." When Calvin was about thirty, friends began urging him to get married (perhaps trying to soften his bristly personality). He told his would-be matchmakers he was not one of "those insane lovers . . . smitten at first sight with a fine figure." No, he announced, "This only is the beauty which allures me, if she is chaste, if not too nice or fastidious, if economical, if patient, if there is hope that she will be interested about my health."

After rejecting three candidates, Calvin noticed a young widow in the church he was leading in Strasbourg—Idelette de Bure Stordeur. She and her husband were Dutch Anabaptists who had fled persecution, landing in this free city and adopting Calvin's Reformed views. Then the husband died in a plague, and Idelette was left with two children, ages twelve and six. She seemed to meet Calvin's requirements, and they were married in August 1540.

Their nine years together were full of pain, sickness, and challenge. Yet, with Idelette's support, John did some of the best work of his life. Both became sick immediately after the wedding. Then John was called away to a theology conference that dragged on for months. When another plague threatened Strasbourg, Idelette trundled herself and the kids out of town for a while. So much for wedded bliss.

A year into their marriage, John felt called to move his work to Geneva, and Idelette had to get used to a new city. The Calvins had three children who died at or shortly after birth. Then Idelette herself became ill in 1545 and never fully recovered. After her death in 1549, John wrote, "I have been bereaved of the best companion of my life. . . . She was the faithful helper of my ministry." He never remarried.

Sometimes God asks a woman or man to change the world. And sometimes he asks us to support someone else who is changing the world. That was Idelette's calling.

The LORD God said, "It is not good for the man to be alone.
I will make a helper who is just right for him."

GENESIS 2:18

CRAZY FOR YOU

Teresa of Avila
1516–82

When Teresa was five years old, she and her brother ran away from home. They planned to go to a foreign land to be martyred for their faith—but an uncle brought them back. Teresa would have to find other ways to suffer for Jesus.

Born in 1515 in the province of Avila, Spain, Teresa lived her life in the shadow of the Reformation and Counter-Reformation, powerful forces trying to cleanse the church in various, often violent ways. Teresa's grandfather, a Jewish convert to Christianity, was suspected of reverting and was condemned by the Spanish Inquisition. That might be why Teresa's parents made their kids as Catholic as possible.

Girls in that time had two major life options: marriage or the convent. Teresa chose the convent—its rules were not as strict as her father's. Her autobiography describes the next two decades as a time of guilt and self-doubt. She regretted the sins of her youth. She wasn't pious enough to be a nun. She had no talent for "great theological thoughts."

She fell ill, and in her recovery, she received visions from God. She was experiencing a level of prayer that seemed real and powerful, but when she discussed it, her friends said the visions came from the devil. So Teresa became focused on suffering, sometimes causing herself pain to do penance for her sins. At one point she stopped praying altogether, but a helpful priest urged her to continue.

And maybe it was the praying that changed her. Somehow, over the following years, this troubled soul turned into a powerful spiritual leader. She still had her opponents. Some fought her as she tried to start new convents, but she persisted. And her writings reflect a relaxed wisdom, a commonsense commitment:

Let nothing disturb you.
Let nothing make you afraid.
All things are passing.
God alone never changes.
Patience gains all things.
If you have God you will want for nothing.
God alone suffices.

It seems God had rescued her from herself.

Why am I discouraged? Why is my heart so sad? I will put my hope in God!

PSALM 43:5

LOVE LIFTED ME

Teresa of Avila
1516–82

"May God protect me from gloomy saints," said Teresa of Avila late in her life. It's ironic because early in her life she was one. A strict upbringing, life in a convent, and a deep sense of her own inadequacy contributed to her gloom. The only way to please Jesus, she figured, was to suffer as he did.

But then something changed. It's hard to know what caused the change, but it's clear she had a different attitude in her later years. It was pointless, she realized, to punish yourself for not being good enough. If you need to grow, grow! Get better. If you're down on yourself, don't stew in it; take a walk and admire the sky. Sure, there's a time for fasting and penitence, but sometimes you just need a good meal.

What characterized the later Teresa is *love*—a deeply devoted love for God that spilled over into love for others and a general joy of life. For years she had struggled to think the proper theological thoughts while praying, but then she realized, "The important thing is not to think much but to love much and so do that which best stirs you to love. Love is not great delight but desire to please God in everything."

It was love that powered Teresa's amazing prayer life. As a nun, she had chosen Jesus instead of a husband—so why shouldn't she give Jesus the attention that other women gave their husbands? In modern terms, prayers could be like dates—when two people in love share their thoughts and feelings.

"It is love alone that gives worth to all things," wrote Teresa, and this truth echoes what we find in Scripture. If you're a "gloomy saint," listen up. The way of Christ is not about rules and regulations. It's about love. Whatever fears you gathered from your upbringing, your early experiences, or your personal insecurity, let them be washed away in the river of God's love. He loves us passionately, and he longs for us to love him back. What's more, he plants a love inside of us that shines forth in the way we live each day. Just ask Teresa.

Love does no wrong to others, so love fulfills the requirements of God's law.

ROMANS 13:10

PRAYER BEQUEST

Teresa of Avila

1516–82

It was a turbulent time: politics and theology clamored and collided across Europe. The sixteenth century saw an explosion of religious reform, but it was also an era in which princes and prelates on all sides scrambled to consolidate power. In the midst of this, a Spanish nun named Teresa found peace in prayer, and ever since, her writings on the subject have been a gift to Christians of all persuasions.

"Contemplative prayer in my opinion is nothing else than a close sharing between friends," she wrote. "It means taking time frequently to be alone with him who we know loves us." Her approach sounds quite modern, even simple. It's not burdened with pious forms. Teresa cut to the heart of what prayer really is.

That's not to say she took it casually. In fact, she scolded others in her convent for caring too much about appearances and human friendships and not devoting themselves to prayer. She applied these same criticisms to herself. One of the great features of her writing is her honesty about her own struggles. "I couldn't wait for the hour of prayer to be over," she admitted at one point. "I would have gladly gone through any penance to get out of the practice of prayer." Distraction was a problem for her. She compared her intellect to a raving madman.

Despite these "interior battles," Teresa provided us with a roadmap for our own prayer journeys. It starts with mental prayer: a withdrawal from worldly concerns and a humble focus on Christ. Then there's the "prayer of quiet," which focuses on the Lord even more exclusively. She also described heightened states of "union" and "rapture," unusual experiences of God's presence and power. But it starts with that "close sharing between friends."

How's your prayer life? If you spend more time on Facebook than on your knees, Teresa might challenge you to consider who your best friend really is. If Jesus is special to you, then why not spend some intentional face time with him—not just squeezing prayers in between the "important" events of your life, but clearing away the distractions and focusing on him for an hour or so?

Never stop praying.

1 THESSALONIANS 5:17

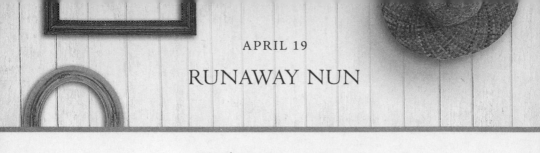

RUNAWAY NUN

Katharina von Bora

1499–1552

She was a runaway nun who couldn't find a husband. She became a wife and a mother and a powerful force behind the man who caused one of the greatest religious upheavals in history.

Katharina von Bora was in a convent in Germany when she read about the fascinating new ideas of Martin Luther: salvation by God's grace, "the just shall live by faith" (Romans 1:17, KJV), every believer having access to God. Along with eleven other nuns, she wrote to Luther, asking for help escaping the nunnery. He devised a plot involving the delivery of twelve barrels of smoked herring—and the removal of those barrels with nuns inside.

Some of these sisters returned to their parents. Others got domestic jobs. Others found husbands. Katie was the last of the lot. A failed romance left her heartbroken, and in desperation she mentioned she wouldn't mind marrying Luther himself.

How's that for a proposal? To everyone's surprise, including his own, the forty-one-year-old bachelor agreed.

It made sense for Martin Luther to be married. He had challenged the Catholic church on many points, including the celibacy of priests and nuns. It might be the calling for some, but he didn't find it biblically necessary. He had often written about the value of marriage in God's eyes—he had just never wed. One problem was that, with all the opposition against him and his Reformation, he feared that any wife he took would soon be a widow. Perhaps a greater problem was that he needed a special kind of woman to put up with him.

Katie was that kind of woman. Independent, sharp tongued, yet deeply loyal, she ran the Luther household like an empress. It is hard to imagine that Martin Luther would have had the same influence without Katie in his home and in his heart.

This was her calling. What's yours? Some women are called to remain unmarried and use their freedom to serve the Lord. Some are led through the difficult straits of divorce or widowhood and emerge with hearts full of mercy. And some are called to marry, leveraging their gifts with those of a husband, to honor God in creative ways.

I, a prisoner for serving the Lord, beg you to lead a life worthy
of your calling, for you have been called by God.

EPHESIANS 4:1

RIPE FOR DISASTER

Katharina von Bora

1499–1552

I f ever a marriage seemed ripe for disaster, it was the Luthers'. Martin and Katie were both quick witted, strong willed, hot tempered, and sharp tongued. They seemed to disagree more than they agreed. The first argument of their married life occurred over a wedding gift. Martin wanted to return the money sent by an arch-rival. His ever-practical bride wanted to use it to pay down his debts.

Martin often wrote about the patience required in a marriage, indicating that he was often irked at his wife, and yet he realized that Katie had to be patient with him, too. For all of their squabbles, it seems that they knew how much they needed each other. He was a genius and a charismatic leader, but a bull in a china shop, making bold statements without worrying about the fallout. She was a manager, full of practical wisdom, welcoming visitors and refugees into their home, and picking up the pieces behind her reckless husband. She possessed a sense of responsibility that he needed more of. He owned a faith that could help her navigate through fretful times.

"We thank you heartily for being so worried that you can't sleep," Martin wrote to her while on his travels, "for since you started worrying about us, a fire broke out near my door, and yesterday, no doubt due to your worry, a big stone . . . would have fallen and crushed us like a mouse in a trap. If you don't stop worrying, I'm afraid the earth will swallow us. . . . Pray and let God worry. 'Cast your burden on the Lord.'"

Like the biblical Martha, Katie Luther was worried and upset over many details, and she needed Martin's chiding. But surely he also needed regular challenges from her to look out for "the interests of others" (Philippians 2:4, NIV).

So how do you match up in your closest relationships? Are you cut from the same cloth, or are you totally different? Whatever the case, see how God can use the unique personalities of you and those around you for his glory.

My dear Martha, you are worried and upset over all these details!
There is only one thing worth being concerned about. Mary has
discovered it, and it will not be taken away from her.

LUKE 10:41-42

CIRCUS ACT

Katharina von Bora
1499–1552

On one occasion, the volatile Martin Luther shut himself in his den for three days, trying to get away from the activity of his bustling home. He and his wife, Katie, lived in a renovated monastery, appropriate for this former monk and former nun. They had six children of their own, and they had welcomed several nieces and nephews to live with them, as well as children of other friends who were going through rough times. Katie invited some of her female relatives to come and help with nannying all these kids. And of course there were regular students and visitors who traveled from afar to learn from the famous reformer.

This wasn't a home; it was a circus.

You can hardly blame Martin for seeking solitude in his den, but for three days? Katie was incensed. Sure, he needed to study, but he was shirking his responsibilities to the rest of the household . . . and to her.

So she had the den door removed.

This is a fitting picture of their relationship. Single until he was forty-one, Martin seemed set in his bachelor ways. When he married Katie, it was more of a business deal than anything. "I'm not madly in love," he told a friend, "but I cherish her." In a way, his sense of romantic love was walled off, shut away.

But through the years of their contentious relationship, in her no-nonsense way, Katie managed to remove the locked door of his heart. She taught him to love her.

Martin once wrote about Jesus' first miracle, turning water to wine at the wedding in Cana. He considered it an apt description of marriage. "The first love is drunken. When the intoxication wears off, then comes the real married love." Maybe the Luthers never experienced that first "drunken" love, but they certainly grew into the latter love. "I will not take the vexation out of marriage," Martin wrote. "I may even increase it, but it will turn out wonderfully." As it was in Cana, the best was saved for last.

What sort of door needs to be removed in your life?

"A host always serves the best wine first. . . . But you have kept the best until now!" This miraculous sign at Cana in Galilee was the first time Jesus revealed his glory. And his disciples believed in him.

JOHN 2:10-11

GOD'S GREEN EARTH

Hildegard of Bingen

1098–1179

The earth should not be injured. The earth should not be destroyed. As often as the elements, the elements of the world are violated by ill-treatment, so God will cleanse them. God will cleanse them thru the sufferings, thru the hardships of humankind.

Surprisingly, environmentalism can be a divisive issue for Christians. Some Christians fear that taking care of the earth can equate to worshiping nature. Yet in their concern to avoid idolatry, many Christians overlook God's command to be stewards of his creation.

The psalmist sings, "The earth is the LORD's, and everything in it. The world and all its people belong to him" (Psalm 24:1). Granted, there have always been people who have "worshiped and served the things God created instead of the Creator himself" (Romans 1:25), but we don't need to follow that path. This earth is God's! Of course caring for it isn't idol worship. It's honoring God's handiwork.

In the 1960s, people looked around and saw that humans were damaging the earth with their massive consumption of natural resources and the pollution and waste it created. US Senator Gaylord Nelson brought those who cared together for the very first Earth Day on April 22, 1970, to shed light on the fact that our earth is in trouble. We were not, and still are not, taking proper care of what is the Lord's.

We may see the 1960s as the beginning of the environmental movement, but the seeds of this concern go far back in Christian history. Back to St. Francis. Back to this amazing twentieth-century prodigy, Hildegard of Bingen, quoted above. She recognized that the earth would be "violated by ill-treatment." She foresaw the "sufferings and hardships of humankind" that this would cause.

It has been a long, uphill battle for the majority of Christians to recognize what Hildegard noticed, but we're finally at a place where Christians and churches are realizing there is a need for creation care and finding ways to "go green" to make a difference.

God may be telling you to lead environmental efforts, or he may simply be asking you to be responsible with what you've been given. What can you do today to help care for God's creation? What can you continue to do every day?

Look, the highest heavens and the earth and everything in it all belong to the LORD your God.

DEUTERONOMY 10:14

THE COMPANY OF WOMEN

Marguerite of Navarre

1492–1549

You might have noticed that the most powerful piece on a chessboard is the queen. That may reflect the reality of Europe in the 1500s. The Renaissance was changing culture, and the Reformation was changing worship. A few privileged families held power throughout the continent, and the women in these families formed an impressive coterie of world changers. In the middle of all this was Marguerite of Navarre, free thinker, writer, and queen.

Her father was a well-born nobleman, but it was her mother, Louise of Savoy, who taught Marguerite languages, philosophy, and theology. This education gave a breadth to the writing she loved to do, and it led to an open-minded attitude amid the new ideas swirling around the Reformation. While Marguerite remained a Catholic, throughout her life she welcomed Protestant teaching, seeking to change the church from within.

Marguerite's brother became King Francis I of France, and she assisted him at court, impressing visitors with her wit and knowledge. She also participated in high-level peace negotiations. All the while, she was writing secular and sacred works of poetry and prose.

It was an era of savvy women. Catherine de Medici would soon become the power behind the French throne. Marguerite's own daughter, Jeanne d'Albret, was a powerhouse of the French Protestant movement. It has also been suggested that Marguerite's Protestant sympathies rubbed off on a young Anne Boleyn as a lady-in-waiting in the court of Francis. And Marguerite's popular devotional book, *The Mirror of the Sinful Soul*, was translated into English by Anne Boleyn's precocious eleven-year-old daughter, who would grow up to be Queen Elizabeth I.

"O my Savior, through faith I am . . . joined with Thee," Marguerite wrote in that book. "O what union is this . . . now I may call Thee son, father, spouse, and brother. . . . O what gifts Thou dost give, by the goodness of those names. . . . Father full of humility. Brother, having taken our similitude. Son, engendered through faith, and charity. Husband, loving in all extremity."

Despite the pressures and politics of that time, this queen understood that true power comes from our connection with the Savior.

May you have the power to understand, as all God's people should,
how wide, how long, how high, and how deep his love is.

EPHESIANS 3:18

LADY WILLPOWER

Jeanne d'Albret

1528–72

Jeanne was so opposed to her first wedding, she literally had to be carried to the altar. She was twelve. The marriage was arranged by her parents for political reasons, and when the political winds changed a few years later, it was easily annulled. Eight years later, she was married again, this time to a dashing prince.

The only child of Henry d'Albret, king of Navarre, and Marguerite de Valois, Jeanne was a princess herself. Their kingdom was a small one, tucked between Spain and France, but it carried some clout. And Jeanne's second husband, Antoine de Bourbon, was a member of the French royal family.

Europe was changing in the mid-1500s, as the Protestant Reformation challenged old loyalties. Calvinism had taken root in Geneva and was spreading into France. Slowly, Jeanne became a supporter of the French Protestants (Huguenots). In 1555, she wrote, "Reform seems . . . right and . . . necessary." She publicly announced her conversion on Christmas Day in 1560.

Though her husband remained Catholic and the French royalty exerted strong pressure, Jeanne never recanted—even when her son was taken away from her. In fact, she became one of the most important Protestant leaders in France, making her little kingdom a haven for Calvinist ministers. While living in Paris, she openly held illegal Protestant services in her home. When civil war broke out, she became a dynamo on the Huguenot side, providing financial support, inspiration, and tactical advice. Her own failing health kept her from doing more. She died in 1572.

Her son later became King Henry IV of France and, while he vacillated between Protestant and Catholic allegiance, in 1598 he issued the Edict of Nantes, granting Huguenots most of the religious freedom his mother had fought for.

It's difficult to find inspiration in historical conflicts pitting Christian against Christian, but Jeanne d'Albret seems to have put her faith ahead of political expediency. By the power of her will, she resisted rulers and armies in order to stay true to God's calling.

What worldly powers do you need to stand up to? Sometimes willpower can be a polite name for stubbornness, but when it conforms to the sovereign will of God, it becomes courageous conviction.

Praise the LORD, for he has shown me the wonders of his unfailing love. He kept me safe when my city was under attack.

PSALM 31:21

THE LITTLE PRINCESS

Jeanne d'Albret

1528–72

Although I am just a little Princess, God has given me the government of this country so I may rule it according to his Gospel and teach it his Laws. I rely on God, who is more powerful than the King of Spain.

She was reportedly a short, frail woman, with great determination. Jeanne d'Albret apparently learned the way of faith from her mother, Marguerite of Navarre, and eventually found a home in the emerging Protestant church. Her "country" was the small kingdom of Navarre, situated in the Pyrenees, between the superpowers of France and Spain. Both those nations were ruled by Roman Catholic royalty, but they squabbled with each other. Jeanne played the political games necessary to keep control of her turf.

As Jeanne became more familiar with Protestantism, she opened her kingdom to Reformed churches, teachers, and literature. One minister in the area reported back to John Calvin, "Preaching is open—in public. The streets resound to the chanting of the Psalms. Religious books are sold as freely and openly at home."

At one point, King Philip II of Spain was seeking an alliance with Jeanne. She was newly widowed, and this pact would involve her marriage to Philip's son. It was politically expedient—her kingdom might be taken by France unless she had Spanish support—but she insisted that the land continue to be open to religious reformers. When Philip rejected that request, Jeanne responded with the words presented above—she would "rely on God" rather than Philip, who reportedly quipped, "This is quite too much of a woman to have as a daughter-in-law."

Consider those moments in your life when you've been tempted to compromise your values in order to get something you want. Maybe a job promotion requires too much time away from your family. Maybe you tend to tone down your faith as you seek the approval of certain friends. Maybe success in your field means lying or cheating or mistreating others. Your "king of Spain" might take different forms.

How will you respond? You have a small turf to "govern"—your life, your career, your home. Will you stay true to God's ways? Will you rely on God more than any earthly power?

If we are thrown into the blazing furnace, the God whom we serve is able to save us. He will rescue us from your power, Your Majesty.

DANIEL 3:17

RE-VISION

Elizabeth Barton

1506?–34

W as she a madwoman, a huckster, a political opportunist, or a prophet?
Historical reports include all these perspectives, and more.

In 1525, Elizabeth Barton was about nineteen, working as a maid, when she fell ill and began to see visions, sometimes while in trances that would last for days. Her utterances had a religious quality. Observers remarked on the "marvelous holiness" of these messages "in rebuke of sin and vice."

Prophecy was no small matter. Her parish priest reported these events to the archbishop, who sent a team to investigate. They discovered nothing amiss. When she publicly predicted her own healing, Barton found popularity among the rich and poor alike. Becoming a nun, she continued to exhort the people of England to remain true to the Lord, the church, and the Virgin Mary. She even met with King Henry VIII.

Then the religious life of England was torn apart. Henry wanted to divorce his first wife in favor of one who could give him an heir. The pope refused to grant an annulment, though this was commonly done for other rulers. So Henry seized control of the Church of England. At this point, Barton's utterances took on a fierce, judgmental tone. The king, she said, was making a grievous error. If he continued, he would die and burn in hell—she had even seen his particular corner of hell.

Because of her celebrity, Barton became a formidable opponent to the king. His advisers eventually arrested her and reportedly forced a confession of fraud. Then she was condemned, along with several sympathizers, and executed in 1534.

It was an ugly business. Partisans on both sides rushed to defend or discredit her, and they still do. Protestant and Catholic historians sharply disagree on who this woman was and what her visions meant.

In this, we find a lesson for today. Our highly partisan culture often makes it hard to hear the true message of God. We quickly look for the political value of any position, rather than listening with open hearts and bowing to God's desires. Love, truth, and wholeness become slogans rather than prophetic directives. Let's stop our partisan revision of God's Word and get a clear vision of his will for our lives.

They tell the seers, "Stop seeing visions!" They tell the prophets,
"Don't tell us what is right. Tell us nice things. Tell us lies."

ISAIAH 30:10

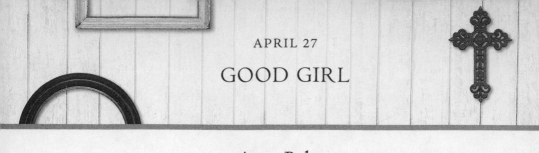

GOOD GIRL

Anne Boleyn

1501?–36

She was the woman behind the English Reformation, praised and vilified, whether or not she deserved it. Anne Boleyn was a person of faith and flaws who got in the middle of issues far bigger than she could control.

Growing up, she dazzled everyone. As she traveled throughout Europe with her diplomat father, people were impressed with Anne's manners and maturity. Queens invited her to attend them. She served in the French court in her youth and later, fatefully, as an attendant to Henry VIII's first wife, Catherine of Aragon.

In those days, fathers married off their daughters to broker deals or pay debts. Anne had one such engagement that was broken off, and there were a few other high-level courtships, but then the king himself took an interest in her.

King Henry wanted to divorce Catherine, and had some legal reasons to do so, but the reigning pope refused to annul the marriage. While this wrangling was going on, Henry was seriously courting Anne Boleyn, who appeared with him in public but reportedly deflected his sexual advances. Detractors claim that Anne was manipulating the king, but there are good reasons to believe that she was sincerely devout, trying to live a chaste life.

Everything changed in 1533. King Henry secretly married Anne, claimed control of the Church of England, got his handpicked archbishop to approve the divorce, and crowned Anne queen. That September, Anne bore him a daughter, Elizabeth. (The timing suggests that Anne was pregnant when they got married.)

In Anne's three years as queen, she proved herself intelligent and politically astute. She also used her influence to support Protestant causes, especially Bible translation. But she failed to provide a male heir, and so the king was soon looking for a new queen. Sentenced to death on trumped-up charges, Anne was beheaded in May 1536. From the scaffold, her final speech ended, "I heartily desire you all to pray for me. O Lord, have mercy on me! To God I commend my soul."

The world can be an exciting and cruel place for any of us. It's hard to stay true to God amid temptations of power and wealth. Like Anne, we all need the Lord's mercy throughout our lives.

We should live in this evil world with wisdom, righteousness, and devotion to God.

TITUS 2:12

QUEEN FOR A DAY

Lady Jane Grey
1536–54

Perhaps you've dreamed of being treated like royalty for a day, just a day—and then you could go back to your ordinary life. Well, Jane Grey had that dream come true for *nine* days, and she paid for it dearly.

When King Henry VIII died in 1547, he left religious turmoil. The Church of England had broken away from the Roman Catholic Church, and now the nation was torn. Henry was succeeded by his sole male heir, ten-year-old Edward VI, who leaned toward the Protestant cause, aided by adult advisers. A sickly child, Edward died at age sixteen, but not before making a will in which he left the throne to his cousin Jane Grey.

Jane was a smart girl, from a good Protestant family, and about Edward's age. Taught by the best tutors, she was respected for her intelligence and manners. Despite her youth, she had corresponded with the Swiss Protestant leader Heinrich Bullinger, who was eager to spread the faith throughout Europe. If Edward sought a leader to protect the newly formed Church of England, Jane might have been a good choice. She was proclaimed queen on July 9, 1553, and did some official business over the next few days, signing documents "Jane the Queen."

But the political machines of the land were in overdrive. Mary Tudor, a Catholic, had been next in line for the throne, and she enjoyed considerable support among the people. On July 19, the Privy Council declared that the new queen should be Mary, not Jane. And so Lady Jane Grey will be forever known as "The Nine Days Queen." Though she insisted that she had taken the throne reluctantly, Jane was seen as a usurper and convicted of treason. She was beheaded the next February, reciting the confessional Psalm 51 from the scaffold and uttering Jesus' prayer from Luke 23:46: "Lord, into thy hands I commend my spirit!"

We might lament the fact that this promising life was cut short. We might rail against the apparent injustice. But we might also recognize that Lady Jane seems to have died as she lived, putting her life in God's hands. Sometimes we are tempted by power and privilege, but they carry empty promises. True value is found in our submission to God.

Restore to me the joy of your salvation, and make me willing to obey you.

PSALM 51:12

MIDDLE GROUND

Queen Elizabeth I

1533–1603

She is one of the giants of English history, largely because no one expected much of her. Her father, King Henry VIII, was disappointed that she was a girl. Her Catholic subjects were disappointed that she was Protestant. Many of her Protestant subjects were disappointed that she wasn't Protestant *enough*. And a number of English noblemen were disappointed that she wouldn't marry them.

Elizabeth shrewdly held on to her power, attracting suitors but remaining unattached—England's "virgin queen." During her lengthy reign, England established itself as a world power. Elizabeth was also shrewd in her management of the volatile religious situation in England. In a time when Catholics were battling several brands of Protestantism across Europe, Elizabeth steered a middle course for the Church of England that remains in effect today. This hybrid of Catholic and Protestant ways drew gripes from nearly everyone, but actually provided a framework for peace and national stability. History hails Henry VIII as the royal founder of the Anglican church, and certainly his brash opposition to the pope provided the impetus, but it was really Elizabeth who grounded the church, who helped it find its unique identity.

We're not saying that she was a spiritual giant. She was primarily a political creature, and she would sometimes deal violently with those who threatened the nation's stability. In general, she seemed rather private about her personal beliefs. She liked the "high" forms of Catholic worship but appreciated the Protestant emphasis on personal conscience. Some say she was ahead of her time in promoting religious liberty, declaring that she had "no desire to make windows into men's souls." Late in her reign, she announced, "There is only one Christ, Jesus, one faith. All else is a dispute over trifles."

The world has changed since then, and it hasn't. Freedom of personal conscience is widely accepted, yet religious violence continues. Even Christians can get caught up in hateful rhetoric against those with other beliefs. We need wisdom and shrewdness to steer a middle course—upholding the truth of Christ, but also expressing his love. Maybe we all need a little more Elizabeth in us—tenaciously guarding a tenuous peace.

Then you will experience God's peace, which exceeds anything we can understand. His peace will guard your hearts and minds as you live in Christ Jesus.

PHILIPPIANS 4:7

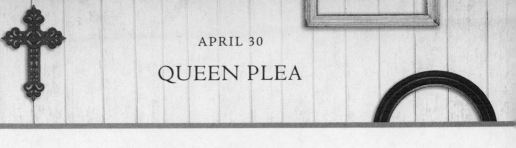

Queen Elizabeth I

1533–1603

Among the actresses nominated for the 1999 Academy Awards were two women playing the same historical figure. Cate Blanchett was stunning as the young queen in *Elizabeth*, but it was Judi Dench who won the Oscar for her supporting role as an older Queen Elizabeth in *Shakespeare in Love*. Both portrayals showed a woman of commanding strength and wisdom.

Historians may debate Elizabeth's wisdom, but few question her strength. The daughter of King Henry VIII and Anne Boleyn (whom he executed), Elizabeth took charge of England at a crucial time, and she held power for nearly half a century. We don't know a lot about her personal faith, but history has left us a small devotional book of hers, with six prayers she composed—two in English and others in Italian, French, Latin, and Greek.

"O Most Glorious King and Creator of the whole world," begins one of the English prayers, "to whom all things be subject, both in heaven and earth, and all best Princes most gladly obey. Hear the most humble voice of thy handmaid. . . . How exceeding is thy goodness, and how great mine offences."

Before you write this off as the false humility of a political speech, consider that this tiny book appears to be for her own private use. She praised God for the blessings he had been "heaping" upon her: her royal blood, her education, and "most gracious deliverance" in times of danger. She also unleashed a surprising confession. In return for God's "benefits," she wondered, "What have I rendered to thee? Forgetfulness, unthankfulness and great disobedience. I should have magnified thee, I have neglected thee. I should have prayed unto thee, I have forgotten thee. I should have served thee, I have sinned against thee. This is my case. Then where is my hope?"

She concluded, "I know no help O Lord but the height of thy mercy, who hast sent thine only Son into the world to save sinners. This God of my life and life of my soul, the King of all comfort, is my only refuge."

In this private prayer, we get a hint of where Elizabeth's strength came from.

This is my command—be strong and courageous! Do not be afraid or discouraged. For the LORD your God is with you wherever you go.

JOSHUA 1:9

GOING POSTAL

Argula von Grumbach
1492–1563

History is full of enterprising women who made a difference by using whatever resources they had. Argula von Grumbach had paper and pen—as well as a keen mind and a knowledge of the Bible.

At age ten, Argula received from her father a Bible in their native German. She studied it avidly. Yet there were no great opportunities for a female Bible scholar in those days. As the Reformation took hold in Germany, Argula supported the dangerous new teachings of Martin Luther. She loved his idea of the "priesthood of the believer," that anyone could have access to God—rich or poor, male or female, educated or not.

In 1523 she heard of a young teacher at the University of Ingolstadt who was arrested for his Reformation views. Outraged, Argula wrote a letter of protest to the school faculty. "When I heard what you had done to Arsacius Seehofer under terror of imprisonment and the stake, my heart trembled and my bones quaked. . . . Where do you read in the Bible that Christ, the apostles, and the prophets imprisoned, banished, burned, or murdered anyone?" In this impressive epistle, she quoted or alluded to Scripture eighty-some times, making a powerful case in support of the reformers. "You have condemned them. You have not refuted them," she claimed, challenging the faculty to argue the case with her from Scripture—in German, rather than ecclesiastical Latin.

When her letter was published, she received both scathing criticism and impassioned defense from various corners of society. Some were scandalized that a woman would dare to confront male authorities. Anabaptist leader Balthasar Hubmaier reiterated his belief that women should generally keep silent . . . but when men are mute with fear, he said, let the women speak.

Maybe you're not an expert or celebrity or leader, but don't let that stop you from proclaiming God's truth and showing his love. What avenues has God given you? Can you send an e-mail, friend someone on Facebook, post a video on YouTube, or just have a good conversation? Argula von Grumbach used what she had, and so can you.

She has done what she could . . . I tell you the truth, wherever
the Good News is preached throughout the world, this
woman's deed will be remembered and discussed.

MARK 14:8-9

OUT OF JOINT

Anne Askew

1521–46

There are certain times of history that just seem, as Shakespeare put it, "out of joint." The sixteenth century in England was one of those times. Christians were fighting, torturing, and killing other Christians. The young preacher-poet Anne Askew lived and died in that world, an imperfect victim of a culture that had gone, well, askew.

Well educated, especially in the Bible, Anne Askew was committed to the Protestant cause. At age fifteen, she was married off to a husband she didn't want. (Her older sister had been engaged to him but died before the wedding. Anne took her place.) The marriage was a mess from the start. Anne wouldn't take her husband's name, wouldn't assume his Catholic religion, and left the home to go "gospelling" (preaching) in London.

Anne's evangelical views—particularly on the symbolic nature of Communion—were suddenly out of favor with English authorities. (King Henry was trying to make nice with the Catholic powers of Europe; evangelical reform was discouraged.) So Anne was arrested, imprisoned in the Tower of London, and tortured on the rack. Her tormentors tried to get her to rat out the ringleaders of the evangelical cause, but this stubborn young woman wouldn't give in. She was burned at the stake on July 16, 1546—her body so broken from the rack, they had to tie a chair to the stake.

While in prison, Anne wrote a ballad that you can still find in poetic anthologies:

Like as the armed knight
Appointed to the field,
With this world will I fight,
And faith shall be my shield.

In her closing stanzas, she imagines God's judgment on her tormentors but then adopts a Christlike attitude:

Yet Lord, I thee desire,
For that they do to me,
Let them not taste the hire
Of their iniquity.

Our world is still "out of joint." Often it's hard for us to do the right thing. But with faith as our shield, we can let the love of Jesus guide us.

Father, forgive them, for they don't know what they are doing.

LUKE 23:34

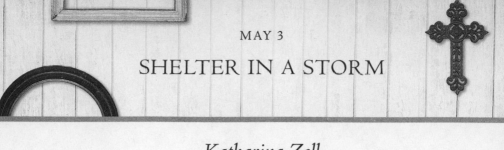

SHELTER IN A STORM

Katharina Zell

1497–1562

Y ou might say that Katharina Zell invented a whole new career: pastor's wife. One of the first to fill that role, she was also one of the best. Her writing, charitable work, and church leadership were key elements in the Protestant Reformation as it took root in central Europe.

Her husband, Matthew Zell, was a Catholic priest who bought into the teachings of Martin Luther and began preaching them in the city of Strasbourg. One of his parishioners, Katharina Schütz, was energized in her faith by Matthew's message. As a challenge to church authority, Matthew decided to marry, and Katharina was willing to become his wife. They wed in 1523, and he was soon excommunicated—despite an impressive letter Katharina wrote to the bishop in her husband's defense.

Their Protestant ministry was just beginning. As civil and religious tensions erupted, many refugees came to Strasbourg, where the Zells offered them relief. Katharina published an open "Letter of Consolation to the Suffering Women of Kentzingen" (a nearby town experiencing a violent crackdown against Protestants). But Katharina Zell used more than words. She worked tirelessly to help these needy ones, offering food and shelter, often in her own home.

When one minister accused her of "disturbing the peace," she responded in self-defense: "Do you call this disturbing the peace that instead of spending my time in frivolous amusements I have visited the plague infested and carried out the dead? I have visited those in prison and under sentence of death. Often for three days and three nights I have neither eaten nor slept. I have never mounted the pulpit, but I have done more than any minister in visiting those in misery."

Labels didn't matter much to her. In a time when Lutherans were fighting Catholics, and everybody was fighting the Anabaptists, she refused to discriminate. Her doors were open to anyone in need. When she was criticized for this, she responded—how else?—by writing an open letter. "It is our duty to show love, service, and mercy to everyone; Christ our teacher taught us that."

The courage, conviction, and charity of Katharina Schütz Zell make her an enduring model not only for pastors' wives, but for all women and men in their personal ministry.

Help her in whatever she needs, for she has been
helpful to many, and especially to me.

ROMANS 16:2

ASSUMPTIONS

Mary Queen of Scots
1542–87

B orn into privilege and power, Mary Stuart became the queen of Scotland upon the death of her father, James V, when she was six days old. Of course, she had some growing up to do, so she was sent off to the French court while others ruled her homeland.

Mary was pampered and prodigious, educated in languages, music, and the Catholic faith. At age fifteen, she married the fourteen-year-old crown prince of France, who became king the next year and died the year after that. By the age of seventeen, Mary, a widow and doubly a queen, had mourned the deaths of several people close to her.

Returning to Scotland, young Mary ruled through six tempestuous years. Presbyterian reformer John Knox railed against Mary's staunch Catholicism. To her credit, she met with him to resolve issues, but she ultimately accused him of treason. Her love life was often wrapped up in political scandal. Her third husband was accused of murdering her second husband, and she was implicated. Mary was forced to abdicate the Scottish throne in 1567, in favor of her one-year-old son, James (yes, *that* King James).

She fled to England, assuming that her cousin, Queen Elizabeth, would welcome her. Not so. England had Protestant-Catholic tensions of its own, and Mary herself had talked with supporters about making England Catholic again (and assuming the throne). Seen as a threat, Mary was imprisoned and eventually executed.

It's hard to see into the soul of Mary, but maybe there are spiritual lessons to be learned. Who knows how she was shaped by the pampering and pain of her youth? It seems that as a young queen, she assumed she deserved respect—and was surprised when she didn't get it. As a devout Catholic, she might have carried similar assumptions into her spiritual life. Many people of different denominations have the same issue today. *Because I am a good Christian, God owes me respect.* But true Christianity is not about deserving God's respect; it's about relying on his mercy.

In Frederick Schiller's insightful play *Mary Stuart,* the proud queen makes a humble confession shortly before her execution: "I tremble to approach, sullied with sin, the God of purity."

All assumptions aside, that is the response of true faith.

Humble yourselves before the Lord, and he will lift you up in honor.

JAMES 4:10

KEEPERS OF THE FAITH

History makers tend to be rulers and warriors. Populations rise and fall at their command. When we consider Christian history, the same holds true, except the battles are often fought over ideas. Martin Luther, John Calvin, and John Wesley made history by changing the way people thought about God.

Focusing on historical women, this devotional book includes a number of powerful rulers and even a few warriors, but we've also included the many different *types* of influence that women have had over the centuries. When Thomas Aquinas was putting church doctrines in order, Mechthild of Magdeburg was describing visions of an unfathomable God. While Henry VIII was consolidating power in England, Teresa of Avila was seeking new ways to be humble before God. And though Martin Luther courageously stood up to a church council, his wife Katharina stood up to *him*, demanding that he come out of his study once in a while to play with the kids.

We might consider Luther, Calvin, and Wesley as "shapers of the faith," but there's also a vast company of Christians we could call "keepers of the faith"—those who practice, model, and teach the way of Christ before their community and the next generation. So we can celebrate the life of, say, Susanna Wesley, who brought up John and Charles (and a dozen other kids) in the faith. Katharina Zell was known for her hospitality as well as her teaching. Anne Bradstreet not only made a home for her family in the world of colonial Massachusetts, but she also wrote poems that revealed the gritty faith involved in doing so. These and countless other women kept the flame of Christianity burning in the hearts of their children and many others.

In today's world, there are two lies women often fall prey to: (1) that marriage and child rearing are *not* an important calling; (2) that marriage and child rearing are your *only* legitimate calling. If you are married and if you have kids, you have a calling to be a good wife and mother, a "keeper of the faith" for the next generation. But there are other ways to keep the faith as well.

What are your callings? Serve the Lord in all the ways he calls you.

Well done, my good and faithful servant. You have been
faithful in handling this small amount, so now I will give you
many more responsibilities. Let's celebrate together!

MATTIIEW 25:21

MAY 6

CHILD'S PRAY

Jacqueline-Marie-Angélique Arnauld
1591–1661

Mademoiselle Arnauld was only eleven years old when she was put in charge of a convent. That's not a reflection of her own brilliance but of her family's string pulling (and they lied about her age on the application). At the time, the Roman Catholic church in France was rife with corruption. It was well known, for instance, that the previous abbess of that convent had borne twelve illegitimate children by different fathers.

"Instead of praying," Arnauld later wrote, "I set myself to read novels and Roman history." She felt no particular calling as a nun. But that changed when she was seventeen. A visiting Franciscan preacher challenged young Jacqueline (who had now taken the name Angélique) to get serious about her faith, and she saw the need for reform—first in herself, and then in the convent. She restored the daily prayer services and restricted visitors—even her own family. A vegetarian diet was introduced, and private property was abolished. Leading theologians of the day came to instruct the sisters.

"Mother Angélique," as she became known, carried on prolific correspondence with leaders throughout Europe, including other abbesses, members of her influential family, and even the queen of Poland (with whom she often discussed the issue of female leadership).

A recurring theme of hers was how hard it is for humans to understand God; therefore we should be careful in interpreting God's actions. "Often . . . what appears to be the result of his wrath and justice is actually the result of his mercy," she wrote to another convent leader. "Blessed are the souls who perceive in every event only God's holy will in order to submit to it."

It seems that the child nun had grown up to embrace a calling of divine submission. In that era, as in ours, people were striving to understand God, explaining his mysteries in brilliant new ways. Such knowledge is a good thing, but it's not the only thing. As Angélique wrote to her brother, "I only desire that God may deign to fill you deeply, not only with the knowledge of the truth, but with a perfect love that you practice faithfully and that gives you a humble patience toward everything."

I pray that your love will overflow more and more, and that you
will keep on growing in knowledge and understanding.

PHILIPPIANS 1:9

HEART-TO-HEART

Marguerite Marie Alacoque

1647–90

At the age of ten, Marguerite took sick with rheumatic fever and was bedridden for about five years. She prayed fervently during these years, promising to become a nun if God would heal her. He did, and she did.

This time of intense spirituality surely paved the way for visions she had later in life. In these visions, she wrote, "He disclosed to me the marvels of His love and the inexplicable secrets of His Sacred Heart." She reported that the Lord called for "a special Feast to honor [his] Heart." There were various promises associated with devotional acts focusing on Jesus' Sacred Heart—success in life and ministry, peace, and well-being. She said that Jesus wanted his people to be "abundantly enriched with those divine treasures of which this heart is the source."

Marguerite had a hard time convincing the leaders of her convent and the church that these visitations from God were real, but eventually she won them over. After her death in 1690, the Jesuits picked up her cause. It was still controversial for a time, but eventually the Catholic church adopted many of the devotional practices Marguerite had called for. She was canonized as a saint in 1920.

Critics might question the validity of her visions or decry some of her recommended practices as superstition. But let's dig down to something we can agree on: the importance of loving Jesus and receiving his love. According to a booklet based on Marguerite's saying and published shortly after her death, "It is impossible to have a lively faith and live in innocence without being at the same time inflamed with a most ardent love of Jesus Christ, or at least with an ardent desire of loving Him."

For some Christians, faith is in the brain. They learn the Bible and believe the truth about Jesus. Others are people of action. They don't just listen to God's Word, they *do* it. Their charitable acts are admirable. But Marguerite leads us into an emotional experience of God's love. Several Scriptures invite us to love and honor God with our whole selves, which would include mind, body, and emotions. How complete is your love for Jesus? Does your heart connect with his heart?

When the Lord saw her, his heart overflowed with compassion.

LUKE 7:13

ROYAL PAIN

Queen Anne

1665–1714

People mocked her for being fat. She was pregnant seventeen times, but bore only five living children, with just one surviving infancy. Anne suffered an eye condition as a child, contracted smallpox as a young woman, and was lamed by gout in later years. Though she was a princess, she watched as others came to power—including her sister and brother-in-law. Anne's own husband was a weak leader and probably an alcoholic. She had a painful public falling-out with her best friend. When Anne finally ascended to the throne of England, her reign was marred by a lengthy and costly war.

Did you ever dream of being a princess, of marrying a prince, of ruling as queen? Well, be careful what you wish for, because Anne Stuart had all of that, and yet she had more than her share of suffering.

England was still smarting from a century of Anglican-Catholic struggle. When Anne became queen in 1702, she strengthened the Anglican identity of the country, favoring the "high church" party—and making life difficult for the "dissenters," those Baptists, Congregationalists, and others who rejected both Catholic and Anglican ways.

But there was one rather amazing thing that Anne did early in her reign. For more than a century, British royalty had been receiving "first fruits and tithes" from churches, a sort of tax that then amounted to about sixteen thousand pounds a year. Anne decided to give these back to the church—expressly for the purpose of helping underpaid clergymen in poor areas. Perhaps her sufferings had nourished some compassion. Well into modern times, this annual allocation was called "Queen Anne's Bounty"—not a bad thing to be known for.

Each of us has an assortment of challenges and accomplishments in our lives. We've all done good and bad things. Who knows how history will remember us? But maybe there's one thing you can do, even now, to help out someone else who's facing more challenges than you are. A gift, a word of encouragement, an opportunity, or maybe just time spent together—this could be your "bounty," something to redeem the past and be remembered for in the future.

There is still one thing you haven't done. . . . Go and sell all
your possessions and give the money to the poor, and you will
have treasure in heaven. Then come, follow me.

MARK 10:21

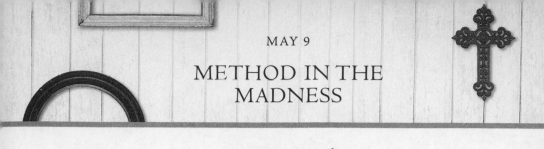

METHOD IN THE MADNESS

Susanna Wesley

1669–1742

She was the youngest of twenty-five children, so she wouldn't think it unusual to bear nineteen children herself. Nine of them died in infancy (not uncommon for that time), but Susanna Wesley still had a house full of kids. Her husband, Samuel Wesley, a minister, left the child rearing to her. There's some irony in the fact that Samuel spent most of his life and finances writing a commentary on the book of Job. While he was studying Job's sufferings, Susanna was *living* them. Besides the deaths of those children, there was a house fire that nearly killed her young son John, and Samuel was thrown in debtors' prison twice, leaving her to scrape by as best she could.

Still, Susanna managed not only to care for her children, but also to teach them. She had learned the Bible, theology, and languages from her minister-father, and she passed all this on to her progeny. Amid the madness of this overflowing household, there was a strict method. At one point Susanna scheduled special times to spend with each child during the week (a method still suggested by parenting experts). The family also had devotional times together, especially on Sundays, sharing in Bible reading and psalm singing. Beginning at the age of five, each child would spend six hours a day in homeschooling, with Mom as the instructor.

Much later, when asked by her grown son John to describe her child-rearing process, Susanna responded with a lengthy essay, including eight "by-laws." Some of her rules would be considered strict by modern standards, but there's wisdom in them . . . and compassion. Consider her fifth bylaw: "That if ever any child performed an act of obedience or did anything with an intention to please, though the performance was not well, yet the obedience and intention should be kindly accepted, and the child with sweetness directed how to do better for the future."

It's hard to argue with the results of Susanna's method. Two of her sons grew up to change history. John and Charles Wesley both went to Oxford University, where they gathered other students into a "Holy Club," and they were soon mocked as "Methodists" for their methodical approach to Christianity. Hmmm. Where do you think they learned that?

Direct your children onto the right path, and when they are older, they will not leave it.

PROVERBS 22:6

"I AM A WOMAN"

Susanna Wesley
1669–1742

Mom had some explaining to do. Dad had gone off on a trip, leaving the church he pastored in the care of a substitute preacher and his large family in the care of their mother, the brilliant Susanna Wesley. Then he started getting reports that Susanna was leading worship services. In an Anglican Church circa 1700, this was scandalous. The Reverend Samuel Wesley demanded to know what was going on.

Susanna's reply (as preserved for us by her son John) reveals her feisty spirit and deep devotion. "As I am a woman," she begins, "so I am also mistress of a large family." She went on to acknowledge her husband's spiritual leadership of the home, but also accepted her own stewardship. "I . . . look upon every soul you leave under my care as a talent committed to me under a trust by the great Lord of all the families of heaven and earth." By "talent," she was referring to Jesus' parable of the talents, sums of money entrusted to servants when the master went away.

This mother was scrupulous in her observance of the Lord's Day. Besides just church attendance, they "fill[ed] up the intermediate spaces of . . . time by other acts of piety and devotion." This meant Susanna would spend time "reading to and instructing my family."

That's where the trouble arose. "Other people's coming and joining with us was merely accidental." The kids told their friends, who told their parents, "so our company increased to about thirty."

Susanna was further challenged by some visiting Danish missionaries. "Though I am not a man nor a minister," she wrote, ". . . yet if my heart were sincerely devoted to God . . . I might do somewhat more than I do." She became even more earnest in her spiritual conversations with her children and her neighbors, and neighbors kept flocking to her meetings. "Last Sunday I believe we had above two hundred, and yet many went away for want of room."

Susanna Wesley was no revolutionary, just a devoted woman with a true zeal. As a result, she pushed the borders of conventional ministry. So how about you? How could you do "somewhat more" than you do?

You must remain faithful to the things you have been taught. You know
they are true, for you know you can trust those who taught you.

2 TIMOTHY 3:14

MOTHER COURAGE

Susanna Wesley
1669–1742

The Methodist revolution of the 1700s forever changed the landscape of Western Christianity. At its helm were two brothers, John and Charles Wesley. Both became popular preachers, though John was better known. Both wrote hymns, though Charles was far more prolific. They dared to preach to the common folk, the laborers and miners, even if that meant challenging the usual practices of the Church of England.

These brothers owed a great deal to their mother, Susanna Wesley, and they knew it. She had taught them as children—including the biblical languages. She also set an example of courageous ministry in their community, even if she ruffled some feathers. And as these two sons developed their own ministries, she cheered them on, offering encouragement, guidance, and support.

As students at Oxford, John and Charles wanted to get serious about their faith, so they joined with like-minded friends for prayer, Bible study, and accountability—and received some mockery from other students. Susanna offered encouragement: "I heartily join with your small Society in all their pious and charitable actions which are intended for God's glory. . . . May you still, in such good works, go on and prosper."

When John and Charles set out as missionaries to the American colony of Georgia, they asked Susanna for her blessing. Transatlantic travel was quite dangerous, and the new colony was still very wild. What's more, Susanna had lost her husband earlier that year. Could she bear to lose these two sons? Yet she responded that she'd be happy to send twenty sons into mission work, even if that meant she'd never see them again.

On one occasion, John returned from a trip and complained that an unordained layman had been preaching in his place. "Take care what you do with respect to that young man," Susanna counseled, "for he is as surely called of God to preach as you are." Perhaps she was remembering times that she had led services in her husband's absence. In any case, that set a new tone for the Methodist movement, in which lay preaching has been a valuable component ever since.

How can you foster courage in young people finding their ministry? That might just be a gift that changes history.

Her children stand and bless her. Her husband praises her: "There are many virtuous and capable women in the world, but you surpass them all!"

PROVERBS 31:28–29

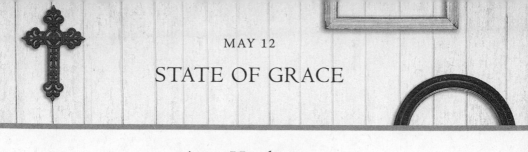

STATE OF GRACE

Anne Hutchinson
1591–1643

You might call it America's first "trial of the century." In 1637, the Puritan leaders of Massachusetts tried Anne Hutchinson on charges of "troubling the peace" and slandering ministers. The real problem was that she taught about God's grace.

Hutchinson had grown up in England, where she married and bore a number of children. When her Puritan pastor, John Cotton, fled to America (escaping Anglican opposition to his evangelical views), Hutchinson gathered up her family and followed. Settling in Boston in 1634, Anne became a model citizen, working as a midwife and leading a small Bible study at her church. That small group, originally just for women, became a large group, including as many as sixty men and women.

Here's where the problem arose. Hutchinson believed in salvation by grace, not by works. According to her reading of Scripture, the Holy Spirit lived within believers, setting them free from the law. Holy living came from the Spirit's guidance, not from a fear of law breaking. This approach threatened the Puritans' "holy experiment" in New England, which was based on personal faith but also collective adherence to God's laws.

When John Winthrop became governor of Massachusetts, he cracked down on the anti-nomian (anti-law) views of Anne Hutchinson and other leaders. As a result of her 1637–38 trials, Anne was placed under house arrest and then banished. She took her family first to Rhode Island, which Roger Williams was establishing as a haven of religious freedom. When she heard that Massachusetts might take over Rhode Island, Anne fled west into Dutch territory. In 1643, she and most of her family were massacred in a territorial dispute with the Siwanoy tribe in what is now New York.

Anne Hutchinson understood something that baffled religious leaders in her day and still baffles many today: grace. It is an outrageous idea, but the Christian gospel is built on it. Intuitively, we expect religion to consist of rules for living, to force us to improve our behavior. But Jesus said that God's Kingdom is not taken by force. Our improvement comes from within, where God's Spirit counsels, challenges, and empowers us.

God saved you by his grace when you believed. And you can't take credit for this; it is a gift from God. Salvation is not a reward for the good things we have done, so none of us can boast about it.

EPHESIANS 2:8-9

INNER FIGHT

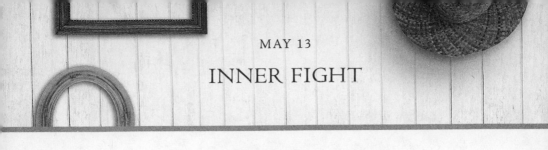

Mary Dyer

1611–60

The study of Christian history can be painful. Oh, we can celebrate the courage of martyrs who gave their lives for their faith, but our hearts ache over the fact that often they were being killed by other Christians. Such is the case with Mary Dyer.

The Puritans had experienced discrimination and persecution from the Church of England in the early 1600s, and so a number of them fled to America, setting up the colony of Massachusetts where they could worship freely. But their sense of religious freedom did not include the toleration of heresy.

When Anne Hutchinson began preaching a bold new theology suggesting that Christians should live by God's Spirit rather than biblical law, she gained many followers, including William and Mary Dyer, who helped to set up Bible study groups. But Hutchinson's teaching was strongly opposed by the Puritan authorities, and in 1638, she was banished from the colony. A while later, the Dyers were banished too. They settled in Rhode Island, a haven for religious freedom.

In 1650, on a trip to England, Mary heard George Fox preach. His description of the "inner light of the living Christ" appealed to her, as did his rejection of many church traditions. He had gathered a "Society of Friends," a group that had already been derisively labeled as "Quakers." This was just what Mary had been looking for.

Returning to New England in 1657, Mary began preaching Quaker doctrine wherever she could—including in the Massachusetts colony. Authorities arrested her, condemned her, and re-banished her, but she wouldn't stay away. Even after she was sentenced to death, she was given a chance to live if she left and promised never to return. She replied, "Nay, I cannot; for, in obedience to the will of the Lord I came, and in His will I abide, faithful to the death." She was hanged on June 1, 1660.

We Christians tend to have strong convictions, and we can vehemently oppose those who disagree. But let's be careful how we treat other believers. Remember that we all serve a Savior who said, "Just as I have loved you, you should love each other" (John 13:34).

God called you to do good, even if it means suffering, just as Christ suffered for you. He is your example, and you must follow in his steps.

1 PETER 2:21

BESIDE STILL WATERS

Madame Guyon

1648–1717

Jeanne-Marie Bouvier's parents were very religious, and they made sure their daughter was brought up in the faith. She was epileptic and couldn't always attend school, but she read a lot, especially the devotional works of Francis de Sales, a French bishop of the previous century.

For a time she dreamed of becoming a nun, but she changed her mind and, at the age of sixteen, married a wealthy older man, Jacques Guyon. His mother made life very difficult for the young bride. What's more, in the following years she suffered the loss of both parents, a sister, and two children. In these troubling times, she turned inward, praying intensely for God's help. She also became aware of the mystical teachings of Father Francois Lacombe, who would be a major influence throughout her life.

After twelve years of marriage, her husband died. A wealthy widow at age twenty-eight, Jeanne-Marie was now free to develop her ideas of the spiritual life. Seeking spiritual direction from Lacombe, she began to write and teach from her own experiences of mystical union with God. Spearheading a new movement that became known as Quietism, Madame Guyon attracted both followers and opponents. One major supporter was Francois Fénelon, a priest and tutor in the royal court, who eventually became a bishop and writer of his own devotional works (though later, under pressure, he retracted support for Quietism).

Madame Guyon's writings about the spiritual life were personal and experiential. In that time and place—Catholic France of the late 1600s—this approach threatened the religious establishment. And yet she gave the church a gift of life. In a ritual-heavy environment, she led people into an authentic relationship with God. In later centuries, her admirers would be many, including the visionary poet William Cowper and the powerful preacher Charles Spurgeon.

The well-known Twenty-third Psalm says the Lord "leads me beside quiet waters, he refreshes my soul" (NIV). In a way, that's what Madame Guyon has done for us. She herself was led by Francis de Sales, Father Lacombe, and others, and she led Fénelon, Cowper, and Spurgeon, who all led countless others. We are a centuries-long procession of believers who lead each other beside the still waters of God's restoration.

So . . . how have you been led here? And who is being led by you?

He leads me beside quiet waters, he refreshes my soul.

PSALM 23:2-3, NIV

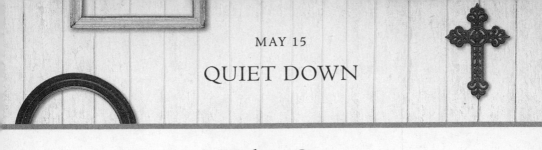

QUIET DOWN

Madame Guyon

1648–1717

Spirituality is dangerous. At least it seemed that way to church leaders in the late 1600s. Religion was about power and ritual. When writers and teachers promoted a personal experience of God's presence, that could only spell trouble.

Jeanne-Marie Guyon was a French mystic, one of several proponents of practices that became known as Quietism. As you might expect, Quietism involved getting quiet before God, praying silently, listening to him, and communing with him in the stillness. Though Madame Guyon's writings seem rather tame today, at that time the Catholic church was cracking down on some other Quietist teachers with unorthodox teachings, so Guyon suffered as well. In order to stay in the good graces of the church, she signed several retractions of her teachings, but she also kept sharing the insights that God was giving her. As a result, she was frequently chastised, confined to a convent for several years, and even locked up in the Bastille.

Several of her writings are still leading Christians into deeper devotional lives. *A Short and Easy Method of Prayer* is an unassuming guide to Christian contemplation. Her commentary on the Song of Songs explores what it means to be the bride of Christ. She also wrote a number of devotional poems, some translated by the hymn writer William Cowper, including one that starts like this:

> *My Lord, how full of sweet content; I pass my years of banishment!*
> *Where'er I dwell, I dwell with Thee, in Heav'n, in earth, or on the sea.*

"We should live in prayer," she wrote, "as we do live through love." For Guyon, prayer was not an activity, but a continual openness to God. God's grace and sovereignty were important elements of Guyon's teaching. We cannot hope to reach God with our own religious efforts; we can only receive what he gives us. This takes a quieting of the spirit and a submissive will. As she put it, "We should forget ourselves, and all self-interest, and listen and be attentive to the voice of God."

Have your devotional times become a chore? Are you just trying to "be a good Christian" by going through your assigned prayer and reading? Then take Madame Guyon's advice and quiet down, slow down, and just listen for what God gives you.

In him we live and move and have our being.

ACTS 17:28, NIV

24/7

Madame Guyon

1648–1717

From a historical perspective, many other women might be more significant than Madame Jeanne-Marie Guyon, a French mystic. But this is a devotional book as well as a history book, and we're indebted to Guyon for opening up new understandings of Christian spirituality. She has had her detractors, then and now—the language of personal experience can seem suspicious—but Guyon was both persistent and sweet spirited in her response.

"Beloved reader," she wrote in the preface to *A Short and Easy Method of Prayer*, "peruse this little tract with an humble, sincere and candid spirit, and not with an inclination to cavil and criticise, and you will not fail to reap some degree of profit from it. It was written with a hearty desire that you might wholly devote yourself to God." She went on to say that all she was trying to do was "to invite the simple and the childlike to approach their Father, who delights in the humble confidence of His children."

That invitation is still needed today. For many, prayer and Bible reading are spiritual chores. *Yes, I ought to do more of all that*, we think, *but it's so hard to find time.* Guyon suggests a different process. When we become "uncentred," she says, "it is of immediate importance to turn again gently and sweetly inward; and thus we may learn to preserve the spirit and unction of prayer throughout the day." She emphasizes the need to make prayer our normal mode of living, not some special task, "for if prayer and recollection were wholly confined to any appointed half-hour, or hour, we should reap but little fruit."

Madame Guyon was living three centuries too early, but we think she would love smartphones, at least the idea of them. They epitomize the kind of nonstop, 24/7 access that Guyon was describing. No longer do we have to turn on a computer and "go online"—we can be continually connected to the Internet. In the same way, we can be continually connected to our loving, living God, involving him in every aspect of our lives. We don't need to "go to prayer" if every moment is a prayer.

The LORD is in his holy Temple. Let all the earth be silent before him.

HABAKKUK 2:20

BE STILL

Katharina von Schlegel

1697–CA. 1768

W e don't know much about Katharina von Schlegel, author of the powerful hymn "Be Still, My Soul," but we can connect some dots. She was born in 1697 and lived in the German town of Kothen, an independent territory ruled by a prince. Her name suggests she belonged to a noble family. The prince, a music lover, employed an up-and-coming organist named Johann Sebastian Bach from 1717 to 1723—so it's possible that Katharina, a promising twentysomething poet with family connections, crossed paths with Johann at some palace function, though we have no record of it.

After the horrific devastation of the Thirty Years' War (1618–48), Germany was certainly undergoing reconstruction. Whatever spiritual gains had been made in the Protestant Reformation of the 1500s must have been severely damaged in this religious struggle.

But along with the rebuilding came a quiet spiritual awakening known as Pietism. Beginning in the 1660s and continuing into the 1700s, certain writers and teachers were calling Christians to get serious about their faith. Following Jesus had to mean more than church membership. It involved a personal relationship with him, meditating on his words, being led by his Spirit into a life of obedience.

Katharina von Schlegel lived just a few miles from Halle, a major center of the Pietist movement, so she might have had some connection there. A number of new hymns were used in Pietist churches, including many of Schlegel's twenty-nine works.

Only one of these is commonly used in English translation:

Be still my soul: the Lord is on thy side.
Bear patiently the cross of grief or pain.
Leave to thy God to order and provide;
In every change, He faithful will remain.
Be still my soul: thy best, thy heav'nly Friend
Through thorny ways leads to a joyful end.

Sung to the dramatic tune "Finlandia," the hymn seems to rise up from the ashes in hope. We may be devastated by war or other disasters, but we can rest secure in our loving Lord. In times of crisis, we're often tempted to *do something*, to get busy, to try anything to fix the situation. But the way of faith is patient. We can quiet our hearts before God and trust him "to order and provide."

Be still, and know that I am God! . . . I will be honored throughout the world.

PSALM 46:10

Mary Fisher
1623–98

In 1651, Quaker founder George Fox spoke with a family in Selby, England, and persuaded them to join his cause. Yet the most influential convert that day was the maid who was listening in, twenty-seven-year-old Mary Fisher. In the following years, she would fearlessly spread the message of Christ on three continents.

The Quakers were shaking things up in England, challenging nominal Christians to get serious about their faith. As they saw it, churches were caught up in wealth and power, preachers were delivering academic lectures rather than an authentic word from God, and the poor were often ignored. As Fox shared his countercultural views, he collected teams of ministers—men and women alike—who would go out preaching wherever God led them.

Shortly after her conversion, Mary was led to the local Anglican church, where she addressed the congregation after a worship service, rebuking the vicar. This got her thrown into jail. In fact, most of the Quaker ministers in those early years (who became known as the Valiant Sixty) spent time behind bars. Later, Fisher challenged students at a seminary and was flogged for it. In transatlantic travels, she and her colleagues got a good reception in Barbados but were terribly mistreated in Boston.

And then she decided to go and see the sultan. The Ottoman Empire, based in Turkey, was a major world power. The sultan, whose brutality was legendary, had thousands of soldiers at his command. Yet Mary Fisher felt that God wanted her to talk to him.

Travel was difficult. The English consul in Turkey was no help, tricking Mary and her companions into boarding a boat headed the wrong way. But finally Mary, by herself, got to the place where the sultan was encamped with his troops. Telling his adviser that she was an emissary of "the Most High God," she was received with high honors, and she gave her gospel message. "There is a love begot in me towards them which is endless," she commented later.

Lots of us are afraid to talk to our next-door neighbors about the Lord. What if we offend them? What if they ask questions we can't answer? Well, if God's love can lead an uneducated maid to stand before the sultan, what can it do for us?

Who knows but that you have come to your royal position for such a time as this?
ESTHER 4:14, NIV

SPRUNG UP IN AMERICA

Anne Bradstreet

1612–72

Eighteen-year-old Anne Bradstreet was a new wife living a new life in the New World. Along with her husband and parents, she had sailed from England in 1630 to join the Puritan colony in Massachusetts. Her husband, Simon Bradstreet, and her father, Thomas Dudley, would both serve as governors of that colony in the coming years.

Life in America was tough. Anne struggled to be a good wife (despite her husband's business trips), a good mother (she would bear eight children), and a good Christian (though her faith was tested by frequent illness and loss). She was also a very good writer, and her disarmingly simple poetry offers a depth of insight on her hardscrabble colonial life.

Winters in New England were downright dangerous, and yet Anne found the perspective to write, "If we had no winter, the spring would not be so pleasant." Every challenge, it seemed, provided an opportunity to connect with God in a new way. One poem describes Jesus' response to her tearful cries: "My hungry soul he filled with good; / He in his bottle put my tears, / My smarting wounds washed in his blood, / And banished thence my doubts and fears."

That might seem like naive, easy-answer faith, until you read on and recognize her visceral experience of suffering. She's not denying her trials; she's committing them to the power of God. There's no naiveté here. One poem, "The Vanity of All Worldly Things," is as crisp a capture of Ecclesiastes as you could find. In "The Flesh and the Spirit," Bradstreet imagines a conversation between two sisters by those names. "How oft thy slave hast thou me made / When I believed what thou hast said," says Spirit, expressing the gritty conflict of, for example, Romans 7.

In 1650, Anne's brother-in-law took a manuscript of her work to London and got it published as *The Tenth Muse Lately Sprung Up in America, by a Gentlewoman of Those Parts*, making her arguably the first published American poet.

Greek myth had nine Muses inspiring creativity. America now had a tenth one. Or maybe that Tenth Muse is actually the God of the Bible, who inspired Anne Bradstreet, as he inspires us, to express deeper faith to meet the challenges of everyday life.

Beautiful words stir my heart. . . . for my tongue is like the pen of a skillful poet.

PSALM 45:1

SMOLDERING FAITH

Anne Bradstreet

1612–72

History has not treated the Puritans kindly. These early American colonists were courageous and devout in their efforts to create a Christian society in the New World. Yet they'll be forever known for their intolerance toward freethinkers like Roger Williams, Anne Hutchinson, and the Quakers. It's not easy to build the perfect society.

One bright light shining from that culture was the poet Anne Bradstreet. Amid the rigid order imposed by the leaders of Massachusetts (including her husband and father), Anne's writings consistently expressed the heart of Puritan faith. Dealing with everyday struggles, spiritual and practical, Bradstreet's poetry reflects a growing maturity—not just "us good, them bad," but, "How can we get to know our amazing God better?"

We see this in a poem she wrote to come to grips with a particular tragedy, "Upon the Burning of Our House—July 10th, 1666." After describing the terror of waking up to the sound and sight of flames, she begins to think about it.

> And when I could no longer look
> I blest his name that gave and took,
> That laid my goods now in the dust; Yea, so it was, and so 'twas just—
> It was his own; it was not mine.
> Far be it that I should repine.

A key feature of Puritan theology is the sovereignty of God. The Lord gives and takes away: we might not understand why, but we are called to accept it. This becomes more than just musing for Anne Bradstreet. She's picking through the ashes with "sorrowing eyes," seeing the places where she used to conduct her life.

> Here stood that trunk, and there that chest;
> There lay that store I counted best;
> My pleasant things in ashes lie,
> And them behold no more shall I.

We feel her sadness palpably; we think of the empty spaces in our own lives, and we appreciate her faith-filled vision of a heavenly house awaiting us, "framed by that mighty Architect." Bidding farewell to all the stuff she has loved and lost, she concludes, "My hope and treasure lies above."

The LORD gave, and the LORD hath taken away; blessed be the name of the LORD.

JOB 1:21, KJV

THE GOOD BOOKS

"Mary" Bunyan

D. 1658

One of the bestselling books of all time was published more than three hundred years ago. *Pilgrim's Progress* sprang from the creative mind of the prisoner-preacher John Bunyan, becoming an instant hit and a Christian classic.

Few would have expected such greatness of this tinker's son from the small English town of Elstow. With his foul mouth and reckless ways, some thought he would (as he recounted later) "spoil all the youth in a whole town." Drafted into the parliamentary army at age sixteen, he saw little action in three years of service, but maybe this helped him grow up a little. Two years after his regiment disbanded, he got married.

We don't know Mrs. Bunyan's first name, but since it was customary for the first daughter to be named after the mother and the Bunyans' oldest daughter was named Mary, we can guess that Mrs. Bunyan was also called Mary. She came into the marriage just as poor as John was. He wrote later that they lacked such "household stuff as a dish or spoon betwixt us both." Yet John treasured the fact that she was born of good parents who had taught her well.

Her dowry consisted of two good books—*The Plain Man's Pathway to Heaven* by Arthur Dent, and *The Practice of Piety* by Lewis Bayly. In retrospect, we can see that these two Christian volumes were as valuable to this writer-to-be as any sum of money. Both came from a Puritan perspective, pushing personal commitment to Christ and not just church ritual. It's also interesting that both depicted the Christian life as a journey. For Dent, it was a pathway, and the subtitle of Bayly's book was "directing a Christian how to walk that he may please God." In *Pilgrim's Progress*, of course, Bunyan would make this "walk" a powerful allegory.

Bunyan's first wife died about 1658, less than a decade after they married, but it's clear she changed his life in major ways. In that time he made a personal commitment to Christ, was baptized into an independent church, and began preaching.

It's hard to know how deeply we influence those closest to us. It might be as simple as a book recommendation—or the way we live out the Word of God each day.

Your lives are a letter written in our hearts; everyone can
read it and recognize our good work among you.

2 CORINTHIANS 3:2

APPEALING

Elizabeth Bunyan

CA. 1641–92

Jesus told a parable of a woman who pestered an unjust judge until he finally ruled in her favor. Elizabeth Bunyan lived out that story. Her husband, John, was imprisoned, basically for preaching without a license. Over the twelve years of his incarceration, she begged several magistrates to release him, or at least to *hear* him. Unlike the judge in the parable, these ones did not relent.

Bunyan had four children with his first wife, who died about 1658. The following year he married Elizabeth, who was seventeen or eighteen. By then, he was already preaching at an independent Baptist church and in surrounding villages. But England was going through big changes. Charles II was the king, and fringe religious groups were not tolerated. As the preacher at an unlicensed church, John Bunyan was convicted and jailed in 1661. While he had a few temporary releases, John refused to promise to stop preaching, and this kept him in the clutches of the law until the law changed.

Though she suffered from poor health, Elizabeth proved tireless in her efforts to win John's freedom. Not only did she pester the local judges in Bedford, but she also traveled to London, appealing to the House of Lords and even the king. "He desires to live peaceably and to follow his calling, that his family may be maintained. He desires a fair trial and freedom; but because he is a tinker and a poor man he cannot have justice," she insisted. While such pleas impressed many along the way, John's obstinate lack of repentance kept the original charges in place.

Meanwhile, in prison, John made shoelaces for his family to sell, wrote devotional material, and kept preaching. Finally, in 1672, King Charles issued the Declaration of Indulgence, decriminalizing the independent churches. John was free. Six years later he published a book he had begun in prison, an allegory of the Christian life called *Pilgrim's Progress*. It rapidly became the best selling book in the English language, apart from the Bible.

As John's book indicates, the Christian life is a journey. We go through swamps of depression, distracting sideshows, and castles of doubt—but there is a heavenly city ahead. No one knew this better than his hardworking advocate, Elizabeth.

Don't you think God will surely give justice to his chosen
people who cry out to him day and night?

LUKE 18:7

CRAZY LIKE A FOX

Elizabeth Hooton

1600–72

At the age of sixty, Elizabeth Hooton traveled with a friend from England to America, but this was no luxury cruise. They had a message for those Puritans who were running Massachusetts: *Stop persecuting Quakers!* The governor heard the message from Hooton and her friend and . . . persecuted them. The two women were imprisoned, beaten, and placed in the stocks. Then they were taken out into the wilderness and left there.

Amazingly, they found their way to safety in Rhode Island and caught a ship back home. There, Hooton decided to tell the king about her mistreatment in Massachusetts. She found him playing tennis and pleaded her case. The king gave her a document allowing her to buy land in Massachusetts as a safe haven for Quakers. But on her next visit to America, that document was pretty much ignored, and the persecution continued.

The Quaker faith began with the teaching of George Fox in the 1640s. Hooton, previously a Baptist, was one of his first converts; some reports suggest that she helped Fox develop his teaching. Fox's focus on the "inner light" guiding the believer seemed mystical and dangerous to the established churches, which found their authority in Scripture and tradition. The equality of all believers was also seen as a threat. Fox and his followers—including Elizabeth Hooton—were often arrested and imprisoned.

Hooton passed away on yet another missions trip, this one to Jamaica. In a published eulogy, Fox called her "a serious, upright-hearted woman," and he added, "receiving the Truth she never turned her back on it, but was fervent and faithful for it until death."

This woman had guts and tenacity. Undaunted by kings or governors, she scored low in meekness but high in faith. No doubt she rubbed some people the wrong way, but Elizabeth Hooton kept going and going in the cause of truth and freedom.

What's your personality style? Don't ever think that God can't use you because you're too . . . what? Quiet? Loud? Abrupt? Antisocial? Shallow? Impulsive? God has crafted you! Put yourself in his service—no matter how crazy that might seem.

If it seems we are crazy, it is to bring glory to God. And if we are in our right minds, it is for your benefit. Either way, Christ's love controls us.

2 CORINTHIANS 5:13-14

NOW IT'S PERSONAL

Margaret Fell
1614–1702

M argaret had a good life—married to an influential judge and member of Parliament, living in a spacious home with a gaggle of children—and then that Quaker showed up and changed everything.

The Quaker in question was George Fox, founder of that movement, who was traveling through England preaching a new style of Christianity. When Margaret Fell heard his message, she wrote later, "This opened me so, that it cut me to the heart; and then I saw clearly we were all wrong. So I sat down in my pew again, and cried bitterly; and I cried in my spirit to the Lord: 'We are all thieves . . . we have taken the Scriptures in words, and know nothing of them in ourselves.'"

Dig through the archaic phrasing to find the gist of the Quaker argument. Scripture is not just a collection of words, but a reality. It's a light that needs to shine from the page and into our hearts, into our lives. The message is as old as James 1:22 (be doers, not just hearers) and Hebrews 4:12 (the "alive and powerful" Word). The Quakers didn't make this up. In fact, many other groups throughout history have tried to awaken sleepy Christians to this reality. In the mid-1600s this approach was new and different—and threatening to the status quo. ("Quaker" was actually a term used by enemies to mock the call to "tremble before the Word of God.")

Margaret Fell bought into it, big time. She opened her house for Quaker meetings and used her high-class status to plead the cause of arrested preachers. Sometimes her pleas worked, sometimes not, and sometimes she herself was thrown in prison. During one incarceration she wrote a pamphlet titled *Women's Speaking Justified*, a Bible-based argument defending the Quaker practice of allowing women to preach. And after her husband died, she married George Fox. Because of this marriage, her courageous protection, and her loving hospitality, she became known as the "Mother of Quakerism."

Does God's light shine in your life? The question is worth considering. Have the routines and rituals of your religious observance ever gotten inside you? Has your Christianity become personal?

Don't just listen to God's word. You must do what it says.
Otherwise, you are only fooling yourselves.

JAMES 1:22

LEARNING CHRIST

Juana Inés de la Cruz

1651–95

S he might be the greatest Mexican writer ever. She was certainly the first internationally acclaimed Mexican poet writing in Spanish. Juana Inés de la Cruz was a child prodigy, a musician, an advocate for women's rights . . . and a nun.

The illegitimate daughter of a Spanish captain and a Creole mother, Juana grew up in her grandfather's hacienda in Amecameca, near what is now Mexico City. She was reading at age three, doing math at five, composing poems at eight, and teaching Latin at thirteen. Described as a very religious child, she would spend a lot of time in the hacienda's private chapel—but she would also sneak from there to read the books in her grandfather's library. This became a pattern for her life. Scholarship was not deemed proper for girls and women, but religious devotion was. Juana practiced both, using each to advance the other.

Soon others took note of her brilliance. The viceroy set up a demonstration, inviting local academics to test the intelligence of this seventeen-year-old whiz kid. She passed with flying colors. Her poetry was published in Mexico and Spain. She received several proposals of marriage, but she wanted freedom to study, so she entered a convent. For two decades, Sister Juana Inés devoted herself to research and writing on all sorts of subjects, not just religious—plays and reviews and many poems. She also gathered an impressive collection of books, musical instruments, and scientific equipment.

Then in 1690 a bishop published an attack on her, saying how scandalous it was for a woman to pursue secular knowledge. Juana responded with a brilliant defense of a woman's right to study. It seems that this provoked her superiors to press for a recantation. The last writing we have from her is a dully worded confession for not being religious enough. Her library was dismantled. The rest is silent.

Today we often draw sharp dividing lines between sacred and secular. While we should avoid the idols and lies of much secular culture, we can still celebrate the truth of our Creator and Redeemer wherever we find it. The example of Juana Inés can lead us into a joyous pursuit of all types of knowledge, as we trust the Spirit to transform and renew us.

Don't copy the behavior and customs of this world, but let God
transform you into a new person by changing the way you think.

ROMANS 12:2

SUPPORTING ROLE

Sarah Edwards
1710–58

"There are no small parts, only small actors." That old theater line affirms the value of supporting roles, on stage and in life. The story of Sarah Edwards brings some clarity to that saying. Sarah played the supporting role to her husband, Jonathan Edwards—a small part, you might think, but actually there was nothing small about it.

Jonathan was a highly influential preacher, a key figure in the Great Awakening, a revival of faith that swept through the American colonies in the mid-1700s. He was a scholar even more than a speaker, and some still regard him as America's greatest theologian.

Sarah was as knowledgeable about the Bible as her husband. Her faith was as strong as his. Yet, while he received recognition for his stirring sermons and deep books, Sarah's contributions were never in the spotlight. She wouldn't have it any other way.

Jonathan respected Sarah's knowledge and wisdom. When he was holed up in his study working, he always welcomed Sarah and listened to what she had to say. The conversations in that study surely influenced the great preacher's sermons.

Legend has it that Jonathan would plan his sermons and books as he went horseback riding through the countryside. He would jot down his thoughts on notes that he'd pin to his coat. Upon his return, it was Sarah who took the notes from his coat to organize them so that Jonathan's thoughts did not get lost.

Without the support of Sarah, Jonathan could not have been the influential preacher that he was. When historians explain the Great Awakening, it's Jonathan they crow about, not Sarah. But she was no "small actor." If she had viewed her role as small and inconsequential, Jonathan could not have had such an influence.

When God puts you in the supporting role to a main character who is doing something big, it's because you are the exact support that person needs. If you see your role as lesser because there's no spotlight, think about Sarah Edwards. She might not have had the lead part, but her role was certainly not unimportant.

I'm not trying to win the approval of people, but of God. If pleasing people were my goal, I would not be Christ's servant.

GALATIANS 1:10

SWEETNESS

Sarah Edwards

——————— 1710–58 ———————

Who were the two most famous preachers in America in the 1700s? The flashy traveling orator George Whitefield and the sober pastor-theologian Jonathan Edwards. These two led what historians call the "Great Awakening," yet their styles were worlds apart. So it's a bit surprising that Jonathan once invited George to preach in his pulpit. Whitefield gladly accepted the invitation, staying in the Edwards's home for a few days.

How did it go? Fine. You might expect the two revivalists to compare notes and maybe wrangle over the finer points of theology. But what impressed George Whitefield the most was . . . Sarah Edwards.

"A sweeter couple have I not yet seen," he wrote afterward. George himself had experienced difficulty finding a suitable wife. Just a few months earlier, he had proposed to a woman who had said no, largely because he was promising her nothing but the challenges of a traveling ministry. Now he saw Sarah Edwards as an enthusiastic partner in her husband's pastorate. "She talked . . . solidly of the things of God, and seemed to be . . . a helpmeet for her husband," he wrote in his journal. Sarah inspired George to "renew" his prayers that God would send him a worthy bride. (In fact, about a year later, he did marry.)

Helpmeet is an archaic term that comes from Genesis 2:18, where God decides to make for Adam a "help meet for him" (KJV). Unfortunately, some use *helpmeet* in a diminutive way—the "little woman" would be the assistant in the important things her husband did—but the actual meaning of that Genesis text is quite different. It uses the same Hebrew word for *help* that's used for God in Psalm 46:1—"a very present help in trouble" (KJV). A "help" is not necessarily weaker, but often stronger—and thus able to provide help. The word *meet* merely means suitable, appropriate, or on the same level. This might be in contrast with the animals that had been created. The man needed someone on his level who could truly offer the help he needed.

Too often we make marriage a power struggle when God made it a partnership. Wives and husbands should give each other the help they need. As George Whitefield recognized, Sarah Edwards did that quite well.

The Lord God said, "It is not good for the man to be alone.
I will make a helper who is just right for him."

GENESIS 2:18

MORE THAN WORDS

Hannah More

1745–1833

A writer needs to get used to rejection. Many successful authors could paper their walls with rejection letters from publishers. Hannah More was a great writer who regularly transformed rejection into redemption.

Her upbringing was humble. At one point, Hannah's father thought he had a substantial amount of money coming to him, but the courts rejected his claim. A highly educated man, he set up a school to teach his children and others. Hannah benefited from this training and became a teacher herself.

Then love got in the way. Engaged to an affluent young man, Hannah gave up teaching to prepare for her roles as wife and mother . . . except she waited six years for the marriage to happen and was ultimately rejected. In a legal settlement, though, the man provided her with a healthy annuity, which enabled Hannah to embark on a writing career.

More's writing style was far ahead of her time, with strong word choices, energetic sentence structure, dramatic themes, controversial opinions, and a tone that could be romantic, preachy, or conversational. Over the following years, she wrote plays, poetry, fiction, and essays that proved to be quite popular in England. She took up with the elite artistic community of London, becoming one of that culture's celebrities for a time.

But fame is fickle, and there were a few more rejections along the way, including an embarrassing accusation of theft from another poet who had been a close friend. Hannah left the London crowd and moved out to the country. But there, an even more important chapter of her life began.

She always was a woman of faith, but she now wrote more books and tracts on faith and ethics, gave her money to charity, and met with evangelical leaders such as John Newton and William Wilberforce. Her poem "Slavery," published in 1788, typified her new commitment. In it, she lambasted so-called Christians who were involved in the slave trade. It was a powerful salvo in the British fight for abolition.

How do you handle rejection? It's no fun to see your dreams dashed, but Hannah More seemed to find new dreams in the ruins of the old ones. Perhaps our best question is, What are God's dreams for us?

---

*"I know the plans I have for you," says the LORD. "They are plans
for good and not for disaster, to give you a future and a hope."*

JEREMIAH 29:11

QUEEN OF HEARTS

Barbara Heck

1734–1804

Sometimes we Christians need a little nudge to get serious about our faith. Sometimes we need a scolding. Barbara Heck delivered a scolding that started a church.

This story starts in County Limerick in mid-1700s Ireland, when John Wesley came to preach. His "Methodist" movement was known for its outreach to common folk who were ignored by the established church. Often preaching outside, drawing huge crowds, the Methodists at this point weren't starting their own churches; they were merely organizing small groups for prayer, instruction, and discipleship. Barbara was part of a German-Irish community that responded well to Wesley's message.

In 1760, many of these German-Irish Methodists sailed to America, settling in New York City. They had no preacher until 1765, when Philip Embury arrived with another group of immigrants. By then their Methodist passion was fizzling out.

As the story goes, one day in 1766, Barbara Heck was shocked to find a group of these friends *playing cards*. This was exactly the sort of worldly activity that Christians—and especially devout Methodists—were supposed to abstain from. Heck threw the cards into the fireplace, saying, "Now look at your idols; there are your gods!" Then she challenged Embury to start preaching the gospel to these people before they all went to hell. When he protested that there was no place to preach, she responded, "Preach in your own house to your own company!"

He did so, and the Methodist movement now had a foothold in the colonies. In a couple of years, the group put up its own chapel, and Barbara was a leader of the building project. The following decades saw several moves for Barbara, her husband, and their friends—largely due to the Revolutionary War. They ended up in Canadian territory, where Barbara is still hailed as a pioneer of Canadian Methodism.

But let's get back to that card table. Put aside the cultural differences. Maybe our modern distractions are sports or fashion or celebrity gossip or, yes, computer solitaire. The question is, How can we get serious about our faith and encourage others to do the same? Maybe scolding isn't the way to do it, but can we use conversation, example, and Spirit-guided nudging to re-instill passion in those who have fizzled out?

Be an example to all believers in what you say, in the way
you live, in your love, your faith, and your purity.

1 TIMOTHY 4:12

Lady Selina Hastings

1707–91

S he was a countess. Her husband, the ninth Earl of Huntingdon, passed away in 1746, leaving his thirty-nine-year-old widow with scads of money and complete freedom to spend it any way she liked. As it turned out, Selina Hastings liked to support Christian ministry. She did so not only with her money, but also with her influence, her time, and her high-level networking.

At that time the Methodist Revival was sweeping through England. John Wesley, George Whitefield, and others gathered crowds in open-air meetings and challenged them to be born again. Those who received this message were usually organized into small groups, where they could get good Christian teaching and encouragement. The Methodists were trying to be a reform movement *within* the Anglican church, not a separate denomination—and this was Lady Selina's goal too.

The countess built various chapels and meetinghouses throughout England for these reform-minded groups to use. She also made George Whitefield her personal chaplain and invited him to speak at parties where she hosted the movers and shakers of society. Selina Hastings was a social dynamo. Everyone knew her; it was hard to say no. For many years, she successfully kept her standing within the Church of England—insisting, for instance, that the meetings in her chapels follow the *Book of Common Prayer*. She even established a curtained-off section in one of her chapels where Anglican clergy could see the proceedings without being seen (it was dubbed "Nicodemus Corner"). But in 1779 the countess finally broke with the Anglicans, officially becoming a "dissenter."

This woman was probably the most important Christian layperson in the eighteenth century. In the next century, Bishop John Henry Newman offered this eulogy: "She devoted herself, her name, her means, her time, her thoughts, to the cause of Christ. She did not spend her money on herself; she did not allow the homage paid to her rank to remain with herself."

Chances are, you don't have the wealth or influence Selina Hastings had. But what resources do you have? And how can you use these for the cause of Christ?

As a result of your ministry, they will give glory to God.
For your generosity to them and to all believers will prove
that you are obedient to the Good News of Christ.

2 CORINTHIANS 9:13

WHEN THE SPIRIT SAYS, "MOVE!"

Women Preachers in New Denominations

In times of spiritual awakening, more women become preachers. This is an observable phenomenon of history, going back to the third-century Montanists and extending to the twentieth-century Pentecostals. It was also seen in the Quakers of the 1600s, the Methodists of the 1700s, and various Holiness groups of the 1800s. Revivals seem to call people of both genders (and all races, ages, and social classes) to use their Spirit-given abilities in every way possible, casting off traditional restrictions.

We recognize that this issue—the biblical role of women in the church—is a hot one. Christians have debated it for centuries, and it has split some denominations. We're not going to provide easy answers in this devotion, but we do want to document this phenomenon. Churches need structure, and the New Testament provides some guidelines, but the church is also a Spirit-powered organism. From day one, exuberant Christians were waving the flag of Joel's prophecy: "Your sons and daughters will prophesy" (Joel 2:28; Acts 2:17). The Spirit has a way of blowing open our closed doors.

In the 1660s, one of the early Quakers, Margaret Fell, wrote a booklet defending the work of women preachers. She concluded, "And so let this serve to stop that opposing Spirit that would limit the Power and Spirit of the Lord Jesus, whose Spirit is poured upon all Flesh, both Sons and Daughters."

Many commentators have focused attention on a few New Testament passages where Paul discourages or prohibits women from teaching men. But the conflict is larger, between two very different visions of how God works in the world. Some see God ordaining a structure in which men and women have distinct roles and the role of leadership falls to men, not women, in the home and the church. Others see God freely dispensing all spiritual gifts to be used by men and women alike, as both are made in his image. Historically, different church groups have emphasized structure at some times and spiritual gifts at other times.

But this struggle should not be about *power* (though, too often, it is). Followers of Jesus should understand that leadership means service, not prestige. Christian men and women alike need to submit to God's calling—wherever that might lead.

[Jesus said,] "Whoever wants to be first must take last place and be the servant of everyone else."

MARK 9:35

HORSE SENSE

Bathsheba Kingsley
D. 1748

Sometimes it's hard to know what the real story is. If you have kids, you know how playground scuffles can get twisted in the retelling. In the modern era, the Internet gives us a huge playground in which facts give way to feelings.

We encounter a similar issue in a strange story from Massachusetts in 1741. Bathsheba Kingsley felt she had a revelation from God and needed to tell people. Taking her husband's horse, she rode from town to town, preaching wherever she could. This is not as unusual as it might seem. The previous year, preacher George Whitefield had come through the area, addressing crowds in open, outdoor venues. Kingsley might indeed have drawn a crowd by riding furiously into the town square and speaking loudly about God. There is also some indication that she went door-to-door, telling people they weren't getting the whole truth from their local pastors.

Kingsley's behavior was, of course, shocking. But why? That's where we enter the playground of history. Was it because she was critical of other preachers? Was it because she spoke in the open, and not in church buildings? Was it because she spoke of a personal experience of God's revelation? Was it because she "stole" her husband's horse? Or was it because she was a woman doing the "man's work" of preaching?

Church leaders—including the respected theologian Jonathan Edwards—counseled her and corrected her. While she was not excommunicated, Kingsley did face congregational discipline. She was asked to stay home, keeping her private revelations private.

Some modern observers see this discipline as a travesty. How dare they silence this courageous woman! But is that the whole story? Certainly the culture of 1741 Massachusetts had little concern for "women's rights," but it seems that those church leaders had an even larger issue to consider—the expression of truth. Should the church allow just anyone to get up and preach whatever they feel God has told them? Doesn't the Bible itself prescribe some checks and balances on the sharing of a new revelation? Perhaps Jonathan Edwards and company did Mrs. Kingsley a favor by reining her in, encouraging her to sort through her God thoughts with family and Christian friends before broadcasting them.

Dear friends, do not believe everyone who claims to speak by the Spirit. You must test them to see if the spirit they have comes from God.

1 JOHN 4:1

A HOUSE WITHOUT WALLS

Sarah Osborn

1714–96

S he didn't want to cause a scandal. She just invited a small group of church women to her home for a Bible study. If their husbands wanted to come too, well, that was on them. She wasn't trying to be a pastor. Sarah Osborn just had a gift for teaching, and she needed to use it.

An active member of the First Congregational Church in Newport, Rhode Island, Sarah found a new dimension of faith when the Great Awakening swept through New England in 1740–41, particularly through the preaching of George Whitefield and Gilbert Tennent. That's when she started the women's Bible study, which proved to be quite popular.

When her husband began to fail in business, she had to earn money by teaching school, so she opened her home to students. But she had such a heart for teaching, she didn't limit her school to only those who could pay. "I educate the children of poor neighbors who gladly pay me in washing, ironing, mending, making, etc.," she explained to a friend. She also began to teach slaves—not that she was an abolitionist; she just knew that God loved slaves, too, and in order to read the Bible, they needed to know how to read.

Her church groups continued. When a friend suggested she was wearing herself too thin, Sarah replied, "I always feel stronger when my companies [meetings] break up than when they come in." She also wrote frequently, keeping regular diaries and composing essays, tracts, and reviews on philosophical and theological issues.

By the 1760s, her home was well known as an education center in Newport, especially for the poor. When revival broke out in the area, as many as three hundred people would attend her Bible studies—men and women, white and black, rich and poor. Yet she insisted she wasn't trying to take leadership from men or change the structure of society—just teaching the Bible to all who needed to learn it.

There will always be those who read ulterior motives into whatever you do. Don't let them stop you. There will be naysayers who somehow feel threatened when you do something good. Press on. Grab the gift God has given you and use it for his glory, even if that means breaking through walls to do so.

If your gift is serving others, serve them well. If you are a teacher, teach well.

ROMANS 12:7

GREAT ADVENTURE

Mary Rowlandson

1637–1711

We're used to it now. Someone goes through a harrowing experience, and a tell-all book is soon on the shelves. A Christian woman named Mary Rowlandson may have started that trend, publishing a bestselling book in 1682 about an adventure that occurred in 1676.

The mid-1600s had seen great expansion for the Puritan colonists in New England, with thousands of new immigrants entering the region. They pressed the frontier westward, into tribal territory. In some cases, the colonists bought land from the tribes and negotiated agreements, but not always. In the winter of 1675–76, Wampanoag warriors attacked Puritan settlements throughout New England—including the village of Lancaster, Massachusetts, where Mary Rowlandson lived with her minister husband and three children. Thirteen colonists were killed, and many others were injured. Mary and her children were taken captive, along with other villagers.

For eleven weeks, the raiding party fled retaliation from Puritan forces, dragging their hostages with them. Ultimately, Mary's release was won with a ransom: twenty pounds raised in an appeal to some church women in Boston.

Years later, Mary wrote about her ordeal in a book titled *The Sovereignty and Goodness of God: Being a Narrative of the Captivity and Restoration of Mrs. Mary Rowlandson.* An instant hit, it went through four printings in the first year. America had never had a book so popular.

Rowlandson frankly described her difficulties but also took every opportunity to mention God's goodness. "So it must be, that I must sit all this cold winter night upon the cold snowy ground, with my sick child in my arms, looking that every hour would be the last of its life; and having no *Christian* friend near me, either to comfort or help me. Oh, I may see the wonderful power of God, that my Spirit did not utterly sink under my affliction: still the Lord upheld me with His gracious and merciful spirit, and we were both alive to see the light of the next morning."

This is the sort of two-fisted honesty we need in our attitude and our conversation. We must not deny the challenges we face, but we can trust "the sovereignty and goodness of God" to provide for us—even in the most harrowing adventure.

Dear brothers and sisters, when troubles come your way, consider it an opportunity for great joy. For you know that when your faith is tested, your endurance has a chance to grow.

JAMES 1:2-3

FREE VERSE

Phillis Wheatley

1753–84

Arise, my soul; on wings enraptured, rise,
To praise the Monarch of the earth and skies.

So begins one of the many religious poems written by Phillis Wheatley in the late 1700s. This highly regarded poet was entertained by George Washington, approved by John Hancock, and published by Thomas Paine. She was only thirteen when her first poem was published, and at age seventeen she wrote a popular elegy to mark the death of preacher George Whitefield.

Three years later, her growing fame took her to England, where she got a book of poems published, met with the Lord Mayor of London, and nearly had an audience with the king. As the Revolutionary War developed, her poems took on a more American slant.

Did we mention that Phillis grew up as a slave? She was seven or eight when the slave ship *Phillis* brought her from West Africa to the American colonies, and she served in the Boston home of John and Susanna Wheatley. Rather progressive for their day, the Wheatleys provided an education for young Phillis and eased her duties so she could practice reading and writing. They recognized her talent and encouraged it. When John Wheatley died in 1778, Phillis was granted her freedom, and though she kept writing poetry, financial woes and health troubles plagued her until she died in 1784.

In modern times, it's hard for us to understand the slave culture of the 1700s. We applaud the Wheatleys for supporting Phillis's poetry—but they were still slave owners! Yet even within that corrupt system, Phillis got some breaks and managed to thrive for a time. While her poetry was generally positive, in a few lines she addressed the slavery issue.

But how, presumptuous shall we hope to find
Divine acceptance with th' Almighty mind—
While yet (O deed ungenerous!) they disgrace
And hold in bondage Afric's blameless race?

We still live in a broken world, but we can use our gifts to offer healing, challenge, and delight.

Live clean, innocent lives as children of God, shining like bright
lights in a world full of crooked and perverse people.

PHILIPPIANS 2:15

FAIR GAME

Hannah Adams

1755–1831

A shy woman, single all her life, Hannah Adams loved to gather knowledge. An avid reader as a child, she learned Greek and Latin from seminary students who boarded in her family's Massachusetts home. The Revolutionary War broke out when she was about twenty, and money was tight. Hannah helped out by making lace and tutoring young men.

Before she turned thirty, she published her first book, *An Alphabetical Compendium of the Various Sects Which Have Appeared in the World from the Beginning of the Christian Era to the Present Day.* This work not only detailed the distinctions of Christian denominations, but also examined the beliefs of Islam, Judaism, Deism, Paganism, and other world religions. Other Christian authors of the time might merely have pointed out all the errors in these competing faiths, but Adams was far ahead of her time in the respect she showed them. She tried to treat each belief system fairly.

This won her the support of a group of influential freethinkers in Boston, who supported her financially as she kept writing. As a result, Hannah Adams is generally considered the first American woman to make her living as a writer. Her books, mostly on religion (*Evidences of Christianity*) and history (*A Summary History of New England*), continued to gather and dispense knowledge.

For instance, *The Truth and Excellence of the Christian Religion* (1804) impressively presents arguments for the truth of the Bible and Jesus as Messiah, quoting extensively from leading Christian authors. Chapters cover the testimony of fulfilled prophecy, of the Resurrection, and of the miraculous growth of the church. Later in life Adams described herself as a Unitarian (possibly influenced by her Boston supporters), but these earlier works seem as evangelical as you can get.

Nowadays, Christians need to steer clear of two pitfalls. One is to go along with the general idea that it doesn't matter what you believe as long as you're sincere about it. It does matter. We can and should, as Hannah Adams did, muster convincing arguments for the truth of the Christian gospel.

But we must also avoid the other pitfall—mistreating those who disagree with us. Church history is full of horror stories along this line—so-called Christians violently abusing others for their beliefs. It makes no sense to hurt people, to slander them or spew hatred, in defense of the one who said, "Love your enemies" (Matthew 5:44).

Anyone who is not against us is for us.

MARK 9:40

ISLAND QUEEN

Elizabeth Ka'ahumanu

——————— CA. 1768–1832 ———————

Hawaii would never be the same. Queen Ka'ahumanu challenged long-held limits on what Hawaiian women could do. She literally rewrote the laws of her island nation. She opened the door to trade with Westerners. And late in her life, she became a Christian.

The queen began her ascent to power as one of several wives of King Kamehameha, but she was his favorite. She advised him in his successful quest to unite the various islands of Hawaii in a single kingdom, and she rallied others to his support. When the king died in 1819, she forced his young son to share power with her.

This culture severely restricted the behavior of women. Men and women did not eat together, and women could not eat certain foods. Ka'ahumanu regularly flouted these taboos. She ate whatever and wherever she wanted, and she even took up surfing. Her very presence as the most powerful person in the islands raised the status of Hawaiian women.

Then the missionaries came. Hiram and Sybil Bingham arrived in 1820 and began learning the local language, translating the Bible, and creating a writing system for the Hawaiian tongue. Ka'ahumanu was interested, but it seems her fierce independence might have held her back at first. Then in 1824, she publicly announced her conversion, encouraging others to embrace Christianity as well. The following year she was baptized, taking the name Elizabeth. Soon she was creating new laws for Hawaii based on the Ten Commandments.

Shortly before her death in 1832, Elizabeth Ka'ahumanu was presented with a copy of the newly translated Hawaiian New Testament. Reportedly, her last words would be translated, "Here am I, O Jesus, grant me thy gracious smile."

Theologians talk about "common grace," the good things that God gives to all people, even if they're not Christians. In this case, it seems that, long before her conversion, Ka'ahumanu had a God-given sense of fairness, as well as the courage to seek justice in her society. She was far from perfect, especially before becoming a Christian. But we might consider her a Christian waiting to happen. All her life, it seemed, God was preparing her to meet him.

God has made everything beautiful for its own time. He has
planted eternity in the human heart, but even so, people cannot
see the whole scope of God's work from beginning to end.

ECCLESIASTES 3:11

THE GOOD OF SOULS

Anne Dutton
1692–1765

Her conversion story is deep and passionate. "The worth of mine own soul, as an immortal spirit, was strongly impressed upon my mind. Again, the misery of my natural estate was set before me, as a transgressor of the holy law: I thought all the curses in God's book belonged to *me*. . . . This raised a cry in my soul (though I kept it as close as I could from others) 'What must I do to be saved?'"

Anne was about thirteen years old at the time.

It was the early 1700s. Anne's parents were good Congregationalists in Northampton, England. A few years after her personal decision to follow Christ, she started going to a Baptist church in town and benefited greatly from the preaching of Pastor John Moore. "The special advantage I received under his ministry was the establishment of my judgment in the doctrines of the gospel," she wrote later.

That spiritual judgment would set her apart in the years to come. Writing books, teaching Bible classes, composing hymn texts and poems, and corresponding with a broad group of friends and acquaintances, Anne demonstrated deep insight about the Christian life. People sought her advice, and she freely dispensed it.

Anne believed firmly that women should not teach men, but she defended her writing ministry on several counts. First, she was writing for "only the glory of God, and the good of souls," not to establish her own power or reputation. But she also likened her books to casual conversations. "Imagine then . . . when my books come to your houses, that I am come to give you a visit." And she wondered in print how women could be forbidden to "tell of the wonders of his love, to seek the good of souls and the advancement of the Redeemer's interest?"

With this sense of ministry, Anne felt empowered to comment on the religious trends of her day, writing gentle critiques and encouragement to popular preachers John Wesley and George Whitefield.

The world has changed greatly, but you might still wonder about your proper ministry within it. Follow Anne's lead and speak courageously to support those around you, to "seek . . . the advancement of the Redeemer's interest."

Let everything you say be good and helpful, so that your words
will be an encouragement to those who hear them.

EPHESIANS 4:29

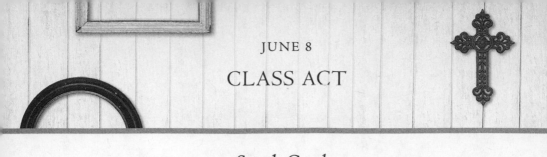

CLASS ACT

Sarah Crosby
1729–1804

There were just too many people. Not that Sarah Crosby was afraid of speaking, but she worried about the propriety of it. She had been a Methodist class leader since 1752, leading a small group, thirty people at most, in Bible study. Now, nearly a decade later, there were nearly two hundred individuals coming to hear her speak. That seemed a lot like preaching, and Crosby wasn't sure a woman should do that. She wrote to John Wesley, the founder of the Methodist movement, for advice.

"I do not see that you have broken any law," he replied. "Go on calmly and steadily." He reaffirmed that the Methodists did not allow women preachers at that time, but these circumstances constituted an "extraordinary" calling, as he saw it. It would not be wrong of her simply to share what was in her heart. If she was uneasy, perhaps she could read sermons from other preachers. "I think you have not gone too far. You could not well do less."

This freed Crosby to continue her ministry. Over the next forty years or so, she spoke throughout England and wrote to hundreds of people, offering spiritual counsel. She became an important voice in the burgeoning Methodist movement.

Crosby also kept a detailed diary of her life, work, and musings. Consider this entry at the end of 1777: "Glory be unto thee, my Lord, who hast brought thy poor helpless creature to the end of another year. How shall I thank thee for all thy multiplied mercies! I have not improved either my time, or talents, as I wish I had, nor profited by my mercies, as I ought to have done. Yet, blessed be my gracious Father, I have great cause to be thankful. . . . Thou hast enabled me [in the past year] to ride 960 miles, to keep 220 public meetings, at many of which some hundreds of precious souls were present, about 600 private meetings, and to write 116 letters, many of them long ones: besides many, many conversations with souls in private, the effect of which will, I trust, be 'as bread cast on the waters.'"

Christian ministry should never be about rights or status. It's a matter of following God's call. Sarah Crosby understood this, and she worked tirelessly to do so.

Cast thy bread upon the waters: for thou shalt find it after many days.

ECCLESIASTES 11:1, KJV

VOICES

Elizabeth Ann Seton

1774–1821

Advice can pour in from many places. Family. Friends. The people in your social networks. Books. Songs. A self-help program on the radio. A sermon. It can be overwhelming.

Some advice comes with an agenda. Some comes out of a genuine concern for you. Either way, in the end you need to weed through all the advice to make your own choices.

Elizabeth Seton was getting advice from many directions. In the early 1800s, she and her husband, William, went to Italy with their five children, hoping for rest for an ailing William. Unfortunately, he didn't recover. Elizabeth found herself a widow with five kids in a foreign country. Fortunately, a Catholic family befriended her and shared their compassion and their faith.

Elizabeth grew up Protestant, but not until she came among the Catholics in Italy did she find her own faith. When she and her children returned to New York and she chose to join the Catholic church, the advice (and the judgment) from friends and family began.

Like all of us, in the end she had to make the right choice for herself. In a memoir, she wrote about how she came to her choice to break her Protestant family tradition and embrace Catholicism. She turned to God for advice. When the advice and opinions of others made her doubt her choice, she wrote, "And here now I am in God's hands, praying day and night for His heavenly direction, which alone can guide me straight."

Once she was able to get everyone else's voices out of her head, she believed that she was to "go peaceably and firmly to the Catholic church. For if faith is so important to our salvation, I will seek it where true faith first began."

This is about more than denominations or church attendance. It's about the voices of others you allow in your head. Friends and family offer advice that is sometimes wise and loving—and sometimes not. God can sometimes use them to guide you . . . and sometimes he'll lead you to go against their wishes. The important thing is to listen for God's voice and follow that.

If you need wisdom, ask our generous God, and he will give
it to you. He will not rebuke you for asking.

JAMES 1:5

THE LEAST OF THESE

Isabella Graham

1742–1814

Jesus once told a brilliant parable about Judgment Day, in which the Son of Man rewards or condemns people for their treatment of him when he was sick, in prison, or needing food, drink, or clothing. On both sides, everyone is puzzled. *When did we ever see you in such need?* The answer has sounded through the centuries: "When you did it to one of the least of these my brothers and sisters, you were doing it to me!" (Matthew 25:40).

Isabella Graham was one of many Christians who have taken that challenge seriously. She grew up in Scotland, joined the church as a teenager, and married a doctor. An army physician, her husband died from an illness about a decade later, and Isabella found herself a widow and a single mom in her early thirties.

It's not unusual to see Christians in dire circumstances reaching out to help others. Graham certainly did—not only teaching school, but also starting a sort of health-insurance union for the poor (the Penny Society). Then she got a visit from an old friend.

John Witherspoon had been the minister of her childhood church. (You might recognize his name because he became a leader in America and signed the Declaration of Independence.) Now in 1785, he was visiting Scotland again, and he convinced Isabella Graham to come to the United States.

There she attained a whole new level of charitable work, founding (or cofounding) organizations to help widows, orphans, the poor, and the mentally disabled. Graham started a Sunday school in New York (at a time when that concept was brand new), as well as a missionary society. She was involved in charities that ministered to prostitutes, visited inmates, and distributed Bibles.

She lived into her seventies, pouring out her life for the needy, in service to God. "The Lord has convinced me that I have nothing in myself on which I can rest," she wrote to a friend, ". . . but this Saviour is provided for sinners. . . . I rest my salvation on his word; God giveth to me eternal life, and this life is in his Son."

Pure and genuine religion in the sight of God the Father means caring for orphans and widows in their distress and refusing to let the world corrupt you.

JAMES 1:27

ALL SHOOK UP

Ann Lee

1736–84

This book includes a number of women who were quite controversial in their times, and few were more so than Ann Lee, who led the group known as the Shakers. Born into a blacksmith's family in England, she got no formal education growing up but worked in a textile mill. She was described as very serious minded, "not addicted to play."

In her midtwenties, Ann joined a new sect led by the preaching team of James and Jane Wardley. Former Quakers, the Wardleys had been influenced by a prophetic group from France that emphasized the second coming of Christ. Over the years, Ann assumed some leadership in this group and also suffered with them, occasionally going to prison on charges of blasphemy or dancing on the Sabbath. The "dancing" was just the group's active worship style; outsiders called them "Shakers."

Their future, they believed, was in America, so Ann led a small group of Shakers to settle in New York, near Albany, starting a religious community there. In New York they found greater acceptance for their ways and beliefs. Arriving in 1774, just before the American Revolution, they took a stance of pacifist neutrality in that conflict. After the war, Lee and others took missions trips into New England to invite others into their church.

America was—and would continue to be—a nation of pioneers. This was true in religion as well as politics or geography. The country's independent spirit led many disaffected believers to leave their churches and start new ones. The Shaker movement, with the charismatic "Mother" Ann Lee at the helm, became a magnet for many of these splinter groups. Like the mystics of old, she had visions and ecstatic utterances that sparked either loyalty or enmity in those around her. Yet the Shakers—or, officially, the United Society of Believers in Christ's Second Appearing—became part of early American culture, known for hard work and hearty worship, with haunting songs and well-crafted furniture. "Put your hands to work, and your hearts to God," Mother Ann exhorted her people.

Despite all the controversy that Ann caused, that's a pretty good way to live, applying hands and heart to fulfill the calling God has given us.

The prize is not just for me but for all who eagerly look forward to his appearing.

2 TIMOTHY 4:8

NEVER BEEN DONE

Ann Judson
1789–1826

I don't know if it can be done. No one has ever done that before."

Have you ever heard those words when you wanted to try something different? Maybe it was a new way to do something at work, a new ministry at church, or even a new hairstyle. Doing something that breaks the mold can be difficult. Just ask Ann Hasseltine Judson, regarded as the first American woman to go overseas as a missionary.

You have to wonder how many people told her she shouldn't do it. It was dangerous, not "women's work." But at the age of sixteen, Anne had dedicated her life to God, and she felt God wanted her to be a missionary.

In 1812, with her husband, Adoniram Judson, she set sail to India to begin missionary work. Shortly after they arrived, they were ordered by the government to leave. Instead of giving up, though, the Judsons went to Burma, a country that had yet to hear the gospel.

Ann wasn't just the wife of a missionary. She herself was a missionary. Together, she and Adoniram translated the Bible into the local language, brought many to faith, and helped to start the Christian church in Burma. It sounds wonderful and romantic, but it came at an immense personal cost to their family.

When war broke out between Britain and Burma, Adoniram was suspected of being a British spy and imprisoned. A pregnant Ann worked tirelessly for Adoniram's release, also sneaking food and supplies to her husband and other prisoners. After eighteen months, he was released, but Ann's health problems took their toll, and she died at age thirty-seven.

Some naysayers might think Ann's early death proved their point. Missions work *was* difficult and dangerous. But consider the impact of Ann's work. Adoniram stayed in Burma, and at the time of his death, that country had sixty-three churches and 163 missionaries. The ministry that Ann helped to start and build was flourishing.

Next time someone says to you, "It's never been done before. It's risky. You probably shouldn't do it," think of Ann Judson. Her ability to listen to God's calling and not society's admonishments made all the difference.

Nothing is impossible with God.

LUKE 1:37

TRIALS

Ann Judson

1789–1826

I f I had not felt certain that every additional trial was ordered by infinite love and mercy, I could not have survived my accumulated sufferings." These words were written by pioneer missionary Adoniram Judson, but they also fit the testimony of his wife, Ann.

Two weeks after Ann married Adoniram, the newlyweds set sail for India. But this was no honeymoon; it was a missionary journey.

When it came to trials, Ann Judson had her share. Shortly after arriving in India, they were forced to leave. They relocated to Burma, but that meant learning a whole new language, one that was especially difficult. On the way to their new mission field, Ann suffered a miscarriage. The Judsons lost another child a few years later. Health problems sent Ann back to the United States for a short time, and when she returned to join her husband, their trials escalated.

Adoniram was taken as a prisoner and suspected of being a spy when the British went to war with Burma. His year and a half of imprisonment was brutal and took its toll on Ann's health.

Ann lost children, saw her husband imprisoned and tortured, and dealt with her own health problems, but she did not question God's love. In fact, she attributed these trials to God's grace.

Talk about a positive outlook! Despite her sufferings, which certainly accumulated over the years, she saw God's "infinite love and mercy" ordering her steps. It's often during times of severe trial, once we've exhausted all other options, that we turn our attention fully on God. As C. S. Lewis said, pain is God's "megaphone to rouse a deaf world." During trials, when we turn to God fully, we open ourselves up to hearing him loud and clear and seeing who he is. And when we come through on the other end, our relationship with him can be deeper.

When problems begin, do you think you can look at them through this perspective—that God's infinite love and mercy will see you through? It might help you turn to him sooner, rather than later.

We can rejoice, too, when we run into problems and trials, for we know that they help us develop endurance. And endurance develops strength of character, and character strengthens our confident hope of salvation.

ROMANS 5:3-4

A BANNER DAY

Betsy Ross
1752–1836

Everyone knows that Betsy Ross sewed the first American flag. Unless, of course, she didn't. Modern historians point out that there's little evidence to support the story, just a family tradition. But they can't really *disprove* it, either.

We know that Betsy Ross was a professional upholsterer, good with a needle and thread. Her husband was an officer in Washington's army, and her assigned pew at Christ Church in Philadelphia was right behind that of the Washingtons—so the general and the seamstress may have passed the peace. Records show that, years later, Betsy Ross was given material to make flags for American ships. So she was definitely a patriot and no stranger to flag making, whether or not her legend is true.

You might not know that Betsy Ross was also a woman of faith. Brought up in a Quaker home, she scandalized her family by eloping with John Ross, the son of an Anglican minister, and she was shunned by the Quaker meeting. (It's ironic that Quakers, who had long fought for religious freedom, would take such a strong stand against a religiously mixed marriage.) John Ross died in battle in 1776, and Betsy's second husband was captured by the British and died in a British prison. Her third husband lived well into the 1800s but suffered greatly from injuries sustained in the Revolution.

Late in life, Betsy reconnected with her Quaker roots, joining a Quaker meeting that was less rigid than the one that had shunned her. An avid Bible reader until she lost her eyesight, she then had her grandchildren read the Good Book to her.

The historical questions about Betsy's flag making call to mind an intriguing Bible verse: "Be careful to live properly among your unbelieving neighbors. Then even if they accuse you of doing wrong, they will see your honorable behavior, and they will give honor to God" (1 Peter 2:12). The point is, the pattern of your life tends to fill in the details. An honorable life is your best defense against false accusations. In Betsy's case, while we may not have solid evidence on the flag story, we know she was a woman of faith and commitment, and so it only makes sense that she would pick up needle and thread to help the country she was devoted to.

So what story does your life tell?

Raise a flag for all the nations to see.

ISAIAH 62:10

OPTIONS

Henriette Odin Feller

1800–68

It's the early 1800s. You're a young woman, born to a wealthy family in Switzerland. What do you expect to be when you grow up? A wife, of course.

Henriette Feller followed the same path most of her contemporaries did—she married and began a family. Her only child died young. Henriette's husband, Louis, died also, leaving her single and childless.

We don't know how she felt about those circumstances, but we do know that after her husband died she was granted "independent legal status." Before she married, she was a dependent of her father. After she married, she was a dependent of her husband. It seems insulting, but that's the way it was in Europe at that time: to make her own decisions, she needed an official court action.

Henriette used her freedom for all it was worth, doing the things she believed God wanted her to do. She preached the gospel in Quebec and later in the United States, using an interpreter (she spoke French). She distributed Bibles in France. She taught school.

Feller's longest-lasting efforts were educational. In 1854, she established Institute Feller, a school for girls. A second school she helped build years later would eventually merge with Institute Feller and educate both girls and boys. That school existed until 1967.

Being married and having children is a wonderful thing, and it seems as if that was Henriette's first choice. When she found herself widowed and childless, she realized that her new situation had its opportunities too.

We all have certain responsibilities and certain freedoms. Sometimes people wish they were married, or wish they weren't. They wish they had kids, or wish they didn't. *If only my life were different, then I could do things that really matter.* On the other hand, there are widows, divorcées, and empty nesters who struggle with their change in status. *What am I supposed to do now?*

You are more, much more than your relationship status. Whatever your family responsibilities are, God wants to use you to do things that matter—in your home, in the wider world, or both. Whether you're married, unmarried, with kids or without kids, how are you running with the freedoms that your status provides?

You are free, yet you are God's slaves, so don't use
your freedom as an excuse to do evil.

1 PETER 2:16

TURNABOUT

Elizabeth Fry

1780–1845

In the late 1600s, Quakers were seen as a dangerous sect in England. Their anti-Establishment ways aroused the ire of—well, the Establishment. They were arrested, imprisoned, humiliated, and even tortured. But only a century later, Quakers—officially "the Religious Society of Friends"—were among the leaders of British society.

Take Elizabeth Gurney, for instance. Her father was a respected businessman, a banker. Her mother came from another famous banking clan, the Barclays. The family faithfully attended Quaker meetings, though their clothing was spiffier than that of most of the other parishioners. Elizabeth was educated at home by her mother, who also brought her along on charitable visits to help the poor.

When Elizabeth was twelve, her mother died. In the following years, Elizabeth continued to attend religious services but lacked enthusiasm for it, finding any excuse she could to play hooky. Her family's resources allowed her to sample the finest entertainment (and fashion) of the culture. But at one Sunday meeting when she was seventeen, wearing purple boots and scarlet laces, Elizabeth's heart was changed forever by a visiting speaker from America. "I have had a faint light spread over my mind," she wrote in her journal. "It has caused me to feel a little religion. My imagination has been worked upon."

This young woman had been struggling with faith for some time. Yet this speaker's message struck a chord with her. "In short, what he said and what I felt, was like a refreshing shower, falling upon earth, that had been dried up for ages. It has not made me unhappy: I have felt ever since humble. . . . I hope to be truly virtuous."

Over the following years, this self-aware teenager got married (to a banker named Joseph Fry) and started a family. She adopted a plainer lifestyle and got involved in Quaker leadership. Eventually she became famous for her charitable work, especially in women's prisons. More than anyone else, Elizabeth Gurney Fry was responsible for improving the deplorable conditions of British penitentiaries. The fashionable teen became a Christlike servant.

Do not love this world nor the things it offers you, for when you love the world, you do not have the love of the Father in you.

1 JOHN 2:15

DEFINING MOMENTS

Elizabeth Fry

1780–1845

I fear that my life is slipping away to little purpose."

So wrote Elizabeth Fry at the age of thirty-two, with six children and another on the way. (She would bear eleven in all.) Elizabeth had become a leader in her Quaker meeting, and she did charitable work when she could, sometimes teaching children in a London workhouse. Yet she was frustrated because there just wasn't enough time to do everything she wanted to do. Maybe you know the feeling.

Fry would soon become famous as a prison reformer, but she didn't know that yet. She was just struggling to get through each day. Fortunately for us, she kept a journal throughout her life.

"I am a bubble, without reason, without beauty of mind or person," she wrote on her seventeenth birthday. "I am a fool. I daily fall lower in my own estimation. . . . I am now seventeen, and if some kind and great circumstance does not happen to me, I shall have my talents devoured by moth and rust."

A teenager dealing with self-esteem issues is no great surprise. Yet long into her adulthood, Elizabeth seemed to struggle with the idea of what kind of person she would be. Shortly after getting married, she wrote about all the deeds she wanted to do, but "my good wishes and good endeavours are of short, very short duration." She took an odd comfort in the fact that even the apostles couldn't pray with Jesus for one hour.

In 1813, she heard a speaker issue a challenge for prison reform. London's Newgate Prison had horrible conditions. Women were crowded there, often with their children, without beds or proper clothing. Elizabeth was moved to visit the prison, bringing clothes and clean straw (for bedding), but further ministry was delayed for a few years while she tended to her own children's illnesses.

In 1817, Fry returned to prison ministry with a dedication and passion that would make a huge difference. Newgate was transformed. She testified in Parliament about prison conditions. Other prisons were improved. The Quaker homemaker was changing the world.

You don't need to become famous for your good deeds. Maybe your calling involves home, family, or a job. But keep seeking God's guidance to be the kind of person he wants you to be.

Don't be selfish; don't try to impress others. Be humble,
thinking of others as better than yourselves.

PHILIPPIANS 2:3

LONDON CALLING

Elizabeth Fry

1780–1845

It was the time Dickens wrote about—manored, mannered gentry and discarded orphans. London in the early 1800s was the most influential city on earth, holding the wealth of a worldwide empire, but thousands of residents lived in abject poverty. Children slaved in workhouses, debtors went to prison, and certain sections of town teemed with a criminal underclass.

Elizabeth Gurney Fry tried to make things better. This affluent Quaker, the wife and daughter of bankers, the mother of eleven children, saw that women were living in deplorable conditions in London's Newgate Prison. She felt God's call to do something about it. First she brought bedding and clothing. Then she asked the inmates what they needed, and in response she started a school for their children. They wanted to be productive, so Fry and her teammates taught them sewing, knitting, and various crafts. Since many of the inmates were illiterate, the Bible was read to them.

It wasn't easy. "I have often thought that, in this little prospect, I must go like David, when he went to slay the giant . . . ," she wrote. "I go not trusting in any power, or strength of my own. . . . I trust the Lord will be with me, and make the sling and stone effectual."

Soon Elizabeth Fry became an expert in prison reform, and her work expanded as she sought other ways to help poor women in society—including starting a nurses' training school that later influenced Florence Nightingale. She wasn't the only Christian reaching out with God's love. Others, like William Wilberforce and the Clapham Sect, had been pushing social reform for some time, including the abolition of slavery. Yet it would be hard to overstate the impact Fry had on British society at that time.

What are you doing to help the needy?

We all have lots of good excuses, as Elizabeth Fry did, for *not* getting around to this, but when God tugs at our hearts, we need to respond. How can we use our talents and resources to do God's work in the world? There are still prisons, and they're still scary places. There are still people suffering in financial, physical, or emotional need. We can walk on past . . . or we can step out in faith, like little David against the giant.

Remember those in prison, as if you were there yourself.

HEBREWS 13:3

TROUBLED SOUL

Dorothy Carey

CA. 1765–1807

The life of Dorothy Carey doesn't offer us easy inspiration. Despite her staunch misgivings, Dorothy was persuaded by her husband, pioneer missionary William Carey, to sail from Britain to India in 1793. Her only two daughters had died, and she had to sail in rough conditions while pregnant and caring for their three young boys. By all accounts, William did not help much with the children.

It seems as if William disregarded the needs of his wife and children to pursue his missionary work. But, as in any troubled relationship, there's his side, there's her side, and then there's the truth. Two hundred years later, it's difficult to know how it really was between Dorothy and William.

We do know this: Dorothy faced many hardships in India. Financial problems, language barriers, lack of emotional support, and health problems—both physical and mental—abounded. History records that for the last twelve years of her life, Dorothy was insane. And in India at the beginning of the nineteenth century, Dorothy had no chance of receiving the mental and emotional care she desperately needed.

What inspiration can we take from Dorothy's life? There's this: life's pressures can get to us, and when there are signs that we need some emotional help, we should never ignore them. Women are notorious for taking care of everyone else before taking care of themselves. We fancy ourselves Wonder Woman but forget that it's a sign of strength to seek and accept help when we need it. And in modern times, we have a wealth of help available to us that Dorothy never had.

Adding to the complexity in Dorothy's case is that William was (and remains) such a hero of the faith. He was attempting great things for God! Did she feel that her needs were pulling him down? That can happen in modern relationships too.

Your needs are important. God wants you and your relationships to be *whole*. You can take a break from caring for everyone else to care for yourself. If you don't, it's quite possible that sooner or later, you won't be able to care for anyone. Take full advantage of the spiritual, mental, and emotional help that's available to you.

---

*Dear friend, I hope all is well with you and that you are
as healthy in body as you are strong in spirit.*

3 JOHN 2

COMING SOON

Ellen G. White

---------- 1827–1915 ----------

William Miller had totaled up the prophet Daniel's seventy weeks and checked all the biblical data, and it kept adding up the same way. Jesus was definitely returning in 1843. Or maybe 1844.

They called it the Great Disappointment. Anticipating a target date of October 22, 1844, many believers had quit their jobs and given away their stuff. Among those disappointed that day was sixteen-year-old Ellen Harmon, who was from a family that had been following William Miller for several years.

Newspapers mocked this false alarm. Many "Adventists" (also known as "Millerites") abandoned the cause. Others, like Miller himself, sought new ways to figure out what God was doing. In December of that year, Ellen was praying with four other women when she had a vision that reassured her. Despite the disappointment, it seemed to say, Jesus was still coming soon. Over the next twenty years, Ellen reported another one hundred to two hundred visions guiding her as she developed her beliefs.

In 1846, after she had gone public with a few more visions, she married James White, an Adventist minister. In the following decades, Ellen White traveled and spoke at Adventist meetings throughout the country. She also became a prolific writer, penning many magazine articles as well as books and pamphlets. Much of her writing is basic evangelical fare, like her classic *Steps to Christ*.

In response to one vision, she adopted Saturday as the Sabbath, casting her lot with the Seventh-day Adventists, with whom she became a respected leader. Another vision in 1863 put her on a health kick. She began writing and speaking about the relationship between physical health and spirituality. Ellen was a driving force as the church established a health institute, a college, and ministry among African Americans in the South.

Ellen has always had her critics, primarily among those who doubt the authenticity of her visions, yet she's a respected figure in the history of the Seventh-day Adventist Church, now more than ten million strong.

But let's get back to where we started, the second advent of Christ. False alarms can tempt us to laugh off the whole matter, but Jesus did promise to come back. We don't know when, but he did ask us to be ready. Are you?

He who is the faithful witness to all these things says, "Yes,
I am coming soon!" Amen! Come, Lord Jesus!

REVELATION 22:20

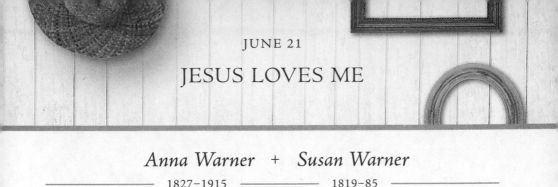

JESUS LOVES ME

Anna Warner + *Susan Warner*
1827–1915 ———— 1819–85

In World War II, an American PT boat was destroyed in the Pacific. The crew, including future president John F. Kennedy, was rescued by natives of the nearby Solomon Islands. On the boat ride to safety, they sang a song they all knew— Americans and islanders alike—"Jesus Loves Me."

It is possibly the best-known Christian song ever, written around 1860 by a novelist named Anna Warner. She and her sister, Susan, lived a riches-to-rags story in which both had to become writers to pay the bills.

They had grown up in a wealthy home in New York City, but their father lost a bundle in the financial "Panic of 1837." The family gave up their city mansion for their country home upstate, on an island in the Hudson River. Eventually the sisters began writing novels, and they turned out to be pretty good at it. Susan often used the pen name "Elizabeth Wetherell" while Anna wrote as "Amy Lothrop." Between them, they churned out more than fifty novels.

At some point in their family's upheaval, both sisters became serious Christians. This came through not only in their writing, which tended to be strongly moral and didactic, but also in their personal lives. They began holding Bible studies for the cadets at West Point, which was just across the river from their home.

"Jesus Loves Me" first appeared in the 1860 novel *Say and Seal*. Anna wrote the lyrics at Susan's request. In the deeply emotional story, a young boy on his deathbed asks for a song from one of the people comforting him. The man picks up the boy and walks gently around the room with him. Softly, "his tone . . . almost as low as his footsteps," the man sings the song we have come to know. (Of course, at that point they were still just words on a page, but composer William B. Bradbury soon created the tune.)

It is a children's song that packs a powerful message for everyone. We are weak, he is strong, and yet Jesus loves each one of us. Let that little tune—and its great message—waft through your mind today.

God loved the world so much that he gave his one and only Son, so that
everyone who believes in him will not perish but have eternal life.

JOHN 3:16

GETTING THE POINT

Anna Warner + Susan Warner

1827–1915 ——— 1819–85

Maybe you're still reeling from the recent economic crisis, but such financial downturns are nothing new. The Panic of 1837 touched off a seven-year recession, creating high unemployment and widespread business failure. Henry Warner, a wealthy New York City lawyer, was one victim. His family had to move out of their luxurious town house and into a Revolutionary-era home on an island in the middle of the Hudson River. Writing about this move, his daughter Anna called the new place "nondescript"—and yet here they would have to "live out our lives, fighting the fight, wrestling with sorrow, gathering up the joy."

If it weren't for their economic necessity, Anna and Susan might never have gotten so serious about their writing—first poems and stories for magazines, and then novels. Susan's book *The Wide, Wide World* (published under her pseudonym, Elizabeth Wetherell) was a huge success, going through fourteen printings in two years. In it, a young woman faces various crises and learns to trust God. While the novel is quite preachy, it is still studied in some college classes as a glimpse into the lives of women in that time. Meanwhile Anna Warner was also writing novels, but she gained her greatest fame for writing the words to "Jesus Loves Me."

The Warner sisters carried out one other remarkable ministry. Beginning in 1875, they held Bible studies for cadets at West Point, the military academy across the river from their home. Eventually it became a much-anticipated Sunday event for the young men who were ferried across to the island for the afternoon. The Warners would teach the Bible, lead discussions on it, and then serve tea and gingerbread. They would also maintain a correspondence with cadets who wanted to know more about the faith. Anna continued this tradition even after Susan's death, until her own death in 1915.

The roster of national leaders who passed through West Point in those years is impressive. How many of them were touched, directly or indirectly, by the faithful ministry of Susan and Anna Warner?

Bad things happen, forcing us in directions we might not want to go. But they can give us the opportunity to see what new talents might awaken in us as we cope with the new circumstances. They can also show us how we can impact the lives of others.

Work for the peace and prosperity of the city where I sent you into exile.

JEREMIAH 29:7

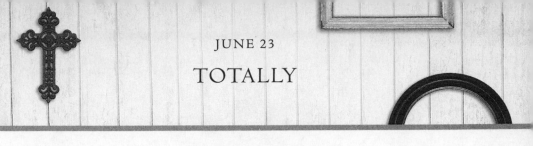

TOTALLY

Phoebe Palmer

1807–74

I do hereby consecrate body, soul, and spirit, time, talents, influence, family, and estate . . . to be for ever, and in the most unlimited sense, the LORD's."

In an 1845 book, Phoebe Palmer urged her readers to make this commitment. Her suggested prayer went on for five more paragraphs, full of the language of totality—putting everything on God's altar, trusting him "unwaveringly."

For more than three decades, Phoebe delivered a message of sanctification, calling casual Christians to get serious about their faith. Historically, she bridged the gap between the great revivalists Charles Finney and Dwight L. Moody. She shaped American Christianity as much as they did, paving the way for social ministries, camp meetings, and the Holiness movement—but unlike those revivalists, she avoided emotionalism. She called for sober decisions from serious believers.

Phoebe Palmer's message came out of her own experience. Brought up as a Methodist, she struggled with her faith. Distracted by the normal activities of life, she worried about her failure to live God's way all the time. Was she lacking something? Did she need to have some emotional experience to be a complete Christian?

After her infant daughter died in a household accident, Phoebe brooded for about a year and then decided that she could commit even this horrific experience to God. One day in 1837, she wrote that her "heart was emptied of self, and cleansed of all idols." God had become her "ALL in ALL."

Phoebe's sister Sarah had started a "Tuesday Meeting for the Promotion of Holiness"—essentially a group where people would share their experiences and encourage one another. In 1840, Phoebe began leading that group. This led to broader influence: editing a devotional magazine, writing eighteen books, and speaking at revival meetings in the United States and Great Britain.

Palmer also put her sanctification to work with some adventurous efforts in social ministry. She dared to enter the crime-infested slums of New York, providing food, clothing, and medicine, starting a church and an innovative settlement house to help people out of poverty.

When God gets hold of your life, he may lead you in all sorts of unexpected directions. Ultimately, it's not about your own religious experience or how you feel about it; it's about letting God have his way with you.

I want your will to be done, not mine.

MATTHEW 26:39

NATURE CALLS

Emily Dickinson

———————— · 1830–86 ————————

You'll sometimes hear people say, "I'm not very religious, but I am very spiritual." Often those people have had a negative church experience. They equate "religion" with the church but "spirituality" with their faith.

The poet Emily Dickinson may not have said those exact words, but they could be used to describe her. Raised in the church, she had experienced much of the religious revival that swept through New England in the mid-1800s, but at some point during her adult life she stopped attending formal religious gatherings. In her poem "Some keep the Sabbath going to Church," she explains that she does church at home, probably outside in nature.

She says her chorister, what we would call a choir member, is a small blackbird called a bobolink. An orchard is her worship space. Emily, it seems, was enjoying a worship service in nature. Not that she was worshiping nature; rather, she found nature a perfect place to commune with and learn about God. The poem goes on to say that God is the preacher in her outdoor service—and he is "a noted clergyman."

Church is good. Listening to and joining with choirs who sing praise to God is good. Hearing sermons from pastors who have studied God's Word and have a desire to teach others is good. Worshiping with other Christians is an essential part of the Christian life (see Hebrews 10:25). But sometimes, sitting out in nature and listening for God's voice is good too.

There may be a time in your life, whether it's for just one week or an extended period, that you find yourself not attending regular church services. That doesn't mean you've abandoned your faith or you're out of touch with God. God uses many methods to speak to those who are listening.

When church isn't happening for you, learning about God and worshiping him doesn't have to stop happening. Find a quiet, natural spot to listen to the "noted clergyman" who speaks through his human servants and through all creation. Let him call you back to worship with others.

Just ask the animals, and they will teach you.
Ask the birds of the sky, and they will tell you.

JOB 12:7

IT'S ALIVE!

Emily Dickinson

1830–86

Emily Dickinson wrote several poems describing faith. In one, she describes faith as a "pierless bridge" that connects what we see and what we don't see. In another, she calls a child's faith "wide—like the sunrise."

Eleventh-grade American literature students, college coeds studying great poets, and scholars through the past century and a half have all tried to explain what Emily meant about faith in these and other works.

When she calls faith "a fine invention / For Gentlemen who *see!*" in one poem, some say she's tearing down religion as something made up, unreal—especially when she goes on to say that microscopes are "prudent / In an Emergency!" Others counter that she's simply carving out space for both faith and science.

Most of Dickinson's 1,800 poems seem simple, even childlike, as she writes about life and death, faith and doubt, nature and culture. But this simplicity gives rise to a multitude of interpretations.

That's the beauty of poetry—the poet can mean one thing, but the reader can take away something completely different. She can learn something about herself, discover some new thought, or see something in a completely new way through the poem. The reader isn't wrong for taking those things away, even if the poet didn't intentionally mean for it to happen. Poetry can be thought of as "living" because something new can always be taken from it.

Kind of like the Bible.

Each time you read a Bible passage, a chapter, or a book, there's an opportunity to take away something new, see something in a different light, and let God speak to you about the situation you're in now. Maybe you're an expert in the Scriptures, with vast knowledge of the text in the original languages, as well as the cultural context—but the Holy Spirit can still teach you something new each day. Are you willing to read the Bible with an open mind to let it say something new?

The word of God is alive and active.

HEBREWS 4:12, NIV

A LITTLE HELP

Emily Dickinson

1830–86

Y ou see them in church—the helpers, the servers, the compassionate people—
and you think, *Wow, I'd like to be like that, but I'm not.* These people quickly
understand when someone is in need and get straight to work. Sometimes they take
care of matters themselves. Sometimes they coordinate the help with others. But
every time, they're on top of it.

If you're not one of those people, don't beat yourself up. God didn't intend
everyone to be like that. He gave you other strengths—perhaps abilities that *other*
people look at and say, "Wow, I'd like to be like that, but I'm not."

From what we can discern about Emily Dickinson, she wasn't someone who
instinctively met others' needs. She kept to herself. By today's standards, she'd be
called a loner. You have to be around people all the time to see and meet their needs,
and she preferred to be by herself. But she understood that she could still help—even
if it was just one person. She wrote a short poem that explained that she felt that if
she could even stop just one heart from breaking, her life wouldn't have been in vain.
At the time, she had no idea how many she would help over generations.

Emily's gift was poetry. She's now a giant of American literature, but she actually
published very little in her lifetime. She seemed to be insecure about the value of her
work. ("I'm nobody!" she said in one of her best-known poems.) Yet in the centuries
since her death, her writing has helped people by speaking deeply to them, connecting with them, helping them to see God, the world, and themselves in a new light.
She had her issues with the organized church, but her poems reflect the reality of
God in honest, personal ways.

God says that all gifts are important. Emily's writing helped people. The shy
person who is happy to photocopy church bulletins but would be uncomfortable
greeting people at the church door helps people too. It's easy to label the person who
coordinates the church food drive as a helper, but there are many others quietly using
their abilities for God's glory.

Don't ever think that what you contribute isn't helpful.

Our bodies have many parts, and God has put each part just where he wants it.

1 CORINTHIANS 12:18

CONNECTIONS

Hannah Whitall Smith

1832–1911

What if you asked everyone you ran into today, "How have you been lately?" How many would answer, "Busy"? We are, as a culture, busy. Very busy.

We can go weeks without seeing the friends and family who mean the most to us. Sometimes we can go days without having a real conversation with the people who live *in our house.* Have you ever texted someone *in the next room* with a quick question? Go on, admit it. You probably have.

We say we want to take the time to form deeper connections with those who mean the most to us, but then we say we don't have the time. In reality, we don't *make* the time. It's easy to have the same problem when it comes to spending time with God. This may seem like a modern problem, but it's not.

In the nineteenth century, Hannah Whitall Smith wrote about this same problem. "How often we say about our earthly friends, 'I really would like to have a good quiet settled talk with them so that I can really get to know them.' And shouldn't we feel the same about our Heavenly Friend, that we may really get to know Him? These thoughts have taught me the importance of the children of God taking time to commune daily with their Father, so that they may get to know His mind and to understand better what His will is."

Author of the devotional classic *The Christian's Secret of a Happy Life,* Hannah was a popular author and speaker. Her "Higher Life" conferences inspired many believers to make time for God.

As we know from our human relationships, just saying we want to spend time with people doesn't make it happen. The deepening of a relationship depends on a commitment to *be with* that person, no matter how busy we are. It's the same with God. We can go a long time without spending serious time with our Creator. Oh, we might shoot quick prayers heavenward, as needed, and that's fine. Better to have *some* communication with God, even if it's quick. But Hannah Whitall Smith would urge us to focus on God, to dedicate the time necessary to truly connect with him—not only calling for help, but also intently listening to his wise guidance.

As the deer longs for streams of water, so I long for you, O God.

PSALM 42:1

WORDS' WORTH

Ella Wheeler Wilcox

1850–1919

A poet, lover of life, musician, and eternal optimist—all these terms could describe Ella Wheeler Wilcox. A prolific American writer in the late 1800s and early 1900s, penning more than five hundred poems in her lifetime, Wilcox earned a healthy income from the sale of her simple poetry. She had a knack for putting complex thoughts and feelings into accessible rhymes and stanzas.

Much of her poetry dealt with the spiritual—God, faith, and human kindness. One of Ella's well-known quotes conveys the biblical principles of treating people (including oneself) with kindness and respect: "A pat on the back is only a few vertebrae removed from a kick in the pants, but is miles ahead in results."

The Bible puts it this way: "Do not let any unwholesome talk come out of your mouths, but only what is helpful for building others up according to their needs, that it may benefit those who listen" (Ephesians 4:29, NIV).

The words we say and hear matter. Wilcox understood this. Over and over, she used words to encourage people to embrace life and see the good in it. To those who saw the earth as only veiled in sin, she said, "I and the bees, and the birds, we doubt it, / And think it a world worth living in."

When starting the morning with prayers, she advised to "ask for your divine inheritance / Of usefulness, contentment, and success. / Resign all fear, all doubt, and all despair."

Whether it's the words that come out of your mouth when you're trying to build someone else up or the words that you allow into your mind when you need to be built up yourself, it might be wise to take a lesson from Ella and make sure those words are a pat on the back, not a kick in the pants.

The apostle Paul challenged believers to make sure their conversation was "full of grace, seasoned with salt" (Colossians 4:6, NIV). Pleasant, tasty, lip-smackingly good. Ella Wheeler Wilcox spent her career putting language together in delicious ways. But you don't need to be a bestselling author to deliver appetizing words.

Encourage each other and build each other up, just as you are already doing.

1 THESSALONIANS 5:11

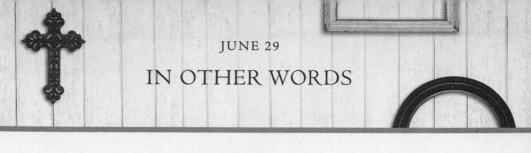

IN OTHER WORDS

Jane Borthwick

1813–97

The book of Revelation paints a glorious picture of a heavenly worship service with multitudes in attendance. There is mention of "every nation and tribe and people and language" being included in praising God (Revelation 7:9). That will be the final reversal of Babel, the continuation of Pentecost, the ultimate gathering of all tongues into one language of praise.

Until then, we need translators to bring us the devotional treasures of other cultures—people like Jane Borthwick, who specialized in the rich tradition of German hymns. This Scottish lass was traveling in Switzerland when a friend suggested she try her hand at translating some of the German hymns she heard there. When she got back to Edinburgh, her father encouraged her further. So she teamed with her sister, Sarah Findlater, to produce a series of four books called *Hymns from the Land of Luther*, which came out between 1854 and 1862. There were more than 120 translations of hymn texts from German to English, including the dramatic "Be Still, My Soul" by Katharina von Schlegel.

Jane and her sister continued to write devotional pieces and poems for magazines and collections, both using the pseudonym H. L. L. (from the title of the hymnbooks). Reportedly, Jane was quite upset when a publisher revealed their true identities. She wasn't writing for fame, just to serve the church. Jane also wrote instructional books for children's Christian education classes, as well as a survey of missions work. It makes sense that a translator would be interested in missions to other cultures.

Among Jane's best-known translations is "Jesus, Still Lead On," by Moravian leader Nicholas von Zinzendorf. One stanza goes,

When we seek relief from a long felt grief;
When temptations come alluring,
Make us patient and enduring;
Show us that bright shore where we weep no more.

Until we all reach that unilingual shore, we need to cope with a multilingual world. Thank God for translators like Jane Borthwick, who offered her linguistic talents to enhance our worship.

Your blood has ransomed people for God from every
tribe and language and people and nation.

REVELATION 5:9

THE POETIC VOICE

There are many female poets sprinkled throughout this book. Emily Dickinson. Grace Noll Crowell. Phillis Wheatley. Marie de France. Madeleine L'Engle. Not to mention the many hymn writers. The poetry these women have written has spanned centuries. Their words inspire and challenge readers. They illuminate who God is and praise him.

What's so special about poetry? Take a look at the Bible. Parts of it are plain and simple. The genealogies draw clear lines from one generation to the next. The stories we learned in Sunday school about David and Goliath, Noah and the ark, Jesus feeding the five thousand—they're all told in plain narrative format.

But the Bible contains poetry, too. Psalms, Proverbs, Ecclesiastes, Song of Songs, and Job are gathered in the center of our Old Testament as poetical works. These books are written in verse with vibrant imagery, deep symbolism, and sweeping emotion. The prophets often wrote in poetic form as well, and there are snippets of poems and songs throughout the historical books and the New Testament.

There are many ways to talk about God and what he has done in the world. Poetry, like other art forms, helps us understand in a creative way. It can turn ideas about God upside down and, when looked at from a different perspective, actually bring a clarity that straight prose would have difficulty conveying.

The poets you discover in this book are fairly traditional, and there's a reason their poetry has resonated for decades or centuries. But there are modern poets, too, who are worth checking out. In every age, literary artists try to craft new experiences of God.

Nowadays, for instance, there is "spoken-word poetry," a performance-art form of poetry that is meant to be heard, not read. Women, particularly urban women, are embracing this form of poetry and recording it, not on paper, but on video. Take a few minutes to search for "Christian spoken-word poetry" online. You'll discover a whole new vibrant poetic voice to make you see God in a new way.

Whether the poetry you read is ancient (as in the Bible), traditional (like that of Emily Dickinson), or modern (like spoken word), interacting with God through the poetic voice gives you one more way to deepen your relationship with him.

Kind words are like honey—sweet to the soul and healthy for the body.

PROVERBS 16:24

SIGHT LINES

Fanny Crosby
1820–1915

In the late 1800s, she was the poet laureate of American Christianity. Well into the 1900s, it was hard to find an evangelical church service that *didn't* feature a Fanny Crosby song. She wrote about eight thousand song lyrics in her ninety-five years, and many of them found their way into church hymnals . . . and Christian hearts, including "To God Be the Glory," "Blessed Assurance," and "Near the Cross."

As a baby, Frances Jane Crosby had an eye infection mistreated by a doctor, blinding her for life. Would she have been any more creative if she could see?

"It has always been my favorite theory that the blind can accomplish nearly everything that may be done by those who can see," Fanny wrote. She accepted her blindness as one might accept being short or blonde or left-handed. You might expect some bitterness to seep through into her writing, but her songs and stories were consistently upbeat, expressing the deep satisfaction of knowing Jesus and her delight in serving him. And she did serve him—not only in her prolific songwriting, but also by helping out in New York City rescue missions.

As a teenager at the New York Institution for the Blind, Fanny had good teachers (she became one there) and made good connections for the future (she found a husband there). The school also encouraged her as a writer. It's possible that her creativity developed there in ways that wouldn't have happened elsewhere.

From ancient times there has been a mystique around the blind poet, the one who "sees" in a way that others don't. That might be what we have here. Surely it was a hardship for Fanny Crosby to be blind, but it might also have been a gift. It enabled her to "see" things that others missed—a whole dimension of God's goodness that many of us never realize.

Maybe you're struggling with a hardship. You can't get around like you used to. You've lost someone close to you. Or you're single and you wish you weren't. It doesn't help to deny the pain, but for a moment, consider what gift God might be granting you—a slowdown, a refocus, a deeper love for Christ.

I pray that the eyes of your heart may be enlightened in order that you may know the hope to which he has called you.

EPHESIANS 1:18, NIV

KNOCKING ON HEAVEN'S DOOR

Fanny Crosby

1820–1915

Fanny Crosby was broke. That's hard to believe, since she was rapidly becoming the most popular songwriter in America. She had already collaborated with some of the best-known composers in the country—sacred and secular—and she had earned some royalties on published lyrics. The problem was, she gave a lot of money away. Fanny was especially committed to the work of New York City rescue missions, which were fighting the scourge of alcoholism in some terrible neighborhoods.

As a result, she was desperately in need of five dollars (a substantial sum in 1875) to pay the rent on her small New York apartment, and her publishers weren't coming through with an advance payment. She had to resort to . . . prayer.

Alone in her apartment, the blind poet knelt to ask God to provide for her needs.

She was just getting up from her knees when she heard a knock at the door. It was a man she didn't know. She didn't recognize his voice or his name. He simply gave her five dollars and left.

Thinking about this later, Fanny wrote, "I have no way of accounting for this, except to believe that God, in answer to my prayer, put it in the heart of this good man to bring the money to me. My first thought was, *It is so wonderful the way the Lord leads me.*" As you might expect, the Lord also led her to write song lyrics about it.

All the way my Savior leads me;
What have I to ask beside?
Can I doubt his tender mercy,
Who through life has been my guide?

The lyrics go on to describe the "heavenly peace" and "divinest comfort" that come from knowing that "Jesus doeth all things well."

So, what do you need from the Lord today? No, it's not like PayPal, where you just type in the amount and God gives it. Think about what the songstress is saying: our Savior *leads* us. He provides us with everything we need to go in the direction he wants us to go.

I am the LORD your God, who teaches you what is good for
you and leads you along the paths you should follow.

ISAIAH 48:17

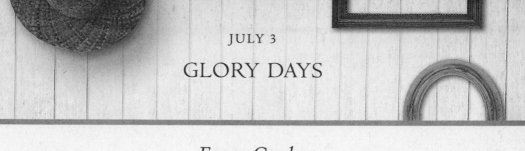

GLORY DAYS

Fanny Crosby
1820–1915

The teenage Fanny Crosby had been summoned to the superintendent's office at the New York Institution for the Blind. Since she was a prize student and already known as a promising writer, she had little fear about this encounter. "My friends had nearly spoiled me with their praises," she wrote later about her school days. She assumed the superintendent would ask her to write a new poem for the school. Not so.

"Fanny," the superintendent began, "I am sorry you have allowed yourself to be carried away by what others have said about your verses. True, you have written a number of poems of real merit; but how far do they fall short of the standard that you might attain?" It was important for her to "shun a flatterer," he said. "Remember that whatever talent you possess belongs wholly to God; and that you ought to give Him the credit for all that you do."

This story helps us understand how influential that school was in Fanny's spiritual and artistic development. It would be easy to pamper a blind student, heaping praise on everything she accomplished, but this educator challenged Fanny to do her best. In retrospect, Fanny herself admitted she had begun "to feel my own importance as a poet a little too much."

In our age of "self-esteem," the issues of praise and humility can get murky. We can and should take satisfaction in the good things we do, but it also helps to challenge ourselves to make maximum use of the abilities God has given us. Make no mistake: we are loved fully by God, even if we fail in our attempts at greatness. In fact, that confidence can set us free to reach even higher. We're not trying to earn God's love— we already have that—but we offer our best efforts for the greater glory of God.

After teaching at the same school she had attended, Fanny Crosby eased into professional songwriting, first collaborating on some popular and patriotic songs, then writing hymn texts. With a knack for expressing the Christian experience, Fanny Crosby changed church worship for the next century. One of her most beloved songs harkens back to that superintendent's office: "To God be the glory, great things he hath done."

Not to us, O Lord, not to us, but to your name goes all the
glory for your unfailing love and faithfulness.

PSALM 115:1

FREE TO BE THANKFUL

Julia Ward Howe
1819–1910

Five dollars. That's what Julia Ward Howe received from the *Atlantic Monthly* when it published "The Battle Hymn of the Republic" in 1862. You're probably familiar with the song.

> *Mine eyes have seen the glory of the coming of the Lord;*
> *He is trampling out the vintage where the grapes of wrath are stored;*
> *He hath loosed the fateful lightning of His terrible swift sword;*
> *His truth is marching on.*

This first verse and every verse of the song is followed by a hearty chorus: "Glory! Glory! Hallelujah!"

The story behind the Civil War anthem goes like this: Julia, already a notable writer and poet, had heard the Union troops singing the song "John Brown's Body." The simple marching song tells the tale of a Union soldier who died in battle so that slaves might be free. While his body "lies a-mouldering in the grave," his "soul goes marching on." So, while riding in a carriage, Julia and some friends were singing patriotic tunes . . . including that one. One of those companions, James Freeman Clarke, challenged Julia to write better words to the tune. Later that night, she awoke with the words in her head and quickly wrote them down.

The song caught on and became a leading anthem for the Civil War, the Union's answer to "Dixie." Soldiers sang it as they marched on in the war—certain that God's lightning from his "terrible swift sword" was on their side in the fight to abolish slavery. The story behind the creation of the lyrics only solidified that idea in the minds of many. From Julia's account, she did not make them up on her own; they were given to her. Some would say she was inspired.

Today is the Fourth of July, a day to show your patriotic spirit and be thankful. While it can be unwise to mix politics and Christianity, it makes sense to offer God thanks for the freedoms this nation affords to us and to others.

Spend some time thanking God today for the freedoms you enjoy.

You have been called to live in freedom, my brothers and
sisters. But don't use your freedom to satisfy your sinful nature.
Instead, use your freedom to serve one another in love.

GALATIANS 5:13

A GREAT GOOD

Harriet Beecher Stowe

1811–96

Her book sold more copies in 1852 than any other book but the Bible. Historians agree that it had great influence on the abolitionist movement and helped fuel the Civil War. Although Harriet Beecher Stowe's *Uncle Tom's Cabin* was instrumental in helping to end the pain and suffering that was slavery, the book was a result of the author's personal pain and suffering.

Harriet lost her infant son Samuel Charles to cholera in 1849. This tragedy gave Harriet a level of compassion for other mothers who had lost their children—not to death but to slave owners. In a letter to fellow writer Eliza Lee Cabot Follen, Harriet explained how her loss helped bring her to this compassion:

> *It was at his dying bed and at his grave that I learned what a poor slave mother may feel when her child is torn away from her. In those depths of sorrow which seemed to me immeasurable, it was my only prayer to God that such anguish might not be suffered in vain. There were circumstances about his death of such peculiar bitterness, of what seemed almost cruel suffering, that I felt that I could never be consoled for it, unless this crushing of my own heart might enable me to work out some great good to others.*

Her deep compassion for slave mothers who were separated from their children did bring about a great good, the novel *Uncle Tom's Cabin*. Harriet told Eliza that the roots of the book were in the "bitter sorrows of that summer."

In his letter to the Corinthians, Paul says God is the source of all comfort. God comforts us in our troubles, and in turn we can comfort others. "When they are troubled," Paul writes, "we will be able to give them the same comfort God has given us" (2 Corinthians 1:4).

Harriet sought comfort in God during her season of grief, and when her season was over, she was able to bring comfort to others.

Has God brought you through a season of heartbreak and sorrow in the past? Think of how you can use the wisdom, strength, and compassion you gained from your season of pain to do great good for someone else.

The LORD is close to the brokenhearted; he rescues those whose spirits are crushed.

PSALM 34:18

WHY, LORD?

Elizabeth Payson Prentiss

1818–78

Wake up, O Lord! Why do you sleep? Get up! Do not reject us forever. Why do you look the other way? Why do you ignore our suffering and oppression?"

Those words of Psalm 44:23-24, probably written by King David, are angry words. The Israelites had been defeated in battle, and it looked as if God had abandoned them.

Elizabeth Payson Prentiss understood feelings like those. In 1852, within a span of four months, she lost two children—a young son and then an infant daughter. Elizabeth was so ill herself that she got to hold the baby only twice.

In a poem about her children, she included this verse:

One child and two green graves are mine;
This is God's gift to me:
A bleeding, fainting, broken heart,—
This is my gift to Thee!

Elizabeth was, understandably, brokenhearted and angry at what God had allowed. Yet that anger didn't change her deepest feelings for God. In her best-known novel, *Stepping Heavenward*, written in 1869, she wrote, "You cannot prove to yourself that you love God by examining your feelings towards Him. They are indefinite and they fluctuate. But just as far as you obey Him, just so far, depend upon it, you love Him."

Broken hearts happen. Loved ones die. Jobs and security are lost. Dreams get shattered. Sometimes no matter how much you pray, no matter how much you get on your knees and beg, God seems to be asleep or looking the other way. Anger, bitterness, doubt, and confusion are natural reactions.

Those feelings, as Elizabeth said, are indefinite, and they fluctuate. At some point, her brokenheartedness lessened, and so did her anger toward God. She went on to write novels for children and adults, poems, and the hymn "More Love to Thee, O Christ."

If you're going through a tough time that has you angry or disappointed with God, it may help to know you're not the first to feel that way, and you won't be the last. Remember that while you're sifting through your feelings, your love for God is still there, and his love for you will never change.

Give thanks to the God of heaven. His faithful love endures forever.

PSALM 136:26

IN THE ARMY NOW

Catherine Booth

1829–90

Catherine Booth and her husband, William, understood something very important: serving the Lord is serious business. It's not a casual, when-you-get-around-to-it thing. It's a war, the church is God's army, and our "weapon" is love.

Reportedly, by the time she was twelve, Catherine had read through the Bible eight times. Though she was often sidelined because of a curvature of her spine, she managed to grow up into a bright, vivacious young woman, quite active in religious groups. Along the way, she fell in love with a talented young preacher named William Booth. They married in 1855.

Over the next dozen years or so, Catherine bore eight children, but she also participated in William's pastoral and evangelistic ministry, first by speaking in children's meetings and eventually by preaching to adults, as well. She had a knack for public speaking, clearly and logically setting forth her case and calling for a response. After hearing her speak, one man remarked, "If ever I am charged with a crime, don't bother to engage any of the great lawyers to defend me; get that woman!"

In 1865, the Booths held tent meetings in a poor section of London, and there they found their calling. Starting the Christian Revival Society (which later became the Christian Mission), they provided not only preaching, but also food.

William was dictating a letter in 1878 when he described the society as "a volunteer army." Hearing this, the oldest Booth boy, Bramwell, said, "I'm not a volunteer. I'm a regular." So the word *volunteer* was scratched and replaced with *salvation*. The organization has been known ever since as the Salvation Army.

The name provided a new theme for the ministry. Workers wore uniforms and were led by "officers." William Booth became the first "general," while Catherine was always known as the "mother" of the Salvation Army.

This was more than a gimmick. The military terms captured the importance of the cause as well as the need for complete dedication to it. They also created an argument for the participation of women in leadership—if our divine Commander-in-Chief is calling for people to serve in a "war effort," why should we care whether the officers are male or female?

Put on every piece of God's armor so you will be able
to resist the enemy in the time of evil.

EPHESIANS 6:13

THE LAST DROP

Catherine Booth

1829–90

As a teenage girl in 1840s England, Catherine Mumford served as secretary of the Juvenile Temperance Society. She used her emerging literary talents to write for a temperance magazine. Alcohol was prevalent in that society, and it was ruining many lives. People of faith, especially Methodists like Catherine, pushed back. Later she got involved with the Band of Hope, an organization promoting total abstinence from alcohol. When she first met William Booth, her husband-to-be, he was reciting a poem about giving up grog.

The Salvation Army, founded by William and Catherine Booth, became known for its opposition to liquor. This was part of its overall outreach to people in poor neighborhoods where drunkenness was common and quite destructive. In England and the United States, the temperance movement grew through the nineteenth century and into the twentieth, with the Salvation Army as a key player. (If you've ever seen the musical *Guys and Dolls*, you've seen this clash of cultures—the serious-minded Salvationist trying to reform the drinking, carousing gamblers.) The movement's greatest victory, the United States' Prohibition amendment in 1919, became its greatest loss. Not only was the amendment repealed in 1933, but the general public seemed to repudiate the whole idea of temperance.

It's a different world today, but many things remain the same. Substance abuse is rampant—not only alcoholism, but also addiction to other dangerous drugs. Once again we're seeing lives ruined through *in*temperate behavior. Self-control is a forgotten virtue.

We might look at Catherine Booth's commitment to temperance as a quaint relic from the past, but she got one thing very right. There is power in a relationship with Jesus Christ. That power can break a person's dependence on alcohol or other substances. We're not ignoring the physical aspects of addiction, but there's a spiritual component as well. And Jesus still works miracles. The Booths preached this in countless meetings in down-and-out neighborhoods. It's just as true today in posh suburbs, office buildings, and red-light districts. Whatever your addiction might be, Jesus calls you to bring it before him. Declare your dependence on him, and trust him to help you put your life back together.

Oh, what a miserable person I am! Who will free me from this life that is dominated by sin and death? Thank God! The answer is in Jesus Christ our Lord.

ROMANS 7:24-25

TROUBLESHOOTER

Evangeline Booth

1865–1950

S he got her name from three other women who appear in this book. Her mother, Catherine Booth, liked the character of Eva in *Uncle Tom's Cabin*, written by Harriet Beecher Stowe. Then, when Eva Booth was nearly forty, the American activist Frances Willard suggested she go by the more religious sounding "Evangeline."

As the daughter of the founders of the Salvation Army, Eva got into the ministry early as a singer and actress at her parents' meetings. At age fifteen, she wore the uniform and began preaching. Few understood the mission as well as Eva did. Her parents learned that they could trust her with leadership. As troubles broke out—persecution from communities or dissatisfaction in the ranks—William would often say, "Send Eva!"

Perhaps her most significant troubleshooting experience came in 1896 when Eva was sent to New York to rein in a breakaway group led by her brother Ballington. Locked out of the Salvation Army building, she climbed a fire escape to get in. Then, jeered by the rebel group, she literally wrapped herself in an American flag and said, "Hiss that, if you dare." Then, in the stunned silence, she began to play her concertina and sing. Order was restored.

In 1904, Eva was named the Salvation Army's commander for the United States, a post she held for thirty years. During that time, she became a US citizen and took the name Evangeline. Among her creative projects was the sending of Salvation Army personnel to support the soldiers on the front lines of World War I. She was named general of the entire Salvation Army in 1934.

With her pedigree, it's no surprise that Evangeline Booth would get such leadership opportunities, but she also made the most of them. Courageous and creative, she was an inspiring leader, a much-needed bridge connecting future generations with her parents' original vision.

Each one of us is a mixture of what we've been given and what we do with it. What sort of birth and upbringing have you had? You may have received certain opportunities or challenges from your parents, but that's only part of your story. What are you and God going to do next?

Direct your children onto the right path, and when they are older, they will not leave it.

PROVERBS 22:6

INFORMATION PLEASE

Angelina Grimke
1805–79

Angelina Grimke was an amazing woman. Born into a Southern slave-owning family in 1805, she eventually moved up north to join the abolitionist movement. Her antislavery stance was very much rooted in her Christian faith. When she spoke out against slavery to crowds of both men and women, she found herself criticized by those who thought that women had no legal or spiritual right to advise men. Soon Angelina was part of the suffrage movement, also.

An educated woman, Angelina cherished her ability to read because it helped her form opinions about things. She also believed in reading before she went to God in prayer. "I have not placed reading before praying because I regard it more important," she said, "but because, in order to pray aright, we must understand what we are praying for."

In today's world, it's easy to form opinions from sound bites on TV, radio talk-show hosts, or headlines linked to our social media pages. We may have a passing knowledge of many trivial subjects, but if we're honest, much of our data is drawn from unsupported conversation threads on the web. Information has never been more readily at our fingertips, yet becoming truly informed from reliable sources seems to be something we have little time for.

This can also be true with spiritual knowledge. We can easily form opinions about spiritual matters in a similar, never-get-past-the-headline manner. We know what our friends in Bible study think. We know what the Christian talk-show host thinks. Their opinions may be worth taking into consideration, but before we form our own opinions, it's best to figure out what God thinks.

That's where Angelina's reading-before-praying strategy comes in. The Bible is sitting right there on your coffee table or waiting to be opened on your phone or tablet. Read it. Inform yourself from God's Word before heading into prayer to ask for further guidance. It's not more important than prayer, but as Angelina pointed out, it helps to understand what you're praying for.

What spiritual matter are you trying to form an opinion about? Find key Bible passages that pertain to the subject, read them carefully, and then make it a matter of prayer.

Open my eyes to see the wonderful truths in your instructions.

PSALM 119:18

FIRST RESPONDER

Elizabeth Blackwell

1821–1910

E lizabeth Blackwell was the definition of a pioneer. She was the first to brave new territory—the previously all-male realm of medical school.

Before her acceptance to New York's Geneva Medical College, Elizabeth applied to twenty-eight medical colleges. None of them had ever admitted a female student. The story goes that Geneva accepted her application because they allowed the male students to vote on it, and the students voted yes as a joke.

Through hard work, Elizabeth earned the respect of her fellow students and teachers, graduating with honors in 1849 and becoming the first woman in the United States to earn a medical degree. And she was apparently a role model. Shortly afterward, her sister Emily earned the same degree.

How does a woman like Elizabeth find the courage to buck an established system like the male-dominated medical profession in the mid-1800s? Certainly she had an inner strength. She also had a family who believed in her and encouraged her. When others outside her family thought her goal was impossible, Elizabeth's family encouraged her to keep trying.

Her father, Samuel, raised his family with progressive ideals. One of her brothers married an abolitionist who kept her maiden name. Another brother married a woman who became the first woman ordained in the United States. Elizabeth was surrounded by people who encouraged women to take professional and spiritual leadership roles. In her efforts to bring genuinely Christian principles into her medical work, she found support from an impressive group of friends.

You may have a family that's as supportive as Elizabeth's was; you may not. We don't get to choose our families. We do get to choose our friends.

Consider the friends that you choose to be close to you. Do they support you and encourage you to excel at home, at work, and in your spiritual life? The Bible says, "As iron sharpens iron, so a friend sharpens a friend" (Proverbs 27:17). The friends you select can sharpen and encourage, even if your family does not. And don't forget that you have the ability to sharpen others too.

Do you have a friend or family member who can use some encouragement to reach a goal? What can you do to help that person today?

Encourage each other and build each other up, just as you are already doing.

1 THESSALONIANS 5:11

CARRYING THE CROSS

Eliza Shirley

1863–1932

A brass band playing gospel songs? Really? Holding religious services on city streets, in front of taverns? It's hard to fully appreciate how outrageous the Salvation Army was when it started. William and Catherine Booth began an innovative ministry in England in the 1860s, but it wasn't until 1878 that they gave this organization its name: the Salvation Army. If they were serious about offering salvation, the Booths reasoned, they would have to go where the sinners were—out to the streets, the slums, the pubs.

At one of these open-air meetings in her hometown, fifteen-year-old Eliza Shirley was dazzled. She saw women offering a call to salvation as fervently as any man would. Her father was a part-time preacher, and Eliza had grown up mimicking his style. Now, perhaps, she could put all that "training" to good use. Answering a call to dedicate her life to Christian service, she eagerly stepped up to join the Salvation Army. Her parents made her wait until she was sixteen.

Shortly after her birthday, she and another young woman were appointed to the Salvation Army's work in a coal-mining town in northern England. It was a difficult area, but they began to see conversions among the miners. Then Eliza received word that her parents were moving to America and wanted her to come along. When she talked with William Booth about the move, he reminded her of her commitment to the ministry. They were doing great work in England; they needed everyone on board. Yet somehow that conversation included the possibility of Eliza starting a new Salvation Army operation in the United States. Booth wouldn't commit any official support or funding, but he let Eliza use the Salvation Army name.

So in 1880, the Shirley family sailed to Philadelphia, where with the help of her parents, Eliza set up a new outreach to the poor and spiritually needy. In time, William Booth recognized her work and sent support. Soon the Army's salvation message was spreading through the cities of a new continent.

Genuine ministry is hard to contain. You can try to limit it to one place, one style, or one type of people, but the Spirit of God keeps expanding outward. Whatever ministry you're involved with, let Eliza's story convince you to consider where it's going *next*.

I will pour out my Spirit upon all people. Your sons and daughters will prophesy.

JOEL 2:28

RESISTANCE

Jarena Lee

1783–?

G o preach the gospel!"
Imagine hearing that message directly from God himself. Would your reaction be something like this? "God, you've got the wrong person. Someone else would be better." It's an excuse as old as Moses.

Now imagine it's around the year 1800, and you're a young black adult—the child of freed slaves, uneducated, poor, and a woman. That woman was Jarena Lee.

Convinced that God was calling her to preach, Jarena Lee ignored her doubts. She went to Richard Allen, the founder of the African Methodist Episcopal Church, and told him what God had said to her. Allen shut her down, insisting that women should not preach. Jarena was silenced by Allen's words . . . for a while. But years later, Jarena couldn't contain herself. While Richard Allen was preaching about Jonah resisting God, Jarena stood up and said that she, too, had resisted God's calling.

The congregation must have been shocked. A woman had interrupted the preacher! Surely there would be consequences. There were, but not as anyone expected. Allen granted her permission to preach. And so Jarena Lee became the first woman preacher in the African Methodist Episcopal Church. At the height of her ministry, she was preaching more than seven hundred times a year.

It's easy to make excuses for ignoring what God says to do, especially when it seems that people are trying to block your path. Their words of doubt can be a good excuse for you to ignore God when he has something uncomfortable or scary for you to do.

The thing is, God can move those people aside. If God has asked you to do something, he will give you what you need to do it. The strongest obstacle may be your own resistance.

What have you been putting off because of doubts that others have put in your head? If you're sure God wants you to do it, take their doubts out of the equation and figure out how to move forward.

Now go! I will be with you as you speak, and I will instruct you in what to say.

EXODUS 4:12

QUICKSILVER

Frances Ridley Havergal

—— 1836–79 ——

This child was so clever, her father called her "Little Quicksilver." Frances Ridley Havergal was reading at age three, memorizing the Bible at age four, and writing poetry at age seven. Poor health kept her from attending school on a regular basis, but her father (an Anglican minister) had a great library, so her homeschooling process was pretty thorough. She learned six or seven languages in her youth, plus biblical Greek and Hebrew.

It was an interesting time for British believers. Many were seeking a deeper knowledge of God—some through academic study, some through tradition, and others through emotional experiences. Frances had grown up as a good Anglican, and she made a personal commitment to Christ at the age of fourteen. This gave Frances something to write about. The rest of her life, she composed faith-filled poems, hymn texts, and even some tracts, in addition to the insightful letters she wrote to friends.

Commitment became a regular theme for Frances, especially in her hymns. In one of her best-known works she wrote the line, "Take my life and let it be consecrated, Lord, to Thee." Consecration involves a complete devotion of one's life—body, mind, money, time, etc. She also wrote "I Am Trusting Thee," "Who Is on the Lord's Side?," and "I Gave My Life for Thee." Each of these texts assumes a simple transaction—Jesus has given it all for us; we can trust him with everything.

Frances described her own songwriting in the same way. "I . . . feel like a little child writing," she wrote in one letter. "You know a child would look up at every sentence and say 'What shall I say next?' That is just what I do; Every line and word and rhyme comes from God." Elsewhere she said that she had to smile when people talked about how clever or gifted she was. "It is neither, but something really much nicer."

She was talking about the process of writing God-directed songs from a God-directed life. When you're trusting God to live through you, you can't take credit for your own works, no matter how clever. You are the vessel for God's amazing activity—and that is indeed "much nicer."

My old self has been crucified with Christ. It is no longer I who live,
but Christ lives in me. So I live in this earthly body by trusting in
the Son of God, who loved me and gave himself for me.

GALATIANS 2:20

PERFECT PEACE

Frances Ridley Havergal
1836–79

In addition to the substantial number of hymns she wrote, Frances Ridley Havergal maintained correspondence with several friends. In today's world of tweets and e-mail, letter writing might already be a lost art form. Fortunately, some of Havergal's friends kept her letters and later shared them. These epistles often contain important nuggets of spiritual wisdom.

For instance, writing to a friend who was struggling with doubt about her salvation, Frances quoted the promise of Romans 5:1—"Being justified by faith, we have peace with God through our Lord Jesus Christ" (KJV). She went on to say that this peace is "yours already, purchased for you, made for you, sealed for you, pledged to you—by the word of the Father and the 'precious blood of Jesus!'" Apparently, Frances recognized the vicious circle that many Christians get into, struggling to feel at peace. The harder they struggle, the less peace they feel, which makes them struggle more. But God's peace is a gift already given. We don't have to fight for it.

Frances developed this idea in the lyrics to one stately hymn that's still sung today:

> Like a river glorious, is God's perfect peace,
> Over all victorious, in its bright increase;
> Perfect, yet it floweth, fuller every day,
> Perfect, yet it groweth, deeper all the way.

Perfectionism was a big issue among Christians in the mid-1800s. Shouldn't we seek to become so sanctified, committed to Christ and led by the Spirit, that we are essentially living sin-free lives? Different churches had different takes on the matter, and new movements were formed on this principle. Without getting too deep into the theology of it all, we should point out the cleverness of Frances's poetry in this song. If something is already perfect, how can it get fuller and deeper? And yet, that's the experience of the growing believer.

Frances Ridley Havergal lived only to the age of forty-two. She wrote the text for about fifty hymns—an impressive number, but far from the output of Watts or Wesley or Crosby. Still, her smart but simple approach to Christian commitment was an important gift to the church at a crucial time.

You will keep in perfect peace all who trust in you, all whose thoughts are fixed on you!

ISAIAH 26:3

COUNTERINTELLIGENCE

Frances Ridley Havergal
1836–79

Every so often, some historian tries to figure out the most influential figures in Christian history. Popes and reformers, preachers and theologians—cases can be made for all of them. But don't forget the hymn writers. These people have shaped Christian worship through the centuries, putting words in our mouths week after week.

It's actually possible to trace trends in Christian thinking through the songs sung in different eras. The Methodist revolution of the 1700s owed as much to Charles Wesley's hymns as to John Wesley's preaching. And Fanny Crosby's experiential lyrics helped to fuel a recovery of personal faith in the late 1800s.

For a rather short time in the mid-1800s, the English hymn writer Frances Ridley Havergal was moving in a slightly different direction. Her songs were not so much about personal feeling but more about individual commitment. Where Charles Wesley was teaching theology and Fanny Crosby was marketing it, Frances was exploring how to *live it out*. Her hymns were embraced by those in the Keswick ("Higher Life") movement that was developing at the time.

Frances's best-known hymn is probably "Take My Life and Let It Be," in which she offers various aspects of her life for the Lord's use—hands, feet, voice, lips, money, intellect, will, heart. She also wrote a sort of commentary on that song: *Kept for the Master's Use*, a booklet with a chapter on each of those aspects of life.

In her section on intellect, she suggested that "two distinct sets of temptations" afflict those who think they're smart and those who don't. The nonintellectuals "are tempted to think themselves excused from effort to cultivate and use their small intellectual gifts," while the intellectuals "are tempted to rely on their natural gifts, and to act and speak in their own strength."

It's a great observation, and it rings true. In her time and place, there were plenty of religious academics who were analyzing Scripture beyond recognition. There were also those who simplified the faith to whatever made them feel good. We still have those extremes today. Frances asserted, "The intellect, whether great or small, which is committed to the Lord's keeping, will be kept and will be used by Him."

So the question for you is not how much "intellect" you have, but what you're doing with it.

May all my thoughts be pleasing to him,
for I rejoice in the LORD.

PSALM 104:34

EMBRACING DIFFERENCES

Frances Willard

1839–98

"A general with an army of 250,000" is how suffragist Susan B. Anthony introduced Frances Willard to a United States Senate Committee in 1895. People were drawn to Frances and her opinions.

And, wow, did this woman have opinions. She championed women's rights, antirape laws, children's rights, suffrage, the eight-hour workday, access to education, unions, prison reform, and sanitation. She held the position of dean of women at Northwestern University and also published a magazine. She preached, too, and was a strong supporter of women's ordination.

What Frances is most remembered for, though, is her work as the president of the Women's Christian Temperance Union (WCTU). The union's purpose was to promote a "sober and pure world." Abstinence from alcohol was part of the movement, but just a part. The WCTU worked to alleviate many social problems. They saw alcoholism as a social problem, but they also saw inequality of rights as a social problem. Frances fought for a wide variety of social reforms. Anyone who thinks of her as simply a woman who wanted to keep people from enjoying a stiff drink is missing the much larger picture.

Nowadays Christians take different stances on the issue of alcohol, and of course on many other issues as well. Often believers on both sides of an issue can cite Bible verses to back their opinions. So how do you handle it when you have a relationship with another Christian who is really great in so many areas but differs with you on an issue or two? Maybe you think a glass of wine is okay occasionally, and he thinks it's never okay. Perhaps she thinks you shouldn't shop on Sunday, and you have no problem stopping to grab groceries on your way home from church. There are dozens of issues like this—social, political, and theological.

In the book of Romans, Paul urges Christians not to condemn people who differ on these issues. If we're all trying to please the Lord, we should live in harmony despite our differing opinions. Do you have room in your heart to "agree to disagree" on issues like this with others who have faith in the same Lord you do?

Why do you condemn another believer? Why do you look down on another believer? Remember, we will all stand before the judgment seat of God.

ROMANS 14:10

WHAT'S IN A NAME?

Sojourner Truth

1797–1893

"What's in a name?" That famous question from *Romeo and Juliet* is one many people think about. *What does my name mean? Does it fit me?* For Isabella, born into slavery and treated harshly for the first three decades of her life, her birth name was no longer meaningful after she was freed. So she changed it.

As a slave in New York State, Isabella had endured all sorts of difficulties. She was beaten by an angry master when she became pregnant by a slave on a neighboring farm. Forced to marry an older slave from her farm, she gave birth to four children. After one of those children was sold illegally and sent to Alabama, Isabella escaped. She found refuge in the home of a kind white couple who paid her master to allow her to work for them, but as a housekeeper and not a slave. In this home, she became a Christian.

New York was in the midst of a long process of emancipating slaves. In 1827, Isabella finally won her freedom. She actually went to court to get back her son, and she won.

After serving in several homes as a housekeeper, she found a new career path in 1843. "The Spirit calls me, I must go," she told her friends. Taking on her new name, Sojourner Truth, she became an itinerant preacher, traveling the country promoting abolition of slavery, women's rights, and religious understanding.

The new name fit her. She was sojourning in the cause of truth. The slave Isabella was gone. The preacher Sojourner Truth, a new person called to serve God and tell others about the gospel, was born.

Have you ever thought of what your name would be if you could change it to one that fits you now? In the Bible, people's names often reflected their characters. If they weren't given those names at birth, they took them on later as nicknames (like Peter the Rock or Barnabas the Encourager).

Based on your strengths, your personality, your experiences, and what God has done for you, what name would you pick for yourself that reflects who you are now?

The nations will see your righteousness. World leaders will be blinded by your glory. And you will be given a new name by the LORD's own mouth.

ISAIAH 62:2

IT TAKES BOTH SUN AND RAIN

Sarah Adams

1805–48

Sarah Adams loved the theater and hoped to be an actress. She even had some success in the field. In 1937 her portrayal of Lady Macbeth on the London stage received very favorable reviews, but poor health kept her from continuing her acting career.

Yet her creativity couldn't be squashed, and she turned to writing poems and hymns. One of her most famous works is the hymn "Nearer, My God, to Thee." She wrote it for a pastor who was working on a sermon about Jacob's dream of a stairway leading to heaven (see Genesis 28:10-17). When the minister complained that he couldn't find an appropriate hymn to accompany his talk, Sarah offered to write one, and she did. The song is still sung in churches today, inspiring people of faith who are seeking to feel physically and spiritually close to God.

Where did Sarah get her inspiration after she was unable to continue acting? How was she able to give up the stage and embrace the idea that there was something else for her—writing? Perhaps one of her poems has some answers.

> He sendeth sun, he sendeth shower,
> Alike they're needful for the flower:
> And joys and tears alike are sent
> To give the soul fit nourishment.
> As comes to me or cloud or sun,
> Father! thy will, not mine, be done!

She recognized that God had plans for her (plans to prosper her and to give her hope and a future, according to the prophet Jeremiah), and that sometimes it takes both sun and rain, good times and bad times, to understand what those plans are and then get down to doing them.

Like Sarah, you might not be doing what you hoped you would be when you got to this stage of life. If you're not, can you get a glimpse of God's larger plan? Can you accept the rain as well as the sun?

How do you know what your life will be like tomorrow? Your life is like the morning fog—it's here a little while, then it's gone. What you ought to say is, "If the Lord wants us to, we will live and do this or that."

JAMES 4:14-15

FINDING YOUR PURPOSE

Mary Lyon
1797–1849

A pioneer is anyone who leads the way to a place where no one has gone before. Mary Lyon was a pioneer in education—women's education, to be exact. At a time when female education was often limited to reading, basic arithmetic, drawing, needlework, and other subjects that were considered suitable for ladies, Mary worked tirelessly to create a women's college that was every bit as academically challenging as a school for men.

After twenty years of teaching, Mary decided to leave her job and devote herself to raising funds to build an institution of higher education for women. Three years later, she opened the doors of Mount Holyoke Female Seminary with rigorous academic entrance requirements and a curriculum equivalent to those at men's colleges. Mount Holyoke was the first of what became the Seven Sisters—seven all-female colleges that became counterparts to the then male-dominated Ivy League schools.

The school also had a spiritual core. Teachers would meet to pray for students, and revival services were common. Time was set aside in the school day for personal prayer and meditation. In those early years, many of the graduates were sent out as missionaries to foreign lands or the American West.

Mary has been quoted as saying, "There is nothing in the universe that I fear, but that I shall not know all my duty, or shall fail to do it." Mary felt it was her duty, her purpose in life, to start a school like Mount Holyoke. She created the type of college that she would have liked to attend as a young woman, if only it had existed.

It can take some time to find your purpose in life; that's not unusual. But when you do find a purpose, are you committed to pursuing it, as Mary did?

In your search for purpose, it's good to consult people you can trust, people who know you and can give you honest feedback about your thoughts and ideas. But there's someone else you need to include too: God.

If you're searching for your purpose or you're already in the midst of fulfilling it, don't forget to spend time consulting God each step of the way.

Seek his will in all you do,
and he will show you which path to take.

PROVERBS 3:6

MAKING THE MOST OF IT

Mary Ann Paton

1840–59

Imagine this. You're eighteen. You marry a man fifteen years older than you. Two weeks later, you set off from Scotland to an island in the South Pacific you've never heard of—all because your husband has accepted a charge to be a missionary. When you arrive, you find natives who have never been reached by anyone from the West before. They're naked. They're painted. And they're cannibals.

This is the situation Mary Ann Paton found herself in during the first year of her marriage. The honeymoon, if there ever was one, was definitely over.

It's not clear if Mary Ann shared her husband's calling as a missionary or if she went out of a sense of duty. Either way, you have to imagine that she was out of her element on that island. And there's one detail that's been left out. By the time she and her husband, John, arrived there, she was pregnant. (Okay, maybe there was a *short* honeymoon.)

Even then, it seems Mary made the most of her situation. She brought women together for Bible study. Sadly, her time on that island (known as Tanna) didn't last long. Shortly after the birth of her son, Peter, she contracted a fever and died. Peter died less than a month later.

Mary Ann's influence didn't die with her, though. Her grave still exists in Tanna, inspiring modern missionaries who are thankful for the foundation that she and her husband laid for them 150 years ago. John stayed four years after her death, introducing the Tannese to the gospel until he needed to leave because his life was in danger.

We never know how much time we have. Sure, there's the old "you may get hit by a bus tomorrow" mind-set, but it's not always death that cuts efforts short. You could get laid off from a job that you love, and where you're doing good work. You could be working in a thriving ministry in your church, and have to move because a job takes you away.

Mary Ann's life and all-too-early death can be a reminder to make the most of the time that's right in front of us, because we truly don't know what tomorrow holds.

Don't brag about tomorrow,
since you don't know what the day will bring.

PROVERBS 27:1

INVESTING IN TOMORROW

Anna Shaw

1847–1919

Considered one of the influential leaders of the women's suffrage movement, Anna Shaw worked tirelessly for women's causes throughout her life. She frequently worked side by side with Susan B. Anthony. But she wasn't just an activist; she was a minister in the Methodist Protestant Church. Her views on equality for women came from her belief that women and men are equal in God's eyes. And even when she resigned from ministry to focus on some of her social causes, her thorough knowledge of the Bible and her skill in preaching proved valuable.

Though Anna dedicated much of her life to women's issues, she died without seeing the final results of her fight. About a year before the Nineteenth Amendment of the US Constitution gave women the right to vote, she died of pneumonia at the age of seventy-two.

If Anna had known that she wouldn't live to see the final outcome, would she have dedicated such a large part of her life to the cause of women's suffrage? Most likely. She believed that what she was fighting for was what God wanted.

When God wants you to do something, he never promises that you'll get to do it from beginning to end, see the fruits of your labor, and get recognition for your efforts. He only promises that he'll be with you during the process.

Maybe you'll jump-start a program at your child's school during his last year there—a program that will end up benefiting other children, but not your own. Or maybe you'll implement a new process at work that will help everyone perform more efficiently—right before you take another job elsewhere. Perhaps you'll start a new ministry at church that someone else will ultimately lead.

Whatever it is, you can only do what God is calling you to do and not worry about how long you'll be doing it, whether you'll get to see it through to the end, or if you'll get recognition for your efforts.

What is God nudging you to do? Don't even think about whether you'll be around to reap the benefits. The benefit comes from obeying God and letting him work through you.

We can make our plans, but the LORD determines our steps.

PROVERBS 16:9

MOON MISSION

Lottie Moon

1840–1912

Three billion dollars—a huge sum of money in any era. In the late 1800s, that was most likely an unimaginable sum to someone like Lottie Moon. A Southern Baptist missionary in China, Lottie struggled to collect even the smallest donations during her early years of ministry, and the needs were great.

Lottie was already thirty-two when she followed the Lord's calling into missionary service. She was frustrated by the restrictions placed on her as a single woman in ministry—basically, she was relegated to teaching women and children—but she soon grabbed this as a unique area of ministry. "Women and children" constituted significantly more than half of the Chinese population, and she could reach them in ways that men never could. Soon she was running herself ragged and imploring the missions board to send more missionaries. There just wasn't enough money.

But in December 1887, Lottie wrote an article that appeared in the denominational missions journal, suggesting that churches take up a special offering for foreign missions the week before Christmas. The idea was picked up, mostly by the women's missionary societies in Baptist churches. That first year, $3,315 was collected in these special offerings—enough to send out three more missionaries.

And the giving hasn't stopped. In the years since then, the annual "Lottie Moon Christmas Offering" has brought in three billion dollars for international missions. And it all started with one overworked woman who didn't mind asking for help.

How good are you at asking for help from others? Or even from God? We're created to need God and each other. It should be natural to ask for help and to give help. But our culture frequently makes us question whether asking for help will make others think less of us. We're told it might make us look needy or weak or unintelligent or unprofessional. Someone might figure out that we're not perfect if we ask for help, and then what would happen?

What *would* happen? Chances are, help would happen. Our friends, family, and neighbors most likely would ask, "What do you need?" Even when help cannot come from other people, God has promised to help, if we just ask.

I look up to the mountains—does my help come from there? My help comes from the LORD, who made heaven and earth!

PSALM 121:1-2

VILLAGE TO VILLAGE

Lottie Moon

1840–1912

As you wend your way from village to village, you feel it is no idle fancy that the Master walks beside you and you hear his voice saying gently, "Lo! I am with you always even unto the end."

Every so often you'll see a Christian interviewed on TV, and in the course of conversation, they'll say something like, "The Lord told me that I should. . . ." It doesn't really matter what the resulting action is. The Lord told him or her to change jobs or to write a book or to call a friend that person hadn't seen for a while. Whatever it is, the interviewer usually finds it strange. There's a smirk, a roll of the eyes. "You mean God talks to you?"

And we, the Christian viewers out there in TV land, are saying, "Well, yes! Of course! Why wouldn't he talk to us?" It's not strange at all. God has always spoken to his people. It's usually not audible—it's a feeling, a whisper in the soul—but we know his voice.

That's what Lottie Moon describes in this simple quote. She was a dynamo of a missionary, reportedly four-foot-three and very smart. When she finally got to the mission field at age thirty-two, she poured herself into the work, dressing and speaking as her Chinese neighbors did. Always outspoken, she challenged her coworkers, her missions board, and the churches back home to do more to win the world for Christ. She often expressed frustration when things weren't being done efficiently. For one thing, she saw that women missionaries were kept from doing effective ministry because of outmoded customs, even though the women of China were a vast, unreached mission field.

So we might picture her power walking to yet another village to do God's bidding, and wondering in her wending what challenges await her there. And there, beside her, she senses the Master himself with a message of comfort, a message of support.

Where are you going to be "wending" today, tomorrow, this week? What will your mind be mulling over as you go? Frustrations? Disappointments? Worries? Look over and see Jesus matching you stride for stride. He is with you, and he'll be with you always.

Go and make disciples of all the nations . . . And be sure of this:
I am with you always, even to the end of the age.

MATTHEW 28:19-20

WHO'S GOT YOUR BACK?

Abigail Roberts

1791–1841

No matter what stage of life you're in, there are people who will give you a hard time. It can happen in school, your neighborhood, the workplace, and sadly, even within the Christian community.

Abigail Roberts had this experience two hundred years ago. Brought up as a Quaker, she attended churches of several different denominations as a young adult. At some point in her twenties, after her marriage, she felt inspired to become a preacher. She joined the Christian Connection Church, a church that had ordained women since the early 1800s.

Dedicated to her ministry, Abigail preached throughout New York and New Jersey, often in churches she had helped to establish. Churches exist today in northwestern New Jersey that can claim Abigail Roberts as a church planter.

What problem could other Christians have with Abigail, who led many people to faith and helped establish churches? She was a woman. Christian denominations that did not approve of women preachers condemned her ministry.

Her son Philetus wrote in his *Memoir of Mrs. Abigail Roberts* that when attending a meeting of another denomination, she "would sometimes hear the professed minister of Christ denounce her, calling her a deceiver, and, at the same time, would unblushingly falsify and misrepresent her views."

It must have been difficult to sit in a pew and listen to someone of her same faith call her names. How did she endure?

Certainly, she was devoted to God. She also clung to her calling as a preacher, committed to her belief that women had a right to exercise their gifts in the church. And she surrounded herself with people who encouraged her and, as we say today, "had her back." Her husband, her friend Nancy Gove Cram (another female preacher), and the members of her church surely provided necessary encouragement.

Whether women should preach remains a contentious issue in many churches today, and we don't mean to shrug it off. We would hope that the debates would be marked by Christian charity rather than name-calling. But Abigail Roberts does inspire a different question for us: When you're doing what you believe God wants you to do but are getting a hard time from others, who helps you sort that out? Who will have your back?

Encourage each other and build each other up, just as you are already doing.

1 THESSALONIANS 5:11

DOUBLE STANDARDS

Josephine Butler

1828–1906

G od and one woman make a majority."

So said Josephine Butler as she fought the double standards of England's Victorian era. On the surface, British society was all very proper. Public standards of behavior were maintained. But there was a hidden hypocrisy that all too often worked against women and children. Josephine sought to expose and eradicate that.

As a devout Christian, she surprised some people by taking an interest in the welfare of prostitutes. While she opposed the business of prostitution, she showed compassion for the women caught up in it, sometimes even bringing them into her home. Politically, she worked to repeal the Contagious Disease Acts—which included a law that required suspected prostitutes, but not those who hired them, to be examined for venereal disease.

After a victory on that front, she turned her attention to forced child prostitution. Her efforts exposed England's rampant but long-hidden problems in this area, changing the legal age of sexual consent from thirteen to sixteen.

Josephine knew right from wrong, but she also understood that Victorian society made it difficult for women trapped in certain circumstances to do the right thing. Society created unfair rules and laws about what women could and couldn't do, leaving them with limited choices. Instead of judging these women for their sins, Josephine looked at the big picture. She saw a society that worked against these women, and she fought for changes, even against strong opposition. Among other projects, she promoted education for women and girls, so they could find a respectable place in this society. Often she was that "one woman" who, with God on her side, would form a majority.

It's easy to judge someone's actions without considering the circumstances. We like to maintain moral standards in society, and that might tempt us to put down those who don't comply. But often there's a story behind the story. We mustn't wink at wrongdoing, but Jesus insists that we show compassion.

When you encounter people who have done wrong, are you able to look past what they've done to understand why they've done it? Even more, like Josephine, are you willing to figure out how to help them into a situation where they don't feel the need to do it again?

You must be compassionate, just as your Father is compassionate.
Do not judge others, and you will not be judged. Do not
condemn others, or it will all come back against you.

LUKE 6:36-37

PRAYING FOR GIRLS

Harriet Winslow

1796–1833

We know it as Sri Lanka, but when the American Board of Commissioners for Foreign Missions sent Harriet Winslow and her husband there, the island was known as Ceylon. The Winslows worked with the people of the region, and Harriet took a special interest in making sure that girls received an education.

Eventually, Harriet was able to open an all-girls boarding school, the Missionary Seminary and Female Central School. The girls attended classes in sewing and household skills as many girls of the time did, and of course they were taught about Christianity. Harriet also made sure they had lessons in arithmetic and geography, subjects that were usually taught only to boys. The school is still in existence today as the Udival Girls' College and has more than one thousand girls, ages five through eighteen, enrolled.

Harriet's care for the girls went beyond school hours, though. It's said that Harriet chose one girl each day to remember while she was saying her prayers. We don't know exactly what she prayed for, other than their general well-being, but she probably prayed that the girls, brought up in a predominately Hindu region, would embrace Christianity.

Harriet's prayers ended when she was thirty-six years old. She died suddenly in childbirth. There's no telling what difference her prayers for those girls and young women made, but we can be assured they did make a difference.

Girls today still need older women to pray for them, and Harriet's example of praying each night for a different girl is an inspiring one. Think about all the girls and young women you come in contact with: daughters, nieces, girls in your church, neighbors, girls from your community, perhaps even students. They need prayer.

If this idea appeals to you, go for it. Make a list of girls you can be praying for, with a few specific requests for each one. Then rotate them into your daily prayers. You might want to tell them you're praying for them or just keep that between you and the Lord. Either way, it will be exciting to see how your prayers impact their lives.

I urge you, first of all, to pray for all people. Ask God to help them; intercede on their behalf, and give thanks for them.

1 TIMOTHY 2:1

CONFIDENCE WITHOUT CREDENTIALS

Nancy Gove Cram

1776–1816

Try making sense of this insult: "She is abundantly gifted with that spirit of her head, which opposes literature, order, and whatever Christians usually have considered, as of vital importance to the interests of religion."

A Presbyterian minister by the name of Gilbert McMaster wrote these words about Nancy Gove Cram. He thought she was crude and an outrage. Why? It was the early 1800s and few women dared to preach, but Nancy did. Not only did she preach, but she did so without the accepted education or credentials. She hadn't formally studied the Bible; she wasn't ordained.

In other words, she had confidence ("gifted with that spirit of her head") that even though she didn't have a formal education ("opposes literature, order"), she had relevant things to say about God even though she wasn't ordained (what "Christians usually have considered, as of vital importance to the interests of religion").

Despite a lack of experience and credentials, Nancy didn't offend everyone with her preaching. Instead, she inspired many. Her preaching began after she said a prayer at a funeral that greatly moved those who heard it. Later she was asked to hold a gospel meeting. When she accepted, her gospel-spreading career was born.

From then on, Nancy spoke wherever she could. She was instrumental in the start of two churches in New York and preached to the Oneida Indians. Seven people she helped become Christians later became preachers. Two of them were women.

Nancy knew that formal study in the Bible was good, but it wasn't necessary for a Christian to be able to talk about God. God teaches us in many ways—through the Bible, through other Christians, through our experiences, and through the quiet time we spend with him. When you want to talk about God with others, don't worry that your credentials might not be good enough. It's okay to trust "the spirit of your head," your confidence in your authentic relationship with God.

The LORD asked Moses, "Who makes a person's mouth? Who decides whether people speak or do not speak, hear or do not hear, see or do not see? Is it not I, the LORD? Now go! I will be with you as you speak, and I will instruct you in what to say."

EXODUS 4:11-12

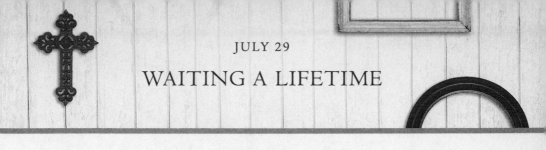

WAITING A LIFETIME

Antoinette Louisa Brown Blackwell

1825–1921

Antoinette Blackwell lived to do something that many of her contemporaries did not. She voted in a presidential election. On November 2, 1920, at the age of ninety-five, she was among the first women to vote for a US president.

The women's suffrage movement can be traced to the late 1700s, but the organized effort began in the mid-1800s. Yet it wasn't until 1920 that women were given the right to vote on a national level.

Many of the pioneers of the women's suffrage movement didn't live long enough to see the passage of the Nineteenth Amendment of the Constitution. They never had the opportunity to cast the votes they worked tirelessly to secure for all women in the United States. But Antoinette did.

It seems she was fighting for women's rights all her life. Graduating from Oberlin College, she wanted to continue at the school and earn a theological degree. Oberlin did not want to admit a woman to the program, but Antoinette fought, and eventually the school compromised. She could take the classes, but with no official credit. (Many years later, the college did grant her honorary Master of Arts and Doctor of Divinity degrees.) Significantly, while there, Antoinette published in an Oberlin journal her analysis of the apostle Paul's writings on women, suggesting that his restrictions on female leadership were merely warnings against "excesses, irregularities, and unwarrantable liberties" in the church's worship services.

She pastored a Congregationalist church in New York State for a time, and she was much in demand as a speaker on women's rights and the abolition of slavery. Antoinette took a break from public life to get married and rear her seven children, but once they were grown, she went back to preaching and fighting for women's suffrage. It took almost her whole life to see the outcome of her fight, but it happened.

When you're fighting for something you know is right, don't give up. Frustrations may arise, people may try to stand in your way, but even if you never see the results in your lifetime, you'll know you were true to what you knew was right.

Let's not get tired of doing what is good. At just the right time
we will reap a harvest of blessing if we don't give up.

GALATIANS 6:9

AN INSPIRING LIFE

Harriet Newell

1793–1812

Harriet Newell is well known for what she didn't get to do. She didn't get to be the missionary she had hoped to be. In 1812, Harriet and her new husband, Samuel, set sail with Ann and Adoniram Judson for India and then for Burma. They were some of the first American missionaries.

Harriet's short story is sad, but not surprising, given the times. When the Burmese government found out the group would be preaching Christianity, they ordered the missionaries to leave. A now-pregnant Harriet and her husband headed by ship to the Isle of France (Mauritius) in the Indian Ocean.

The trip was brutal. During those three months at sea, Harriet gave birth two days before her nineteenth birthday. The baby died a few days later. By the time the ship finally reached land, Harriet had contracted tuberculosis and doctors were unable to help her. By November 30, she, too, had died, leaving Samuel alone in a strange land. Harriet became known as the first American missionary martyr.

Right about now you're probably wondering, *Why am I being told this sad story? Where's the inspiration?*

From the age of thirteen, Harriet kept a journal. She also was a prolific letter writer. In 1814, her memoirs were published, including parts of her journals and letters. The book was so inspirational that for twenty-five years, a new edition was published almost annually. People loved to read about how Harriet's faith guided her in the years leading up to her missionary adventure.

> *Providence now gives me an opportunity to go myself to the heathen. Shall I refuse the offer—shall I love the glittering toys of this dying world so well, that I cannot relinquish them for God? Forbid it heaven! Yes, I will go. However weak and unqualified I am, there is an all-sufficient Saviour ready to support me.*

Some historical Christians seem larger than life—we could never hope to act with their courage, skill, or stamina—but not Harriet Newell. She faced a choice we all face in one way or another—to follow God's leading or to play with the "glittering toys of this world"? The promise she clung to is ours as well. We may be "weak and unqualified," but the Savior supports us, too.

My grace is all you need. My power works best in weakness.

2 CORINTHIANS 12:9

GO YE

Women and the Missionary Impulse of the 1800s

Since the church began, there have always been missionaries. After the apostle Paul's journeys, Christians kept taking the Good News of Jesus to other lands. In medieval times, Irish monks replanted Christian tradition on the European mainland. In the 1600s, men and women known as Quakers took their simple teachings to the New World. In the 1700s, a group of Moravians banded together in an evangelistic enterprise.

But the 1800s saw a new momentum for missions, especially among Christians in England and America. William Carey seemed to get the ball rolling in 1792 as he preached and wrote about missions, then left for India the next year. Many men and women would follow him into missionary service.

Actually, missions work opened up significant new opportunities for female believers. While women were still expected to attend to domestic duties, who could object if they got involved outside the home in activities supporting missions? In fact, a number of "women's missionary societies" were formed in this era. If a husband was called to be a foreign missionary, of course that meant his wife would be one too—sometimes reluctantly (like Dorothy Carey), but often as a valued teammate (like Ann Judson). Once on the missions field, a woman might take on a number of leadership tasks that needed to be done, including teaching and even preaching. The importance of the missionary effort trumped any gender limitations. When souls need to be saved, does it matter whether it's a man or woman delivering the message of salvation?

For many women who struggled with their self-worth, the missions movement was, well, a godsend. After meeting a seminarian who was eagerly headed into mission work, Sarah Joiner Lyman began to ask herself, "What am I doing? What are my plans, and what my prospect of usefulness? Who has been or who will be benefited by my existence? . . . O that a way might be opened whereby I may labour for the good of souls." Soon afterward she found her calling as a missionary to Hawaii.

So what are *you* doing? Who is benefiting by *your* existence? God might be calling you to serve him in another land . . . or he might want you to shine for him where you are.

Whom should I send as a messenger to this people? Who will go for us?

ISAIAH 6:8

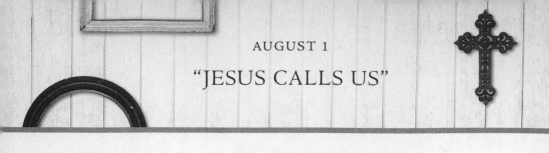

"JESUS CALLS US"

Cecil Alexander

1818–95

A minister's wife from Ireland, Cecil Alexander was a prolific poet and hymn writer, specializing in songs for children. "Once in Royal David's City," "There Is a Green Hill Far Away," and "All Things Bright and Beautiful" were among the songs she penned to teach parts of the Apostles' Creed. But some of her work was directed more toward adults, like "Jesus Calls Us," written to accompany her husband's sermon on the calling of the disciple Andrew.

> *Jesus calls us from the worship*
> *Of the vain world's golden store,*
> *From each idol that would keep us,*
> *Saying, "Christian, love Me more."*

Cecil not only wrote those words, but she also lived them out, showing her love for Christ by caring for the poor and sick—even donating much of the money she earned from her writing. As one writer said about her, "Day after day she rode over the wet moorlands in all weathers, carrying food, warm clothing, medical supplies to the impoverished and sick." In this way, she showed she loved Jesus more than whatever gold the world stored up. She understood the biblical teaching that money can become an idol, and that we break free of it by giving it away.

But this song isn't just about money. It's about hearing the call of Christ amid the chaos of our daily lives. It's about following him rather than the passing fancies of our culture. It's often used as a missionary hymn, inviting people to dedicate their lives to the Lord's work, but it's even larger than that. We all are called to follow Jesus wherever we are, at work or at play, in our neighborhoods and homes. We reject the idols of our culture and put Christ first.

Do you have anything in your life that you're holding on to, something of the "world's golden store" that you're worshiping, that's keeping you from showing Jesus that you love him? Ask God to help you loosen your grip on it. Ask him to show you how rich your life can become if you let go of your idols and follow him.

> *After breakfast Jesus asked Simon Peter, "Simon son of John, do*
> *you love me more than these?" "Yes, Lord," Peter replied, "you*
> *know I love you." "Then feed my lambs," Jesus told him.*

JOHN 21:15

"DAY BY DAY"

Carolina Sandell Berg

1832–1903

You never know what the day is going to bring, do you? Your to-do list can be neatly organized on your smartphone, but life's unexpected events might make a mockery of your list. Some days go as planned, some are better than planned, and some days . . . well, they just blow up.

That reality's not unique to this generation. Carolina "Lina" Sandell Berg, a Swedish hymn writer in the 1800s, had her share of unexpected days. She had no to-do list on a smartphone, but she probably woke each day with things she wished to accomplish. Sometimes she got them done. Sometimes the unexpected occurred.

As a child, she suffered from a mysterious paralysis that doctors expected to be permanent. One morning while her parents were at church, the paralysis miraculously disappeared. In her twenties, Lina was traveling by boat with her father. The boat pitched, and her father fell overboard. No one was able to save him. Lina watched helplessly as her father drowned.

Like most people, Lina Berg had some sensational days, some traumatic days, and many that were just regular days. No matter what the day brought, Lina looked to God for her strength. The evidence is in the 650 hymns she wrote, including "Day by Day and with Each Passing Moment," which is still popular.

Day by day and with each passing moment,
Strength I find to meet my trials here;
Trusting in my Father's wise bestowment,
I've no cause for worry or for fear.

In her lyrics, Lina models for us a great sense of balance:

He whose heart is kind beyond all measure
Gives unto each day what He deems best—
Lovingly, its part of pain and pleasure,
Mingling toil with peace and rest.

Life, she knows, is full of both pain and pleasure, and the Lord is there through all of it, comforting us, strengthening us, teaching us lessons, surprising us. In all days—good, bad, and ordinary—we can trust that God knows best.

Great is his faithfulness;
his mercies begin afresh each morning.

LAMENTATIONS 3:23

"SO SEND I YOU"

Margaret Clarkson

1915–2008

If you've ever thought, *I've read the Bible enough to understand it fully*, think again. The Bible is alive; it says so in Hebrews. As you read more, pray more, gain more life experience, have growing relationships with other Christians, and most important, have a growing relationship with God, you'll find your understanding of the Bible grows and changes too.

Margaret Clarkson, a Canadian hymn writer, experienced this. A look at her popular missionary hymn "So Send I You" shows how her thinking and understanding of the Bible changed as she grew closer to God and to other Christians and became more knowledgeable about the Scriptures.

Margaret wrote two versions of the hymn, one when she was twenty-two, depicting the loneliness, sorrows, and difficulties that she imagined a missionary would have—although, because of physical disabilities, she knew she would never be a missionary. This version speaks of the rebuke, scorn, suffering, loneliness, hard work, and hatred missionaries will face on the mission field.

Almost ten years later, she rewrote the hymn, calling it "So Send I You, by Grace Made Strong." The second version speaks of conquering, breaking bonds of sin, the promised presence of God, and the fruits of missionary service. Its final stanza refers to the Lord's biblical commendation, "Well done, my faithful servant."

Why the change in her point of view? Margaret said that after more life experiences and contact with actual missionaries, she rewrote the hymn into a more biblical one.

Over time, our understanding of what the Bible is saying to us may change. When we're new to reading it, we'll likely understand just a little of it—and that's okay. With life experience, Bible study, and deeper relationships with Christians and God, our understanding can deepen. We'll never know it all. We'll never have the Bible "down pat." It will keep speaking its truth into our lives in fresh ways—and we need to be open to that, just like Margaret Clarkson was.

The word of God is alive and powerful. It is sharper than the sharpest two-edged sword, cutting between soul and spirit, between joint and marrow. It exposes our innermost thoughts and desires.

HEBREWS 4:12

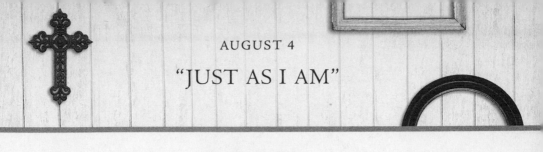

"JUST AS I AM"

Charlotte Elliott

1789–1871

What does it take to be worthy of God? Do you have to stop some bad habit before you can come before him? If you need to be forgiven for something, do you need to do something good first before you ask?

Or does God take you just the way you are, without your efforts to fix yourself?

"Just As I Am" is a hymn that helps answer those questions. Its author, Charlotte Elliott, came to a point in her life when she realized she wanted to be a Christian, to know the saving grace of Christ and have a relationship with God. She had conversations with family friend Dr. Caesar Malan, a minister, and she expressed to him that she wasn't sure how to go about becoming a Christian. She wondered if she needed to fix a few things in her life before entering into a relationship with Christ.

Dr. Malan gave her this simple, freeing advice: "Come just as you are." Charlotte believed her friend's words. She accepted Christ, just as she was.

Of the many things Charlotte was, she was also an invalid. In her early thirties she fell ill, and this left her weak and depressed for much of her life. Becoming a Christian didn't automatically cure her of feeling depressed and useless, and she often struggled with those feelings. Out of that struggle came "Just As I Am."

As the story goes, one day her family and friends went to a fund-raiser to raise money for a school for underprivileged children. Too sick to go with them, Charlotte stayed home, feeling useless because she was unable to help raise money for the cause. In her depression, she turned to writing and penned the words, "Just as I am, without one plea, but that Thy blood was shed for me."

When you need to come to God, whether it's for the first time as a new Christian or the thousandth time to ask for forgiveness, God says, "Come to me, just as you are." Are you holding back on coming to God because you think you have to fix things first? Don't. Come as you are.

Those the Father has given me will come to me, and I will never reject them.

JOHN 6:37

"HE GIVETH MORE GRACE"

Annie Flint
1866–1932

I'm at the end of my rope."

Most people have said that at one time or another, or at least felt it. It means things are really tough. You don't know what to do. You're not sure you have the strength to keep on going.

Annie Flint reached the end of her rope several times. By her early twenties, she had been orphaned twice—first by her natural parents, who died when she was young, and then by her adopted parents, who died within a few months of each other. She didn't have much money, and she had a younger sister to support. Teaching provided income until she developed debilitating arthritis. Doctors told her she would live the rest of her life as an invalid.

She turned to writing poetry and creating handwritten cards and books. Holding a pen for long periods of time could not have been easy for someone with severe arthritis, but she found the strength to do it. Eventually, she wrote for magazines and she published some books. Most of her earnings went toward her medical care.

What kept her going when she probably wanted to throw away her pen and paper because of the pain? Her well-known hymn "He Giveth More Grace" might contain the answer.

The gist of the text is that when we face difficult circumstances, God gives us even more ability to cope. When our problems pile up, his grace grows even greater. As Annie put it, "When we have exhausted our store of endurance . . . our Father's full giving is only begun."

This concept is consistent with biblical teaching. Jeremiah laments the destruction of Jerusalem but pauses to note that the Lord's mercies "begin afresh each morning" (Lamentations 3:23). Paul prays for the removal of the painful "thorn in my flesh" that's apparently hurting his ministry, but God offers him grace instead—that should be enough for him (see 2 Corinthians 12:7-10). James assures us that our trials are "an opportunity for great joy" (James 1:2), because we grow through them.

When you've reached the end of your rope, or in the words of the song, "the end of [your] hoarded resources," it's good to know that God's lifeline has no end to it. He keeps giving and giving and giving.

My grace is all you need.

2 CORINTHIANS 12:9

"THERE IS A REDEEMER"

Melody Green
1946–

She was a Jewish hippie and then a Jesus freak; a hardworking designer and then a ministry leader; a loving wife and then, tragically, a single mom. Melody Green was only thirty-six when her husband, singer Keith Green, died in a plane crash, along with two of their children. (She was caring for her third child at home and was expecting a fourth.) Melody soldiered on, continuing the ministry they had started together.

Both Keith and Melody were children of the sixties, caught up in the Southern California counterculture of drug use and spiritual searching. They met and married and continued their quest together. Melody was designing clothes, and Keith was singing in clubs when they were invited to a small Bible study in 1975. Through the Bible study, they turned their lives over to Jesus.

The Greens took their newfound faith seriously. They opened their modest home to people in need. When that proved to be too small, they bought and rented other homes in the area, offering shelter, food, and support to runaways, recovering drug addicts, pregnant teens, and so on. This was the beginning of an enterprise they called Last Days Ministries. Keith became a popular Christian singer, with Melody cowriting some of his songs, but he shied away from celebrity status.

In 1979, Last Days Ministries moved to a ranch in East Texas. They continued to shelter people in need, but they also developed a national, even international, outreach. Melody edited the group's magazine. Keith went on concert tours. Both were invited to speak at Christian gatherings. Their message was prophetic, challenging Christians to live what they claimed to believe. By 1982 there were about one hundred people working for Last Days Ministries. And then the plane crashed.

That fall, Melody spearheaded a Keith Green Memorial Concert tour. He was gone, but their message still needed to be heard. One key element of that tour was a challenge to young people to become missionaries. Hundreds responded.

Melody Green is known as the writer of several songs still currently used by churches, notably "There Is a Redeemer," but her story is much richer. And the Greens' challenge still confronts us. *How serious are we about our faith? Are we living what we claim to believe?*

Anyone with ears to hear must listen to the Spirit and understand what he is saying to the churches.

REVELATION 2:7

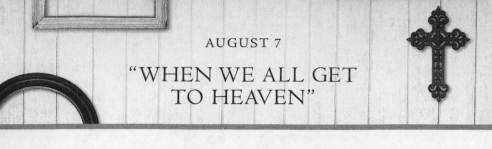

"WHEN WE ALL GET TO HEAVEN"

Eliza Hewitt

1851–1920

Christians have an amazing promise—the promise of spending eternity in heaven. The Bible gives us glimpses of a heaven where the streets are paved with gold; angels are singing nonstop; and there is no pain, no crying, no sorrow. In heaven, we will be in the presence of God. It's something to look forward to, for sure, and that's what Eliza Hewitt wrote about in her well-known hymn "When We All Get to Heaven."

> *When we all get to heaven,*
> *What a day of rejoicing that will be!*

A well-educated woman, Eliza graduated as valedictorian of her class. She became a schoolteacher and taught until a spinal injury made it too painful to work. From her bed, where she faced a long recovery, she studied and wrote. Her output included the text for some seventy hymns—including "Stepping in the Light," "Sunshine in My Soul Today," "More about Jesus," and "My Faith Has Found a Resting Place." After some recuperation, she was able to teach Sunday school again at her church, where she continued to influence young people.

Sometimes Christians are criticized for being "so heavenly minded that they're no earthly good." Not Eliza. It might have been easy for her to languish on her sickbed and wait for glory, but she didn't. In spite of her ailment, she found ways to contribute to God's glory on earth. The hymns she wrote during her recovery have brought countless people closer to God. Eliza was certainly looking forward to heaven, but she knew she still had lots of life to live here on earth. Her original plans of being a schoolteacher weren't working out anymore, but she kept on living and learning.

We're here on earth for a reason. This is where God has put us for this specific time. We have jobs to do, things to learn, a relationship to build with God, and relationships with other people to enjoy. Sure, it will be great when we all get to heaven, but here on earth it can be pretty wonderful too.

If we live, it's to honor the Lord. And if we die, it's to honor the Lord. So whether we live or die, we belong to the Lord.

ROMANS 14:8

"THE GATE AJAR FOR ME"

Lydia Baxter

1809–74

If you've spent a lot of time around other Christians who love to share the story of Jesus and how he paid the price for our sins with his death on the cross, then possibly you've heard something like this: "Yes, Jesus died to save everyone, but even if you were the only person in the world, he still would have died just to save you. He loves you that much."

That can be a hard concept to accept, can't it? Jesus would have gone through the humiliation of his trial, the pain of being beaten, and the agony of hanging on the cross just because you can't get your act together? Overwhelming, isn't it?

Lydia Baxter found that concept to be overwhelming too. She was an invalid for most of her adult life, spending much of her time bedridden. Like many others in those circumstances, she spent a lot of time with her thoughts and turned to writing poetry and hymns to express them. She's best known for the lyrics to "Take the Name of Jesus with You," but a more obscure hymn, "The Gate Ajar for Me," expresses both her awe and her gratefulness that what Jesus did, he did for her.

> There is a gate that stands ajar,
> And through its portals gleaming
> A radiance from the cross afar,
> The Savior's love revealing.
>
> O depth of mercy! Can it be
> That gate was left ajar for me?

Jesus did die for you, and the gate is open for each one who accepts him. That gate stays open, even if you seem to wander out of it every once in a while. When you get far away from God—when you neglect spending time in prayer or give in to a habit you know you shouldn't—the gate remains open. It's ajar, just waiting for you to return.

---

*If a man has a hundred sheep and one of them gets lost, what will
he do? Won't he leave the ninety-nine others in the wilderness
and go to search for the one that is lost until he finds it?*

LUKE 15:4

"FACE TO FACE"

Carrie Breck
1855–1934

Most biographical information about Carrie Breck will include this fact: while she's known for being the author of many hymns, she had no sense of pitch and was not able to carry a tune. Her hymns came from poems she wrote that were set to music by others.

One of her best-known hymns, "Face to Face," was the result of that kind of partnership. The story goes that Carrie sent a poem to a family friend, Grant Tullar. As it happened, just the night before, Grant had composed a new tune. When he put Carrie's words to his music, they were a perfect fit.

The hymn deals with something that many of us have wondered from time to time: When we finally meet Jesus face-to-face, what exactly will it be like? Now we see him only "faintly," Carrie's text observes, with a "darkened veil" obscuring our knowledge of him (picking up on the dark glass of I Corinthians 13:12, KJV). From Scripture and from the Spirit's whispers, we have hints of what Jesus is like, but we can't know fully—not yet. But one day we will be face to face with him, and the reality will surely be far more amazing than we can imagine.

Carrie's lyrics also refer to the "grief and pain" of our current lives that will be "banished" in that moment of connection with Christ. It's natural to be frustrated with our own frailty. All of creation groans, waiting for that redemptive moment (see Romans 8:22). We look forward not only to the sight of our Savior, but also to our own transformation. John says that "we will be like him, for we will see him as he really is" (I John 3:2).

As we wait for that glorious day, we can still get to know Jesus better now. Prayer and meditation on Scripture can draw us closer to him. Following his teachings and connecting with other believers can also bring us a fuller understanding of who Jesus is. And that will make us all the more eager to see him face to face.

My heart says of you, "Seek his face!" Your face, LORD, I will seek.

PSALM 27:8, NIV

"SHOUT TO THE LORD"

Darlene Zschech
1965–

On Sunday mornings, millions of Christians go to church and worship. We sing songs of praise and maybe an old hymn or two, listen to a soloist sing a beautiful song (and envy her voice), perhaps see a drama group enact a scene with a message, and spend a little time in prayer. And, with the exception of a quick song at the end of the service, once the pastor gets up to give the sermon, the worship is over.

Or is it?

Maybe during one of your worship times you've sung Darlene Zschech's praise song "Shout to the Lord," one of the most popular songs of the modern worship music genre. In a few lines of this song, Darlene suggests that worship is never ending.

Let every breath, all that I am
Never cease to worship you.

How is that possible to "never cease" worshiping God? How can we do so with "every breath"? You've got a job to do. A family to spend time with. Friends to be social with. Laundry that keeps piling up. Are you supposed to sing hymns throughout all of that, only stopping for times of prayer?

Not exactly. If you think of worship as only singing and praying, then you probably won't be able to worship God without ceasing. But if you consider worship to be anything you give to God, then it becomes easier to see how you can worship all the time.

Just how do you give the time you spend with family or friends to God? How about making the effort to speak and act around them the way you know God would like? How do you give your laundry duties to God? Instead of treating it as a hassle, you can choose to be grateful that you have a closet full of clothes and a washing machine to make cleaning them easy. You can look at your job as an offering to God as well.

Where can you add a little non-singing and non-praying worship in your life?

Give to the LORD the glory he deserves!
Bring your offering and come into his presence.
Worship the LORD in all his holy splendor.

1 CHRONICLES 16:29

"THE NINETY AND NINE"

Elizabeth Clephane

1830–69

She had plenty of reasons to be bitter, but Elizabeth Clephane had a cheerful manner that dazzled the people of the Scottish town where she grew up. They called her Sunbeam. A sickly girl, she had lost both parents at an early age, but Elizabeth didn't waste a lot of time feeling sorry for herself. Instead, she and her sisters became known for their charitable efforts, serving the poor of the region and giving away any excess income.

It would have been a quiet, devout life, except that Elizabeth also wrote poetry. A few of her works were published during her lifetime in a Scottish Presbyterian magazine, which published a larger collection of her poetry after her untimely death at age thirty-eight. Among these poems was the text of "Beneath the Cross of Jesus," which has since become a beloved hymn. There, in the third stanza, the woman known as Sunbeam wrote: "I ask no other sunshine than the sunshine of His face." Elizabeth had a knack for expressing rich human emotion in simple phrases.

Another hymn from her hand became a powerful part of revival meetings led by Dwight L. Moody in the late 1800s—"The Ninety and Nine." Song leader Ira Sankey once picked up a newspaper for a train ride through Scotland, noticed a religious poem printed there, and clipped it. A few days later, Dwight L. Moody was preaching about the Good Shepherd and asked Ira to sing an appropriate song. Put on the spot, the song leader heard an inner voice saying, *Sing the hymn you found on the train.* He placed the clipping on the organ in front of him and improvised a tune for it.

There were ninety and nine that safely lay in the shelter of the fold.
But one was out on the hills away, far off from the gates of gold.

It had been five years since Elizabeth's death, but in the revival meeting that night, hearing these words sung for the first time, was her sister, surprised and delighted to hear Sunbeam's old poem in this fresh, new way. When we follow the Lord's leading, there are no accidents.

Seek his will in all you do,
and he will show you which path to take.

PROVERBS 3:6

"MORNING HAS BROKEN"

Eleanor Farjeon
1881–1965

The song "Morning Has Broken" hit the pop charts in 1972, but it was written some forty years earlier as a children's hymn for the first day of spring. British poet Eleanor Farjeon penned this beautiful ode to God's creation and chose a traditional Gaelic tune as its melody.

Of course there was no way Eleanor could have anticipated the immense popularity her hymn would eventually have. It was surprising when, in the heyday of rock music, people could turn on their radios and hear words that clearly expressed a sense of wonder and praise at the beauty of what God had made.

> *Praise for the singing, praise for the morning,*
> *Praise for them springing fresh from the Word.*

Eleanor saw the dawn of each new day as a reminder that creation is one of God's masterpieces. Her song eventually inspired millions to think about creation, the beauty surrounding them, and where it all came from.

Do you ever look at creation and become inspired by the beauty surrounding you? What catches your attention? The sunrise? Sunset? New buds on the trees in the spring? The power of the ocean? The silent stillness of a night after a snowfall? The scent of basil growing in the garden in the summer?

When you're inspired by creation, do you respond with creativity? Perhaps you could write a poem like Eleanor's. Perhaps not. But you could also use that garden basil to create a fresh, home-cooked meal for family or friends. Or you could preserve a beautiful sight by snapping a photo with your phone. Maybe you could improvise a praise song or compose a "creation rap." The important thing is to respond. Let God know that you don't take his masterpiece for granted.

O Lord, what a variety of things you have made!
In wisdom you have made them all.
The earth is full of your creatures.

PSALM 104:24

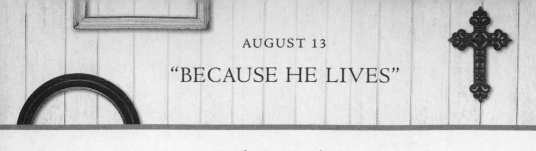

"BECAUSE HE LIVES"

Gloria Gaither

1942–

Wе wake each morning to uncertainty. Even on the days we look forward to, we never know what's going to happen.

Your boss could call you in and tell you the company has to lay off employees and your job is being eliminated. Your doctor could tell you your health, or the health of someone you love, is in danger. You might find that a relationship—with a family member, a friend, or your sweetheart—has struggles you were unaware of. Those are the days when you realize you need more than just your own strength to get you through the day and quite possibly many, many days to come.

Everyone has days like that in their lives, and songwriter and singer Gloria Gaither is certainly no exception. One of Gloria's best-known songs, "Because He Lives," was written with her husband, Bill, anticipating the birth of their third child in 1970. It was not a good time to welcome a new life into the world. The recent years had seen riots in the streets, wars across the world, and a moral slide in society. Who could say what kind of world this child would grow up in?

The song powerfully affirms that we can face the future without fear. We don't know what the future holds, but we know who holds the future. And, as the song's chorus concludes, "life is worth the living—just because He lives."

Churches often use this Gaither song on Easter Sunday. While it mentions the "empty grave," it doesn't focus on the *process* of the Resurrection, but the result. Christ is alive, and that changes everything for us. He arose victorious over death, and so we can count on him to win victories for us. Not that he reverses the trials we face, but he sees us through them. We can face tomorrow *not* because the future looks rosy, but because our Savior stands with us no matter what.

So turn to him in your times of uncertainty. He'll listen to you through your tears and your fears and your questions, and he'll reassure you that although you may be unsure about your future, he is not. He holds it—and more importantly, he holds *you*.

My future is in your hands.

PSALM 31:15

"I AM NOT SKILLED TO UNDERSTAND"

Dora Greenwell

1821–82

God only knows. God makes his plans. The information's unavailable to the mortal man." You may be familiar with those lyrics from Paul Simon's hit song "Slip Slidin' Away." But a century earlier, the same sentiments were expressed by an English poet named Dora Greenwell. Her poem "I Am Not Skilled to Understand" was later put to music by William J. Kirkpatrick and used widely as a hymn.

> *I am not skilled to understand*
> *What God hath willed, what God hath planned.*

It's a common notion. What on earth is God doing? If only we were smarter or more spiritual, we think, we might begin to grasp the plan. But for now, for us, it's a mystery.

This feeling often occurs in times of sorrow, as it did with Dora Greenwell. Her father's death put the family in dire financial straits. She herself struggled with health problems. At one point she was working with disabled children, daily facing the question, Why did God let this happen?

As a writer, Dora began to focus on themes of patience and hope. We might not be able to understand God's plans, but we can trust that he has them. When his plans for us include difficult times, we can be sure he's not abandoning us, but that he's giving us strength when we have none of our own left.

> *Yea, living, dying, let me bring*
> *My strength, my solace from this spring;*
> *That He who lives to be my king*
> *Once died to be my Savior!*

God's plans for Jesus' death on the cross might have seemed inexplicable to those who loved Jesus. His disciples, his followers, his family couldn't understand why Jesus would have to go through what he went through. But now, much later, we see God's plan—that Jesus died to save us. That brings us strength and solace in our own times of questioning.

Oh, how great are God's riches and wisdom and knowledge! How impossible it is for us to understand his decisions and his ways! For who can know the Lord's thoughts?

ROMANS 11:33-34

"JESUS PAID IT ALL"

Elvina Hall

1820–89

You're in church, listening to the sermon, and an idea hits. You feel the idea is good—inspired even—and you don't want to lose it. You pull out your smartphone, open up the notes section, and record it quickly. Maybe the person next to you gives you a little disapproving look, or maybe the person next to you is doing the same thing.

Elvina Hall was in that position 150 years ago. With no smartphone, and no spare paper either, she grabbed a hymnal and scribbled on its flyleaf a poem that came to her during her pastor's sermon. When she showed it to the pastor, he paired it with a tune the church organist had given him, resulting in the hymn "Jesus Paid It All."

We're not sure what the pastor's sermon was about that day, but it led Elvina to contemplate strength—how little she felt she had on her own and how much she had in Jesus.

> *I hear the Savior say,*
> *"Thy strength indeed is small;*
> *Child of weakness, watch and pray,*
> *Find in Me thine all in all."*

We are often tempted to trust in our own power. We try to impress God with our righteousness. We face temptation with our own moral willpower. We easily forget that we are, indeed, "child[ren] of weakness." We must trust Christ for everything.

"Jesus Paid It All" is still sung in many churches today. Not long ago it was recorded by popular Christian artist Kristian Stanfill, reaching a generation that Elvina never could have dreamed would find new comfort from her hastily scrawled verses.

And that hymnal flyleaf carries another lesson for us: inspiration doesn't always strike at convenient times. When it comes, write it down, record it, text it, or pray it—just don't lose it.

It is not by force nor by strength, but by my Spirit, says the LORD.

ZECHARIAH 4:6

"OPEN MY EYES, THAT I MAY SEE"

Clara H. Scott

1841–97

You might say there was a music explosion in the United States in the last half of the nineteenth century. Midwestern music teacher Clara Scott was in the middle of it. There had always been folk songs, and there were anthems sung in churches, but this was the era that mashed the two together. Through singing schools and music festivals, the common folk were learning how to read music, write it, sing it, and play it. Advances in printing, manufacturing, and transportation brought sheet music and instruments into many American homes. If you've seen *The Music Man*, with a salesman starting a brass band in a small Iowa town, you get the picture.

As a teenager, Clara attended a music institute in Chicago led by renowned music educator C. M. Cady. Later she went to a small Iowa town to teach music to young women. She also wrote and published music: a number of instrumental pieces as well as some hymns. Her *Royal Anthem Book* in 1882 became the first book of anthems published by a woman. In 1897, after publishing two more collections, she died in a traffic accident—thrown from a buggy pulled by a runaway horse.

Clara's enduring contribution is one song still sung in many churches: "Open My Eyes, That I May See." In succeeding verses, the lyrics offer God open eyes, open ears, an open mouth to proclaim his truth, and an open heart to share his love. Churches often use this hymn before the sermon to express a congregation's receptivity to God's Word. But it can also serve as preparation for one's own quiet time.

> Silently now I wait for Thee,
> Ready my God, Thy will to see,
> Open my [eyes, ears, mouth], illumine me,
> Spirit divine!

Isn't this what a devotional time is all about—laying ourselves open for whatever God has for us? Sure, God invites us to speak to him with thanks and praises, confessions and concerns, but we also need to be still and know that he is God. We need to let him share himself with us, in whatever way he wants.

Take a moment now to open up to the Lord. Use Clara's words if you like.

Elisha prayed, "O Lord, open his eyes and let him see!"

2 KINGS 6:17

"I NEED THEE EVERY HOUR"

Annie Hawks

1835–1918

Annie Hawks was, by her own account, a rather ordinary homemaker from Brooklyn who got a taste of fame through one of the hymn texts she wrote, "I Need Thee Every Hour." Born in upstate New York, she began writing poetry at age fourteen, getting a piece printed in the local paper. Over the years, she contributed other verses to newspapers, but it was hardly a career. She got married, had kids, and settled in Brooklyn, where she and her husband attended a Baptist church pastored by Robert Lowry. This pastor was also a musician, and he had composed the music for a number of church hymns. When he learned of Annie's gift for poetry, he suggested she apply herself to hymn writing. If she would supply the words, he would write the music.

This arrangement worked well, as Annie wrote text for hymns such as "All Thine," "The Cross for Jesus," and "Why Weepest Thou?" Robert Lowry got these works published, but they found little popularity. Then one balmy June morning, seated by an open window, Annie Hawks put pencil to paper and wrote a new song. "In the midst of the daily cares of my home," she wrote later, ". . . I was so filled with the sense of nearness to the Master that, wondering how one could live without Him either in joy or pain, these words, 'I need Thee every hour' were ushered into my mind, the thought at once taking full possession of me."

With Robert Lowry's music, the hymn debuted at an 1872 Sunday school convention in Cincinnati and soon was used regularly in D. L. Moody's evangelistic services. In Annie's words, it was "wafted out to the world on the wings of love and joy." She remained quite humble about her lyrics. "Now when I hear them sung, as I have sometimes by hundreds of voices in chorus, I find it difficult to realize that they were ever, consciously, my own thoughts or penned by my own hand."

No matter how "ordinary" you are, God can use you to waft his wonders in the world.

God chose things despised by the world, things counted as nothing at all, and used them to bring to nothing what the world considers important.

1 CORINTHIANS 1:28

"TELL ME THE OLD, OLD STORY"

Katherine Hankey

1834–1911

A group of affluent, influential British Christians banded together around 1790 to try to change the world for Christ. Over the next forty years, they set a moral course for their country. Because of their connection to Holy Trinity Church in London's Clapham Common, they later became known as the Clapham Sect. William Wilberforce, a member of Parliament, was a driving force as the group strove to eradicate the slave trade, free current slaves, and reform prisons. This was more than do-goodism; it was Christ-following.

Kate Hankey was a generation late for that party. Her family was involved in the Clapham Sect, but by the time she reached adulthood, the group's influence had waned. Yet nothing could stop her from following Christ into active ministry among the poor and disenfranchised.

This was the world of Charles Dickens, with shabby orphanages and brutal workhouses. Despite her upper-class upbringing, Kate entered a rough part of the city to teach a Bible study to poor "factory girls"—young women who couldn't get a normal education because they were forced to work.

Then Kate got sick, seriously enough that the doctor prescribed a year of bed rest. While it frustrated her to be removed from her ministry, she used her convalescence for a new type of ministry—writing. During that year she composed two long poems, fifty stanzas each, about the story of Jesus. Each of these formed the basis of a hymn—"Tell Me the Old, Old Story" and "I Love to Tell the Story." When she recovered, Kate was able to return to the "factory girls."

Through both her writing and her serving, this young woman teaches us an important lesson. The "old, old story, of Jesus and His love" is central to everything we do—or it should be. We love to tell the story because we recognize its life-changing power, because it has changed *our* lives. Evangelism is more than just a membership drive for God's Kingdom. It's not a debate we're trying to win. It's a gift we offer from a loving Lord to people he deeply wants to know.

If sharing your faith has become a chore, then stop. Go back to the old story, and let the Spirit write some new chapters in your life.

Everyone will share the story of your wonderful goodness;
they will sing with joy about your righteousness.

PSALM 145:7

"GRACE GREATER THAN OUR SIN"

Julia H. Johnston
1849–1919

History shines its spotlight on the people in charge, the movers and shakers. But observers of *Christian* history need to be aware of the upside-down phenomenon. Jesus repeatedly said that the first shall be last. True leaders are those who serve. And the ones who are actually setting the tone for the church are not necessarily the preachers and prophets, but often the Sunday school teachers, custodians, and secretaries.

Take Julia H. Johnston, who lived in Peoria, Illinois, quietly serving the Lord in various ways. Over the years, she taught Sunday school, worked in a church office, led a missions agency, and wrote curriculum for other church teachers to use. Oh, yes— she also wrote words for hundreds of hymns. Most of these lyrics are long forgotten, but one of her hymns has become a favorite: "Grace Greater Than Our Sin."

In 1911, when this hymn came out, evangelistic meetings were common. D. L. Moody had dominated the late 1800s with his services of powerful preaching and heart-tugging music, and he inspired a pack of followers to carry the tradition into the new century. So "Grace Greater Than Our Sin," put to music by Moody Bible Institute songsmith Daniel B. Towner, met a ready market. It's a hymn of invitation, calling people to receive God's grace. No matter how immense our sin, God can forgive it. As Julia expressed it, the "crimson tide" of Jesus' blood can cleanse the "stain that we cannot hide." Her text, anchored in New Testament theology, was emotionally appealing to lost souls.

But God's grace doesn't just save us; it empowers us. The Bible describes various gifts of God's grace showered upon the followers of Jesus. That means we don't have to sit around and wait for D. L. Moody or Billy Sunday or Billy Graham to make things happen. God has gifted *us*, all of us, and we can put our gifts together to do his work in the world. Whether teaching a class or organizing mission work, Julia Johnston used the gifts God had graced her with, and she left us a song we're still singing. That's how grace works. As Christians, we write history not merely with headlines but with day-to-day faithfulness.

How are you going to make history today?

In his grace, God has given us different gifts for doing certain things well.
ROMANS 12:6

"TURN YOUR EYES UPON JESUS"

Helen Howarth Lemmel

1864–1961

Perhaps you're at a point where, when people ask, "How are you?" your usual response is "Busy!" We might imagine that Helen Howarth Lemmel had that kind of life too. The daughter of a Wesleyan Methodist pastor, as a child she came with her family from England to America. With music as her passion, she studied voice in Germany, performed as a soloist throughout the Midwest, and later taught voice at Moody Bible Institute in Chicago and the Bible Institute of Los Angeles. For a time, she also served as a music critic for a major newspaper. Helen also wrote hundreds of songs, both lyrics and music.

One day in 1918, in the midst of this busy life, she was handed a small booklet with the title *Focused*—written by another multitalented woman, the artist-turned-missionary Isabella Lilias Trotter. In it was a challenge to pay full attention to Jesus, putting away other distractions.

Helen got the message . . . and created the song we know as "Turn Your Eyes upon Jesus." She recounted the process later: "Suddenly, as if commanded to stop and listen, I stood still, and singing in my soul and spirit was the chorus of the hymn with not one conscious moment of putting word to word to make rhyme, or note to note to make melody. . . . The verses were written . . . the same week, after the usual manner of composition, but none the less dictated by the Holy Spirit."

Within a few years, the song was published in England and America and was finding considerable popularity—especially at the Keswick Bible Conferences. Helen's full life continued until she was ninety-seven. And it is said that in her later years, she developed a unique reply to the common question, how are you?

"I am doing well," she would say, "in the things that count."

Perhaps you're humming along these days at three speeds: busy, really busy, and crazy. Our world doesn't seem to be slowing down much. But when we're busy with many responsibilities, obligations, and distractions, we often lose our focus on the things that matter most. Turn your attention back to Jesus, and let him put the rest of your life back in order.

How are you? Doing well, you could say, in the things that count.

Seek the Kingdom of God above all else, and live righteously,
and he will give you everything you need.

MATTHEW 6:33

"WE WILL GLORIFY"

Twila Paris

1958–

At the tender age of seven, she recorded her first album, a collection of songs her family sang in their evangelistic meetings. Twila Paris grew up surrounded by faith. Her father was not only an evangelist, but later also became founder and chancellor of a Christian college in northwest Arkansas.

Twila's next album didn't come out for another fifteen years, in 1980, but that one quickly put her on the map of contemporary Christian music. Over the next quarter century, she released nearly an album a year, but she wasn't just another pop singer. Early on, she found that her lasting gifts to the church were in worship music. "We Will Glorify," "We Bow Down," "Lamb of God," and "He Is Exalted" all came from her pen and her voice.

Christian worship was changing in the 1980s and '90s, and Twila provided the playlist. Many churches were experimenting with "contemporary" worship styles, using guitars and drums rather than organs, singing modern choruses instead of old hymns. Some folks objected to this new direction; Christian magazines were writing about the "worship wars." But in the midst of the debate, Twila's worship songs had a majesty to them. Modern, but very singable, and strongly focused on God, to many these songs felt far more *worshipful* than the old favorites, and thus they provided the best possible argument in favor of contemporary worship.

Today's worship leaders should take a lesson from Twila's work. Though she has always been a fine singer and a popular performer, her lasting significance comes from the fact that her music has consistently led Christians before God's throne. Worship is not ultimately a performance, but a bowing, a humbling, an offering. And worship must never focus on the skill of the leader but on the Lord's greatness.

Individually, we can fall into that same trap. We can start concentrating on how well we're praying, or studying, or meditating, or obeying. If only we were more disciplined, more focused, or more spiritual, we think, *then* we'd be great Christians. The music of Twila Paris reminds us that it's not about us. God is the one we're exalting. He gets the glory. We're just bowing down.

Not to us, O LORD, not to us,
but to your name goes all the glory
for your unfailing love and faithfulness.

PSALM 115:1

"GOD WILL TAKE CARE OF YOU"

Civilla D. Martin

1866–1948

Civilla Martin was sick in bed one Sunday. Her husband, a minister and musician, had a preaching engagement some distance away, but he thought he should cancel it to stay home with her. As they discussed this, their nine-year-old son piped up, "Father, don't you think that if God wants you to preach today, he will take care of Mother while you are away?"

The kid's logic was solid. So Walter Martin kept his preaching gig and returned late that night to find Civilla feeling much better. She also handed him some new song lyrics. Taking her cue from their son's precocious comment, Civilla had written "God Will Take Care of You."

Walter rushed to his keyboard and quickly created a tune. Some friends came over, and they sang it together. He managed to get the new work into a hymnal he was compiling, and the rest is history. Thousands of believers have taken comfort from Civilla's sickbed song.

Another comforting song from Civilla's pen had its genesis beside another sickbed. As the Martins were tending to an ailing friend, they asked if their friend ever got discouraged by her illness. How could she remain so positive? The friend referred to Jesus' comment about God caring for sparrows . . . and a song began brewing in the lyricist's head.

"His Eye Is on the Sparrow," written in 1905, became a hit in the following decades, primarily in the African American community. Gospel singer Ethel Waters popularized it, but many other singers have covered it. Beginning in 1957, Ethel Waters sang it often at Billy Graham rallies.

Civilla Martin's lyrics express joy in the midst of difficulty. To cynical minds, that might seem like denial, but it's actually built on a sober trust in a God who cares for us more than we could ever know. Discouraging things happen; there are times of loneliness. You might be going through such a time right now. But God has not abandoned you. He draws close to you in your time of need. The God whose eye is on the sparrow is certainly watching you with love.

What is the price of five sparrows—two copper coins?
Yet God does not forget a single one of them.

LUKE 12:6

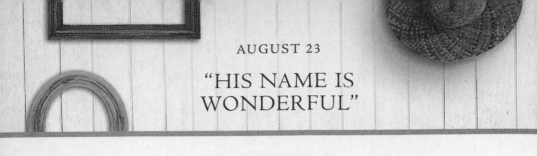

"HIS NAME IS WONDERFUL"

Audrey Mieir

1916–96

Children in bathrobes were playing shepherds and angels in a church nativity play. The prophecy from Isaiah 9:6 was read: "His name shall be called Wonderful, Counsellor, The mighty God, The everlasting Father, The Prince of Peace" (KJV). Afterward, the pastor reiterated, "His name is Wonderful."

From her place in the congregation, musician Audrey Mieir saw and heard all of this. "I felt as if I heard the rustle of angel wings and a musical chorus came to my mind," she said later. She quickly wrote the words inside her Bible: "His name is wonderful." In the next few days, a song took shape. It soon became a favorite of churches everywhere.

In her youth, Audrey Mieir had moved from Pennsylvania to California, where she got involved in the church led by Aimee Semple McPherson. In 1939, Audrey was ordained in the Foursquare Gospel denomination (which McPherson founded), but music remained her major ministry. There in Southern California, she was at the hub of a growing Pentecostal movement, working with a number of well-known preachers and musicians.

Besides her work as a choir director and songwriter, Audrey played an important role as a promoter. She helped to run a regular "Monday Night Sing," in which up-and-coming Christian musicians could share their gifts. In the 1960s, she encouraged a young singer named Andraé Crouch. "God is using you to bring out things people want to express," she told him. Mieir helped Crouch get started on an impressive career. (And he made a memorable recording of Audrey's song "To Be Used of God.")

This is a role we can emulate—helping others to be used by God. Sometimes we focus only on the gifts we ourselves can offer the Lord. We want to be the best speakers, writers, singers, helpers, or whatever. That's all well and good, but sometimes the best gift is encouraging someone else, as Audrey Mieir did with several young musicians.

Look around you. Do you recognize any "diamonds in the rough"? Are there those with musical or artistic gifts, or perhaps raw communication skills or unfocused creativity? What could you do to support them and develop their gifts? Could you be a "wonderful" counselor to someone else?

A child is born to us. . . . And he will be called: Wonderful
Counselor, Mighty God, Everlasting Father, Prince of Peace.

ISAIAH 9:6

"I'D RATHER HAVE JESUS"

Rhea Miller

1894–1966

Martin Ross was a drunk who had no interest in the Christian faith, despite the prayers of his devoted wife, Bertha. And then, suddenly, everything changed. He gave in to Jesus, and he didn't do it halfway. He gave up alcohol and went into the ministry. Ever after, as he preached at the Baptist church in Brooktondale, New York, he would tell his story. Looking back on the change in his life, he would say that he'd rather have Jesus than anything the world offered.

His daughter was listening. And one day, when she was twenty-eight, Rhea Ross Miller was walking in the fields near home, reflecting on her father's story, when a song began to form in her mind and soul: "I'd Rather Have Jesus." The lyrics describe the various lures of the world—riches, power, fame, etc.—and announce the decision to follow Jesus instead.

A decade later, these lyrics came to the attention of a young singer named George Beverly Shea, who put them to his own music. It would be another decade or so before he would start working with Billy Graham. As the main soloist at Billy Graham's evangelistic services, George Beverly Shea often performed this song, and it has inspired millions to examine their own priorities.

Meanwhile, Rhea Miller was a pastor's wife, using her musical gifts in the church. By the way, she approved of George's new tune and helped him publish it. She didn't need any fame from this song; she preferred to keep serving Jesus quietly. And as her husband became a superintendent in their denomination, overseeing other pastors, Rhea found a new way to serve. She offered piano lessons to the families of these pastors, free of charge.

There is a vast network of people who would rather have Jesus—and *serve* Jesus—than to enjoy any kind of worldly success. They're pastors, missionaries, and social workers instead of CEOs. They're worship leaders instead of Hollywood stars. This isn't to say that "successful" people can't serve Jesus. Of course they can. But some callings practically ensure a *lack* of worldly success. Rhea Miller decided to reward some of these folks by donating her services. What could you do to support those who would "rather have Jesus"?

---

*Everything else is worthless when compared with the
infinite value of knowing Christ Jesus my Lord.*

PHILIPPIANS 3:8

"FREELY, FREELY"

Carol Owens

1931–

It was a team effort from the start. Carol Owens partnered with her husband, Jimmy, in life and in songwriting. In the 1960s, he was working as a church music minister and an arranger when the two of them decided to write something new.

Understand that Christians were about twenty years behind the times in their musical tastes, maybe more. The rock 'n' roll revolution of the fifties and sixties was largely ignored by churches. There were moral reasons for this, but it still left young believers in an artistic time warp. For the most part, "modern" church music meant peppy choruses sung at Youth for Christ rallies in the 1940s.

Slowly things began to change with musicals written by Ralph Carmichael, Kurt Kaiser, and others. They were still pretty tame musically, but they had a pulse. Jimmy and Carol Owens joined that group of groundbreaking composers in 1971 with *Show Me!*

This dramatic musical told a story of evangelism and conversion. It was notable for its honesty. The Owenses had the nerve to criticize the church establishment and its failed attempts at sharing the gospel. *Show Me!* showed a genuine respect for spiritual seekers. Songs like "Break Down the Walls" were downright prophetic in their challenge to Christians to get out of their holy huddles and show God's love to outsiders.

A few years later, Jimmy and Carol offered a new musical, *Come Together*, calling churches to unity and worship. It was the first of its genre, the large-scale "praise musical." *Come Together* included Carol's song "Freely, Freely," which has been picked up by a number of modern hymnals.

The Owenses went on to write *If My People* and *Heal Our Land*, as well as the children's musical *Ants'hillvania*. They've also thrown their energy into teaching other Christian songwriters, worship leaders, and performers. Their two children are both involved in ministry. Daughter Jamie Owens Collins went on to be a noted singer-songwriter in her own right.

Jimmy and Carol are a team, devoted to helping that larger team, the church, do what God has called us to do. We don't need to go it alone, drumming up our own talents to try to make a difference. Find your team, and come together to honor God.

Make me truly happy by agreeing wholeheartedly with each other, loving one another, and working together with one mind and purpose.

PHILIPPIANS 2:2

"HAVE THINE OWN WAY"

Adelaide Addison Pollard

1862–1934

The 1890s saw a new excitement among American Christians about missions. International travel was becoming ever easier, and many converts from D. L. Moody's revivals were looking to put their faith into action. The Student Volunteer Movement had taken shape in the late 1880s with a stated goal of "evangelization of the world in this generation." In many churches, if you were truly serious about following Christ, you'd be headed for the foreign missions field.

Such was the attitude of Adelaide Pollard, a young woman from Iowa. She felt called by God to be a missionary in Africa, but her attempts to raise financial support fell short. For a number of years, her missionary dreams languished, leading to serious discouragement.

Then one night in 1902, she attended a prayer meeting and heard an older woman say, "Lord, it doesn't matter what you bring into our lives—just have your way with us." This inspired her to turn to the extended metaphor of the potter and the clay in Jeremiah 18:6—"As the clay is in the potter's hand," the Lord said, "so are you in my hand."

Putting pen to paper, Pollard wrote the text for what became a well-known hymn of dedication, "Have Thine Own Way."

Mold me and make me after Thy will,
While I am waiting, yielded and still.

She went on to teach at the Nyack, New York, training school of the Christian and Missionary Alliance, also becoming known as an evangelist and healer. Then she finally got to Africa for a short time but had to leave when World War I broke out. After the war, poor health kept her stateside.

Face it—some of us are very good at telling God what we want to do for him. We have our dreams of conducting certain ministries, and when they don't pan out, we're confused. *Why, Lord? I'm doing this for you! Why are you making it so hard to serve you?*

We forget that he's the Boss, we're the servants. He's the Potter, we're the clay. He gets to decide when, where, and how we serve him.

Who are you, a mere human being, to argue with God? Should the thing that was created say to the one who created it, "Why have you made me like this?"

ROMANS 9:20

"LET JESUS COME INTO YOUR HEART"

Leila Naylor Morris

1862–1929

Leila Morris told an interesting, but not unusual, story of her conversion: "When I was ten years old I was led to give my heart to God. . . . I knew then that I needed a Saviour. Three different years I went forward to the altar and prayed and prayed, until a man came and laid his hand on my head and said, 'Why, little girl, God is here and ready to forgive your sins.'"

Her life was a challenge even then. Her father had died, and her mother struggled to bring up five kids on her own. Leila helped out by knitting and sewing things they could sell in the family millinery shop. She also took piano lessons at the home of a neighbor who had a piano. These skills she learned in childhood proved valuable throughout her life. Leila kept sewing for a number of years, and she played piano and organ for the churches she attended.

She also wrote songs. "Nearer, Still Nearer," "Sweeter as the Years Go By," and "Let Jesus Come into Your Heart" all came from her pen. She didn't start song-writing until she was about thirty, but over the last thirty-seven years of her life, she churned out about 1,500 hymns—even though she was blind for the last fifteen years. (When her eyesight began to fail, her son built a twenty-eight-foot blackboard with large musical staff lines. Later she composed hymns in her head and sang them to her daughter, who transcribed them.)

You won't find deep theology in Leila's songs, just an honest expression of an authentic relationship with Jesus. In a way, she takes us back to that childhood altar—and the lesson she learned there. Human beings strive to attain God in various ways, but the gospel of grace invites us to stop striving. At ages eight and nine, little Leila tried to pray hard enough to please God. The message broke through the next year: God was already eager to welcome her.

That's the most powerful theological statement we can make. "Let Jesus Come into Your Heart." He's there, knocking. We just need to open up.

Look! I stand at the door and knock. If you hear my voice and open the door, I will come in, and we will share a meal together as friends.

REVELATION 3:20

"WE HAVE AN ANCHOR"

Priscilla Owens
1829–1907

She taught children for half a century—for the city of Baltimore and for the Sunday school of Union Square Methodist Church. Before we consider the enduring contribution of Priscilla Owens to our hymnals, let's consider the quiet impact she would have had on two, maybe three, generations.

There's a hidden history written in the lives of students. If they somehow get famous, they might give thanks to a special teacher who helped ground them in the truths that guide their lives. More likely, the grounding happens without fanfare. Teachers prepare children for adulthood, when some have their own children and send them to teachers for more grounding. Thus civilization is preserved.

Besides teaching, Priscilla wrote songs. In 1882 she penned the lyrics for "We Have an Anchor," clearly an expression of its era. She lived not far from Baltimore's Inner Harbor, and in that time before air travel, ships were a common part of life. The song begins with a question—"Will your anchor hold in the storms of life?"— and that storm imagery continues throughout the song. Priscilla assures us that our faith is "grounded firm and deep in the Savior's love."

Flip through an old hymnal, and you'll find a bunch of songs about storm-tossed ships. Almost all of them come from the 1880–1900 era, and that makes sense. It was a turbulent time. The industrial revolution was going full throttle. Society's changes were fast and furious. Everything was unsettled. People needed an anchor "fastened to the Rock which cannot move."

Life is still hurtling past us, fast and furious. If you are feeling unsettled, join the club. Fortunately, we still have an Anchor, as we put our faith in Jesus. New hymns will have to use newer metaphors—perhaps images of drifting in space—but we will always need to cling to something solid. We always need to get grounded in the Savior's love.

More than a decade after she penned "We Have an Anchor," Priscilla Owens was asked to write something for a church anniversary celebration focusing on missions. For this one, she looked past the insecurities of her age and offered the solidity of Jesus to the wider world. "We have heard the joyful sound: Jesus saves! Jesus saves!"

This hope is a strong and trustworthy anchor for our souls.

HEBREWS 6:19

"'TIS SO SWEET TO TRUST IN JESUS"

Louisa Stead

1850–1917

Tragedy struck suddenly for Louisa Stead when she was on a Long Island beach with her husband and four-year-old daughter. Her husband dived into the water to save a child, but the child dragged them both under and they drowned. It happened right in front of Louisa and her daughter, Lily.

Imagine it. One minute you're enjoying a perfect family afternoon, and the next your husband is gone because he tried to do something good. Louisa's husband, the father of her child, the provider of her home, was there and then he wasn't. It seems unfair. To add to the tragedy of it all, Louisa and her daughter were left in poverty. She had no money to take care of them, but she had her faith. Out of that faith came a poem, and that poem became the hymn "'Tis So Sweet to Trust in Jesus."

As the story goes, one day when there was nothing to eat and no money to buy food, Louisa opened her door and found food and money that someone had left. She wrote the poem in response to that particular kindness, but the thoughts she expressed in it go deeper. This profound trust in Jesus must have been what she clung to daily as she dealt with the loss of her husband, the nurturing of her daughter, and the practical necessities of life.

"'Tis So Sweet" speaks of the gifts that come from trusting Jesus: resting on his promises, freedom from relying on self, and the ability to take "life and rest, and joy and peace" from him. Louisa concludes the hymn with the assurance that Jesus would "be with me to the end." That's a recurring promise in Scripture. Clearly, it's what kept Louisa going.

What do you trust in when the hard times hit? Do you take comfort in knowing that you can trust in Jesus? That he is your Friend and Savior? Do you remind yourself that he is there with you until the end? It's not always easy to turn your focus from the problems at hand and refocus on Jesus and his promises, but when you do, you will find that it is very sweet.

The LORD is my strength and shield. I trust him with all my heart. He helps me, and my heart is filled with joy. I burst out in songs of thanksgiving.

PSALM 28:7

"BREAK THOU THE BREAD OF LIFE"

Mary Artemisia Lathbury
1841–1913

A commercial artist by trade, Mary Lathbury designed layouts for magazines and wrote poetry on the side. She was also an enthusiastic student of the Bible. Few, if any, would consider her an important historical figure, but she got involved in a history-making movement, and she left us a hymn that many still sing today.

The movement became known as Chautauqua. It launched in the 1870s as a continuing education program for Sunday school teachers, held each summer on the shores of Lake Chautauqua in western New York. This was a brilliant idea hatched by a businessman and a pastor, and it actually worked. Over the next fifty years or so, Chautauqua became an important part of American culture.

Over time, these summer classes evolved beyond Bible training. A wide variety of experts would be invited to speak on literary, social, or scientific subjects; writer Mark Twain and orator William Jennings Bryan made frequent appearances. Spin-off gatherings were held around the country. President Theodore Roosevelt called Chautauqua "the most American thing in America."

But let's get back to Mary Lathbury. She often attended the conference in its early years, when it was still focused on training Sunday school teachers. One of the Chautauqua founders, John Vincent, learning that Mary wrote poetry, asked if she could compose a text for a Bible study hymn, something the crowd could sing before a Bible teacher addressed them. She came through.

Break Thou the bread of life, dear Lord, to me,
As Thou didst break the loaves beside the sea;
Beyond the sacred page I seek thee, Lord;
My spirit pants for Thee, O living Word!

In a big way, the Chautauqua movement recognized the American hunger for knowledge and found many ways to meet it. In a smaller way, Mary Lathbury captured the soul's desire for knowledge of God.

As you read Scripture, you can make it a history lesson or a literary study, but if that's all it is, you're missing the point. God breaks open his Word like a piece of warm pita, and he shares himself with us in that sacred page.

---

*Jesus replied, "I am the bread of life. Whoever comes to me will never
be hungry again. Whoever believes in me will never be thirsty."*

JOHN 6:35

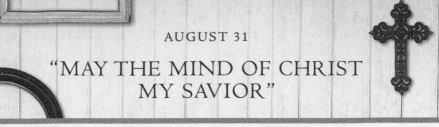

"MAY THE MIND OF CHRIST MY SAVIOR"

Kate B. Wilkinson

1859–1928

Christians often seek a greater experience of God. They want more joy, an extra blessing, or a more serious commitment. At various points in history, groups of believers have gathered around this search for something extra. In the late 1800s, the Keswick Convention in England was promoting the "Higher Life," as they called it. Kate Wilkinson, an Anglican involved in a ministry to girls in West London, often attended Keswick meetings.

The longing for a higher level of Christianity can get tricky, however. It quickly devolves into a focus on our own works as *we* discipline *ourselves* to be better Christians through study and obedience. While Scripture does call for study and obedience, it also emphasizes God's work in transforming us. The spiritual disciplines seem to be merely a matter of putting ourselves in a position to receive God's work of renewal.

Kate nicely captures this sense of openness in her hymn "May the Mind of Christ My Savior." Its opening lines seem to be a reflection on Philippians 2:5—"In your relationships with one another, have the same mindset as Christ Jesus" (NIV).

In this hymn, Kate explores what it means to have the mind of Christ. She wants his love and power to control all she does and says. Echoing Colossians 3:14-16, she wants the Word of Christ to dwell richly in her heart, Christ's peace to rule everything in her life, and the love of Jesus to fill her. This is not a determination to be more religious; it's a prayer for Christ to do his work within us.

Some modern folks might take issue with a line in her fourth verse: "Him exalting, self abasing, This is victory."

Wait—what? Self-abasement? That can't be right, can it? To abase is to degrade or belittle, to put down. In our age of self-esteem, are we really expected to put ourselves down?

Consider the Philippians 2 passage, which says Christ made himself like a servant and humbled himself so that he could be obedient to God's will. This is certainly what Kate was getting at. Our goal is not to be "great Christians," but to honor the Lord with our lives, and to let his presence fill us.

The LORD delights in his people;
he crowns the humble with victory.

PSALM 149:4

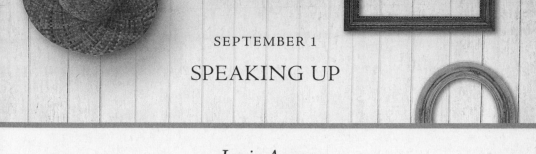

Jessie Ames

1883–1972

Jessie Ames didn't want much. She simply wanted to "create a new public opinion in the South" about racism in the 1930s. How difficult could that be?

What popular belief was she looking to change? She was challenging the notion that lynching black men was justifiable. Those who participated in or condoned lynchings said they were necessary because these executions protected women from being raped by black men. Jessie didn't believe this was true. She knew that rapes of white women by black men were rare. She believed the lynchings were motivated by race and hatred, not by a true protective instinct. She couldn't stand to have women's safety used as a cover-up for hate.

As a devout Methodist active in church women's groups, Jessie had already been involved in the fight to win women the vote. Now she organized women to speak out against mobs and lynching. She founded the Association of Southern Women for the Prevention of Lynching (ASWPL). The thousands of women she inspired to join her in the anti-lynching campaign spoke to whomever would listen—law-enforcement officials, churches, social clubs, politicians—and their voices were heard. Through their efforts, eighty-one organizations throughout the country endorsed the anti-lynching pledge that declared lynching was an "indefensible crime, destructive of all principles of government, hostile to every ideal of religion and humanity, degrading and debasing to every person involved." The number of lynchings in the country decreased dramatically.

Lynchings may no longer be a part of our day-to-day reality, but there are still plenty of injustices. As you look around, what do you see that is unfair in your world that your heart is saying you need to help change?

It doesn't always have to be a fight. Maybe you see a single parent who is struggling to meet their kids' needs, and you can help out. Or maybe it's something bigger that God has laid on your heart, and like Jessie and her racism-fighting sisters, you know you need to speak out, to educate, and to sway the minds of others.

What injustice, small or large, can you help to alleviate?

The LORD has told you what is good,
and this is what he requires of you:
to do what is right, to love mercy,
and to walk humbly with your God.

MICAH 6:8

POOR VISION

Dorothy Day

1897–1980

It seems hard to imagine, but Dorothy Day, the cofounder of the *Catholic Worker* newspaper and a national movement that served the poor in the 1930s, would sometimes be given a hard time about her work.

What possible justification could people have for objecting to meeting the needs of those in poverty? Ironically, some used the Bible as "proof" that Dorothy didn't need to help the poor. "Jesus said that the poor will always be with you," they'd say. They took the attitude that if having a poor population was inevitable, what point was there in trying to do anything about it?

Dorothy's response to her detractors didn't deny what Jesus said, but she knew Jesus didn't advocate throwing in the towel when it came to the poor. "We are not content that there should be so many of them," she said. "The class structure is our making and by our consent, not God's, and we must do what we can to change it. We are urging revolutionary change."

Have you ever come up against someone who uses an out-of-context verse or two from the Bible to try to prove that you're doing something wrong? What's the best way to handle that? Pull out your Bible. Find the verses that are being used to try to sway you. Read the whole story, the entire chapter, or even the entire book—and put those verses in their context.

If you read the entire story surrounding Jesus' words about the poor, simply finishing Jesus' sentence would convince you that Jesus wasn't saying it was pointless to help the poor. In fact, in Mark 14:7, Jesus says, "You will always have the poor among you, *and you can help them whenever you want to*" (emphasis added). In Mark 14:1-11, Jesus was saying that his time on earth was short, so it was important to pay attention to him for the moment. When he was gone, the poor would still be there to take care of.

Bible verses taken out of context can convince anyone of almost anything. Always go back to the source to determine the truth.

The godly care about the rights of the poor;
the wicked don't care at all.

PROVERBS 29:7

SAVING SOLES

Gladys Aylward

1902–70

Gladys Aylward, whose life was the inspiration for the 1958 film *The Inn of the Sixth Happiness*, was a missionary to China who worked with orphans and wounded soldiers. It was a rather unmissionary-like job, but it earned her the trust of the Chinese people, paving the way to effective ministry.

In the early decades of the 1900s, there were a number of missionaries in China—this was before the Communist takeover—but they were quickly labeled as foreigners. Their size, appearance, language, and way of carrying themselves kept them from fitting in. But Gladys Aylward was different. Though she was British, she was less than five feet tall, with dark hair, and she had no desire to look and act British. Her appearance made the Chinese people comfortable.

The Chinese government had recently forbidden the ancient practice of binding the feet of girls, and they needed a foot inspector to help enforce the ban—a woman who would agree with the new law and still be trusted by the people. They asked Gladys.

Foot inspection. Probably not what Gladys had envisioned as missionary work. But she willingly visited the homes of the Chinese families where she could examine the feet of young girls. While there, she had the opportunity to share her faith. The people came to accept her, not as a missionary, but as someone simply doing her job well and talking about something that was important to her. Her later work with orphans and soldiers (featured in the film) might not have been possible if she had not won acceptance by inspecting feet.

Do you ever look at missionaries or ministers and wish that you could have such a holy calling? Wouldn't it be great to make a living caring for people's souls? Are you frustrated with the mundane, unspiritual nature of your current work? Then take a lesson from Gladys Aylward. Even something as down-to-earth as foot inspection can be a ministry. Do what God has given you to do, and do it for his glory.

Work willingly at whatever you do, as though you were
working for the Lord rather than for people.

COLOSSIANS 3:23

THRILLER

Gladys Aylward
1902–70

She was no Ingrid Bergman. Missionary Gladys Aylward was short and dark haired, with a Cockney accent. So in 1958, when Hollywood created a film about her life, of course they cast Ingrid Bergman, a statuesque Swedish blonde. And that wasn't the only liberty the filmmakers took. They manufactured a romance that never existed and changed the name of Gladys's base of operations. There were actually *eight* "happinesses" in the name of her hotel, since eight is a Chinese number of good fortune. Oddly, Hollywood made it *The Inn of the Sixth Happiness*.

The true story of Gladys Aylward has enough adventure for several films. As a maid in England, Gladys longed to go to China as a missionary. But the China Inland Mission rejected her application because they thought she wasn't smart enough or young enough (she was in her late twenties) to learn the language. So in 1932, she spent her own savings to take the Trans-Siberian Railway across two continents—but when passenger space was needed for soldiers, she was put off the train in the middle of nowhere. By foot, bus, and mule, she finally got to the Chinese town where she began her work. At first she was running an inn for traders passing through the town. Later it became an orphanage.

Slowly, this working-class Brit won the respect of the townspeople. She learned the language and adopted the fashion and customs of the locals, even becoming a Chinese citizen in 1936. On one occasion she was summoned to quell a prison riot. Why her? "You have been preaching that those who trust in Christ have nothing to fear," the warden explained. She waded into the melee, quieted the prisoners, took their complaints to the authorities, and accomplished some meaningful prison reforms.

Nothing to fear. What a great way to be remembered! That's what makes this adventure story so thrilling. Called by God, this ill-equipped woman crossed the world to find her place of service. In a number of harrowing situations, she did what was necessary, and she led people closer to Christ.

What fears are holding you back? Are you worried about losing your money, your reputation, your free time? Are you afraid you might fail? As the prison warden learned from this plucky saint, those who trust in Christ have nothing to fear.

Even when I walk through the darkest valley, I will
not be afraid, for you are close beside me.

PSALM 23:4

SECOND CHOICE

Gladys Aylward
1902–70

That courageous missionary to China, Gladys Aylward, described herself as "insignificant, uneducated and ordinary in every way." She was amazed that God could use her, but he did.

Gladys spent sixteen years in China, during one of that country's most turbulent times. The inn she ran soon became an orphanage, and she worked in many other ways for the good of her neighbors. It was a time of growing suspicion toward Westerners, but Gladys immersed herself in Chinese culture, even becoming a citizen. After Japan invaded China in 1938, she stood with the Chinese and suffered with them. There are reports that Gladys even did some spying for her adopted country. In advance of one invasion, she led one hundred orphans across the mountains to safety.

This was *incarnate* faith. Gladys spoke freely about Jesus, but she is remembered for her sacrificial actions. Her Christlike actions. One local leader said he was converting to Christianity in her honor. Was he convinced of the truth of the gospel by her persuasive preaching? No, he saw Christ in her actions.

With the Communist revolution brewing, Gladys Aylward had to return to England in 1948. After repeated efforts to move back to the Chinese mainland, in 1958 she finally moved to Taiwan, where she started another orphanage and served until her death in 1970. The 1958 movie *The Inn of the Sixth Happiness* made her a minor celebrity, but she hated the limelight.

Looking back on her life, Gladys made a curious comment: "I wasn't God's first choice for what I've done for China. There was somebody else. . . . I don't know who it was—God's first choice. It must have been a man—a wonderful man. A well-educated man. I don't know what happened. Perhaps he died. Perhaps he wasn't willing. . . . And God looked down . . . and saw Gladys Aylward."

As she saw it, she was just filling in. The *perfect* missionary was out there, but unavailable. As a replacement, Gladys didn't have much to offer—except everything.

Whatever God is asking you to do, there's no use complaining that you're not perfectly suited to the task. Maybe you're God's second choice, or third. It doesn't matter how brilliantly you preach or teach or sing or lead or whatever. Just be the face of Christ in that place.

The Word became human and made his home among us.
He was full of unfailing love and faithfulness.

JOHN 1:14

BROADCAST NEWS

Aimee Semple McPherson
1890–1944

By the 1920s, Pentecostal preacher Aimee Semple McPherson had tens of thousands of devoted followers. She had raised funds to build Angelus Temple, a five-thousand-plus-seat church in Los Angeles. Nowadays, we'd call it a megachurch. And she was the preacher.

Aimee was equal parts evangelist and performer. Her theatrical method of bringing God's Word to people was both entertaining and inspiring. Thousands responded. On any given Sunday, the celebrities of the day—luminaries like Jean Harlow, Charlie Chaplin, and Anthony Quinn—might be in the congregation. In addition to her temple, Aimee started a Bible college that trained more than eight thousand ministers who went out and started hundreds of churches.

Several scandals threatened to take down her ministry, but none succeeded. In 1926, the already once-widowed and once-divorced female preacher was accused of faking her own kidnapping, perhaps to spend a month in seclusion with a man. Several lawsuits were filed against her because of mismanaged investments, and it took her a decade to pay off the debt. Still, her following grew and her ministry spread.

One of the reasons her ministry grew so rapidly was Aimee's wise use of the newest technology of her day. Her radio broadcast of the services at Angelus Temple reached twenty thousand people weekly. It's interesting to imagine what someone with Aimee's energy, theatrical talent, and forward thinking would be able to do with today's technologies. Would she have an incredibly popular blog? A YouTube series? A podcast? A digital magazine?

Aimee had to raise large sums of money to take advantage of the technology that was available to her during her lifetime. Today, reaching thousands of people with technology is not such an expensive proposition. Anyone with a smartphone can make videos or start a blog. Even you.

But technology is just a tool. We still need a message, a story to tell. So what's your story? What is God doing in your life? And how will you use the technological tools available to you in sharing that story?

The word of the Lord is ringing out from you to people everywhere . . .
for wherever we go we find people telling us about your faith in God.

1 THESSALONIANS 1:8

FOCUS

Isabella Lilias Trotter

1853–1928

In an 1883 lecture, art critic John Ruskin announced, "For a long time I used to say . . . women could not draw or paint. I'm beginning to bow myself to the much more delightful conviction that no one else can." Who changed his mind? A talented young Briton named Lilias Trotter.

Born into a wealthy home in 1853, she grew up enjoying fine art and international travel. Yet she also had a deep sense of spirituality. As a young woman, she attended deeper-life conferences and volunteered with the YWCA.

On a trip to Venice, her mother arranged a meeting with John Ruskin, who was staying at the same hotel. Seeing the young artist's watercolors, the hard-to-please critic raved. It was "extremely right minded and careful work." If Lilias kept at it, he suggested, she could become the "greatest living painter," producing art that was "Immortal."

This was a big break for her. With John Ruskin's coaching, Lilias applied herself to art. But he was increasingly demanding that she give up distractions—like her YWCA ministry on the streets of London. Lilias reached a difficult decision: "I see clear as daylight now, I cannot give myself to painting in the way he means and continue to 'seek first the Kingdom of God and His Righteousness.'"

Finally her life was in focus. In 1888, she went to the North African nation of Algeria as a missionary, and for the next forty years she served there, reaching out to the largely Muslim population. She used her immense creativity to pioneer new methods that were far ahead of her time.

This comment from her writings still rings true for modern believers: "Never has it been so easy to live in half a dozen good harmless worlds at once—art, music, social science, games, motoring, the following of some profession, and so on. And between them we run the risk of drifting about, the 'good' hiding the 'best.'"

You don't have to be an art prodigy to experience the pull of different activities. We are a generation of multitaskers. It's harder than ever to focus on what God truly wants from us. But when we seek him first—his Word, his desires, his Kingdom—everything else falls into perspective.

Seek first his kingdom and his righteousness, and all
these things will be given to you as well.

MATTHEW 6:33, NIV

STRANGERS IN THE NIGHT

Ida Scudder

1870–1960

Ida Scudder didn't want to be a missionary. Her grandfather was the first American missionary doctor to serve in India, and his seven sons, including Ida's father, were all missionaries. Everyone assumed Ida would be one too, but she had other ideas.

After graduating from school in the States, Ida was visiting her parents in India when she had a strange night that changed everything. A man came to the door pleading for help. His wife was in labor and having difficulty. Ida promised to send her father when he got home, but the man protested. Only a woman would be permitted to tend to his wife. Ida explained that, unlike her father, she was not trained as a doctor. She could do nothing to help. The same thing happened twice more the same evening, with news of different women having trouble in childbirth. The next morning, drums beat out a message of death. All three young women had died.

"I shut myself in my room and thought very seriously about the condition of the Indian women," Ida wrote later, "and, after much thought and prayer, I went to my father and mother and told them that I must go home and study medicine, and come back to India to help such women."

That was the beginning of a lifelong commitment. Ida Scudder not only returned to India, but she also brought money she had raised to build a women's hospital. She had to train her own nursing staff, and then she trained new doctors, too. That one awful night of death led to decades of giving life. Ida worked tirelessly, not only at the hospital, but also visiting the outlying villages to offer medical care. The people she served loved her. Gandhi visited. She won honors from British and Indian leaders. She raised up a new generation of doctors and nurses, forever changing the landscape of health care in that massive country.

Consider this: What unique quality do you bring to the Lord's service? Ida realized that, as a woman, she could have an impact that male doctors couldn't. What people can you reach, what service can you perform, that maybe no one else can?

He broke the power of death and illuminated the way to
life and immortality through the Good News.

2 TIMOTHY 1:10

PONDER, THEN DARE

Ida Scudder

1870–1960

Ida Scudder made things happen. Moved by the medical needs of India's women, she got trained as a doctor. She also built a hospital. It turned out that she was a pretty good fund-raiser, setting high goals and working hard to reach them. She was never shy about asking for money, and as a result her hospital project (and the medical college that followed) received donations small and great.

Did we mention that this project began when she was just in her twenties? It's not unusual to see naive confidence in someone so young; it's rare to find such wisdom.

Ida was both practical and rich in faith. She wrote:

First ponder, then dare. Know your facts. Count the cost. Money is not the most important thing. What you are building is not a medical school. It is the kingdom of God. Don't err on the side of being too small. If this is the will of God that we should keep the college open, it has to be done.

We need more of that combination of practicality and faith these days. Some Christian leaders follow impossible dreams with a reckless bravado. Others reduce ministry to budget proposals, measuring God's leading by its effect on the bottom line. We need to ponder first, and then dare.

The Kingdom of God is not about money. Sadly, some churches have gained a reputation as cash-mad enterprises. Aren't we always begging for donations? Here's where we need Ida's reminder that, whatever we're raising money for, it's far more than a building, a program, or a utility bill. It's God's Kingdom. That has several major implications. As Ida notes, we don't want to set our sights "too small." But we also want to observe godly principles in our fund-raising efforts—no manipulation of data, no coercion, no deceit. It makes no sense to try building God's Kingdom with worldly methods. We can trust him to tug at donors' heartstrings in appropriate ways.

So take a moment to ponder the possibilities of your own life. How are you building the Kingdom of God? And what practical aspects come into play? Your family? Your home? Your income? Your savings? Your education? What sort of "dare" is God giving you?

Don't begin until you count the cost. For who would begin construction of a building without first calculating the cost to see if there is enough money to finish it?

LUKE 14:28

DISCARDED

Evelyn Brand
1879–1974

She was too old to return to the missions field she loved. That's what the missions board told Evelyn Brand after decades of ministry. She must have felt crumpled up and discarded. At age sixty-eight, what was left for this widow?

From a well-to-do English home, Evie had been a Christian since childhood. A talented artist, she helped out in some local ministries to the poor in her twenties, but it wasn't until some overseas travel at age thirty that she felt called to foreign missions. She went to serve in India, where she married another missionary, Jesse Brand.

Together they developed a difficult ministry to mountain villages. It took years to build trust. The local Hindu priests offered strong opposition, but the Brands faithfully shared the gospel by their words and actions, tending the sick, building houses, teaching new farming methods, and helping the locals interact with national authorities. Jesse shared with Evie his dream to reach the people on five Indian mountain ranges.

Then Jesse died of blackwater fever in 1929. Evelyn tried to carry on the ministry, but her new coworkers weren't as effective as Jesse. Reassigned to an area in the plains, she was frustrated, cantankerous. And as political tensions in India arose, everyone decided that retirement was her best option. But she never gave up the dream.

In 1947, a new era dawned in India, and missionaries were returning (including Evie's son, Paul, a doctor at Ida Scudder's Vellore hospital). Evelyn begged the missions board to send her back to the mountains, and they refused. She promised to play well with others, if they'd just send her back, even to the plains, even for just one year. Finally they agreed.

And after one year, she retired *again* from that missions board but launched an independent mission, starting new ministries on the mountain ranges of India, as Jesse had dreamed. Over the next two decades, "Granny" Brand became a legend. Her son said she kept looking younger. "This is how to grow old," he wrote. "Allow everything else to fall away, until those around you see just love."

Ever feel discarded? Don't let anyone tell you you're finished. God loves you, and he *still* has a wonderful plan for your life.

The LORD will work out his plans for my life—for your
faithful love, O LORD, endures forever.

PSALM 138:8

THAT'S HOW WE ROLL

Lisa Beamer

1969–

September 11 has become a strange sort of "holiday" in the United States, a time of collective grieving as we remember the 2001 attacks on our country. Some find it odd that we would "celebrate" our losses, but we have found something else to be proud of: the willing sacrifice of those who put themselves in danger to save others.

Among these heroes are the passengers of Flight 93 who gave their lives to thwart the hijackers' plans to attack another national target. And among those passengers was a Christian man named Todd Beamer.

His widow, Lisa, was thrust into the spotlight, making hundreds of media appearances in the months following the attacks. She also put out a book entitled *Let's Roll*, named after her husband's favorite catchphrase. Fame can be cruel sometimes, and fickle. Some criticized her for trying to profit from this national tragedy. Some distrusted the charitable foundation she set up. But Lisa was processing her own grief in a very public way, and she hoped that her Christian witness and that of her departed husband would somehow be heard through the din. Eventually the media machine was finished with her, and she sank back into relative anonymity.

In 2011, she gave the commencement address at the school from which she and Todd had both graduated, Wheaton College in Illinois. Introducing herself as "a suburban mom from New Jersey," she challenged the students to be agents of redemption. "This is how we know redemption: when we see broken things made whole; when what's been discarded is restored to its rightful place; when those in peril are brought back to safety; when a path of restoration becomes clear; when love shines in the place that's been starving for it."

She noted that some of these students might find fame for great accomplishments, or perhaps for stupid YouTube videos, but their true *significance* might come without fanfare. "What an honor we've been given to cooperate with God as he works in the world!"

In closing, she gave the audience—and us—some questions to ask: "Who is becoming whole again on your watch? What is being healed through your influence? How is God redeeming his creation by way of your life?"

There is no greater love than to lay down one's life for one's friends.

JOHN 15:13

THE KIDNAPPER

Amy Carmichael

1867–1951

Amy Carmichael always had an eye for the down-and-outers. As a teenager in Ireland, she began a Sunday morning Bible study for women who worked in the local mill. Known as "shawlies," these women wore shawls to church because they couldn't afford hats, which all respectable women were expected to wear. While uppity churchgoers sneered at the shawlies, Amy welcomed them to her meeting, which eventually became its own church—appropriately called Welcome Evangelical Church. When family circumstances required a move to England, Amy started another ministry to mill workers there.

Increasingly, though, Amy was drawn to foreign missions. One problem: she suffered from neuralgia, a disorder that left her bedridden for weeks at a time. One missions board rejected her application because of this, but she persisted, serving briefly in Japan and Sri Lanka before finding her new base of ministry in India.

This ministry involved kidnapping.

At the time, young girls were often dedicated to the "gods" and forced into prostitution in Hindu temples. Amy was appalled, of course, and sought to change this practice. Even the Christians around her thought this was too big a task. Temple prostitution was deeply rooted in the culture. How could an Irish missionary change that?

Then a girl named Preena showed up. She had escaped from the temple and needed shelter. Amy welcomed her in and then stood up to the "employers" who tried to get her back. Soon there were other runaways seeking shelter. Amy found and protected them. Whenever she could get a child out of that peril, she did—despite threats and danger, fatigue, and even arrest. Over the years, some nine hundred children found refuge with Amy's Dohnavur Fellowship.

Her failing health increasingly confined her to bed, but then she found a new ministry in writing. She penned a number of devotional and instructional books, most notably the classic *If*, which explores the depths of Christ's love. It would seem that was her favorite subject, in life as well as art. "You can give without loving," she once said, "but you cannot love without giving." From the shawlies of Ireland to the temple girls of India, people saw divine love in her life.

Christ will make his home in your hearts as you trust in him. Your
roots will grow down into God's love and keep you strong.

EPHESIANS 3:17

BROWN EYES BLUE

Amy Carmichael

1867–1951

As a young girl, Amy Carmichael learned an important lesson about prayer. But she didn't really get it until decades later.

Her parents were solid Irish Presbyterians, and they had been teaching young Amy to trust the Lord. If you pray, they always said, God will answer. Well, as the story goes, young Amy was dissatisfied with her ordinary brown eyes. She wanted dazzling blue eyes.

You guessed it. Amy prayed fervently all night, begging the Lord to turn her brown eyes blue. In the morning, she rushed to the mirror and let out a mournful wail. Still brown. In this teaching moment, her mother explained that sometimes God answers by saying no. Sometimes he has a better idea about what we should have.

Flash forward a couple of decades. An adult Amy Carmichael is serving as a missionary in India, doing everything she can to fight the scourge of child prostitution in the Hindu temples. She wants to find out what's going on, to visit the temples, to talk to people in the know, to get the inside story. She knows the doors will be closed to a meddling missionary from Ireland—so she tries to pass herself off as an Indian, wearing a sari and even dyeing her skin with dark coffee. And that's when she realizes *it's a good thing my eyes are brown, not blue.*

Prayer confuses us sometimes. How can we get what we want? Jesus talked about praying in his name and about being persistent. In various Scripture passages we are told that God will give us the desires of our hearts, that we should make our requests known with thanksgiving, and that the prayer of the righteous can be very effective. But what's the secret to successful prayer?

Depends what you mean by success.

If prayer is, at its most basic level, a connection with God, then there is great value in telling God what we want, in waiting for his response, and in submitting to what he wants. A connection is made. We learn, we grow. Jesus himself concluded a prayer with "not what I want but what you want" (Matthew 26:39, NRSV).

Amy Carmichael learned this connection early, and all her life she kept connecting her desires to God's desires. The same thing can happen with us.

Take delight in the LORD, and he will give you your heart's desires.

PSALM 37:4

LETTING GOD'S VOICE BE THE LOUDEST

Carrie Judd Montgomery

1858–1946

Taking a chance can be scary, even when you believe it's something God wants you to do. People around you may try to dissuade you, often thinking they're looking out for your best interests. It can be difficult to ignore their well-meaning words of caution.

In the early 1880s, Carrie Judd Montgomery had an idea she believed God wanted her to act on. She wanted to publish a monthly journal about divine healing.

As a teenager, Carrie had been bedridden for two years. She experienced an immediate healing though prayer, and she quickly was able to walk. When news of Carrie's healing spread, she wrote a pamphlet, *The Prayer of Faith*, about her experience.

People began to ask her about healing prayer. There was much more to be written about healing, more people to encourage, and more stories than just her own to be told. A monthly journal was the way to do it.

Of course she asked the opinion of those she trusted. Not everyone was as enthusiastic as Carrie. One trusted minister didn't think it would be a success, so he discouraged her. But Carrie wasn't looking for success. She was looking to do what she believed God wanted her to do. She took the chance. In January 1881, the first issue of *Triumphs of Faith* was published.

Financially, it was an all-or-nothing deal. A second issue could be published only if those who had received the first issue paid for a subscription. They did. *Triumphs of Faith* had a sixty-year run.

Carrie became an influential leader in the divine-healing movement of the late 1800s because she took what others saw as a chance. But is it ever really taking a chance when you do something God has planned for you to do? Obedience to God doesn't always lead to financial or critical success, but it does lead you closer to being the person that God means you to be.

When you hear God's voice, do you let the voices of well-meaning people become louder than his? Or do you trust God's voice and your own relationship with him and follow his lead, knowing that whatever the outcome, you've done God's will?

---

*Peter and the apostles replied, "We must obey God
rather than any human authority."*

ACTS 5:29

RUN WITH YOUR DREAMS

Mary McLeod Bethune

1875–1955

As a child, Mary McLeod had opportunities her parents hadn't. But it still required personal strength and self-discipline to take advantage of those opportunities.

She was the daughter of former slaves, one of seventeen children. The family was impoverished, and everyone worked from the time they were young to provide the family with basic necessities.

Education was something Mary's parents couldn't provide all their children. When a missionary school for African American children opened near their home in South Carolina, Mary was the only one of her siblings allowed to attend. Each day she walked several miles to school and back. Once she learned to read, there was no stopping her. Her thirst for education was great, and she shared what she learned with her family.

But she didn't educate just her family. After attending Scotia Seminary and Moody Bible Institute, Mary became a teacher. She married Albertus Bethune, and they moved to Florida. In Daytona Beach, she started her own school, now known as Bethune-Cookman University, a private university that still educates students today.

That would be enough for anyone to be impressed with Mary's accomplishments, but there's much more. She became a civil rights activist and a special adviser on minority affairs to President Franklin D. Roosevelt. She opened a hospital in Daytona Beach to serve the black community. She worked to find jobs for African Americans in the first half of the 1900s. The list of her accomplishments could go on and on.

Mary was inspiring to those who knew her. She's an enduring example of someone who didn't allow circumstances to keep her from accomplishing her dreams. Her family gave her what they could. They gave her faith, and they sent her to the missionary school. Mary took those things, trusted God, and ran with them.

Sometimes it's easy for us as adults to blame the circumstances of our upbringings for blocking us from our dreams. But Mary didn't allow her circumstances to hold her back, and we don't need to either.

Do you have a dream that you've been afraid to go after because of the circumstances of your youth? Can you choose to trust God and run with it now?

God has not given us a spirit of fear and timidity, but of power, love, and self-discipline.

2 TIMOTHY 1:7

DIG THIS

Kathleen Kenyon
1906–78

There are two main ways to study history. One is to study it in books; the other is to dig it up. Kathleen Kenyon's father was a Bible scholar who became director of the British Museum, but his daughter preferred to play in the dirt. Kathleen became one of the foremost archaeologists of the twentieth century.

After conducting some important excavations in Zimbabwe and England, Kathleen moved to Jerusalem, directing the British School of Archaeology there. She turned her attention to the site of Jericho. Recent developments in carbon dating and site management led to a number of new (can we say "groundbreaking"?) discoveries. Kathleen pioneered a method of stratigraphy—analyzing layers (strata) of a dig. Since ancient cities were usually built on the rubble of older cities, archaeologists can find artifacts from different periods of history in different layers of the same site. Using stratigraphy and other methods, Kenyon determined that Jericho was probably the oldest continuously occupied settlement on earth, dating back to the 7000s BC or earlier.

The field of biblical archaeology was forever changed by Kathleen's work—though some Christians criticized her for challenging the scriptural record. At Jericho, Kathleen did *not* find evidence of Joshua's famous conquest, and this made her wonder publicly if there were other ways to read the biblical text. While she was a Christian, she was also a historian, and she had to report honestly what she found—and didn't find.

In our lives, we are sometimes tempted to "sell" the gospel by making claims that aren't entirely true. Will Jesus make all your problems go away? No. Has he turned you into a perfect person? No. Will he make you rich, powerful, and better looking? Probably not.

We need to speak truthfully about what God is doing in our lives. Excavate what's really going on in your heart and soul, and that should give ample testimony to the reality of Christ. Don't polish the story. Don't "market" the truth. Just dig through all your layers of personhood and share your story as a flawed but faith-driven follower of a forgiving Savior. People will reject a sales pitch. They'll respond to your honest story.

It was by faith that the people of Israel marched around Jericho
for seven days, and the walls came crashing down.

HEBREWS 11:30

TRUST THE ENGINEER

Corrie ten Boom
1892–1983

When you were a child and you first learned about the Holocaust, you were probably in disbelief that such horrors could happen. The thought that everyday people would allow it to happen makes most kids think, *I wouldn't have gone along with it. I would have said it was wrong.*

Yet everyday people did go along with it—but not Corrie ten Boom and her family. She and her family were Christians, part of the Dutch Reformed Church. Their church protested the Nazi persecution of the Jews, even though the Nazis claimed they were acting in the name of God.

Knowing the danger it would put them in, Corrie's family hid Jews in their home during the Holocaust. They were successful for a while, but eventually they were arrested. Corrie and her sister Betsie were imprisoned in Ravensbruck concentration camp. Betsie died there, but because of a clerical error, Corrie was released a few days after her sister's death.

After the war, Corrie created a home where survivors of the Holocaust could live and recover from their ordeal. Traveling extensively to talk about her experiences, she was never afraid to tell others what had happened to her. She freely expressed her faith in God, a faith that remained strong even in the concentration camp.

In the midst of the most difficult times, you might be tempted to wonder where God is—if he's there at all. Sometimes you have to make choices during those tough times, even though you're in the dark about what the outcome of those choices will be. Corrie had some thoughts about those times. She believed that "when the train goes through the tunnel and it gets dark, you don't throw away your ticket and jump off. You sit still and trust the engineer."

Trusting God when you have no idea what will happen next is a huge part of what faith is all about. If you knew what was going to happen, how much faith would you really need?

Don't be afraid, for I am with you. Don't be discouraged, for I am your God. I will strengthen you and help you. I will hold you up with my victorious right hand.

ISAIAH 41:10

THE TRIO

Mildred Cable + *Evangeline French* + *Francesca French*

—— 1878–1952 —————— 1869–1960 —————— 1871–1960 ——

The adventurous life of a foreign missionary—that was all young Mildred ever dreamed of. She found a potential husband who said he shared that dream, but then he changed his mind, and he pressured Mildred to change hers. She refused. At the age of twenty-three, she joined the China Inland Mission.

And there she found a new family. Immediately she teamed up with Eva French, another Englishwoman who had already served in China for a few years. Later they were accompanied by Eva's sister, Francesca. Together, they were known as "the trio," and their exploits became the stuff of legend.

Missionaries should keep moving, they thought. Start a new ministry, encourage local believers, and then let them run the show while you move on—that was the plan. The trio kept pushing westward, from the safer coastal regions toward the untamed desert. Mildred wrote that they "spent long years in following trade-routes, tracing faint caravan tracks, searching out innumerable by-paths and exploring the most hidden oases. . . . Five times we traversed the whole length of the desert, and in the process we had become part of its life." While other explorers fitted out large caravans for their journeys, these missionaries traveled light, with a few Chinese guides and a few pack animals to carry their Christian literature. Along the way they stopped, of course, to share the gospel. In the last city inside the Great Wall, they started a Bible school. As they crisscrossed the Chinese terrain, they were often in danger and occasionally suffered injuries, but they regularly experienced miraculous protection from God.

Who's on your team? These three women supported one another through thick and thin. Who does that for you? This trio seemed to instill bravery in each other, working together to follow their mutual calling. Do you have friends who call out the best qualities in you? Can you do that for them?

Find your "trio" (or whatever number you have). Talk about your common calling and how you can help each other follow it. Get past small talk and start knitting yourselves together into a strong fabric of adventurous service to God.

A person standing alone can be attacked and defeated, but two can stand back-to-back and conquer. Three are even better, for a triple-braided cord is not easily broken.

ECCLESIASTES 4:12

SEEKING AND SPEAKING

Agnes Ozman

1870–1937

I t's one of the sad ironies of the modern church. "There is one body and one Spirit," the apostle Paul wrote (Ephesians 4:4), and yet Christians in the twentieth century regularly fought about the Holy Spirit! The Pentecostal movement dawned in the early years of the century, with its flamboyant gifts of healing and tongues-speaking, and that brought about a backlash of suspicion and criticism from *non*-Pentecostals.

Agnes Ozman is often considered the first person in this modern Pentecostal movement to speak in tongues. Does that make her a hero or a troublemaker, a saint or a pawn? Who knows? Yet we can't deny her significance as the firstfruit of a huge religious culture.

Agnes was a seeker. Brought up in a Methodist church in Wisconsin, she yearned for a fuller experience of God, and she traveled across the country following different preachers. At a Bible school run by A. B. Simpson, she became acquainted with Holiness teaching—that sanctification involved a second blessing of the Spirit. Agnes was a woman of faith who prayed for divine healing on a few occasions and received it. She sought to follow God's leading in her life—and in 1900, he led her to Bethel Bible College in Topeka, Kansas.

Charles Parham was the founder and driving force of that new school. He and his students were exploring what it means to "receive the gift of the Holy Spirit" (Acts 2:38). On New Year's Eve 1900, the students prayed to receive this gift. The next evening, Agnes Ozman spoke in tongues. A halo seemed to surround her head. Her words sounded like Chinese. "I had the added joy and glory my heart longed for and a depth of the presence of the Lord within that I had never known before," she wrote later. "It was as if rivers of living waters were proceeding from my innermost being."

This was just the beginning. The next day, other students spoke in tongues, and there would be other outbreaks over the next few years.

Sort out the theology as you will, but we can learn this from Agnes: be open to God's leading, wherever that might take you. How can you let the Spirit guide you?

He is the Holy Spirit, who leads into all truth. . . . You know him,
because he lives with you now and later will be in you.

JOHN 14:17

PASS IT ON

Lettie Cowman

1870–1960

When you find words of encouragement—in the Bible, a book, a friend's e-mail, a song—do you ever share those words of encouragement with others? It stands to reason that if you found something encouraging in those words, others might too.

Lettie Cowman certainly found encouragement through the words of others, and she wrote them down to encourage her friends. In the process, she ended up encouraging generations of Christians.

After spending twenty years as missionaries in Japan, Korea, China, and Taiwan, Lettie and her husband, Charles, returned to the United States because of his failing health. Lettie spent the next six years caring for Charles until his death. During that time she devoured the writings of other Christians.

In devotionals, poems, and sermons from Harriet Beecher Stowe, Charles Spurgeon, Christina Rossetti, George MacDonald, and many others, Lettie found strength and encouragement each day as she sat with her ailing husband. She would read to him each morning from the various Christian books available to help them both through the long days.

After Charles's death, Lettie took the encouraging passages from the writings she had collected and put them together in a book called *Streams in the Desert*. She wove together Bible verses, her own words, and the words of other Christian writers to encourage fellow missionaries when they were struggling. She didn't know that her book would go beyond its intended readers and become one of the bestselling devotional books of all time. It's never been out of print.

When you're encouraged by someone else's words, don't keep them to yourself. Put them out there to encourage others, too. And think of how much easier it is for you today to share words of encouragement than it was for Lettie. Today, you can send those words quickly through e-mail to friends they might touch. You can post them as a Facebook status and wait to see who might comment. At your favorite coffeehouse, you can text the words of a song that moved you before the foam on your cappuccino has even disappeared. Maybe those words are exactly what someone needs to read.

Encourage each other and build each other up, just as you are already doing.

1 THESSALONIANS 5:11

IT'S THE JOURNEY

Coretta Scott King

1927–2006

Coretta Scott King stood for peace. Even after her husband, Martin Luther King Jr., was violently assassinated, she spent her life dedicated to finding avenues of nonviolent change. After her husband's death, she founded the Martin Luther King Jr. Center for Nonviolent Social Change, spoke at peace rallies around the world, organized and participated in rallies for civil rights, and inspired people across the globe to embrace peace and love rather than violence and hatred.

Coretta's husband, as we all know, had a dream. Coretta had a dream too. She had a dream of what she and her husband called the Beloved Community—an inter-religious, interracial, and international community that embraced tolerance and respect for all cultures.

The Coretta Scott King Book Awards were created to recognize African American authors and illustrators of children's books that demonstrate the values that Coretta and her husband stood for. Christian, Judaic, Islamic, Hindu, and Chinese symbols are all represented in the seal that is affixed to any book that wins the King Award. Coretta was a Christian, but her influence reached people of all religions.

The Bible makes it clear that one day there will be peace on earth. True peace. Of course we know there isn't peace right now. In fact, Jesus said that although we can have a spiritual peace in him, we will still have trials and sorrows (see John 16:33).

If trials and sorrows are inevitable, what's the point of working toward peace—the type of peace where all cultures tolerate and respect each other? Won't our efforts be futile?

Have you heard the saying "It's the journey, not the destination"? Practicing and embracing peaceful tolerance and respect will do you good. The apostle Paul tells us to do all we can to live in peace with everyone (see Romans 12:18). Peter tells us that if we want to enjoy life and be happy we must "search for peace, and work to maintain it" (1 Peter 3:11).

Being a peacemaker may not change the world, but it will change you, and it may change the lives of some of the people you come in contact with. That's a pretty good outcome for your journey, isn't it?

God blesses those who work for peace,
for they will be called the children of God.

MATTHEW 5:9

FOR THE BIRDS

Ethel Waters

1896–1977

S he was the first African American woman to receive equal billing in a Broadway show. For her role in the 1949 film *Pinky*, she received an Academy Award nomination, the second African American woman ever to receive one. She sang in jazz clubs, performed with the likes of Duke Ellington on stage and Sammy Davis Jr. in movies, had roles on television in its early days, and was eventually inducted into the Grammy Hall of Fame.

Ethel Waters had a successful public career, but her personal life was frequently tumultuous when she was young. But in the last twenty years of her life, her career took a turn. She rededicated her life to Jesus and toured with the Billy Graham Evangelistic Association from 1957 until 1976. Her signature song was "His Eye Is on the Sparrow." In fact, the song became the title of her autobiography.

That title refers to a passage in Matthew 10, where Jesus was giving his disciples the authority to go out in his name to drive out impure spirits and heal every disease and sickness. No big deal, right? Actually, it was probably incredibly scary, overwhelming stuff for twelve men who until recently had been fishermen and laborers.

To calm their fears, Jesus told them that not even a sparrow, a bird of very little value, ever falls to the ground without the Father being aware and caring about it. If God cares so much about a sparrow, Jesus assured them, how much more would he care about these twelve men, each of whom was much more valuable than a sparrow?

Ethel Waters understood that in the scary, lonely times, God's "eye is on the sparrow, and I know He watches me," as the song says. Do you understand that too? The Bible frequently reminds us that we can give our fears to Jesus. "Don't let your hearts be troubled," we're told. "Give all your worries and cares to God, for he cares about you" (John 14:1; 1 Peter 5:7). If there's something that has you worried or fearful right now, remember that God cares, you are valuable to him, and he's watching over you.

What is the price of two sparrows—one copper coin? But not a single sparrow can fall to the ground without your Father knowing it.

MATTHEW 10:29

SITTING DOWN FOR WHAT'S RIGHT

Rosa Parks

1913–2005

On December 1, 1955, Rosa Parks did something that unintentionally inspired a group of committed citizens, and it was the beginning of change in the world. You may already be familiar with the story. After a long day working as a seamstress in Montgomery, Alabama, Rosa boarded a segregated city bus to go home and took a seat in the back. The bus filled up, and when a white man got on and found there was no seat, the bus driver told the African Americans to give up their seats. Rosa refused . . . and was arrested.

The incident is considered the beginning of the civil rights movement in the United States. Within days, African Americans in the city stopped taking the bus in protest. For a year, they boycotted the buses. They walked, took cabs owned by African Americans, or carpooled to their destinations. The city retaliated, using an old law that prohibited boycotts to arrest some of those who stopped taking the bus.

Members of the African American community went a step further when they went to court and challenged the separate-but-equal law that allowed the bus company to segregate whites from blacks. Less than a year after Rosa refused to give up her seat, the US Supreme Court declared the segregation law unconstitutional.

What you might not know is that the woman who started all this was a devout Christian, brought up in a faith-filled home. "Prayer and the Bible became a part of my everyday thoughts and beliefs," Parks wrote later. "I learned to put my trust in God and to seek Him as my strength." She certainly needed God's strength for this ordeal.

Rosa had no intention of starting a movement that day. She was just tired of the injustice. Is there an injustice that you're tired of giving in to? It may seem overwhelming, but one small act of standing up (or in Rosa's case, sitting down) could be just what it takes to start the ball rolling toward change.

Learn to do good. Seek justice. Help the oppressed. Defend the cause of orphans. Fight for the rights of widows.

ISAIAH 1:17

WORDS WITH WINGS

Grace Noll Crowell

——— 1877–1969 ———

She was poet laureate of Texas. She published over thirty-five books during her lifetime. In the mid-1900s, she was so wildly popular that her husband quit his job to manage her career and answer the hundreds of letters she received monthly from an admiring public. Grace Noll Crowell had a life that many must have looked at and said, "It would be nice to have a life like that."

Her life was not as easy as it must have appeared from the outside, though. In 1906, she became very ill, and her recovery took years. During her years of sickness, she began to write poetry.

If you spend some time in her poetry, you get a glimpse of the hope and faith that she had, even though she was suffering while writing much of it. Her poetry was a way for her to express her continuing trust in God during her sufferings and a way to encourage others. She's quoted as saying, "I would like to write poetry that will help others who are suffering as I am."

In some of Grace's poetry, she wrote about angels. But not angels that sit on clouds, playing harps and singing all day long, like those often depicted in modern folk art; she wrote about angels that God sends to help us through trials and dangers. She wrote of angels that can loose the "yoke of weariness" and make hurts grow "faint and dim as some forgotten song." She imagined someone at the end of a struggle finding an angel "bent above him in the night to strike his chains away and set him free."

Biblically, angels are God's warriors, God's messengers, and they offer the Lord's protection in dangerous situations. Grace Noll Crowell vividly depicted this reality in exalted language.

When you're facing difficult times, do you ever think about the angels that are sent to fight for you and protect you? It can be a great comfort to know that a celestial support team has your back.

If you make the LORD your refuge, if you make the Most High your shelter, no evil will conquer you; no plague will come near your home. For he will order his angels to protect you wherever you go.

PSALM 91:9-11

YOUR PATH TO FOLLOW

Katharine Drexel

1858–1955

In May 1889, a Philadephia newspaper ran this headline: Miss Drexel Enters a Catholic Convent—Gives Up Seven Million. In truth, Katharine Drexel, a well-to-do Philadelphia native, didn't give up her family fortune; she used it for ministry.

Katharine was raised to believe that her family's wealth should be employed to benefit others. When she was a child, she learned charity from her father and step-mother when they would help people who came to their house. They gave food, clothing, and even money to those who needed it.

Their wealth gave the Drexels the luxury to travel, and when Katharine toured the country, she became aware of the problems of Native Americans. She saw that many of them were uneducated and impoverished. She also had a place in her heart for African Americans and their hardships.

Katharine felt God wanted her to help these specific people. A Catholic, she chose to become a nun. She founded the Sisters of the Blessed Sacrament and dedicated her life to serving the populations of the United States that she felt called to serve.

She understood that her calling was not necessarily the calling that God has for everyone, though. "It is a lesson we all need—to let alone the things that do not concern us," she said. "He has other ways for others to follow Him; all do not go by the same path. It is for each of us to learn the path by which He requires us to follow Him, and to follow Him in that path."

That's a very freeing lesson to learn, isn't it? God does not expect all Christians to take the same path. Some Christians are called to do full-time ministry. Some are called to jobs outside ministry. Some are called to take time away from work to raise a family.

Don't look at the path that God has set for someone else and assume that path is somehow more godly than yours. Follow the path of service he has set for *you*.

In his grace, God has given us different gifts for doing certain things well.

ROMANS 12:6

NO LIE

Katharine Bushnell

1856–1946

S he's lying. Are you going to believe a woman?"
Katharine Bushnell probably had to face verbal attacks like that when she testified before the Wisconsin legislature in the 1880s. Guards had to surround her for her own safety. She was testifying about women held against their will for sexual purposes in lumber camps. Having managed to get into these camps to investigate "white slavery" (as it was known), she knew she had to bring it out into the open, no matter the risk.

Her actions were controversial. Some state officials denied her accusations and accused her of telling lies. Still, she did what she believed was right, leaning upon the promise of a favorite Bible verse, Philippians 4:13. Christ would keep her strong while she fought for women who couldn't fight for themselves.

Katharine's bold testimony led to a Wisconsin law that outlawed the practice of white slavery, but the fallout from the controversy led her to go to England, where she worked with Josephine Butler. There, she learned the British army was supporting forced prostitution in India. Once again, she gathered evidence and gave testimony to officials despite a threat to her safety. Her testimony led to an independent investigation, and her accusations were proven to be true.

Beyond this social activism, Katharine was also a doctor, a medical missionary in China, and a Bible scholar. Her 1921 book, *God's Word to Women*, made a strong biblical case for the equality of the sexes. Throughout her life, this talented woman strode directly into controversy to try to make life better for others.

What do you do when faced with a situation like Katharine's in Wisconsin? Do you do what is right and risk your reputation and safety, or do you keep quiet and allow others to be hurt? It can be a tough call, but you can rely on the same promise from God that Katharine relied on: God will give you the strength to do what must be done.

Does this mean you'll feel no fear, no doubts, when you're in the middle of a difficult situation? Of course not. But faith keeps us clinging in spite of our fears and doubts.

I can do everything through Christ, who gives me strength.

PHILIPPIANS 4:13

WHAT YOU ARE

Henrietta Mears

1890–1963

Today, many churches have committed ministries for children, youth, and young adults, all of which have well-written curricula and trained leaders. Not all churches are able to provide this, but it's certainly not unusual to find those ministries in healthy churches.

In the early and mid-1900s, that wasn't always the case. Some churches had well-run ministries for their younger members, but curricula for Sunday schools and youth wasn't abundant.

It took a public school teacher, Henrietta Mears, to help change that. A devout Christian, she had taught various Sunday school classes since she was a teenager. Then she left full-time teaching to become director of Christian education at the Hollywood Presbyterian Church. She was almost forty years old when she made this career change.

Inadequate and uninteresting. That's how Henrietta described the materials the church's Sunday school teachers were using. She started to write her own. Soon other churches sought the materials she was writing. To meet the demand, she founded Gospel Light Press to publish the lessons she created.

Innovation seemed to come naturally to Henrietta, and that's one reason that young people were attracted to her. She became known as "Teacher" to thousands of youth and young adults during her ministry. She met them at the level where they were, but she had a knack for helping them grow greatly spiritually. Some of the young people she influenced included evangelist Billy Graham and Campus Crusade for Christ founders Bill and Vonette Bright.

Why was she so influential? It might have had something to do with her basic philosophy. She once said, "You teach a little by what you say. You teach most by what you are." Young people are quick to pick up on hypocrisy. Henrietta lived out the faith she talked about, and the young people of her time appreciated that. Young people still do.

Are you involved in ministry with youth or young adults? Do you have influence over youth—your own kids, nieces or nephews, or kids in the community? Remember that it's not just a cliché: your actions will definitely speak louder than your words.

You yourself must be an example to them by doing good works of every kind.
Let everything you do reflect the integrity and seriousness of your teaching.

TITUS 2:7

AT ANY COST

Betty Stam

1906–34

Betty Scott grew up as the daughter of missionaries in China. At the age of ten she wrote a poem that began with these words:

> I cannot live like Jesus
> Example though He be
> For He was strong and selfless
> And I am tied to me.

Those are wise words for a child. While Betty certainly never became just like Jesus, she did prove to be very strong and selfless as an adult. By the age of eighteen, she wrote that she was willing to give up all her own plans and purposes, give herself to Jesus, and accept his whole will in her life "at any cost."

While attending Wilson College in Pennsylvania, she met John Stam. They wanted to marry but gave up their own plans because John was involved with a mission in China that sent only single men. Even though Betty was also headed to China for missions work, they didn't think they'd see each other for a long time. Through a series of unexpected circumstances, they ended up in the same place. They were married a year later, in 1933. Their daughter, Helen, was born the next year.

Three months later, Betty made good on her decision to give her whole life to Jesus at any cost. Communists seized the city where the Stams ministered, abducted the missionaries, and executed them. They did not harm baby Helen, and somehow Betty had managed to slip some provisions and money in the baby's blanket. Another missionary found the child two days later, and he was able to use the money to get her and his own sick son to safety.

After the martyrdom of Betty and John, Christian colleges in the United States saw an increase in students preparing for missions in foreign lands. Betty's adult life as a missionary may not have lasted as long as she had hoped it would, but her influence as a missionary is still felt today as others step up to serve.

What influence does the story of Betty and John have on you?

Dear brothers and sisters, I plead with you to give your bodies to God because of all he has done for you. Let them be a living and holy sacrifice—the kind he will find acceptable. This is truly the way to worship him.

ROMANS 12:1

PUTTING GOD IN HIS PLACE

Duk Ji Choi

1901–56

Duk Ji Choi holds the honor of being the first woman in Korea ordained as a pastor. Before she received that honor, though, she endured quite a bit.

By her early twenties, Duk Ji was both an orphan and a widow. Her parents had died when she was in her teens; her husband died early in their marriage. Deciding to dedicate her life to Christ, she attended Pyongyang Women's Seminary in what is now North Korea.

Korea was occupied by Japan during this time, and Christians were ordered to worship the Japanese emperor. Duk Ji knew that the Ten Commandments forbid worshiping any god but the true God, so she refused to comply.

Along with others who refused, she was imprisoned and severely tortured, but she still refused to submit. She was released but arrested twice more, and both arrests involved more torture. Not only did she not give in, but she also openly worshiped God several times a day and held services in her cell.

She was not out of danger until the Japanese occupation ended. Later Duk Ji was ordained, and she preached all her life.

Chances are, you've never had anyone order you to worship an idol or false god and threaten you with torture if you refused. But if you think about it, idols are all around—not threatening, but enticing. It's easy to get lulled into making something the center of your attention and giving it greater importance in your life than your relationship with God. Your job, the love of your life, your kids, a hobby—or even the smartphone in your pocket that you're unable to live without—can become idols.

Putting these idols back in their proper places may seem like torture, but when you consider the actual torture that Duk Ji and other Christians endured to stay true to God, you may have a better perspective.

Is there something that's been pushing God out of his proper place in your life lately?

The idols of the nations are merely things of silver and gold, shaped by human hands. They have mouths but cannot speak, and eyes but cannot see. They have ears but cannot hear, and mouths but cannot breathe. And those who make idols are just like them, as are all who trust in them.

PSALM 135:15-18

IT'S YOUR SERVE

The Changing Face of Church Leadership

We really don't want to stir up controversy, but in our overview of women in Christian history, we have to mention this modern development: more churches are ordaining women for ministry than ever before. Some readers will cheer this fact; others will rue it. Women's ordination was one of the most divisive issues in Protestant denominations in the twentieth century, and it remains so today.

On one hand, some see strong biblical commands to keep women out of church leadership. A key passage is I Timothy 2:12: "I do not let women teach men or have authority over them." Many would argue for a basic order in God's creation: not that men are better than women, but that the genders have different roles. They see the increase in women's ordination as a dangerous compromise with worldly trends.

On the other side are those who preach gender equality, based on Galatians 3:28: "There is no longer . . . male and female. For you are all one in Christ Jesus." They cite the many New Testament examples of women in ministry as proof that the Bible's occasional restrictions on women pertain to specific cases and temporary situations. What's more, they say, all Christians are called to use their gifts in God's service. How can we deny opportunities to women who are gifted in leadership, prophecy, or teaching?

We won't resolve this debate in these short paragraphs, but we will offer one insight: the Kingdom of God is not about human power or status. Jesus said this repeatedly, in many different ways. *The first shall be last. If you want to lead, serve.* Men and women in our churches should not be jockeying for power. We should be seeking to serve one another.

We follow a Savior who did not cling to his divine privilege, but became a servant (see Philippians 2:6). It makes no sense for Christian men to hoard their power or for Christian women to grasp for it. If that's what's going on, we've all missed the point.

We admire the selfless service of the women we've written about who poured their lives into God's work. And we invite you to seek your place of service, regardless of power or position. How can you give your life for your Lord?

Whoever wants to be first must take last place and be the servant of everyone else.

MARK 9:35

THE MOST TERRIBLE POVERTY

Mother Teresa
1910–97

Mother Teresa of Calcutta was of course not always Mother Teresa of Calcutta. As a child growing up in a devout Catholic family in Skopje, Macedonia, her name was Agnes Gonxha Bojaxhiu. After her father died when Agnes was eight years old, her mother continued to raise her with a deep faith and a deep commitment to charity. Her mother encouraged her to always share with others—especially meals.

At age eighteen, Agnes went to Ireland to join the Loreto Sisters of Dublin, taking the name Sister Mary Teresa (after Thérèse of Lisieux, a patron saint of missions). In 1931, she was sent to Calcutta to teach at a school for some of the city's poorest girls. It wasn't until she made her final vows in 1937 that she became known as Mother Teresa.

A decade later, she left the Calcutta school to go into the poorest areas of the city to care for the unloved. Sensing a special calling from God to work with people who had no one to care for them, she believed that loneliness and being unloved were the most terrible poverty, and it was a type of poverty felt all over the world.

"The greatest disease in the West . . . is being unwanted, unloved, and uncared for," she wrote in *A Simple Path*. "We can cure physical diseases with medicine, but the only cure for loneliness, despair, and hopelessness is love. There are many in the world who are dying for a piece of bread but there are many more dying for a little love."

We know that God is love and that there is nothing in the world that can separate us from his love (see Romans 8:31-38). That doesn't mean we don't feel unloved and lonely at times, and this feeling can be very difficult to endure. To whom can you reach out today to help relieve some of the terrible poverty of loneliness and let them know that they are loved by both God and you?

---

*I am giving you a new commandment: Love each other. Just as
I have loved you, you should love each other. Your love for one
another will prove to the world that you are my disciples.*

JOHN 13:34-35

SOULS OF GREAT SILENCE

Mother Teresa

1910–97

Mother Teresa had been a nun and a schoolteacher for several years in the city of Calcutta before, on a bus ride, she sensed God telling her that he wanted nuns who would be his fire of love to work with the poor, sick, dying, and children. She heard him say to her, "I want to use you for my glory. Wilt thou refuse?"

It took Mother Teresa a year and a half after hearing God's request to get permission from her order to change her position from teacher to missionary to the poor. Once she had permission, she went to work helping those she'd heard God name—the poor, sick, dying, and children. For the children, she established an open-air school. She received medical training so she could help the sick. She created a home for people who were dying and destitute.

She also established the Missionaries of Charity, a Catholic church made up of women dedicated to the poor. It started with twelve members, but by the end of Mother Teresa's life, the Missionaries of Charity had four thousand members in congregations all over the world.

All of this came because she listened to God's voice one day while she was riding on a bus. We don't know how quiet that bus might have been, but we do know that Mother Teresa believed in seeking out quiet to be able to hear the voice of God. She believed that God could be found in the quiet, and silence was necessary to communicate with God.

"In the silence of the heart God speaks," she said. "If you face God in prayer and silence, God will speak to you. Then you will know that you are nothing. It is only when you realize your nothingness, your emptiness, that God can fill you with Himself. Souls of prayer are souls of great silence."

In our busy, noisy world, making the time to find a place to be in silence and remain quiet can be a challenge. Imagine how difficult it must have been for Mother Teresa, who knew there were always more people to tend to, more mouths to feed, and more sick to care for. If she could find the time, do you think you can?

Let all that I am wait quietly before God, for my hope is in him.

PSALM 62:5

Mother Teresa
1910–97

When you think of Mother Teresa, do you think of luxury? Probably not. The Catholic nun is known for her work with the poorest of the poor in Calcutta, India. She's known for working with lepers, those with AIDS, the homeless, and the dying. Luxury is not part of the Mother Teresa legacy.

It's not that there wasn't opportunity for Mother Teresa to indulge in some luxury during her life. As her ministry grew and she gained recognition in both the church and the world at large, she was, from time to time, offered some ways to make her life easier.

In 1965, Pope Paul VI gave her a Lincoln Continental limousine. It was the ceremonial car he had used on his trip to India. Instead of using the limousine as transport for herself and others who helped her with her work, she raffled the vehicle and used the money to help those she cared for in the leper colony.

When she won the Nobel Peace Prize in 1979, she didn't partake in the traditional banquet that would normally be given in honor of a Nobel Prize winner. Instead she asked that she be allowed to use the money that would have been spent on a banquet to help feed the poor in India. The banquet money was added to the $190,000 in prize money to help feed countless starving people.

As part of her choice to become a nun, Mother Teresa took a vow of poverty, which isn't necessarily a promise to be poor, but a promise to share everything you have with others so that a quest for wealth and stuff does not become a goal. It's clear that Mother Teresa took that vow to heart.

Our lives are full of small luxuries—four-dollar cups of coffee, TV channels we pay for but barely watch, pizza delivery on Friday nights. . . . Have you ever considered giving up one of those small luxuries once in a while and using the money saved to help others?

Don't store up treasures here on earth, where moths eat them and rust destroys them, and where thieves break in and steal. Store your treasures in heaven, where moths and rust cannot destroy, and thieves do not break in and steal.

MATTHEW 6:19-20

AN ENCOURAGING WORD

Ruth Bell Graham

1920–2007

Growing up, Ruth Bell was taught that ministry was a family thing. Her parents were missionaries in China, and Ruth spent most of her childhood there. Planning on missions service herself, she attended Wheaton College—where she met a young preacher named Billy Graham. She married him.

Instead of becoming a traditional missionary, as she had planned, Ruth found herself the wife of a pastor. After a few years, she was the wife of one of the country's most prominent evangelists. Billy's ministry took him all over the country for weeks at a time.

It didn't make sense for them to take their growing family on the road. Ruth chose to support her husband's ministry by staying home to care for their family. When her five children were young, caring for them in their North Carolina home was a full-time job. As they grew, Ruth began writing books of poetry and reflections about the things that her chosen path had taught her, and this became her ministry. It wasn't the ministry she had imagined when she was young, but it's the ministry that her choices led her to.

In her book *It's My Turn*, she wrote about something she learned as she was raising her children: "Never let a single day pass without saying an encouraging word to each child. Particularly wherever you have noticed any—even the slightest—improvement on some weak point. Some point at which you have been picking and criticizing. And never fail to pass on any nice thing you have heard said about [the child] to that child."

That's important advice for parents or anyone who cares for children, but it can certainly apply to others besides children, can't it? We hear so many negative things each day about ourselves. And, being harsh self-critics, we probably think even more negative things about ourselves than we hear.

Why not make this a priority—finding genuine reasons to tell other people what they're doing well, giving them something positive to dwell on? Children and adults alike need encouragement.

To whom can you give a genuine encouraging word today?

Let us think of ways to motivate one another to acts of love and good works.

HEBREWS 10:24

THIS IS MY REALITY

Joni Eareckson Tada

1950–

Why me? It's a question Joni Eareckson Tada must have asked herself constantly in the months following her accident. Paralyzed from the shoulders down after a diving mishap at age seventeen, Joni faced years of rehabilitation and a lifetime in a wheelchair.

Depression understandably ensued. In her bestselling book *Joni*, she recounts her despair and suicidal thoughts when she realized God was not going to answer her prayer to be physically healed. Her spinal cord was permanently damaged.

Joni learned to depend on other people for all her physical needs . . . and to depend on God for her spiritual and emotional needs. With the help of Christian friends and family, she accepted her new reality and understood that even with her disabilities, she had a lot of life to live.

After she learned to paint by holding a brush between her teeth, her artwork sold well. She also started to talk to others about what she had been through. Joni's story gained even more attention when she starred in a movie based on her life. With fame came opportunities to help more people. She started Joni and Friends, a ministry focused on those with disabilities. The ministry, now international, provides wheelchairs for those who need them, hosts retreats for families with disabled members, educates churches on how to minister to those with disabilities, and much more.

There's no way to know what life Joni might have had if she hadn't had her accident. We do know that eventually her question of *Why me?* turned into *Okay, this is my reality. How can you use me?* More than most people, she had to learn to trust both God and others in order to accomplish the things she found God had planned for her.

Sometimes God puts things in front of us to overcome or accomplish that we can't imagine we'll ever be able to do. Can you learn to rely, as Joni did, not only on God but also on other Christians to get them done?

Those who trust in the LORD will find new strength. They will soar high on wings like eagles. They will run and not grow weary. They will walk and not faint.

ISAIAH 40:31

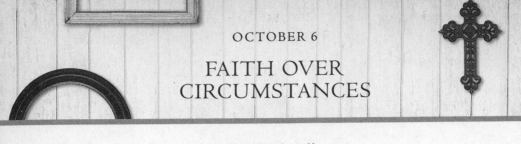

FAITH OVER CIRCUMSTANCES

Elisabeth Elliot

1926–

Elisabeth Elliot's story makes many people wonder, *Could I ever have done what she did?* She grew up in a missions-minded family and felt a call to use her talents to translate the New Testament for a tribe that didn't have the Bible.

At Wheaton College, Elisabeth met Jim Elliot, who felt called to reach a tribe that had never heard the gospel. The two were married in Quito, Ecuador, in 1953. They began to work with the Quichua tribe. Then an opportunity arose to make contact with the Aucas (now known as Huaorani), an unreached tribe that had killed all outsiders who tried to make contact.

In 1955, ten months after Elisabeth gave birth to their daughter, Jim and four other missionaries made contact with the dangerous Huaorani. They had some encouraging, friendly encounters with a few tribe members, but suddenly things changed. The five missionaries were speared to death.

It was big news. America mourned its "missionary martyrs," and many Christians were inspired to reach unreached peoples. But the most powerful inspiration might have come from Elisabeth Elliot and some of the other widows, who kept seeking ways to reach the Huaorani.

This is where the *Could I have done what she did?* question comes in. Elisabeth's faith must have been tested by those tragic circumstances, but she remained faithful. She was called to serve God there, and Jim's death didn't change the call. Eventually Elisabeth connected with the tribe that had killed her husband. She was able to tell them of the forgiving love of God.

In *These Strange Ashes*, a book about her first year in Ecuador before her husband's death, she wrote, "Faith's most severe tests come not when we see nothing, but when we see a stunning array of evidence that seems to prove our faith vain."

Elisabeth didn't see Jim's death as a stunning array of evidence that her faith was vain. Certainly, there were times when she was afraid for herself and for her young daughter, but her faith was stronger than her fear.

When the evidence against your faith seems to mount, do you allow it to sway you? Or do you choose faith over circumstances?

The LORD is my light and my salvation—so why should I be afraid?
The LORD is my fortress, protecting me from danger, so why should I tremble?

PSALM 27:1

YOUR CALLING

Elizabeth O'Connor

1928–98

Before 1952, Elizabeth O'Connor was "unchurched," as she would put it. She wasn't a churchgoer and didn't hold any particular Christian beliefs. But then friends who had helped her care for her sick brother invited her to the Church of the Saviour in Washington, DC. Out of respect for them, she went. It took just that one visit to the church, just that one time hearing the gospel, for Elizabeth's life to be changed. After that day, she made that city and that church her home.

Elizabeth became very involved in her church and its ministries, and she spread the church's story through her books and articles. She felt it was her calling.

Having a calling was a common theme in Elizabeth's writings. God has a call for everyone, a good work that they need to do. Those who choose to obey the call help others while benefiting themselves. Through the process of obeying the call, an individual becomes more of the person God wants him or her to be.

This wasn't just Elizabeth's belief. It was also embraced by the church's other members. They would spend time in prayer and meditation, listening closely to what God called them to do. In the mid-1970s, the church as a whole felt called to start six new churches. Through this new network of churches throughout DC, members helped others (and themselves) discern their own personal calls.

These believers understood that church wasn't just for their personal benefit. They lived out their belief that the insights they received at church were messages they should carry into the world to benefit others.

What programs or classes does your church offer that you can attend to help you gain the knowledge and give you the encouragement to tackle what God calls you to do? Are you willing to get involved at church so you can get involved in the world?

We keep on praying for you, asking our God to enable you to live
a life worthy of his call. May he give you the power to accomplish
all the good things your faith prompts you to do.

2 THESSALONIANS 1:11

NEVER TOO LATE

Laura Ingalls Wilder

1867–1957

Most of us know Laura Ingalls Wilder from her "Little House" books and the 1970s television show, *Little House on the Prairie*, that they inspired. The books are based on Laura's life as a girl growing up in a family that worked hard to provide for themselves in the Midwest in the mid-1800s.

At eighteen, Laura married Almanzo Wilder and lived and worked with him on a farm. They had children, a daughter, Rose, and a son who died after birth. Shortly after that tragedy, Almanzo developed diphtheria and was partially paralyzed from the illness. Not long after that, their home burned to the ground.

A drought further complicated their situation, putting them in dire financial straits. They moved from place to place trying to find somewhere they could prosper. When they landed in Mansfield, Missouri, it took them twenty years to become truly prosperous on their new farm.

Their hard-earned prosperity lasted until the stock market crash of 1929, when they lost their investments, but not their farm. Laura had written some before 1929, but it wasn't until after the crash that she tried to publish an autobiography, *Pioneer Girl*. It was rejected, but she didn't give up. She edited and edited, and eventually *Little House in the Big Woods* came to be. The $500 royalty check she received from the book was the first of many that finally brought lasting financial stability to the Wilders.

Through her autobiographical stories, readers get a glimpse of the spiritual education woven into Laura's childhood. The family attended church, and the children learned the Bible. This foundation must have been a comfort to her as she faced tragedy during the early years of her marriage.

Knowing Bible stories and verses and drawing on our understanding of them can be a great comfort when we are going through difficult times. If, unlike Laura, you didn't receive that type of education as a child, it's never too late. Bible stories and Scripture memorization aren't just for children in Sunday school.

Do you feel the need to be more familiar with the Bible? If so, set aside a few minutes each day to read it on your own.

When I discovered your words, I devoured them. They are my joy and my heart's delight, for I bear your name, O Lord God of Heaven's Armies.

JEREMIAH 15:16

DOING WHAT YOU GOTTA DO

Louisa May Alcott

1832–88

Young Louisa May Alcott was surrounded and educated by an impressive crowd. Formally, Louisa and her three sisters were homeschooled by their father, Bronson Alcott. Informally, family friends like Henry David Thoreau, Ralph Waldo Emerson, Margaret Fuller, and Nathaniel Hawthorne took an interest in sharing their knowledge with the Alcott children.

It was the time of the New England transcendentalist movement. Louisa's father spent most of his time involved with this philosophical and religious movement that emphasized self-reliance and independence. Louisa embraced these traits, but she also embraced much of what she learned from her mother.

From her mother, Abigail May, Louisa was taught Christianity and social responsibility. You can see this influence in Louisa's classic novel, *Little Women*, which is based on her family experiences. Jo, the independent tomboy who loves to write and becomes a teacher, was modeled after the author herself.

The things her parents taught her served her well. Louisa was self-reliant, independent, and faithful. She took care of her family. Although her father believed deeply in education and educating others, the transcendentalist beliefs that encouraged simple living often left him unconcerned about making money. As a result, Louisa had to work as a seamstress, a woman's companion, a teacher, a governess, an actress, and of course, a writer, to support the family. Some of her early novels were thrillers, a scandalous genre for a woman to be writing at the time, so she used the pen name A. M. Barnard. Hey, they helped pay the bills.

Although the saying "You gotta do what you gotta do" didn't exist at the time, Louisa certainly understood the sentiment. She even rolled up her sleeves during the Civil War and worked as a nurse, though she had no formal training.

When life gets tough, sometimes you have to take on tasks that aren't what you had imagined for yourself. You can resent it, or like Louisa May Alcott, you can draw on your strengths and do what you gotta do. Be grateful that you have those strengths, along with a God to draw strength from, to take care of yourself and those you love.

Work willingly at whatever you do, as though you were
working for the Lord rather than for people.

COLOSSIANS 3:23

LIFE'S DISAPPOINTMENTS AND ANNOYANCES

Catherine Marshall

1914–83

If you're not familiar with Catherine Marshall's books, perhaps you're familiar with the 1990s television series *Christy*, based on her book of the same name. Catherine's mother, Leonora, was the inspiration for the novel. Like the title character, she taught in Appalachia in the early 1900s. *Christy* was just one of more than twenty-five books the author wrote during her lifetime.

Catherine, the daughter of a pastor, grew up in Tennessee and later West Virginia. She attended Agnes State College to study history during the years of the Great Depression and learned to rely on faith that her tuition needs would be met even though times were tough financially. After graduation in 1936, she married a minister, Peter Marshall. The couple moved to Washington, DC, where Peter eventually became chaplain of the United States Senate.

Struggles came when Catherine contracted tuberculosis and battled for three years with the disease, depression, and recovery, all while trying to raise her young son, Peter John. In 1949, her husband died suddenly of a heart attack, and Catherine found herself a single mother with a nine-year-old son. To provide for him, she turned to writing.

Her first book was a biography of her husband, *A Man Called Peter*, published two years after his death. In 1955, it was made into a movie. Catherine continued to write books of fiction, instruction, and inspiration. Ten years after Peter's death, she married Leonard LeSourd, longtime editor of *Guideposts*. Together they founded a Christian publishing company, Chosen Books.

Catherine faced many disappointments after her first husband's death, but her faith brought her through, and she was able to provide support to other strugglers. In *Christy*, one of the characters gives this advice: "My father always told us . . . that if we will let God, He can use even our disappointments, even our annoyances to bring us a blessing. There's a practical way to start the process too: by thanking Him for whatever happens, no matter how disagreeable it seems."

Can you think back on a time when a setback or annoyance eventually brought you a blessing? The next time you face a disappointment, can you trust that God can use it to bring more blessings?

Give thanks for everything to God the Father in the name of our Lord Jesus Christ.

EPHESIANS 5:20

ARRANGING THINGS

Evelyn Underhill

1875–1941

As a mystic, Evelyn Underhill embraced the Bible as the *living* Word of God, something to be experienced, not just read. Mystics place an emphasis on having a spiritual relationship with God through intensely personal experiences.

Evelyn wrote extensively about mysticism. Her writings came not only from studying the practice through the ages, but also from her own mystical experiences. Early in her life, she wrote the classic *Mysticism*. Another classic, *Worship*, written toward the end of her life, has had tremendous influence on many modern authors and worship leaders. Mysticism can seem scary to some Christians who might have difficulty with some of Evelyn Underhill's ideas. But it becomes helpful as it leads us to bow down in worship in the unfathomable presence of God.

Evelyn made the pursuit of a relationship with God her highest priority. Her mentor, theologian Baron von Hügel, served as her mentor and encouraged her to learn of God's love both within the institutional church and by going out and helping the poor. He also advised her to pray at least one hour every day. If having a relationship with God was going to be her highest priority, spending time in prayer was a must. She passed on this wisdom to a friend: "Try to arrange things so that you can have a reasonable bit of quiet every day and do not be scrupulous and think it selfish to make a decided struggle for this. You are obeying God's call and giving Him the opportunity to teach you what He wants you to know, and so make you more useful to Him and other souls."

In our hectic world it can seem selfish to take time daily, especially as much as an hour, for quiet and prayer. There always seems to be something else to do, something urgent. We can easily convince ourselves that we'll make sure we'll find the time for God . . . soon.

How can you arrange things so you can have a "reasonable bit of quiet every day"? Can you make it a priority to carve out a time for quiet and prayer?

When you pray, go away by yourself, shut the door behind you, and pray to your Father in private. Then your Father, who sees everything, will reward you.

MATTHEW 6:6

MIRROR, MIRROR

Madeleine L'Engle

1918–2007

How do you know what's true about yourself? Whose words and opinions do you take into consideration when you create a mental self-portrait of who you are and what you're worth? It's tempting to absorb the words of everyone you come in contact with and create your self-portrait from those opinions.

Madeleine L'Engle, author of Newbery Medal–winning *A Wrinkle in Time*, cautioned about the people we use as mirrors of our inner selves. There was a time in her life when her books weren't selling, and she felt as if she wasn't meeting the standards set by other women in her community. Looking into other people's eyes for her reflection, she saw herself as a failure—until she realized that those people shouldn't have had that much influence on her opinion of herself. Later she wrote in *A Circle of Quiet*, "I try to be careful whom I use as a mirror: my husband; my children; my mother; the friends of my right hand."

Do you make conscious decisions about whom you allow to be your mirror, or do you just take in everyone's opinions about you? Coworkers, neighbors, casual friends, and even relatives who don't spend a lot of time with you will all have opinions about who you are and why you do the things you do. It's easy to fall into the trap of giving equal weight to the opinion of the person in the cubicle next to you and that of your best friend you've known for decades. But do they really deserve equal weight? Of course not.

Choose your own "mirrors." Make a list of those people whose eyes reflect the real you. Who knows you best? Whose opinion do you cherish the most? Who will be honest with you but also considerate?

And don't forget the one who knows you better than anyone else—the one who made you. Spend time with God in prayer. Through meditation and Scripture reading, look into his eyes and get a true picture of yourself.

O LORD, you have examined my heart and know everything about me. You know when I sit down or stand up. You know my thoughts even when I'm far away.

PSALM 139:1-2

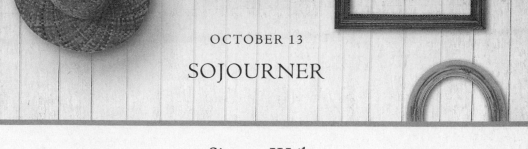

SOJOURNER

Simone Weil

1909–43

S imone Weil covered a lot of territory in her thirty-four years—spiritually as well as geographically. Born into an agnostic Jewish family in France, she had a keen mind, learning classical Greek as a child and Sanskrit as a teenager. She also had a deep-seated ethic of compassion for the needy.

Simone became well known among European intellectuals as a philosopher, teacher, and writer. Many admired her for throwing herself into causes she believed in. Once she left a teaching position to work at a factory for a year in order to connect with the working class. She publicly debated the Communist leader Leon Trotsky but also graciously hosted him at her parents' home. A few years later, she fought in the Spanish Civil War against an oppressive dictator. It turned out she was not a very good soldier, and soon she was in Assisi, Italy, recuperating from injuries. There, in the hometown of St. Francis, Simone had a mystical experience of Jesus. A year later, reading a poem by George Herbert, she had another—reporting that "Christ Himself came down and took possession of me."

Faith did not tame her wild intellect. It seemed to give her a whole new dimension to roam in. Many of her existentialist friends weren't sure how to handle her conversion. There were questions—was this for real, or some kind of soul experiment?—but also admiration. Camus called her "the only great spirit of our time."

During World War II, Simone left France for the United States and then England, but she still tried to support the French Resistance. She limited her diet to the meager rations eaten by those under the German occupation, and this severely weakened her, keeping her body from fighting off tuberculosis, from which she died in 1943.

Many of her writings were published after her death, including *Waiting for God* and *Gravity and Grace*. Few would agree with everything this freethinker wrote, but it's clear that God was in her thoughts.

The apostle Paul wrote about how God transforms us by the renewing of our minds (see Romans 12:2). How is that happening with you? Has Christ taken possession of your thinking? Is he inspiring you, exciting you, and energizing you to throw yourself fully into his abundant life?

[Jesus said,] "You must love the LORD your God with all
your heart, all your soul, and all your mind."

MATTHEW 22:37

HOW DOES JESUS VIEW IT?

Dorothy Sayers

1893–1957

Dorothy Sayers grew up in academia. Born when her father was headmaster of Christ Church Cathedral School in Oxford, England, Dorothy spent her life around education, learning, and books.

One of the first women to graduate from Oxford University, Dorothy earned highest honors in modern languages. After graduation, she chose to go into the world of words, first working for a publisher, then as a copywriter, and eventually authoring many books, essays, and plays. Her fictional character Lord Peter Wimsey was the hero of a series of detective novels and short stories that made Dorothy a bestselling author in the 1920s and '30s.

Yet Dorothy's talents went beyond fiction. She learned Italian so she could translate Dante's *Divine Comedy*. She considered it her greatest work, and the translation is still popular today. She also wrote books that centered on her faith and often looked deep into the connection between the Creator and his created people.

In *Are Women Human?*, a collection of some of her essays, Dorothy makes some thought-provoking observations about the relationship between Jesus and women. The women who knew Jesus had never known another man like him, she suggests. He never nagged, flattered, coaxed, or patronized them. He didn't make jokes about them. He "rebuked without querulousness and praised without condescension."

He "never urged them to be feminine or jeered at them for being female," Dorothy notes, adding that Jesus himself had "no uneasy male dignity to defend." She remarked that the church in her day (and some could argue that some churches still in this day) found something "funny" about being a woman even though one could never find that funniness by looking at how Jesus treated and interacted with women.

Jesus treated men and women truly equally.

Have you ever thought of looking at an issue by seeing how Jesus looked at it? Instead of accepting the way the culture views it, or the way a particular church denomination views it, or even how your family views it, pick an issue. See if you can, through reading the Gospels, determine how *Jesus* viewed it. It might give you a whole new understanding.

God created human beings in his own image. In the image of God he created them; male and female he created them.

GENESIS 1:27

MAKE IT FRESH AND MEANINGFUL

Flannery O'Connor

1925–64

T he only child of devout Catholic parents, Mary Flannery O'Connor was very bright, an avid reader, and often described as shy. At the age of twenty, she graduated from Georgia State College for Women with a degree in social sciences. Her studies were certainly useful for the two novels and dozens of short stories she wrote.

Displaying a keen understanding of the culture of the American South, the stories were strongly character driven, and these often quirky characters usually underwent transformation. O'Connor would frequently bring her characters around to a closer understanding of God, providing fresh insight on timeless themes.

At the age of thirty-nine, Flannery died of lupus, the same disease her father had died of when she was fifteen. Several of her works were published posthumously—some letters, a collection of book reviews she wrote, and, almost fifty years after her death, an early journal of her prayers.

In the fall of 2013, *A Prayer Journal* was published, containing her private writings from the times she attended the Iowa Writers' Workshop in 1947 and 1948. Included in this book are some important talks with God from O'Connor's early twenties, the beginning of her writing career. The journal gives great insight into the writer's thoughts, hopes, and dreams. It also shows that, like many people, she struggled at times with prayer.

"I do not mean to deny the traditional prayers I have said all my life," she mused, "but I have been saying them and not feeling them."

Can you relate? From a young age, many people are taught prayers to repeat over and over. Bedtime prayers, mealtime prayers, and the Lord's Prayer are examples of worthwhile prayers, but sometimes after the same words get repeated again and again, we can stop thinking about what they mean. When that happens, it helps to find a way to make prayer fresh again.

One way Flannery did that was to write her prayers—to journal her conversations with God. If your prayer life is a little stale, do you think writing your prayers could freshen it up?

When you pray, don't babble on and on as people of other religions do. They think their prayers are answered merely by repeating their words again and again.

MATTHEW 6:7

CHALLENGED AND CHANGED

Gracia Burnham

1959–

Y ou never know when you might make history. Sometimes history just happens to you. Such was the case with Gracia Burnham and her husband, Martin.

They had been serving in the Philippines as missionaries with New Tribes Mission since 1986. Martin was a jungle pilot, flying into remote areas with supplies and ferrying sick folks to medical centers. Gracia worked in a number of support roles and also homeschooled their three kids. In 2001, they were celebrating their eighteenth wedding anniversary, splurging on a trip to a resort hotel. That's when everything changed.

A militant group of Muslims stormed the complex and captured a number of guests, including the Burnhams. Some of the captives were released when their families or companies paid ransoms; others were killed. The kidnappers demanded a payment of about $1 million (US) for the Burnhams. This was not paid.

The couple was held for just over a year. According to Gracia's website, they faced "near starvation, constant exhaustion, frequent gun battles, coldhearted murder—and intense soul-searching about a God who sometimes seemed to have forgotten them." Then the Philippine military stormed in. Martin was caught in the crossfire and died, along with another hostage. Gracia was freed.

In the years since then, Gracia has candidly told her story in books and interviews. "I speak my mind," she told one journalist, joking that "everyone is entitled to my opinion." Gracia often gave her captors an earful, and after her release she openly wondered about the handling of the matter. Yet the ordeal changed her. "I think I saw my heart for what it is," she told *Christianity Today*, "the selfishness of my heart and always wanting my own way. I'd like to think that my heart has changed a bit. A lot of my self-will and my drive and always having to be right—I think that's what changed."

Jesus promised his disciples that trouble would come—especially when they were representing him to the world. Elsewhere, Scripture reminds us that our difficulties help to hone our character (see Romans 5:3-4). We get changed by our challenges.

I have told you all this so that you may have peace in me. Here on earth you will have many trials and sorrows. But take heart, because I have overcome the world.

JOHN 16:33

WISDOM OF YOUTH

Modern Young Women of Faith

Even at young ages, women can be inspirations to others. Three young Christian women in particular come to mind, each with a story that influences people of all ages.

Cassie Bernall was a seventeen-year-old student at Columbine High School in 1999 when two teenagers went on a shooting spree. Reportedly, one of the shooters accosted her and asked if she believed in God. She said yes, and she was shot and killed.

While the facts about the exact exchange of words have been disputed, Cassie's Christianity has not. According to *She Said Yes*, a biography written by her mother, Cassie had dabbled in the occult and had a difficult relationship with her parents. But then she found support in the local church youth group and eventually trusted Christ. The book has inspired and comforted many young adults with similar teenage experiences and parents who deal with troubled teens.

Bethany Hamilton was a thirteen-year-old surfer with professional aspirations, but in 2003 a tiger shark bit off her arm. Instead of being bitter about this tragedy, she became even more determined to go pro . . . and she achieved her goal in 2007. Throughout her journey, she spoke of how her faith in God helped her. Her book, *Soul Surfer*, has inspired many other teenagers and injury survivors.

Emma Sleeth was fifteen when she wrote *It's Easy Being Green* in 2008. The book for teens delivers the message that it's their job to care for the earth. Now she travels the country speaking about creation care, a modern environmental movement that emphasizes taking care of the planet so you can live out Jesus' commandment to love your neighbor—even if your neighbor is halfway around the world.

Sometimes it's easy to overlook what young adults can teach us. Cassie, Bethany, and Emma are just a few examples of girls with inspirational faith. Look around at the young adults you know. Are there any whose faith inspires you? Encourage them by telling them so.

Don't let anyone think less of you because you are young.
Be an example to all believers in what you say, in the way
you live, in your love, your faith, and your purity.

1 TIMOTHY 4:12

Martha Williamson + *Roma Downey*

———————— 1955– ———————— 1960– ————————

It's commonplace to complain about the decadence of TV shows, but these two women did something about it. Individually and together, they have offered some bright spots in bleak lineups. Martha Williamson and Roma Downey have reminded Hollywood that there's still a substantial market for wholesome entertainment.

Martha was a TV writer and producer, mostly in comedy, when CBS brought her in to work with a troubled project, *Touched by an Angel*. She had earned a reputation as a script doctor, someone who could breathe new life into a flawed story. That's what happened with *Angel* in 1994. Martha, a Christian, became executive producer of that new show, which ran for nine very successful seasons.

The program was consistently positive and inspirational, depicting angels sent by God to redeem bad situations and offer messages of hope. It was not aggressively evangelistic, but it was generically spiritual. The goal, expressed often by Martha and the show's breakout star, Roma Downey, was to share God's love. The series also featured Della Reese, another active Christian.

Martha and Roma both went on to produce other programs with spiritual and explicitly Christian messages. Along with her husband, Mark Burnett, Roma produced *The Bible* miniseries for the History Channel; it aired in 2013. In it, she played Mary, Jesus' mother. The series was a stunning success, with a reported viewership of more than 100 million.

Jesus told his disciples they were "the salt of the earth" and "the light of the world" (Matthew 5:13-14). Ever since then, Christians have tried to find ways to season and enlighten their society. How are you doing that? Are you bringing flavor to your workplace through your God-given joy and creativity? Is your home a beacon of caring and compassion in your community?

You don't have to be a TV star to do any of that. But you can have a major effect on your Facebook friends and Twitter followers and even your next-door neighbors—not by telling them how wrong they are, but by touching their hearts with a word of hope.

You are the salt of the earth. . . . You are the light of the world—
like a city on a hilltop that cannot be hidden.

MATTHEW 5:13-14

PRISONER OF LOVE

Mathilda Wrede

1864–1928

A life placed in the hands of God will be used by Him," Mathilda Wrede believed. As the daughter of a well-respected governor in Finland, she was officially a baroness. She could have lived in luxury her whole life, but she preferred to place her life in God's hands.

As a child, Mathilda had seen prisoners coming to the governor's mansion to do repairs. Even then, her heart went out to them. After having a religious experience at age nineteen, she decided to do what she could to help prisoners. Over the next four decades, Mathilda Wrede became a legend of charitable work. Without concern for her own safety, she visited prisons and befriended hardened criminals.

The inmates came to love and respect her. She wasn't some rich do-gooder parading her own righteousness. She left her fur coat at home and shivered with the rest of them. Dropping her baroness title, she became known as a "friend of prisoners." She ate prison rations. She dared to sit down with them and talk. She handed out Bibles and spoke of God's love, but she never seemed preachy.

Stories circulated about this courageous woman. One murderer warned her that she'd be wasting her time to talk with him: "My heart is as hard as a stone and my sins as big as a mountain." Mathilda surprised him by sitting beside him and asking about his time in Siberia. She asked if he knew some of her friends who had been shipped off there. She didn't preach to him that day, or on her next several visits. Eventually he begged Mathilda to tell him about her faith. He ended up asking God for forgiveness.

"I believe that the secret of success in our work . . ." she wrote, "is to love those whom we seek to save without waiting until we find something lovable in them. What would become of us if Christ had not loved us and come to our help?"

Our modern society loves to label people. We divide up generations, social classes, religious groups, and political leanings—ultimately breaking it all down to "us" and "them." We love our neighbors—those who are like us—and hate our enemies. But that's not God's way, as Mathilda would quickly tell us. He doesn't wait for people to become lovable before he loves them, and neither should we.

I was in prison, and you visited me.

MATTHEW 25:36

LET YOUR ACTIONS DO THE TALKING

Clara Swain

1834–1910

Clara Swain was known as a helpful child. A cousin once said that, at seven, Clara was "always eager to help someone." By the age of twelve she was helping to take care of another family's baby. In her midteens she helped nurse an aunt who had broken her ankle.

Clara taught for several years, but it wasn't what she wanted to do forever. She moved from teaching to medicine, accepting a job at a sanatorium and training under Dr. Cordelia A. Greene. With a female doctor as a teacher, Clara gained experience, and eventually she entered the Women's Medical College of Pennsylvania in Philadelphia. There she learned about women who served as medical missionaries in India.

After Clara completed her studies, God called her to India. She was thirty-five when she left for India to become a medical missionary, and she dedicated her life until retirement to caring for the physical and spiritual needs of that country's people. She's recognized as the first female missionary doctor to be sent to a non-Christian nation. For thirty years, she trained Indian women in Western medical practices.

Because of Clara's pioneering medical intervention in India, lives were changed. Women, who often were not given the same care as men in the country, learned to care for each other and for children. They learned how basic hygiene could improve their health. Clara created places to train women to give medical care and pass that information on to others. Later, she became the personal physician to the wife of a raja, and out of gratitude for Clara helping his wife, the raja allowed Clara to open a dispensary for women.

Throughout her time in India, Clara also dispensed Bibles and taught those around her about Jesus. That was part of her job as a missionary. Maybe you're not a missionary, but no matter what your job, you, too, can teach people about Jesus, even if it's just by your behavior. Hmmm . . . that's something to think about. What are people learning about Jesus by watching you?

Imitate God, therefore, in everything you do, because you are his dear children.

EPHESIANS 5:1

TEACH YOUR CHILDREN WELL

Catharine Beecher

1800–78

T alk about pressure! Catharine Beecher grew up as the daughter of a famous minister (Lyman Beecher), and her younger brother Henry gained even more fame as a church leader and abolitionist. Sister Harriet wrote the bestselling book *Uncle Tom's Cabin*, which further energized the abolitionist movement. Other brothers and sisters also became notable as activists, preachers, authors, and academics. This was one talented family.

As the oldest child, Catharine participated in the upbringing of her prodigious siblings, especially after their mother died when Catharine was just sixteen. But she was destined to make her own mark on society. In the United States at that time, the education of girls was not a high priority. Why would they need to learn philosophy or math if they would just grow up to marry and bear children?

Catharine had higher goals, not only for herself but for a whole generation of young women. After teaching herself many of the subjects normally reserved for boys, she became a teacher. At the ripe age of twenty-three, she cofounded a school for girls that would teach an ambitious curriculum, preparing young women to teach others. Promoting education for girls became her calling, as she continued to write, speak, teach, and establish new schools.

"If all females were not only well educated themselves," she wrote, "but were prepared to communicate in an easy manner their stores of knowledge to others; if they not only knew how to regulate their own minds, tempers, and habits but how to effect improvements in those around them, the face of society would be speedily changed."

And she did change the face of society, along with a few other like-minded educators. In that era, the country was growing westward, so Catharine started a program to train women to teach school in the "Wild West." As she saw it, women had a general inclination to teach children. They just needed to receive a good education in order to educate others.

That raises a good question for us: What do we do with the things we learn? As we gain insights about Scripture, glean hard lessons from life, or read fascinating articles online, do we keep these to ourselves, or do we dare to share with others?

Instruct the wise, and they will be even wiser. Teach the righteous, and they will learn even more.

PROVERBS 9:9

THUNDERSTRUCK

Rebecca Cox Jackson

1795–1871

At thirty-five years old, she was still terrified of thunderstorms. As Rebecca Cox Jackson wrote in her autobiography, "In time of thunder and lightning I would have to go to bed because it made me so sick." But this time as she prayed for deliverance, God answered. It was as if a cloud burst within her, she said. The thunderstorm—what she called "the messenger of death"—held no more threat for her. It was now "the messenger of peace, joy, and consolation."

That event was more than meteorological. It was a profound conversion that dramatically affected Rebecca's life. Now relying fully on God, she began hearing his voice inside her, telling her about her spiritual gifts and how to use them. Responding to this guidance, she began to lead regular "Covenant Meetings" with people from the neighborhood—mostly women but also a few men. There she would share her messages from God.

Of course, the local church authorities were skeptical about these meetings, especially since Rebecca refused to join a church or urge her followers to do so. Yet after Bishop Morris Brown of the African Methodist Episcopal Church visited her gathering, intending to admonish her, he said, "If ever the Holy Ghost was in any place, it was in that meeting. Let her alone now."

Rebecca's religious activity took a toll on her personal life, however, leading to the breakup of her marriage and an estrangement from her brother (an AME minister). Still she continued to work as she felt God was leading her, eventually connecting with the Shaker movement and starting a Shaker community in Philadelphia. This group followed the simple theology of the Shakers but added worship elements from African prayer circles. "Mother Jackson" was apparently pretty good at empowering African American women in their own interactions with God.

Have you ever had a "thunderstorm moment" in which God helped you face your fear? Do you need one? For Rebecca Cox Jackson, in a flash, terror turned to trust, and that changed her life forever. Realizing that she desperately needed God's guidance, she developed the habit of listening for his voice.

That's a good habit for us as well.

Listen carefully to the thunder of God's voice as it rolls from his mouth.
It rolls across the heavens, and his lightning flashes in every direction.

JOB 37:2-3

PRAY ON, DEAR ONE

Mary Slessor
1848–1915

Growing up in the slums of Dundee, Scotland, Mary Slessor was accustomed to hard work and long hours at a young age. Both her parents worked in the mills to provide for the family, but they were unable to make ends meet, partially because her father spent much of the money they earned on liquor. Mary went to work in the mills at the age of eleven to help bring in money.

Mary was fourteen when her father died of pneumonia, and she went to work full-time while attending school at night. On Sundays, her family always attended church. Mary's mother raised them to have faith despite their circumstances, and Mary embraced that faith.

In 1876, she went to work in the mission field of Calabar, a region of Nigeria, and ministered there until she died. Witchcraft, poverty, and alcoholism were prevalent, yet she slowly, very slowly, gained the trust of the people.

Mary did more than just preach to them about God. She changed their way of life. She taught them how to care for their sick. She created churches and schools. She took unwanted children into her home. The people believed that twins brought evil, and they abandoned them to the wild. So Mary took in those unwanted children as her own, becoming known as "White Ma." She went deeper and deeper into the region to areas where the currency was guns and liquor and violence, and she settled every grievance peaceably.

Because of her kindness, patience, and the grace of God, the local people accepted Mary's teachings and began to change their ways. She eventually was accepted as one of the people, taking on roles in the local government of Okoyong, an area where other missionaries had been killed.

Mary attributed her success to God and to the people who prayed for her. She once wrote to a friend, "It is all beyond my comprehension. The only way I can explain it is on the ground that I have been prayed for more than most. Pray on, dear one—the power lies that way."

Praying for people in the missions field is one powerful way that anyone can contribute to their work. Do you know anyone in ministry who could use your powerful prayers?

Pray in the Spirit at all times and on every occasion. Stay alert and be persistent in your prayers for all believers everywhere.

EPHESIANS 6:18

FLOWING LIGHT

Mechthild of Magdeburg

1207–97?

Mystic poet Mechthild of Magdeburg was well ahead of her time. Born around 1207 in a German castle, presumably from a well-to-do family, she decided to simplify her life in her twenties, joining a religious community, the *beguines*. The focus of this movement was Christian service, spiritual deepening, and voluntary poverty. *Beguines* were not officially nuns, and this gave them some freedom from the church hierarchy.

Since the age of twelve, Mechthild had experienced ecstatic visions. She said once that she saw "all things in God and God in all things." These visions continued throughout her life, and at the *béguinage*, she was encouraged to write them down. This resulted in some beautiful poetry and stunning prose, full of stark imagery and punchy phrases—very modern in its style. She wrote in the Middle Low German dialect, the speech of the common folk, not the church's high Latin. She was not shy about criticizing church leaders, and this earned her some official opposition.

Among other subjects, she wrote extensively about purgatory and hell. Some of her ideas may have been picked up in Dante's *Inferno* in the next century, and some scholars think that Dante's character Matelda is based on Mechthild.

But Mechthild's major theme was oneness with Christ. Borrowing styles from the biblical Song of Songs, she penned love poems that were both highly romantic and deeply devotional.

> *The tender caress between God and the soul,*
> *The Lord in the highest makes all things whole. . . .*
> *The undiluted joy of unity*
> *Vibrant love through eternity*

Ill health forced her to take refuge in a convent in her seventies. There she completed her book, *The Flowing Light of the Godhead*. She also mentored two other women, including another visionary who became known as Gertrude the Great (see the February 28 devotion).

The love and light of God flowed through Mechthild's life—into some amazing words, and into the lives of others. May that the same vibrant love flow through us.

Place me like a seal over your heart, like a seal on your arm.
For love is as strong as death.

SONG OF SONGS 8:6

REWRITING HISTORY

Faltonia Proba

FOURTH CENTURY

What if you took various lines of Shakespeare and put them in a different order to tell a biblical story? That's essentially what was done by Faltonia Proba, a Roman noblewoman. The middle of the fourth century was a time of great change. Under Emperor Constantine, Rome was now officially Christian, though there were still many who honored the traditional gods. Faltonia was brought up in a pagan family, and some of her early poetry apparently reflected those beliefs. But then she became a Christian, and that new commitment inspired her masterpiece, "De Laudibus Christi" (essentially, "In Praise of Christ").

This epic poem begins with creation, moves through some Old Testament stories, and continues with the ministry of Jesus. But here's the tricky part: Faltonia used lines from Virgil's *Aeneid*, pulling them out of order and reassembling them (and changing a few names) to tell the biblical stories. It's called a "cento," from a Greek word meaning "needle." This form was occasionally used by ancient writers, sometimes in theatrical comedies, stitching together lines from a well-known text to tell a new story.

Faltonia's "needlework" proved quite popular—and controversial—in the following centuries. Jerome panned it. Popes banned it. Emperors asked for copies of it. Historians praised Faltonia's "ingenuity" and included her in an early "Who's Who." Her masterwork was studied in medieval schools. In the fifteenth century, it was probably the first printed work written by a woman.

So let's think for a moment about what she did. Rather than completely rejecting non-Christian culture (as many Christians have done, then and now), she used it to create a new story: the Good News of Jesus. Her work had a ring of familiarity in the ears of the pagans who heard it, but it communicated far more than the lines originally did. Isn't this something like Paul's strategy in Athens, where he quoted Greek poets to express truth about the Creator?

How can we do this sort of thing in our day? Can we take bits and pieces of our culture—hashtags and sitcoms, ads and rap songs—and stitch them together to communicate the amazing story of Jesus? You don't need to write an epic poem; just start seeing the whole culture as a grab bag of gospel sharing.

This God, whom you worship without knowing, is the one I'm telling you about.

ACTS 17:23

SONGS FROM THE HEART

Mahalia Jackson

1911–72

"Gospel music is nothing but singing of good tidings—spreading the good news," said songstress Mahalia Jackson. "It will last as long as any music because it is sung straight from the human heart."

She grew up in New Orleans, singing in her Baptist church. Mahalia moved to Chicago at the age of sixteen, quickly connecting with a prestigious church choir and touring with another gospel group. She became famous for singing the songs of composer Thomas A. Dorsey, often considered the father of gospel music. His "Precious Lord, Take My Hand" became a standard for her. In 1947, her "Move on up a Little Higher" became the best selling gospel single ever. A decade later, she connected with composer Doris Akers to record a number of new gospel songs.

From the 1930s into the 1970s, Mahalia Jackson dominated the world of gospel music, making many records and winning many awards. She sang at President Kennedy's inaugural ball, the 1963 March on Washington, and Martin Luther King Jr.'s funeral. All the while, Mahalia refused to sing secular music, though she had no problem bringing jazz stylings into her gospel songs.

"I sing God's music because it makes me feel free," she's quoted as saying. "It gives me hope. With the blues, when you finish, you still have the blues."

So, what songs are you singing?

This question isn't just about music. It's about your attitude, your emotions, your expression of what's most important to you. In your Facebook posts, do you join with all your friends who are "singing the blues" about some issue or another? In your daily conversation, do you let others call the tune? Or do you express what's truly in your heart, the good news of gospel truth? Do you "sing" your own jazzy rendition of life with God-given creativity?

Mahalia Jackson knew poverty firsthand, and she used her remarkable gift to bring hope and help to those who continued to struggle. A strong supporter of the civil rights movement, she lent her voice to the cause whenever she could. According to one report, before Martin Luther King spoke at the March on Washington, she said, "Tell them about the dream." She shared her own dream of God's love and redemption every time she sang.

I will sing of your love and justice, LORD.
I will praise you with songs.

PSALM 101:1

HOMEMAKING

Edith Schaeffer

1914–2013

She was a missionary kid from China, attending college near Philadelphia, when she met a fascinating student from Westminster Seminary. Edith Seville married Francis Schaeffer, and together they made history.

The Schaeffers went into missions themselves, sent to Switzerland after World War II. In 1955, they had a new vision for ministry, and they had to break with their conservative missions agency to make it happen. In the Swiss Alps, the couple set up a shelter for travelers, where Francis could carry on intellectual discussions that turned evangelistic and Edith could show God's love through hospitality. They called it L'Abri (French for "the shelter").

This bold experiment bore fruit early. By their second year, they were averaging thirty-one visitors per week. By the late 1960s, they would occasionally house one hundred individuals—mostly young people. The Schaeffers caught the wave of the counterculture, the wondering wanderers backpacking through Europe in search of enlightenment. Many met Christ at this mountain retreat.

Those who couldn't travel to the Alps could still read Francis Schaeffer's books, first *Escape from Reason* (gathered from his talks) and then *The God Who Is There*, both published in 1968. Several other books would follow, up to his death in 1984. Francis offered a Christian critique of culture and society, vividly showing the need for hope—a hope that could be realized only in Jesus. In a time when many Christians were distancing themselves from the world, Francis promoted engagement with it, academically, socially, and politically. He was certainly one of the greatest influences on the evangelical movement in the last half of the twentieth century.

Edith wrote more than twenty books herself, including *The Hidden Art of Homemaking* (1971) and *What Is a Family?* (1975). Her subject was often Christian hospitality, which makes sense, since that was her specialty at L'Abri. In her writings and by her example, she elevated the value of marriage and motherhood as a creative calling. She had made a home not only for her husband and children, but also for thousands of needy travelers. One historian noted that Francis Schaeffer would never have gained prominence without L'Abri, and without Edith "there would have been no L'Abri."

Accept your calling—in a career, in ministry, in your home, or all of the above—and use your God-given creativity to make it a work of art.

Always be eager to practice hospitality.

ROMANS 12:13

QUEEN ANNE'S GRACE

Anne of Bohemia
1366–94

When King Richard II of England married Anne of Bohemia, many were left scratching their heads. Yes, she was daughter of the Holy Roman Emperor, Charles IV, but she brought no dowry into the English coffers. In fact, Richard had to pay a substantial sum to wed her. European politics was always a tricky business, and marriages often served to forge important alliances, but the English historians couldn't figure this one out. One of them described the fifteen-year-old bride as a "tiny scrap of humanity." Yet Richard, just sixteen, seemed to love her.

There were widespread complaints about this foreign queen—and about the entourage of attendants she brought from Bohemia—but Anne won the people over with her kind heart and gracious ways. (The ladies of England even began to copy her fashion choices.)

Though there had recently been insurrections, the young queen urged her husband to pardon the troublemakers. She became known as a peacemaker in various disputes. Anne was also an avid student of Scripture, and this brought about a significant connection in Christian history. One of the earliest Reformers, long before Martin Luther, was John Wycliffe, an English scholar who translated the Bible into English, completing the text in the same year Anne became queen. Some of Anne's attendants learned from Wycliffe and later returned to Bohemia, where they influenced another major Reformer, Jan Hus. In God's grand design, maybe this was the reason the English king married the Bohemian princess.

In her late twenties, Anne died in an epidemic. Grief-stricken, Richard wrote her epitaph, which included these lines: "To Christ were her meek virtues devoted: His poor she freely fed from her treasures; Strife she assuaged, and swelling feuds appeased; Beauteous her form, her face surpassing fair."

Have you ever been troubled by people saying nasty things about you? Have you been treated as a "tiny scrap of humanity," disregarded, dismissed, or discarded? Keep your focus on Christ. Offer him your "meek virtues." Win over your detractors with God's love and sweet peace. Who knows what impact you could have?

Look at those who are honest and good,
for a wonderful future awaits those who love peace.

PSALM 37:37

REST ASSURED

Phoebe P. Knapp

1839–1908

History books are full of examples of sons growing up in the shadow of famous fathers. From Solomon to Charlemagne, from Adams to Bush, we see the drama played out in various ways. But what are the dynamics in mother-daughter relationships? When the mom is prominent, how does a young woman find her own way? We get a glimpse of this in the life of Phoebe P. Knapp, daughter of religious leader Phoebe Palmer.

The mother was a dynamo, a popular speaker in the mid-1800s, author of a Christian classic (*The Way of Holiness*), a founding force in the Holiness movement.

Young Phoebe was the only child of Walter and Phoebe Palmer to live past infancy. You can imagine the pressure she might have felt to live up to the achievements of her well-known mother. From an early age, she poured herself into music, a gift she used in church ministry.

At age sixteen, Phoebe married Joseph Knapp, the president of a big life insurance company, and moved into a Brooklyn mansion. Phoebe Knapp became a popular hostess in town, and together this couple directed the Sunday school program in their Methodist church, becoming famous for their charitable giving. But Phoebe's greatest contribution to history was yet to come.

Phoebe Knapp knew the songwriter Fanny Crosby from church and often invited her over. On one such visit, Phoebe played for the famous lyricist a bit of music she had just composed, asking, "What does this tune say?"

Hold that thought. One of the issues that Phoebe Knapp's mother, Phoebe Palmer, had struggled with all her life was *doubt*. She preached a gospel of grace, but discipleship required a certain commitment to holy living, didn't it? And if your life wasn't holy enough, wasn't that an indication that your faith wasn't strong enough? Don't we need some sort of experience that assures us we're saved? The daughter must have had a front-row seat to her mom's struggle.

Back in the Knapps' music room, we find Fanny Crosby kneeling in prayer, listening to the new tune. Then she gets up and announces, "That says, 'Blessed assurance, Jesus is mine.'"

Christians have been reassured by this hymn ever since.

I give them eternal life, and they will never perish.
No one can snatch them away from me.

JOHN 10:28

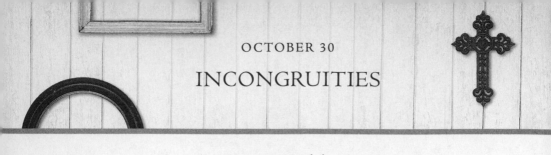

Augusta Pulcheria

CA. 398–453

For a part of the fifth century, Augusta Pulcheria wasn't just the most powerful *woman* in the world, but the most powerful person. Her father was Roman Emperor Arcadius, who died when she was about ten. Though her younger brother became the next emperor, she ruled with him. When he died in 450, Pulcheria seized power for a few tumultuous years.

It was a Christian empire at the time, based in Constantinople (what is now Istanbul). Pulcheria herself was known for her charity to the poor and her regular involvement in worship. She even took a vow of virginity. (Though this may have been a sincere religious commitment, it was also shrewd politically, since it kept her from being dominated by an ambitious husband. When she did marry, late in life, her husband promised to protect her virginity, and she maintained her power.)

The church was fighting fierce battles theologically and politically. Bishops in Alexandria and Constantinople vied for power with the pope in Rome and, to a lesser extent, bishops in Antioch and Jerusalem. Emperor Theodosius (probably pushed by sister Pulcheria) convened a church council in Ephesus in 431 to discuss the nature of Christ—human, divine, or both? The role of Mary was also at issue—if she was the "God-bearer," wouldn't she be divine herself?

That council devolved into violent riots, and a second Ephesus council in 449 didn't go much better. But in 451, Pulcheria and her new husband, Emperor Marcian, called the Council of Chalcedon, at which some four hundred church leaders agreed that Jesus was "fully God and fully man." This has remained official church doctrine.

The Confession of Chalcedon is a beautiful statement of Christian faith. It's strange that it would come out of such ugly rivalries. History often leaves us shaking our heads at its incongruities. Pulcheria herself, a devoted Christian leader, could be brutal toward her enemies. With one hand she gave to the poor; with the other she shut down synagogues. One day she would raise her voice in worship, and the next she'd be ordering violence against an opponent.

So don't model your life on Pulcheria's, or anyone else's. All of us are deeply flawed. Keep your focus on Jesus, the perfect God-man, who showed us the way and helps us follow it.

We all fall short of God's glorious standard. Yet God, with
undeserved kindness, declares that we are righteous.

ROMANS 3:23-24

MATCH MAKING

Women of the Reformation

While many today are celebrating the eeks and shrieks of Halloween, October 31 is also Reformation Day. Protestants commemorate Martin Luther's act of posting ninety-five complaints against the church establishment of his time. You think that tweets can be controversial? Luther's text, nailed on a church door in Wittenberg, Germany, started a religious revolution that spread worldwide.

Luther, Calvin, Zwingli, Knox—historians rattle off the names of Reformation leaders like kids thumbing through baseball cards. And the Reformers are all men. Where are the women of the Reformation?

At home, mostly. And in many cases, their supporting role was crucial to the cause.

Remember that the Catholic church required celibate priests. For a religious leader to be married was, in itself, a revolutionary act—so it was crucial for Reformers to marry women who would help rather than harry them. Like Katharina Luther, who brilliantly managed not only their home, but also Martin.

We see similar dynamics in the marriages of other Reformers. Before he married Idelette, John Calvin conducted a lengthy search for a wife who would share his reforming values. It's likely that Idelette also softened the hard edges of this lawyerly theologian.

It wasn't easy for these male Reformers to find wives who would mesh with their unique calling. Wibrandis Rosenblatt married *four* different Reformers, including Lutheran leader Martin Bucer. When each of her husbands died, there was another Reformer ready to marry her. Weird, yes, but it may testify to her own unique ability to support the Reformation cause.

Still, there was no particular model for these women to follow. In Strasbourg, Katharina Zell matched her husband's pastoral ministry with her own work of radical hospitality and prolific letter writing. In Geneva, another pastor's wife, Marie Dentière, wrote letters and spoke publicly in the Protestant cause. Each woman used her God-given abilities in teamwork with her husband to do God's work.

One key teaching of the Reformation was "the priesthood of all believers"—that any Christian could connect with God without having to go through a priest. This was a bold new concept for men; perhaps even more so for women. These "women of the Reformation" understood that they, too, could honor God with their abilities.

There is one God and one Mediator who can reconcile
God and humanity—the man Christ Jesus.

1 TIMOTHY 2:5

SAINTS ALIVE!

The Extraordinary Ministry of Ordinary Women

The term *Halloween* comes to us from Hallow Evening or Hallows Eve—designating the night before All Hallows Day or, as November 1 is often known, All Saints' Day.

A number of the women featured in this book are revered as saints by Catholic or Orthodox churches. Many of them faced persecution, refused to deny Christ, and died as martyrs. Others were sainted for their great works of compassion. We find their examples inspiring, but here we want to focus on a larger definition of sainthood, the kind we can all attain to.

The apostle Paul often began or ended his letters with references to "the saints." He used the Greek word *hagioi*, which is often translated as "holy ones" in Scripture. (*Saint* derives from the Latin word *sanctus*.) "All the saints greet you," he told one church before signing off (2 Corinthians 13:13, NKJV). He addressed another letter to "the saints who are in Ephesus" (Ephesians 1:1, NKJV). He wasn't writing to some superspiritual subset of the congregation but to all the believers. He could call them saints, or holy ones, because God had made them holy through the sacrificial blood of Christ.

Remember that some of these churches had major problems—scandals, factions, heresies—and yet Paul addressed them as "holy ones." How come? Perhaps you've seen this on a bumper sticker: "Christians aren't perfect, just forgiven." That's the essence of sainthood. Saints are sinners who kneel before God and receive his forgiveness.

But that's not the end of our story. God's love does amazing things in our lives. We begin offering it to others, stepping out courageously in faith, empowered by the Holy Spirit (the *Sanctus Spiritus*). So, yes, we admire the saints of old for their faithful actions, but we also practice sainthood ourselves as we humbly serve others and honor Christ.

So join in the celebration of All Saints' Day by exhibiting your own sainthood today!

You are no longer strangers and foreigners, but fellow citizens
with the saints and members of the household of God.

EPHESIANS 2:19, NKJV

Georgia Harkness

1891–1974

Georgia Harkness grew up in an upper-middle-class progressive family in New York. As a teenager, Georgia embraced her family's Methodist faith and felt a calling to do something in the church. She attended Cornell University and earned a BA in philosophy, going on to earn a PhD in philosophy of religion at Boston University. She taught philosophy and religion at Elmira College in New York while making time to study theology at Harvard Divinity School, Yale Divinity School, and Union Theological Seminary. She had to audit those classes because women were not allowed to take them for credit.

The Methodist Church ordained her in 1926, but she was not able to be a minister in the church—no woman in the denomination could at that time. Yet she continued to teach, becoming the first woman in the United States to teach theology at a seminary (Garrett Biblical Institute outside of Chicago).

Georgia's efforts were significant in the advancement of women in the male-dominated world of theology. Considering herself a feminist and a liberal (a subscriber to "chastened liberalism," she said), she worked for changes in both the church and society, particularly women's rights, civil rights, pacifism, and social justice.

Outspoken about the things she believed in, Georgia also chose to be patient. She would praise small changes in the right direction instead of condemning people or institutions for not changing quickly enough. Her patient, positive attitude helped to bring about large changes, one small step at a time. Thirty years after her ordination, she was instrumental in bringing about the revisions in the Methodist denomination that allowed women to become ministers.

Thirty years is a long time, and certainly not all issues take that long to resolve. But in our fast-paced world, even a few months can seem too long to wait. We tend to grumble about what hasn't been done yet instead of praising the efforts that are being made to work out the problem.

When changes need to happen, are you able to see the small steps toward change as positive things?

Let's not get tired of doing what is good. At just the right time
we will reap a harvest of blessing if we don't give up.

GALATIANS 6:9

NO RETIREMENT FROM LIFE

Maggie Kuhn

1905–95

Maggie Kuhn is known for what she did after retirement. At sixty-five, after decades of service, she was forced to retire from the Presbyterian Church. An activist, she had taught at a YWCA before working for the church. She had always encouraged women to get involved in social and work issues. She spoke about sexuality at a time when women weren't encouraged to admit that sexuality was important to them. In various eras, she vocally opposed segregation, McCarthyism, and war.

Once she retired, Maggie took on another issue—ageism. With other retirees, she cofounded the Gray Panthers in 1970 with a firm belief that older citizens had the responsibility to be fully involved in all aspects of life. Yet this was more than a special-interest lobby. Maggie felt strongly about working side by side with younger people to effect change in all areas—not just areas that affected older Americans. The Gray Panthers' motto is "Age and Youth in Action."

While she fought for justice for people of all ages, Maggie became a voice for the older generation. She once said our society "scrap-piles old people as it does automobiles" with policies like mandatory retirement. Old age is not a disease, she maintained. Senior citizens are far from useless. "We elders have all sorts of skills and knowledge," she said in the 1970s, "and I submit that if we got our heads together, there wouldn't be a single problem that could not be solved."

Maggie helped pioneer changes in the way older Americans thought about themselves and the way society viewed the elderly. She didn't think retirement from a job should mean retirement from life, and she embodied that principle herself. Through the Gray Panthers, the work she did *after* retirement has had a very positive effect on society.

Let's not lose sight of what people at every stage of life can contribute to society, to our families, and to the church. When you look around your family and your church, do you see the older members encouraged and invited to contribute as much as they possibly can? Is there someone you can invite to contribute more of the experience and wisdom that they've gained over the years?

Wisdom belongs to the aged, and understanding to the old.

JOB 12:12

THE LITTLE FLOWER

Thérèse of Lisieux

1873–97

Thérèse of Lisieux felt called to religious life from a very young age. She joined the Carmelite order in Lisieux, France, when she was fifteen years old. The young nun is now one of the Catholic faith's most recognizable saints because of the influence her autobiographical writings had after her death.

When she was only twenty-four years old, Thérèse died of tuberculosis. Her writings were compiled and published posthumously in a book called *The Story of a Soul*. She wrote frequently about flowers and the lessons she learned as she contemplated them—so much so that she's become known as "The Little Flower" or "The Little Flower of Jesus."

One of the things that flowers taught her was that everyone is important in God's eyes. "I realised that if every tiny flower wanted to be a rose," she wrote, "spring would lose its loveliness and there would be no wild flowers to make the meadows gay."

It's the same in "the world of souls—which is the garden of Jesus," she said, comparing some "great saints" to lilies and roses, while other people "must be content to be the daisies or the violets which rejoice His eyes whenever He glances down."

Her biggest revelation from her careful contemplation of flowers was that each person can be perfect when she is "that which He wants us to be."

Whether or not you believe that someone can be "perfect," Thérèse made a good observation. God has created us each to be different. He's given us different personalities, different temperaments, different talents, different desires. It's to our benefit to be who God created us to be and not look at others and wish we had been created like them.

Whether you consider yourself a rose or a daisy, you are exactly the way God intended you to be. Stop envying the other flowers in the field and embrace your unique, God-given identity.

Look at the lilies of the field and how they grow. They don't work or make their clothing, yet Solomon in all his glory was not dressed as beautifully as they are.

MATTHEW 6:28-29

THE FREEDOM TO LEARN

Helen Kim

1899–1970

When Helen Kim, whose birth name was Kim Hwal-lan, grew up in Korea, she was educated in church-related schools. She came to the United States for college, supported financially by American women missionaries in Korea. Helen earned a BA from Ohio Wesleyan University and an MA from Boston University Graduate School. In 1931, she became the first Korean woman to earn a PhD. With it, she returned to Korea to expand women's education in her home country.

She took the job as dean of Ewha Womans College, a private Methodist school in Seoul, South Korea, becoming its president in 1939. Not long after that, during World War II, Korea came under the control of Japan. Helen cooperated with the Japanese to keep the college open. When the war ended and Korea gained its independence from Japan, the school flourished into a full university, adding more schools and departments as well as a hospital.

Helen's achievements weren't limited to the educational field. In 1948, the Korean president selected her to represent the nation before the General Assembly of the United Nations. She spoke to many other international bodies as a Korean delegate, including the International Missionary Council and the World Council of Churches. She also served as publisher of the *Korean Times,* a daily English-language newspaper that reported on the political landscape in Korea so the US and UN allied forces could be informed of what was going on. Somewhere in there, she found time to serve as vice president of the Korean Red Cross for a while too.

In the male-dominated society that Korea was at the time, Helen dedicated her life to advancing the freedoms of her people, particularly the educational freedoms of women.

It's easy to take for granted the education that's readily available to us. Even when the choice is ours to attend college, get continuing training for a job, or commit to formal Bible study, we can grumble about the work. When you're tempted to grumble about your freedom to learn as much as you want, think about Helen Kim and how she fought to get educational freedoms for Korean women.

How much better to get wisdom than gold, and good judgment than silver!

PROVERBS 16:16

YOUR SPECIAL PLACE

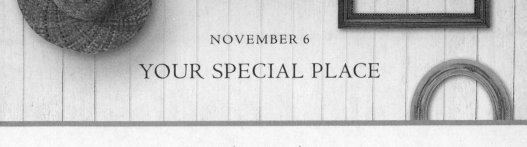

Bernadette Soubirous

1844–79

Bernadette Soubirous grew up in Lourdes, France. Her childhood was not remarkable. Her family was poor, and Bernadette was frequently ill. At the age of fourteen, the Catholic girl had yet to make her first Holy Communion.

But God doesn't need to use someone who has a lot of money or good health or has made their first Holy Communion. He can use anyone, and when Bernadette was fourteen, God used her to inspire the community of Lourdes. From February to July of 1858, Bernadette had several visions of who she believed to be Mary, the mother of Jesus.

In her visions, the young woman who came to her was sixteen or seventeen years old, wearing a white robe with a blue sash. The visions always occurred when she was at the same place, a grotto where she gathered firewood. Each time she returned, a "small young lady" would appear to her. No one else could hear or see this lady, but as the visions continued, people became interested. Some believed Bernadette; some did not. At one point, the authorities interrogated her to see if she was perpetrating a fraud. They found no evidence of deceit.

The Catholic church officials were skeptical at first too. Cynics were amazed when the vision told Bernadette to "drink of the water of the spring," and Bernadette swallowed mud because there was no spring there. The next day, clear water miraculously flowed from the grotto, and the spring still exists today. After the last appearance in July of 1858, Bernadette never saw the vision again. She entered a nunnery to live out the rest of her years.

Lourdes has become a place where Christians travel for pilgrimages, and millions of people have visited the grotto and its spring. Some people claim to have been healed from illness after experiencing the waters from the Lourdes spring.

Heading to France to make a pilgrimage to Lourdes may or may not be on your bucket list, but perhaps you have a special place where you've experienced God particularly deeply. Have you ever thought of making a pilgrimage to your special place to pray, be still, and listen to what God has to say?

What an awesome place this is! It is none other than the
house of God, the very gateway to heaven!

GENESIS 28:17

FAITHFUL PRAYER

Genevieve

_422–512_

Although he lived 1,500 years ago, Attila the Hun's reign of terror was so brutal and far reaching that his name is still familiar today. The empire he conquered stretched across eastern and western Europe. When he entered what is now France, the people knew what kind of destruction to expect. In Paris, the people planned to flee, but they were persuaded to stay.

What could persuade people to face Attila the Hun and his army? Did they have an even bigger, more powerful army? Did they have a clever strategy thought up by a military genius? No. They had a nun named Genevieve who persuaded the people of Paris that God would intervene. The men prepared to fight, but the women fasted and prayed. The Huns did not invade.

Some sources say the nun who became Saint Genevieve was born a peasant, but others suggest she had wealthy parents. Whatever her family's financial status, all reports say that when she was seven, she attracted the attention of Bishop Germain, who spoke with her for some time and declared that she would be consecrated to God. So Genevieve prepared to become a nun, entering the convent at age fifteen.

Genevieve was known to pray almost continuously once she entered the convent. Maybe her habit of earnest prayer inspired her to trust God with such conviction. The more you pray, the more likely you are to trust that prayer can make a difference.

You might not be able to pray almost continuously as Genevieve did. Yet you probably can make time to add just a little more prayer to each and every day. Where can you find five or ten minutes each day to spend time with God? You may just find that when difficult times threaten, you'll have a stronger, more trusting relationship with him.

He will rescue you from every trap and protect you from deadly disease. He will cover you with his feathers. He will shelter you with his wings. His faithful promises are your armor and protection.

PSALM 91:3-4

REVISITING CHILDHOOD STORIES

Patricia St. John

1919–93

P atricia St. John was born to parents who had been missionaries, but she never lived on the missions field with them; they returned to England right before she was born. There they raised her and her four siblings with a desire to help others.

After becoming a nurse, Patricia found herself in London during World War II, attending to the wounded during the Blitz. After the war, she worked for a while as a housemother at a boarding school, looking after thirty children. Eventually she made her way to Tangier, Morocco, to work with her brother for many years at a hospital. Then she went farther into North Africa to work at a village clinic. In all, she spent twenty-seven years as a medical missionary in Africa.

Even after she left Africa, Patricia dedicated herself to caring for people. When she returned to England, she cared for elderly relatives and used her home to minister to youth, single parents, and older people.

She ministered in another way too. Throughout her life, she wrote dozens of books, both fiction and nonfiction. She honed her storytelling skills when she worked as a housemother, telling bedtime stories to kids. Many of her works are children's books, including *Treasures of the Snow*, which was made into a movie. Written shortly after World War II, the book has a theme of forgiveness.

She wrote in her autobiography that she saw many who could not forgive others for the atrocities that happened during the war. "I knew that this generation of children needed, above all things," she said, "to learn the meaning of forgiveness." The book is still in print today; many of Patricia's books are. Readers find them relevant because the themes are timeless. The characters get into realistic situations where they must make important choices.

C. S. Lewis once said, "A children's story which is enjoyed only by children is a bad children's story." Adults and children alike enjoy Patricia's stories.

Are there books with Christian themes that you remember from your youth? Are they worth revisiting? Why not grab a copy (or download one) and see if you learn something as an adult that you didn't as a child?

My children, listen to me, for all who follow my ways are joyful.

PROVERBS 8:32

THE PRIMARY SOURCE

Maria Woodworth-Etter

1844–1924

When she was young, Maria's family often went without. As she wrote in her autobiography, her father was "addicted to the accursed cup." Both parents converted to Christianity in 1854, but her father died a year later, creating even more financial stress for the whole family. Along with some of her older siblings, Maria had to work to support the family, though she longed to be able to go to school and learn.

When she was thirteen, Maria professed her own faith in Christ, and her deepest desire was to go into ministry. Somewhere along the way, she formed the belief that it wasn't possible unless she had a husband who wanted to be in the ministry too. She married Philo Harris Woodworth and had six children. Five of those children died—some as infants, others when they were older. Maria and Philo traveled and ministered together—although Maria did most of the preaching. The stress of the deaths of their children took its toll, though. In 1891, Philo had an affair. Maria's marriage ended in divorce. Her life up to that point certainly had been rough.

Maria eventually married Samuel Etter, and the two of them traveled together, evangelizing. She led meetings where thousands of people worshiped and prayed, often praying for healing. Sometimes she led three meetings a day as people experienced great power, healing, visions, speaking in tongues, and occasionally trances. Maria became known as the grandmother of the modern Pentecostal movement.

In her autobiography, Maria wrote about realizing that God uses women—apart from men—to minister. She had second thoughts about her youthful belief that women could minister only alongside men. "As I continued to read my Bible," she wrote, "I saw that in all ages of the world the Lord raised up of his own choosing, men, women and children—Miriam, Deborah, Hannah, Hulda, Anna, Phoebe, Narcissus, Tryphena, Persis, Julia, and the Marys, and the sisters who were co-workers with Paul in the gospel . . . are mentioned with praise."

Notice what Maria did here. She had a long-held opinion that she thought was biblical—and then she went back to the Bible to see if it really was. That's a good practice for all of us, on any issue.

Your word is a lamp to guide my feet and a light for my path.

PSALM 119:105

AN OPPORTUNITY FOR GENEROSITY

Eva Burrows

1929–

Here's something interesting you might not have known: the Salvation Army, the Christian charitable organization that cares for the poor and homeless, is organized like the actual military, with both soldiers and officers. From 1986 to 1993, the general of the Salvation Army was Eva Burrows.

You might say she was born for the job. Her parents, Robert and Ella Burrows, were officers. Eva was eighth of their nine children, born when they lived in Australia. Her large family did not have a lot, but neither did the people around them. She never thought of herself as poor.

Eva went through a period in her life when she wasn't sure she wanted to follow in her parents' footsteps, but eventually she dedicated her life to the Salvation Army. After graduating from college, she entered service in the organization with the intent of becoming ordained and being a missionary in Africa. She worked in Zimbabwe for nearly twenty years, followed by a period of going from place to place, from England to Sri Lanka to Scotland to Australia to other regions. She worked with the poor in many, many countries.

In 1995, Eva began promoting a rather novel concept she called "Banking with the Poor," sometimes known as microfinancing. When Jesus said, "The poor you will have with you always," according to Eva, he was "indicating that those who have plenty will always have an opportunity for generosity in helping those living in poverty." She encouraged banks to provide small loans to people who don't have access to traditional banking.

At that time, participating in microfinancing wasn't easy for individuals. Today, there are many online organizations that provide microloans to entrepreneurs all over the world who don't have access to traditional loans. These loans help them start businesses and give them a chance to climb out of poverty. Anyone now has the "opportunity for generosity in helping those living in poverty" by investing a small amount in microloans, sometimes as little as twenty-five dollars.

A quick online search for microloan organizations will turn up several you can research to see if investing in microfinancing is a good way for you to help the poor. Next time you're online, consider checking it out.

If you help the poor, you are lending to the Lord—and he will repay you!
PROVERBS 19:17

TO LIVE AND LOVE LIFE

Florence Nightingale
1820–1910

Her name is synonymous with helping the sick and injured. Even today, someone who nurses people back to health is sometimes called a "Florence Nightingale."

Against her family's wishes, the original Florence Nightingale dedicated her life to nursing when she could have had a life of privilege. Hearing the voice of God when she was seventeen, she confidently claimed her calling: to help others.

Florence was educated and talented. She chose not to marry so she could devote her attention to her ministry. Although her family and friends had plenty, she saw hunger, poverty, and sickness around her in England. Wanting to relieve this suffering, she became a nurse in London.

You might say she gave up the good life to be a nurse, but Florence felt she *gained* a good life by becoming a nurse. For her, this service to God was a way to live and love life, so she gladly threw herself into her work.

It was mostly her work with soldiers during the Crimean War that made her famous. Traveling to Crimea to supervise volunteer nurses, she found a bad situation—a hospital severely neglected and poorly managed. Florence worked patiently to improve conditions and to comfort patients, becoming known as "the Lady with the Lamp" because she made rounds after hours to talk and pray with ailing soldiers. After discovering that many of them died from illnesses they picked up in the hospital, she became an advocate for more sanitary medical practices.

When she returned to England, she continued in nursing and also began to write. Her first book, *Notes on Nursing*, was written as curriculum for a nursing school she founded. It sold well to the public and helped to change the way patients in all hospitals were taken care of. She spent the rest of her career promoting and improving nursing, and she inspired generations of others to enter the profession.

Following God's call may take us out of our comfort zone, and it may mystify the people who are in that comfort zone. Could you, like Florence, give up "the good life" for a truly good life?

If someone has enough money to live well and sees a brother or sister in need but shows no compassion—how can God's love be in that person?

1 JOHN 3:17

POWER OF EDUCATION

Pandita Ramabai

1858–1922

In India, there is a mission that has stood for over a century, serving hundreds of thousands of India's poor and needy. Today, an orphanage gathers girls into families where they are given a future. A school at the mission combats India's high illiteracy rate, teaching thousands to read.

This is only a portion of what Mukti Mission provides. There are medical services on site and traveling medical personnel who go to villages to treat people. A home for India's unwanted—widows, unwed mothers, and special-needs children—provides outcasts with a place to live and vocational training. Mukti also has a two-thousand-seat church. It was all founded by an Indian woman known as Pandita Ramabai.

Pandita Ramabai had been brought up by a father who believed in female education. He taught his wife to read and write Sanskrit as well as several other languages, and she taught their daughter, who excelled in all her studies. By the way, Pandita is not her name; it's a Sanskrit title awarded to scholars that means "learned." She earned the title when men at Calcutta University discovered her education was equal to theirs.

By the time she was twenty-four, she'd been married, had a child, and was widowed. Ramabai decided to dedicate her life to improving the lives of Indian women. She had come into contact with some Christians in India and had read parts of the Bible, but while studying in England she finally converted to Christianity. Lodging there with a community of nuns, she was especially impressed with their grace-filled mission to prostitutes.

Before leaving England, she began raising funds for a new enterprise back in India—what eventually became Mukti Mission. And toward the end of her life, she translated the Bible into the local language so those at the most basic reading level could read it.

Education was obviously important in Ramabai's life, and it came from many directions—unconventional parents, organized schooling, and a group of sisters sharing the grace of God. It all raises these questions: What are you learning these days? And what are you teaching others?

Feed the hungry, and help those in trouble. Then your light will shine out from the darkness, and the darkness around you will be as bright as noon.

ISAIAH 58:10

FRENEMIES

Eudokia of Heliopolis

D. 107

Fantastic tales are told of a Samaritan woman, Eudokia, who lived in Phoenicia at the turn of the second century. Historians don't know much about Christianity in this immediately postbiblical time, and so they're not sure how much of the Eudokia story is fact and how much is legend. Still, this woman is revered in the Orthodox tradition, and the accounts—even if they're merely legend—tell us something of the character of Christianity in that pivotal period.

It is said that Eudokia lived a sinful life until she awoke one midnight to hear singing from the home of a Christian neighbor. Asking about it the next day, she met a traveling monk, who led her to Christ. She renounced her loose lifestyle, gave away her wealth, and joined a monastery herself. (This is one of the historical problems with the story, since it's generally accepted that the monastic movement began in the late third century. Still, there might have been ascetic Christian communities in her time.)

Then an old boyfriend showed up, trying to seduce her. Not only did she reject his advances, but she also uttered a prayer that struck him dead. At the urging of the other Christian women there, Eudokia prayed for his resurrection, and he revived . . . and soon converted.

Later, persecution broke out against the Christians. Eudokia was arrested and tortured—but then the torturer got word that his wife had died. He begged Eudokia to pray for his wife's resurrection. It happened, and the family converted.

Several other Eudokia stories involve resurrections. She even urged an assistant to raise someone. While historians question the legitimacy of these accounts, there's still something striking about them. Eudokia was showing love to her enemies by giving them new life. For the next two hundred years, Christians would be locked in a struggle for survival, but they did not take up arms to fight the authorities. Instead they relied on the power and love of God.

Nowadays many Christians feel embattled. They're fighting for their rights, for freedoms, against cultural decay, against sins of various sorts. But we can all learn a lesson from Eudokia, who loved her enemies—sharing with them a new life in Christ.

Love your enemies! Pray for those who persecute you! In that way,
you will be acting as true children of your Father in heaven.

MATTHEW 5:44-45

A NEW DIRECTION

Olympia Brown
1835–1926

Olympia Brown was raised in a family that valued education for women. By the age of fifteen she was teaching school, but she was determined to continue her own education too. After graduating from Antioch College, Olympia searched for a seminary that would admit women, finally finding the theological school at St. Lawrence University, which admitted her reluctantly. She excelled at her studies and gained the respect of her classmates.

Receiving ordination in 1863, Olympia then pastored several churches. She married, keeping her maiden name, and had two children. She was dedicated to her family and to her ministry until she felt a call to something different.

In 1887, she resigned as a minister to take up a more political cause—women's suffrage. It was a cause she'd always been involved with, but Olympia felt she now needed to dedicate herself full-time.

Olympia and her fellow suffragists chose to focus on the issue at a federal level. She fought for decades, and in 1917 (at the age of eighty-two!) she joined one thousand other women who picketed the White House demanding a constitutional amendment that guaranteed women the right to vote. Three years later, the Nineteenth Amendment was ratified. Olympia and her peers had fought for voting equality and won.

Though her two careers may seem very different from each other, they were rooted in Olympia's belief that men and women are equal in the eyes of God and should have equal rights in the home, in the church, in education, and in politics. When she felt God wanted her to be in full-time ministry, she did it to the best of her ability. When she felt called to fight for women's suffrage, she put herself fully behind that.

God doesn't always have just one thing planned for you in your lifetime. He can use you for a time in one place and then use you somewhere else. If you find your interests changing in your job or a ministry at church, take some time to pray and ask God if he's moving you in a new direction.

Take delight in the LORD, and he will give you your heart's desires.

PSALM 37:4

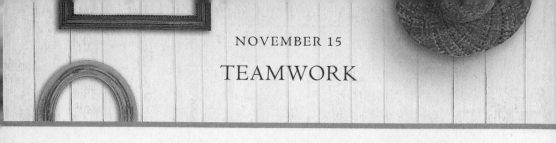

TEAMWORK

Lucy Peabody + *Helen Barrett Montgomery*
1861–1949 — 1861–1934

The New Testament describes the church as a body, with different members doing different tasks. Throughout history, we've seen this played out in many ways. Some people are on the front lines of ministry; others do whatever they can to support those people. Lucy Peabody was on the front lines for a while as a missionary, but then she seemed to find her true calling in a support role as a mission executive. She teamed with Helen Barrett Montgomery, a gifted writer, to promote an explosion of Baptist missions.

Lucy first went to India as part of a missionary couple, but her husband soon died, and she returned to the United States with her two young children. After she began speaking to church groups about foreign missions, she got a job with the Women's Baptist Foreign Missionary Society. Soon she was leading that group.

In that role, Lucy employed the writing talents of Helen Montgomery, commissioning several books that helped to raise millions for missions efforts. Lucy and Helen were a great team, traveling the world to see missionaries in action and reporting back to US churches what was going on. Helen went on to become president of the Northern Baptist Convention, the first woman to lead a major denomination. Using her classical language training, she also produced a modern translation of the New Testament, published in 1924 as the Centenary Translation.

These women helped to lead American missions into the twentieth century, upholding the work of women missionaries and promoting a wide range of missions work. In a time when men were bickering over the "social gospel," with some fearing that doing good deeds was growing more important than preaching, Lucy and Helen (like many other women) understood that our biblical calling involves both. In a disarming response to the controversy, Lucy wrote that women in general "did not bother themselves with sophisticated arguments about the social gospel vs. preaching. . . . They simply responded to what were obvious needs and that response was their witness."

Who do you want on your team? Start looking around for people whose abilities complement yours, people who help you do your best, even as you help them.

We are many parts of one body, and we all belong to each other.
ROMANS 12:5

WE ARE NOT AMUSED

Queen Victoria
1819–1901

Queen of Great Britain for most of a century, Victoria was the figurehead of a culture that saw major developments in science, technology, and scholarship. Her royal tenure was the longest of any British monarch. Crowned shortly after her eighteenth birthday, Queen Victoria ruled until her death at age eighty-one.

By Victoria's time, the power of British royalty had faded. Victoria's role was largely ceremonial, more public relations than genuine statecraft, but this was a role she played well. The nation had seen its share of playboy kings, but Victoria's reign was decidedly family friendly. Even today, people speak of "Victorian morality."

Victoria herself was brought up in an extremely sheltered environment. The granddaughter of King George III, she was several steps removed from the throne. Her mother, a German-born princess, still handpicked her friends and set strict limits on her activities. Victoria seems to have maintained such restraint throughout her life. When those ahead of her in the line of succession died, she became queen, transmitting her own moral code to the nation.

It was a time of great development for the British Empire, which had colonies across the world. Christian morality and British customs were indistinguishable. Many colonists saw themselves as redeeming their adopted lands by introducing British order and moral values. They could ride roughshod over the local culture "for queen and country."

The problem is, "Victorian morality" easily leads to hypocrisy. People judge others for not toeing the line, but they themselves find loopholes. Certain sins are avoided, but others are winked at. If morality is not based on a heart-changing relationship with Jesus, it has no real strength.

The elderly Queen Victoria reportedly heard a sermon on Christ's return and said, "I wish that the Lord might come during my lifetime. . . . I should so love to lay my crown at His feet."

This is where authentic morality comes from: not a desire to be "civilized" or to receive approval from others, but an encounter with Jesus and a recognition that he is ultimately our King.

Why do you keep on following the rules of the world? . . . These rules may seem wise because they require strong devotion, pious self-denial, and severe bodily discipline. But they provide no help in conquering a person's evil desires.

COLOSSIANS 2:20, 23

TRAVEL MERCIES

Egeria

FOURTH CENTURY

She took the vacation of a lifetime, traveling to the Holy Land from her home in what is now Spain. Of course it was more than a vacation—it was a pilgrimage. Traveling in the years 381 to 384, Egeria kept a record of her journey and sent it to her girlfriends back home.

Exploring the sites of biblical events, she wended her way through Egypt and the Sinai Peninsula and finally to Palestine, visiting monasteries along the way. (The monastic movement itself was quite new, but this was where it had started, in the biblical lands.) Remember that Christianity had become legal in the Roman Empire just seventy years earlier. Since then, there had been sort of an explosion of interest in this "new" religion. Emperor Constantine's mother had taken an entourage to the Holy Land earlier in the century, but for a woman like Egeria, apparently with no great wealth or position, to make the trip without an armed escort—that was remarkable.

As you might expect, her travelogue is full of descriptions of the places she saw, along with references to the biblical events that occurred there. But what stands out is her devotion. Each new site provided the occasion for a worship service. She wrote, "It was our practice, whenever we managed to reach our destinations, that there would first be a prayer offered, then a reading from the Bible, then one appropriate psalm, and then another prayer." Historians love this report because it provides a glimpse of worship in the fourth century. Even more than that, it helps us understand the spiritual discipline that drove a woman like Egeria on this quest.

Will you or your loved ones be traveling for the holidays? After waiting in security lines, cramming into airline seats, or driving hours on the highway, it can be hard to get in the mood for Thanksgiving or Christmas. Surely Egeria's travel was just as stressful. But she managed to reorient herself at each new stop by means of a mini-worship service. Prayer, reading, psalm, prayer. Nothing fancy, but this customary practice kept reminding her of the reason for her journey.

Wherever you go this season, that's not a bad habit to get into.

The LORD says, "Stop at the crossroads and look around. Ask for the old, godly way, and walk in it. Travel its path, and you will find rest for your souls."

JEREMIAH 6:16

FREE AGENT

Rebecca Protten

1718–80

Aslave girl of mixed race on a tiny island in the Caribbean—how could young Rebecca ever hope to change the world? But she did. She learned Christianity from her master, a Dutch planter on the island of St. Thomas. Shortly after he died, Rebecca gained her freedom, but she didn't give up her faith.

In 1732, a group of missionaries arrived from Europe and began preaching the gospel to slaves. (This effort, led by Leonard Dober and David Nitschmann, was the first foreign outreach launched from the Moravian community of Herrnhut. Moravians would become famous for their missions work around the world.)

Still a teenager and already a Christian, Rebecca joined their cause, actively sharing her faith with slaves on her island. This was downright dangerous. White planters feared a slave revolt, and they didn't appreciate a former slave—and a girl, no less—speaking out so publicly. Yet Rebecca persisted, helping to establish a local church whose traditions would later impact the African American church in the United States.

After more than a decade of ministry on the island, Rebecca went to Europe with some of the missionaries, and there she married David Protten, who later evangelized the Gold Coast region of Africa.

If someone had told twelve-year-old Rebecca that she would speak out for Jesus in two hemispheres, changing lives and establishing a rich religious tradition that would remain strong for centuries to come, she'd probably have laughed. Or maybe, with a childlike faith already taking root in her heart, she might have said, "Good. Let's make it happen."

You may have all sorts of reasons why you can't do anything of great importance for God. You lack the talent or discipline. You're not as strong a Christian as you ought to be. There are so many others who would do better. You have responsibilities to your community, your family, your job. You're not the right race or age or gender. So *of course* you can't be expected to do anything great.

But then consider Rebecca—or about a hundred other women described in this book. Like them, you can be an agent of God's redemption—in big ways or small, it doesn't matter. Don't let your circumstances convince you otherwise.

Moses again pleaded, "Lord, please! Send anyone else."

EXODUS 4:13

YOU NEVER KNOW

Gertrude Chambers

1884–1966

Gertrude Hobbs had a skill, a very specific skill. She was an expert at shorthand, recording up to 250 words per minute. At the time, that was a very accomplished speed. She aimed to be a professional stenographer, but after she married Oswald Chambers, she used her skill for a different purpose: recording her husband's sermons and speeches.

You may be familiar with Oswald Chambers's classic *My Utmost for His Highest*, one of the bestselling devotionals of all time. Millions of readers have spent their daily quiet time—or whatever quiet time they may have been able to steal from their hectic lives—reading his words and discovering new things about God.

Here's something interesting about the book. Oswald Chambers died before it was written—sort of. The words and the thoughts were Oswald's, but they weren't originally intended to be a book. He may have intended to publish his thoughts eventually, but his untimely death at age forty-three due to complications from surgery prevented that. If it weren't for Gertrude's shorthand notes, everything her husband said would have been lost.

Gertrude spent years transcribing her husband's words, and the culmination of her hard work was the 365 entries in *My Utmost for His Highest*. Imagine what she learned along the way, poring over her husband's thoughts and words about the God they both loved. Imagine how close it must have made her feel to the man that she lost too early.

When Gertrude learned shorthand, she didn't know how God would use her skills later in life. None of us knows how God will use our skills or talents. We might study something with the goal of getting a job and find that later, like Gertrude, we get to use what we learned for some sort of ministry.

Maybe your best skills seem like things God can't use, but you never know what he has planned. As you go through your days, doing the things that you're good at, take encouragement in knowing that at any moment God could use your abilities to achieve his purposes.

Work willingly at whatever you do, as though you were
working for the Lord rather than for people.

COLOSSIANS 3:23

AMAZING LOVE

Polly Newton

1728–90

John Newton was an ambling, directionless teenager when he fell madly in love. Polly Catlett was three years younger, one of the children of his late mother's dearest friend. He was visiting the Catletts before going off to sea to seek his fortune, but he stayed longer than expected and missed the boat—literally.

The twists and turns of John Newton's life are dramatic. Pressed into naval service, he kept misbehaving and running away. Eventually he got a job on a ship transporting slaves from Africa. This latter-day Jonah was trying to sail away from the God of his youth, yet God kept rescuing him from danger. A stormy experience in 1748 finally forced him to his knees. John Newton turned back to God.

Through it all, he remembered Polly back home and often wrote to her. She seldom replied. John was frustrated: *Did she love him or not?* Maybe she was just looking for some stability on his part. Back in England at age twenty-four, and now a ship captain, he proposed to her. Three times. In 1750, she finally married him.

John had a lot of growing to do, both as a Christian and as a husband. He continued as a slave trader for a while but later gave that up and eventually became a respected minister. John and Polly faced their share of difficulties, including Polly's poor health, but they seemed to continue a smoldering love affair, wrapped up in a love for God.

"When I indulge myself with a particular thought of you," John wrote Polly, "it usually . . . brings me upon my knees to bless the Lord for giving me such a treasure, and to pray for your peace and welfare."

Later in life, when Polly was beset by worries, John reminded her of God's blessings: "We have traveled together near twenty-six years; and though we . . . have seen almost every thing change around us, he has preserved our affections."

John Newton is well known as the author of "Amazing Grace," yet his life might have been much different without Polly's amazing love.

You have captured my heart, my treasure, my bride.

SONG OF SONGS 4:9

FAITH FIRST

Eva von Tiele-Winckler

1866–1930

A German orphanage with a hundred children was facing a food shortage. They generally grew their own potatoes, but the previous year's crop had been badly stored, and by March they had nothing edible left, with several months until their next harvest. An inquiry was sent to a neighboring farmer: How much would it cost for *x* amount of food? He misunderstood the message and brought wagons full of produce. The leaders explained they had no money to pay him. No problem—he could wait until May 1.

This was a great blessing, but as the weeks passed, the orphanage still lacked the money to pay that bill . . . so they prayed about it each day, trusting that God would provide three hundred German marks to pay that bill. And when the mail arrived on May 1, it contained a sum of 304 marks.

Eva von Tiele-Winckler had many stories like that from the network of forty orphanages she founded throughout Germany, housing about two thousand children. Yes, she was born into a noble family with affluent connections, but it took Eva years of prayer and pleading before her own father would help her. Caring for the poor just didn't fit his Prussian sensibilities, yet his daughter was called to it. At age seventeen, as she described it later, she encountered Christ and her charitable calling simultaneously. "I was changed in a moment from an unbeliever without knowledge of salvation into a follower of Christ. At the same time He who is love poured into my heart a deep love for the poor and forsaken ones and gave me a vivid impression of the great need."

As she started orphanages, new needs came to light, and new resources arose to meet those needs. Often money arrived in the nick of time. Evicted from its building, one orphanage received a beautiful summer home from a widow who no longer needed it. Eva's work spanned some very difficult times in Germany—money was tight for everyone—but the Lord kept providing regardless.

Perhaps you've been through some tough times yourself. These times teach us to trust God more. So let your material needs drive you to your knees in prayer.

Don't worry about anything; instead, pray about everything.
Tell God what you need, and thank him for all he has done.

PHILIPPIANS 4:6

GOING BACK

Anne Piggot
CA. 1895–1935

It is one of the blessed ironies of the last century: while denominations in the United States and United Kingdom have debated the role of women in the church, many women have taken on the very biblical role of missionary. Women have been at the forefront of missions efforts, especially in difficult areas.

The gospel penetrates many cultures through their women. Perhaps men have too much at stake; their conversion would be problematic. But women can respond eagerly to the Christian message of love, joy, and freedom, and they often hear this message from other women.

When she was about twenty-five, Anne Piggot went to India to serve with a Church of Christ mission. Much of her work involved teaching the local "Bible women," who joyfully studied, discussed, prayed, and sang the Scriptures. These Indian women were already affecting their culture for Christ. The mission also operated some schools for local children.

In her excellent book, *Pen Pictures from India*, Anne tells of her experiences, including her interaction with a young convert she calls Jaswa. This girl was like Nicodemus, very curious about Jesus. But when she announced her decision to follow Christ, her family pressured her to recant. After emotional appeals, magic charms, and even violent threats, Jaswa backed down, returned home, and seemingly forgot about Christianity. But one night she awoke to see a vision of two men in shining white robes. "Are you going back?" they asked her. These heavenly messengers were inviting her back to the mission—and a short time later she did go back.

In her account, Anne goes on to tell about a school picnic in which a girl of the "untouchable" caste fell into a pond and nearly drowned. It was Jaswa who courageously dived in to save her. "Up Jaswa came," Anne writes, "dragging the girl she would not have touched a month before." Later, Jaswa said, "I always feel God called me for something."

Consider this "pen picture" that Anne Piggot gives us. Anne touches the life of Jaswa, who literally touches an untouchable girl, saving her life. God's love is transmitted from one to another to another.

You don't need to preach or teach in a foreign land. You just need to touch those around you with the love of God—and see what sort of chain reaction begins.

No matter what their diseases were, the touch of his hand healed every one.

LUKE 4:40

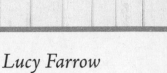

THE GO-BETWEEN

Lucy Farrow

1851–1911

One of the most important religious developments of the twentieth century occurred in its first decade: the beginning of the Pentecostal movement. Historians often point to the explosion of speaking in tongues in April 1906 at a church meeting on Azusa Street in Los Angeles, but those events had been brewing for a number of years. William J. Seymour pastored that church and led the burgeoning movement. He had been influenced by the Bible teaching of Charles Fox Parham, who had started a school in Kansas. But it was an African American woman—Lucy Farrow—who introduced those two men. Her contribution to this important movement has too often been overlooked.

Born a slave in Virginia (and a niece of the famed abolitionist Frederick Douglass), Lucy grew up in the Reconstruction-era South. Details of her early life are sketchy, but she landed in Houston in the 1890s and at some point began pastoring a small mission church there. Hearing Charles Fox Parham's teaching on the Holy Spirit at a crusade in Houston, Lucy traveled with the crusade to Kansas, leaving her church in the care of a friend, William Seymour. She came back excited about this new direction.

After William Seymour met Charles Fox Parham and moved to a new church in Los Angeles, he invited Lucy to visit him and share his ministry. People respected her connection with God. Some would come to her for prayer, asking that she lay her hands on them. Many considered her the channel through which they received the outpouring of the Holy Spirit.

As you read this, you might be applauding these events or be skeptical about them. For the moment, try to put aside any questions and consider the character of this significant woman. She saw herself as a servant of God. Her whole ministry involved making connections between others and the Holy Spirit. She connected Charles Fox Parham with William Seymour. She connected Houston with Kansas and later with Los Angeles. Even later, she traveled around the country and to Africa, connecting others through her preaching and praying. (It is said that in Liberia she was miraculously able to communicate in a tribal language she did not know.)

Obviously she wasn't seeking her own fame. History has largely forgotten about her, but we suspect that she wouldn't mind. She was just a channel for what God chose to do.

As are we.

Peter and John laid their hands upon these believers, and they received the Holy Spirit.

ACTS 8:17

REVIVE US AGAIN

Clarissa Danforth

1792–1855

Churches can get crusty. Over time, the supple movement of the Spirit is hardened into rules and traditions that are strictly followed. People forget whom they're worshiping, or why.

You can trace a pattern of revival through history. Men like John Wycliffe, Martin Luther, George Whitefield, and the Wesleys—as well as a number of the women mentioned in this book—stepped up to remind Christians of the immensity of God's grace, the power of his Spirit, and the joy of a life lived in his love. Virtually all of these "revivers" broke the rules in some way. They often faced serious opposition from those who claimed to be guardians of the true faith.

For a half-dozen years in the early 1800s, Clarissa Danforth was the hottest revivalist in New England. A historian of the time described her as "a lofty, vain young lady" before she came to know Christ at age seventeen. People in her Freewill Baptist church soon recognized her speaking ability. Though there was resistance to women preaching in church, "social meetings" were held in which Clarissa was asked to expound on the Scriptures. Eventually the demand grew greater, and this young woman began preaching throughout the region. As the historian noted, "Whoever could divest himself of prejudice against a woman's appearance in public, listened to her preaching with profit as well as delight."

In 1819, Clarissa began a revival in Smithfield, Rhode Island, which continued for sixteen months. An estimated three thousand people came to Christ. Her popular preaching style could be emotional—she reportedly "warned the people with tears"— but also full of "common sense." It's clear that God used her to get his message across.

Most Americans in that time would have considered themselves Christian, and yet for many, it was merely a formal faith, a matter of customs and traditions—not a lively relationship with God. Clarissa was one of numerous preachers who revived people from their religious slumber, who "woke them up" into a new life in Christ.

Today's world is different, but this issue remains the same. Many people claim a Christianity that's merely formal, not personal. What can you do to wake them up?

---

*I have this complaint against you. You don't love me or
each other as you did at first! Look how far you have fallen!
Turn back to me and do the works you did at first.*

REVELATION 2:4-5

THE NEW WORLD

Pocahontas

1595–1617

She's an American legend: the Native American princess who saved an English settler and fell in love. The problem is, the details of the Pocahontas story are sketchy at best. It's hard to know what exactly happened.

The English were settling Virginia, beginning with the Jamestown colony in 1607. Over the next few years, they had numerous encounters with the native population—some peaceful, some not. Powhatan was chief of the local Algonquin nation. He had a daughter who sometimes went by the name Pocahontas, which may mean "playful little one."

Captain John Smith ventured into native territory and was captured. He later told of being spared from death by the brave actions of young Pocahontas. While the captain and the chief's daughter became friends, she was far too young for a romance. (She called Smith "older brother.") Later she was captured and held by the English as a pawn in their negotiations with tribal leaders. During this time, the local minister taught her English, reading, and Christianity. In 1614, she married an Englishman, John Rolfe, and took the name Rebecca. He later took her to England, where she was introduced to many gawking nobles. As the Rolfes prepared to return to America, she took sick and died. On her deathbed, she reaffirmed her Christian faith.

The conversion of Pocahontas remains a matter of historical debate. Was it authentic? Could a hostage make a free choice to follow Jesus? Wasn't she really just a victim of a domineering European culture?

Maybe so. We can't know her heart. Yet we know that Jesus saves people of every culture, so it's no surprise that a "playful" Algonquin girl might discover fulfillment in the joy of Christ. Jesus does not belong exclusively to Europeans, or to Americans, or to any particular race or sect. He's the Savior of the world, and he invites us all into a new world where cultural boundaries are broken down in his name.

Take a moment to reflect on your own background. Do you consider yourself a Christian merely because you live in a "Christian" culture or go to a Christian church? Perhaps you were even brought up in a Christian home. But none of those things makes you a follower of Jesus. You need to talk to him directly.

Christ himself has brought peace to us. . . . He broke
down the wall of hostility that separated us.

EPHESIANS 2:14

GIVING THANKS

Sarah Hale

1788–1879

W hy do Americans celebrate Thanksgiving Day? Because the editor of a leading women's magazine pushed the idea.

A Christian woman named Sarah Hale edited *Ladies' Magazine and Literary Gazette* from 1827 to 1836 and then *Godey's Lady's Book* for the next forty years. Under her leadership, *Godey's* circulation soared to 150,000, making it the most popular periodical of its kind. Avoiding political controversy, Sarah published poems and stories, fashion articles, recipes, and household hints. This was a formula for success.

Things had not always been so positive for Sarah. Her husband had died after only nine years of marriage, leaving her a widow at age thirty-four—and a single mom of five young children. She turned to writing, publishing a book of poetry and a novel. Her most famous literary output, however, was a nursery rhyme—"Mary Had a Little Lamb." (This became all the more famous in 1877 when Thomas Edison used it for the first phonograph recording.)

After becoming an editor, Sarah used her magazine to promote several ideas, including education for women. She supported Christian missions, serving with two women's missionary societies. She was especially interested in training and sending women as medical missionaries. Patriotism was dear to Sarah, and she worked for the preservation of several historic sites, including the Bunker Hill Monument in Boston.

And then there was the idea for a national day of thanks. She wrote about a "deep moral influence" that would come from such "seasons of rejoicing in which whole communities participate. They bring out . . . the best sympathies in our natures." For more than fifteen years she lobbied, in print and in person, for this holiday—until Abraham Lincoln made it happen in 1863.

Sarah was right: gratitude is good for us. All sorts of psychological studies in recent years have proven the value of a "positive outlook," but thankfulness goes deeper. It recognizes that we are recipients of grace. This is true even for atheists and agnostics, by the way. When people feel thankful, whether they're thanking the universe or society or their own family, they are acknowledging that they've received something good. Their souls are activated, you might say.

And for Christians, it's another opportunity to bow before our gracious Father in heaven.

Be thankful in all circumstances, for this is God's will for you who belong to Christ Jesus.

1 THESSALONIANS 5:18

MINISTERING TO PHYSICAL NEEDS

Jackie Pullinger

1944–

G et on a boat and get off where God tells you" was the advice that Jackie Pullinger took when she was in her early twenties. A graduate of music college, where she studied the oboe, Jackie wanted to be a missionary. After many missions organizations turned her down, a vicar gave her the advice to just go. She did, starting her journey in Great Britain and getting off the boat in Hong Kong.

She got work as a music teacher in the Walled City, one of Hong Kong's most dangerous slums. In the 1960s, the police had no jurisdiction in the Walled City, and criminals would go there to hide. Opium-producing gangs, drug addicts, and prostitutes made up a large portion of the population.

Jackie started a youth club for drug addicts, gang members, and others. At first she ministered to their physical needs. She fed them. She took boys who had been hurt in gang fights to the hospital. She visited those who ended up in prison. She spent time with them, and eventually they began to trust her, realizing that her concern for them was genuine.

It was awhile before they responded to her words about Jesus, but when they did, amazing things started to happen. She helped them to break their addictions cold turkey. Jackie recalls in her autobiography, *Chasing the Dragon*, that some of the addicts never experienced symptoms of withdrawal when they were being prayed over.

Through the contributions of other Christians and the government, she established St. Stephen's Society, a series of rehabilitation homes for drug addicts, gang members, and prostitutes. She is still ministering in Hong Kong, and recently she added human trafficking to the societal problems she's trying to solve.

Jackie's example shows how important it is to first establish genuine relationships with the people we want to share Jesus with. Is there someone you're trying to tell about Jesus who needs your help or your friendship first?

The King will say, "I tell you the truth, when you did it to one of the least of these my brothers and sisters, you were doing it to me!"

MATTHEW 25:40

SHARING YOUR PAIN

Lydia Sexton

1799–1894

She must have felt like Job. Lydia Sexton bore more than her share of pain, as one relationship after another was torn from her. When her father died, Lydia and her siblings were parceled out to various relatives. She married at age twenty, but her first husband died in a fall, leaving her with a young son. Feeling ill equipped to care for her child, she gave him to a wealthy couple and visited him weekly. A few years later she remarried and relocated for her new husband's job, but he soon died too, and now she had another son. She fought to get her first son back, and she succeeded, but she found the boy had been neglected and badly injured in a household accident. Fortunately, God had a third husband for her, and this marriage lasted some fifty years.

But Lydia's struggles weren't just due to tragic loss. She fought to find her spiritual footing in the midst of these crises. The early 1800s offered a broad menu of religious experiences for the seeker, and she tried several different churches. She landed at a United Brethren church that felt like home. "Although I had not a relation on earth that would join the church with me, I soon found fostering fathers and nursing mothers there."

The church discovered her gift for speaking, and they encouraged her to do more of it. Though she refused at first, she soon was licensed to preach. In this role, Lydia traveled throughout the Midwest for several decades. At age seventy, she took on a new task, as a chaplain at the Kansas State Penitentiary. Here she used not only her speaking skills, but also her knack for organization to build a thriving ministry.

Perhaps it's appropriate that the final act of Lydia's too-tragic life involved ministry to people shut away from relationships and often forgotten. Her own pain might have enabled her to understand theirs.

It's tempting to think that your struggles disqualify you for God's work. But the tragedies you have faced, the temptations you have fought, the turmoil you have muddled through—God can use it all.

God is our merciful Father and the source of all comfort. He comforts us
in all our troubles so that we can comfort others. When they are troubled,
we will be able to give them the same comfort God has given us.

2 CORINTHIANS 1:3-4

GREAT DANE

Karen Jeppe

1876–1935

Some Christians are known by their words, others by their deeds. Karen Jeppe, the Danish schoolteacher-turned-relief-worker, was one of the latter. Hearing about the needs of Armenian Christians in Turkey, she traveled to the town of Urfa in 1903 and began to teach Armenian children. Reportedly, she was quite good at this, but she also helped organize businesses—carpentry, weaving, shoemaking, etc.

It was the middle of what some historians call the Armenian Genocide. The Turks were systematically impoverishing, oppressing, and killing off the Armenians. The people of Urfa spoke of a massacre there in 1895, years before Karen arrived, but she saw continuing havoc in the years leading up to World War I. In some cases, Armenian men were slaughtered and women and children forced to march across the desert to "death camps." Karen worked tirelessly to provide relief to those in need and to rebuild Armenian society. Often she hid children in her home for their safety.

As conditions grew worse for the Armenians, so did Karen's health. She went back to Denmark to recuperate, but soon she returned to Turkey, helping however she could. When she learned that captured Armenian girls were being sold into prostitution, she jumped to action again, mobilizing an effort to rescue those girls and house them safely.

While dying of malaria in 1935, she spoke of being ready to go "home." She who had provided a home to so many was now headed for her eternal shelter. She who had brought light into this dark corner of the world was memorialized at the Church of Gregory the Light Bringer. One Armenian mourned, "A messenger from God has left us."

Karen Jeppe did not start a church, preach to multitudes, or write inspirational verses. She just used her God-given gifts of teaching and organization to make her mark on the world. She stood up against an overwhelming tide of oppression, and while she didn't stop it, she brought the love of Christ to suffering Christians.

We hope that you will never have to face such atrocities, but you may still have opportunity to care for someone in need, to comfort a sufferer, or to stand up against an oppressor. You can be a "messenger from God" in any situation you encounter today.

Unless it produces good deeds, [faith] is dead and useless. . . . I will show you my faith by my good deeds.

JAMES 2:17-18

TRIPLE PLAY

Eliza Grew Jones + *Anna Leonowens* + *Margaret Landon*

—— 1803–38 —————— 1831–1915 —————— 1903–93 ——

The American missions movement was still young when Eliza Jones and her husband, John, sailed to Burma in 1830. It had been just two decades since the Judsons had made that same journey, and Adoniram was still serving there.

Eliza had a knack for languages, and she put it to good use after being transferred to Siam (modern-day Thailand) in 1832. First she produced a Siamese-English dictionary. Then she created a Romanized script for the Siamese language, making it easier for Westerners to learn. Eliza also wrote songs, poems, and school lessons in Siamese, as well as translating some portions of Scripture.

Her work gave Eliza a deep appreciation for the Siamese culture. She talked about Christ in ways that Buddhists could understand. And she certainly opened doors of communication between Siam and the West.

Fast-forward to 1862, when a young widow named Anna Leonowens moved to Bangkok, hired as a governess to teach Western language and culture to the multiple wives and many children of the King of Siam. Though she was asked to keep religion out of it, Anna often let her Christian faith inform her teaching. "If any germ of love and truth fell from my heart into the heart of even the meanest of those wives and concubines and children," she wrote later, ". . . I did not labor in vain among them."

Move on into the next century, when Margaret Landon and her husband went to Siam as Presbyterian missionaries. Hearing Anna's story, Margaret thought it might make a good novel. She published *Anna and the King of Siam* in 1944, inspiring the Rodgers and Hammerstein musical *The King and I*.

Maybe you've seen that show or heard its music—"Shall We Dance?" or "I Whistle a Happy Tune"—without realizing that part of its heritage was the faithful work of these three Christian women. And it makes us wonder what the impact of our own Christian service might be a generation or two from now. Will that kid you're teaching in Sunday school translate the book that inspires a person to help someone else do something amazing? You may never know . . . but it could happen.

You have heard me teach things that have been confirmed by many reliable witnesses. Now teach these truths to other trustworthy people who will be able to pass them on to others.

2 TIMOTHY 2:2

BEAUTY CONTEST

Theodelinda

570–628

She sounds like a character out of *The Lord of the Rings*: Theodelinda, queen of the Lombards, daughter of Garibald, king of Bavarians, married to King Authari. Sounds very Middle-earth, or at least very medieval, doesn't it?

In fact, Theodelinda did live during the early medieval period. She is widely credited with converting the Lombards to Christianity, making her sort of the St. Patrick of northern Italy.

Although she was never declared a saint, she's become somewhat of a religious icon. Artistic images of her, which weren't created until hundreds of years after her death, often portray her as unattractive, yet there is evidence to the contrary. Some records indicate that before her marriage to King Authari, he traveled to see her to make sure that he liked what he saw. When he met the tall, blonde, beautiful young woman, he agreed to make her his queen.

This has created a minor debate among scholars. Did artists have difficulty creating a beautiful image for a serious religious leader? Or were historians overstating her beauty? Of course that leads to further questions about the value of looks in our society—both now and fourteen centuries ago.

There's no question—we live in a beauty-crazy age, but maybe there's nothing new about that. Have beautiful women always attracted attention . . . while having trouble getting respect? Does this happen in the church as well as in wider society? If so, what can possibly be done about it?

The New Testament promotes modesty in women's appearance and a beauty based on good deeds rather than hip hairstyles or bling (see I Timothy 2:9-10). There's no place for vanity, of course. But we wonder if there's a sort of "reverse vanity" going on these days, as people openly fret about their looks. How often do you hear a compliment—"Hey, you look great!"—answered with a litany of flaws—"Thanks, but my hair isn't cooperating, and I tried on four different outfits to find one that doesn't look horrible"? Self-debasing sounds more spiritual than vanity, but it still reflects a preoccupation with outward appearance.

Can we begin to grasp the idea that we were all created in God's image—inside and out?

Thank you for making me so wonderfully complex! Your workmanship is marvelous—how well I know it.

PSALM 139:14

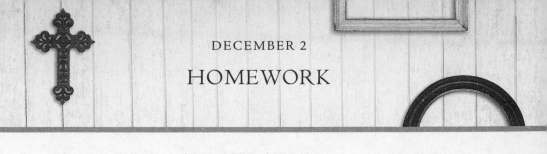

HOMEWORK

Annie W. Armstrong
1850–1938

When you think of missions, what comes to mind? Missionaries who dedicate years in other countries to help people and share their faith? Teams of adults or teens who take a week's vacation and fly off to where the latest natural disaster has occurred to help rebuild homes and lives?

Many people assume missionaries serve only in foreign countries. This adds to the exotic image of their work. But what about those who serve closer to home?

Annie W. Armstrong was a champion for "home missions." Born in the mid-1850s, she grew up in Baltimore and saw the needs of immigrants, children, the sick, and the poor. There were people right in her city who needed help, and she felt compelled to do what she could for them. Her missions field was right in her backyard.

Along with other Southern Baptist women, Annie helped to form the Woman's Missionary Union. Still in existence today, it has become a very powerful force in the church, raising what has amounted to more than $800 million for missions work in the United States.

The principle behind home missions is a valuable one: find your missions field, no matter how close or far away it might be. Not everyone will go on an overseas missions trip, but everyone has the opportunity to do something nearby. There are missionaries serving the Lord in your state, perhaps in your town. You can rather easily provide resources, encouragement, or even volunteer efforts. See if your church can make such a connection for you.

Annie once challenged people in this way: "The future lies all before us . . . shall it only be a slight advance upon what we usually do? Ought it not to be a bound, a leap forward, to altitudes of endeavor and success undreamed of before?"

Surely that quote belongs on your refrigerator or in your daily planner. You can cautiously tiptoe forward into the future, she says, or you can leap forward. With all that God has given us—resources, talents, compassion, etc.—why not leap?

Don't forget to do good and to share with those in need.
These are the sacrifices that please God.

HEBREWS 13:16

NOT KNOWING

Joy Davidman
1915–60

I t's the not knowing that's killing me."

That's a common response to an unresolved problem—physical pain, a relational conflict, or waiting to find out about a job layoff. There's no way to know at the moment what the outcome will be.

It can feel like torture, can't it? The not knowing. The uncertainty.

Joy Davidman was a woman familiar with the uncertainties of life. Born into an American secular Jewish family, she identified herself as an atheist at the age of eight. As a young adult, she relied on her own intellect and abilities until life got exceedingly difficult—until the uncertainties hit.

Although she's known to many as the wife of C. S. Lewis, the *Narnia* author was not Joy's first husband. Her first marriage, to Bill Gresham, was a strained one with many problems. One day her husband phoned, telling her he was having a breakdown and couldn't come home. She did what she could to find him, but no one knew where he was. That evening, after she put her small children to bed, the not knowing got to her. She said she felt helpless for the first time in her life, and in her helplessness "God came in." Her atheism was no more, and she understood that God had always been there.

Later in her life, during her marriage to C. S. Lewis, Joy was struggling with the cancer that would eventually take her life at age forty-five. It was difficult to deal with the uncertainty of which direction the cancer would go. How long did she have? Would there be pain? There were no definitive answers. Eventually, she came to terms with the uncertainty and wrote to a friend that "uncertainty is what God has given us for a cross."

When things are uncertain, of course we want to know the eventual outcome. We may grow frustrated when God doesn't seem to provide answers. Yet he provides something far more important—a relationship with him. Even in your uncertainty, draw closer to him.

Don't worry about anything; instead, pray about everything. Tell God
what you need, and thank him for all he has done. Then you will
experience God's peace, which exceeds anything we can understand. His
peace will guard your hearts and minds as you live in Christ Jesus.

PHILIPPIANS 4:6-7

WORKING THROUGH YOUR THOUGHTS

Martha Stearns Marshall

1726–CA. 1793

In the mid-1700s, Martha Stearns Marshall preached alongside her husband Daniel, a Separatist Baptist pastor. But when Daniel was called to lead the Abbotts Creek Baptist Church in North Carolina, he ran into some trouble with his ordination process. Most other ministers disapproved of women preaching and praying before the congregation, and they gave Daniel grief for allowing it. Yet he was eventually ordained, and the congregation became accustomed to the husband/wife team.

There's a story of a time when the Marshalls were arrested in Georgia. Some accounts say they were arrested because Daniel preached something that was against the Anglican church, the state church in the colony at the time. Other accounts say they were arrested for allowing Martha to preach. What's consistent in the accounts is that while they were under arrest, Martha did not stop preaching. The constable who arrested them was so moved by Martha's words that he became a Christian. It's fun to imagine this woman, so sure of her divine calling to preach that she simply could not shut up about God, even under arrest.

Recently, in honor of this pioneering woman preacher, the Baptist Women in Ministry started the Martha Stearns Marshall Month of Preaching. Every February since 2007, the organization has invited Baptist churches to have a woman preach sometime during the month.

Perhaps you don't share the calling—or the tenacity—of Martha Stearns Marshall, but here's an interesting thought: If you were invited to speak before your congregation, what would you say? What thoughts about God could you share? What experiences could you relate? What Bible verses have challenged you recently? Having to prepare a sermon, whether for real or for fun, is an opportunity for anyone to work through what's in her head about God and Scripture.

So how *will* you express these ideas? You could do so privately in a journal, but you could also share them with a Bible study group. Nowadays you could blog your God-thoughts, or perhaps tweet them. Martha Stearns Marshall could not be stopped from talking about God. Neither should we.

The word of God is alive and powerful. It is sharper than the sharpest two-edged sword, cutting between soul and spirit, between joint and marrow. It exposes our innermost thoughts and desires.

HEBREWS 4:12

AFRICA THANKS GOD

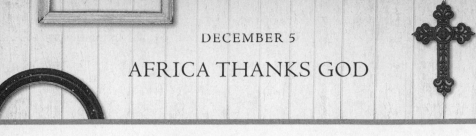

Charlotte Manye Maxeke

1872–1939

Charlotte Maxeke was a stout lady with a striking face, with sharp penetrating eyes which could strike terror into those who crossed words with her and yet be gentle and kind to those who needed her sympathy." So wrote one historian about one of the major figures in modern South African history. Before Nelson Mandela, before Desmond Tutu, there was Charlotte Maxeke, a Christian woman fighting for the rights of all Africans, and especially African women.

Her journey started in adolescence, as she and her younger sister sang in a choir that toured England—even singing for Queen Victoria. Another choir tour took her to Canada and the United States, where she made connections that landed her at Wilberforce University in Ohio. There she impressed her teachers, including the famed scholar W. E. B. Du Bois. She paved the way for other South African students, including her future husband, to attend Wilberforce. After graduation, the couple returned home as missionaries of the African Methodist Episcopal church.

There, Charlotte founded the Wilberforce Institute, which still exists as Wilberforce Community College, near Johannesburg. She was also elected president of the AME's Women's Missionary Society, which gave her a platform from which to speak out against the prejudicial treatment of blacks in South Africa, especially the pass laws that enforced segregation policies. She founded the Bantu Women's League to work for women's rights and to promote education for girls. Dr. Du Bois considered her "a pioneer in one of the greatest of human causes, working in extraordinarily difficult circumstances to lead a people, in the face of prejudice, not only against her race but against her sex."

One African leader (A. B. Xuma) made this simple summation: "Africa thanks God for Charlotte."

God loves justice. That seems to go without saying, but it's remarkable how often supposedly "Christian" societies forget. Scripture overflows with commands to care for the needy, to seek justice for all, to extend God's mercy. We need prophetic figures like Charlotte Maxeke to point out our errors and remind us of our obligations.

So look around you. Where do you see injustice? Who is being bullied, held down, kept from having a fair chance to succeed? And what does God ask you to do to help?

---

*Learn to do good. Seek justice. Help the oppressed. Defend
the cause of orphans. Fight for the rights of widows.*

ISAIAH 1:17

EQUIPPED FOR THE JOB

Jessie Penn-Lewis

1861–1927

According to her spiritual autobiography, Jessie Penn-Lewis grew up "in the very heart of the religious life of Wales." Her grandfather was a Methodist minister, and her home was a "rendezvous for the ministers as they passed hither and thither on their Master's work."

Growing up around religion and having ministers constantly in your home doesn't automatically mean you'll make their faith your faith. It wasn't until Jessie was older that she embraced Christianity. She was about nineteen years old when she realized that if Christ returned, she wasn't ready. It was then that she made her family's faith her own faith.

Right about that time, Jessie contracted tuberculosis, but she was healed. She saw this as a miracle and chose to use the health she regained to serve God. In her early thirties she began to teach all over the world and, along with her husband, became a central figure in the Welsh Revival of the early 1900s.

Jessie was a gifted speaker, and she traveled to countries like Russia, India, and the United States to speak at conferences. She was also a prolific writer, authoring fifteen books and starting a magazine, the *Overcomer*, that is still being published today.

Despite her evident gifts, Jessie struggled to believe she was qualified for what she was doing. She felt that God had given her a specific commission, but not everyone saw it that way. She said that some doors "were fast closed to the message I bore, purely, and only, because I was a woman." At times, she wondered if she was only supposed to teach until a qualified man could take her place. God finally showed her that there was no man who would be taking her place. No woman either. God had given her the job, and he was the only judge of her qualifications.

That's an important lesson for everyone to embrace. Do you believe that when God chooses you to do a job, you can be assured that you're qualified—or as the Bible puts it, *equipped*—to do that job?

May he equip you with all you need for doing his will. May he produce in you, through the power of Jesus Christ, every good thing that is pleasing to him. All glory to him forever and ever! Amen.

HEBREWS 13:21

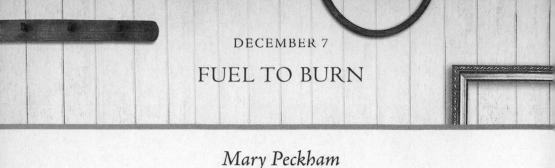

FUEL TO BURN

Mary Peckham

1932–2010

As she grew up on Lewis, one of the small islands in the group of Scottish Hebrides Islands, morning worship was a part of Mary Peckham's life. Families on the island would gather together in homes to read the Bible and pray. When children got to school, they prayed again and learned more Bible stories. After school, there was usually a psalm to memorize.

In 1949, the people of Mary's village found themselves discouraged after the horrors of World War II. But they were so steeped in the Scriptures, they were ready when revival swept through Hebrides. As Mary put it, "When the Spirit of God fell on our island, there was fuel there to burn."

Scottish preacher Duncan Campbell led the revival, traveling from village to village calling people to turn from sin and get saved. Thousands came to faith.

At the time of the revival, Mary lived on the Scottish mainland. Gaelic singing was now her passion; she had left her interest in God back home. When she heard about the revival in her village, at first she stayed away. Why should she care if the people of Lewis were even more religious than when she left? When her parents became ill, however, she returned to her home.

Mary attended a revival meeting with her parents reluctantly at first, but she found herself returning the next night. And the next. She saw old schoolmates who were changed, and those changes were attractive to Mary. She was "being drawn irresistibly to God." After months of prayer and struggle, she gave in to God. The Scriptures she had learned in her youth now helped her to break through her struggles. She went on to become a missionary in Africa.

Knowing God's Word is valuable when you're struggling with something. It helped the people of the island of Lewis when they were discouraged, and that knowledge of Scripture was the fuel for a revival. It guided Mary when she struggled with her faith. Are you willing to commit time to getting to know God's Word better, so when you struggle, you'll have it as fuel to help you get through?

They delight in the law of the LORD, meditating on it day and night.

PSALM 1:2

TEEN CHALLENGE

Anna Nitschmann

1715–60

The religious community of Moravians needed to select a "chief eldress," someone to provide spiritual guidance for the women and girls. As was the custom, four finalists cast lots to determine God's choice. It was Anna Nitschmann . . . only fourteen years old. The Moravians' leader, Count Zinzendorf, suggested that Anna refuse the position, since she was so young. She reminded him that it was the Lord who had selected her.

Anna had, in fact, shown amazing maturity in the preceding years. When her family had come to this community two years earlier, Anna was somewhat rebellious. Then, in a community-wide revival, Anna committed herself fully to Christ. She grew rapidly in her own faith and also organized the other girls to do acts of service and worship. The grown-ups took notice and put her on the short list for the eldress position. In that role, she continued to lead and organize the Moravian women for several decades, even creating a "single sisters" group that put Christian service ahead of marriage and, in fact, led to the sending of numerous female missionaries.

It's hard to say enough about the impact of the Moravians in Christian history. This little band, often squeezed by the major powers of European politics, committed itself to disciple making and had a huge missional impact, especially in the Americas. And among the core leaders of this world-winning group was Anna Nitschmann.

Anna also wrote a number of hymns that were sung by Moravian congregations for centuries. In one, cowritten with the son of Count Zinzendorf, she prayed,

> *I am needy, yet forgiven;*
> *With Thy blood my heart enliven:*
> *Give me, Jesus, of Thy passion*
> *An abiding, deep impression.*

As a teenager and as a mature leader, Anna Nitschmann made an impression, but it was never about her own reputation—it was a passion for Jesus.

What challenges has the Lord set before you? Stop making excuses—that you're too young (or old); that you don't know enough; that you lack the resources. God knows exactly how needy you are. Just let him enliven your heart with his blood, his passion.

Don't let anyone think less of you because you are young. Be an example to all believers in what you say, in the way you live, in your love, your faith, and your purity.

1 TIMOTHY 4:12

SHARING YOUR GIFTS

Lucy Wright
1760–1821

Equality of the sexes was a part of Shaker beliefs from the group's inception in the 1770s. Founder Ann Lee preached and led the church, something almost unheard of for a woman at that time. When Ann died, leadership was taken over in part by Lucy Wright.

Lucy wasn't always a Shaker. She and her husband, Elizer Goodrich, were Baptists. Once Elizer converted to the Shaker faith, Lucy had to decide if it was for her. She took some time to weigh this, perhaps because converting would mean giving up her husband. The Shakers believed in celibacy. Married couples who converted became "brother and sister." Despite this major drawback, she agreed to convert.

Lucy became part of a Shaker community in New York. Elizer was sent on the road as a preacher. In New York, Lucy worked closely with Ann Lee, seeing firsthand how a woman could hold a position of authority. After Ann's death, Lucy co-led the Shakers with Joseph Meacham. Together they organized the various Shaker communities, and after Joseph Meacham's death, Lucy became the sole leader of the Shakers.

Under Lucy's leadership, the Shaker community grew and thrived. She sent out missionaries to establish new Shaker communities in Ohio, Indiana, and Kentucky. She organized their communal living and their way of earning money. Shortly before her death, she helped draft the Millennial Laws, a document that guided Shaker communities in all areas of worship and living. Lucy had a natural gift for organizing, and she helped her community thrive because she was given free rein to use it.

Organizations function best when their members are working to their strengths, doing jobs where their talents and natural abilities are best suited. You may already be using your gifts in your church, but have you thought of how you can use those same gifts to serve in your community? The gifts that you use in ministry can be used in a civic group, a community theater, a parent/teacher group, and other organizations that benefit the community you live in. Where can you share your gifts outside of your church?

God has given each of you a gift from his great variety of
spiritual gifts. Use them well to serve one another.

1 PETER 4:10

TIES THAT UNITE

Salome Lincoln Mowry

1807–41

Salome Lincoln Mowry wrestled with her desires. She was bright. She was eager to learn and to read everything she was able to, including her Bible. Salome had even been baptized as a Free Will Baptist when she was about sixteen. What troubled her was that she believed she was supposed to be doing something for God, but what? She desired to speak publicly about her faith but wasn't sure it was acceptable for a woman to do that. She wanted to be faithful to her calling but also obedient to God's restrictions.

An opportunity came when she was twenty, and she took it. At a religious meeting, the preacher who was supposed to speak never arrived, so Salome chose to deliver a sermon. It must have been nerve racking for her, but God put the desire in her to preach, and after a while she couldn't deny it.

She continued to preach after that first experience, and of course she faced opposition. A woman preaching during that time was bound to come up against people who thought her actions weren't theologically sound. She had come to believe, however, that she would be disobeying God if she *didn't* embrace her desire to speak about him.

Still, Salome never went to seminary and didn't seek ordination. Although she was Baptist, she spoke to any denomination. Minor differences in theology didn't bother her. She embraced all Christians. In compiling Salome's memoir, Almond Davis said, "Whenever, or wherever she found the image of Christ, soul mingled with soul, and to such a one, she felt that she was bound by a cord stronger than earthly, and by ties dearer than those which unite parties, sects and denominations."

Not all Christians will agree on theological matters. Your Christian brothers and sisters may belong to different denominations and hold different views on things they read in the Bible. Are you able to remember, as Salome did, that as Christians we're bound by a cord, Christ, who ties us together? He is certainly stronger than theological differences that threaten to divide us.

There is one body and one Spirit, just as you have been
called to one glorious hope for the future.

EPHESIANS 4:4

POWER WALK

Mary Jones
1784–1864

This poor Welsh girl would be unknown to history except for one determined journey. Mary Jones, daughter of a weaver in what is now Gwynedd, used to walk two miles to a neighbor's farm in order to read the Bible. Her family was Calvinistic Methodist, and she had professed faith at age eight, but the Scriptures were scarce in her native language. She knew how to read, thanks to a traveling education program initiated by clergyman Thomas Charles, but how could she read God's Word with no copies available?

Mary decided she wanted to buy a copy for herself, so she saved up her money. She heard that Thomas Charles had some Bibles for sale, but he lived in the town of Bala, twenty-five miles away. No matter—she would walk there. Barefoot, this fifteen-year-old navigated the hills and streams of the Welsh countryside until she reached the Charleses' home, only to be told that all the Bibles were sold or spoken for.

But a couple of things happened in the heart of Thomas Charles as he encountered this resolute girl. First, he took pity on her, and he sold her a Bible he had been holding for someone else. Second, he was inspired to launch a ministry that would make Bibles available to people everywhere.

This became known as the British and Foreign Bible Society, which has pioneered Bible distribution around the world. The organization still tells the story of "Mary Jones and her Bible." And that very Bible now sits in the society's archives in the Cambridge University Library. Mary herself proudly inscribed it: "I bought this in the 16th year of my age [that is, before her 16th birthday]. I am Daughter of Jacob Jones and Mary Jones His wife. The Lord may give me grace. Amen."

Sometimes we Christians treat the Bible as a textbook. There's nothing wrong with earnest study, but that can often replace something even more important—a passion for God's Word. The Bible speaks of Scripture as sweeter than honey, an object of desire. That's where we encounter the Lord we adore!

Mary Jones knew this, and her passion drove her twenty-five miles on bare feet. Surely we can reach for a book on the shelf and plunge into an experience with God.

---

*Make me walk along the path of your commands, for
that is where my happiness is found.*

PSALM 119:35

HATCHET JOB

Carrie Nation
1846–1911

One of the most aptly named people in history, American Carrie Nation went on a religious crusade and carried the nation into Prohibition. Born Carrie Moore (her father sometimes spelled it Carry), she married a lawyer-minister-editor named David Nation. He was her second husband; her first had died from the effects of alcoholism.

Carrie found her calling as a fierce opponent of alcohol. She started a chapter of the Women's Christian Temperance Union in Kansas and then worked hard for the enforcement of that state's laws against drinking. This usually involved vandalism. Sometimes she would lead a group of women to sing hymns inside or outside bars, and sometimes they would heckle the staff and patrons. But there were other times when Carrie would throw rocks through windows. When her husband quipped that she would do better with a hatchet, she replied, "That's the most sensible thing you have said since I married you"—and that became her new weapon.

With her imposing six-foot frame, her perfect name, and now her hatchet, Carrie Nation became a celebrity. Cartoons mocked her. Bar owners feared and hated her. Audiences flocked to her lectures. Police arrested her but then asked her to speak at civic events. Her husband divorced her, citing abandonment. Churches weren't quite sure what to do with her. She was disfellowshipped from her Disciples of Christ congregation, yet they gave her a letter of commendation.

Through it all, Carrie felt she was following a call from God, and she seemed to love all the attention, good and bad. Meanwhile the temperance movement was growing—because of her or in spite of her. But at a 1911 rally in Eureka Springs, Arkansas, her career was cut short. Midspeech, Carrie blurted out, "I have done what I could," and lapsed into a coma. She died five months later, less than a decade before the United States adopted Prohibition.

Nowadays Christians get involved in various social causes. We are often tempted to use the world's weapons—not just hatchets, but slander, cheating, vandalism, or violence—in order to win. But in the service of Christ, winning isn't the main thing. Loving is.

We are human, but we don't wage war as humans do. We use God's mighty weapons, not worldly weapons, to knock down the strongholds of human reasoning and to destroy false arguments.

2 CORINTHIANS 10:3-4

TRAVELING LIGHT

Saint Lucia

D. 304?

There were many dark days for Christians in the Roman Empire at the beginning of the fourth century. For many years, Christianity had been an illegal religion, but it had continued to grow as various rulers busied themselves with other matters—wars, plagues, the economy, and so on. Now Emperor Diocletian decided to put an end to the Christian threat once and for all, unleashing a widespread persecution throughout the empire, and especially in Rome. Christians were arrested, their property seized, and many were tortured or killed. They had to go underground to hold worship services—sometimes literally, in burial vaults beneath the city.

From this desperate time comes the story of a young woman named Lucia, or Lucy, who brought a bit of light into that darkness in several ways. Legend has it that she brought food to fellow Christians who were hiding out in the catacombs. And here's the coolest part: in order to keep her hands free to carry more food, she crafted a wreath for her head that could hold candles.

Imagine that scene. You're cold, hungry, and terrified of getting caught; you are under the surface of a city that doesn't know you're alive, and you want it that way. Suddenly you hear light footsteps in the passageway, and you see a girl bringing food, with what appears to be a blazing halo on her head.

The historical details are murky, but tradition holds that Lucy was martyred for her faith around AD 304, after being tortured multiple times. Yet that image remains—the girl who brought light into the darkness—and it's celebrated in many churches every December 13, St. Lucia's Day. Sometimes there's a procession of girls bearing food, led by an older girl selected to play the role of Lucia, with a wreath of candles on her head.

How do you bring light into the darkness around you? Do you provide food for people in need, as Lucy did? Do you encourage people, reminding them of a God who loves them? Do people perk up when they see you, knowing that you'll enlighten their lives?

Consider also the creativity Lucy showed, fashioning a newfangled candle carrier. Can you use your God-given creativity to find some new way to shine with God's love?

Live clean, innocent lives as children of God, shining like bright lights in a world full of crooked and perverse people.

PHILIPPIANS 2:15

SEEING THE UNSEEN

Dorothea Dix

1802–87

The history of asylums for the mentally ill in the United States hasn't always been pretty, but those institutions largely originated from one woman's desire to provide compassionate and respectful treatment.

In the mid-1800s, America had few, if any, asylums. Those who were mentally ill and had no one to care for them were often imprisoned. Dorothea Dix discovered that imprisoned women had been abused, beaten, chained, kept naked, and housed in small, unclean spaces. When she challenged this treatment, she was told it was okay to treat the women this way because the "insane" didn't realize what conditions they were kept in. Dorothea didn't believe that.

She heard God tell her that she needed to do something about this. For many years of her very full life—she had been a teacher before her crusade for the mentally ill and a nurse afterward—she visited the places where people with mental illnesses were kept and recorded what she found. With this information, she lobbied state governments to set up humane homes and hospitals for the mentally ill instead of sending them to prison.

This required a radical shift in public thinking. "Insanity" was often considered criminal; some considered it punishment from God. True, some of the mistreated mentally ill people did engage in criminal activity. But Dorothea believed that the mentally ill could be helped and that better living conditions could go a long way in achieving that goal.

"Man is not made better by being degraded," she said. "He is seldom restrained from crime by harsh measures, except the principle of fear predominates in his character; and then he is never made radically better for its influence."

Her efforts paid off. This dedicated woman helped establish some of the first asylums and schools for the mentally ill in the United States.

Throughout his ministry, Jesus saw the invisible people, those forgotten by the rest of society, left by the side of the road. He challenged his followers to see and help those sick and imprisoned. These are our neighbors too.

---

*I was hungry, and you fed me. I was thirsty, and you gave me a drink. I was
a stranger, and you invited me into your home. I was naked, and you gave me
clothing. I was sick, and you cared for me. I was in prison, and you visited me.*

MATTHEW 25:35-36

FOUND IN TRANSLATION

Catherine Winkworth

1827–78

You may know some of the great hymn writers in Christian history—Isaac Watts, Charles Wesley, Frances Ridley Havergal, Fanny Crosby—but sometimes there are other names attached to the songs we sing. When hymn texts come from German or French or Latin, as many do, we need a translator. This is an art form in itself, since the hymn translator needs to match the rhyme and meter of the work as well as the meaning.

Catherine Winkworth was one of the best at this, specializing in German hymns, especially those originating in the rich devotional tradition of the early Pietist movement.

A trip, a book, and a family friend got her interested in German translation. She grew up in Manchester, England, but her father, a silk merchant, had international connections. In her teens, Catherine traveled to Dresden and became fascinated with German culture and language. Back home, she came in contact with Baron Christian von Bunsen, the German (Prussian) ambassador to England. The Winkworth family developed a strong friendship with this well-respected Christian statesman. He even hired Catherine's sister, Susanna, as his translator. At one point in the early 1850s, the baron gave Catherine a book of German devotional writings. This fed the young woman's passion for all things German, and it gave her something of substance to translate.

Soon she was publishing her new renderings of the German poems and hymn texts. She set her verses to traditional tunes and published a hymnal. Now the English-speaking church had a new treasure trove of worship materials. Among Catherine Winkworth's best-known translations are "Now Thank We All Our God," "All Glory Be to God on High," and "Praise to the Lord, the Almighty."

But Catherine's life wasn't just about words. She also worked hard to provide educational opportunities for girls in northern England—something that could not be taken for granted in that era.

Does it ever seem to you, in our world today, that Christians and non-Christians are speaking different languages? We speak of God's salvation, and people hear only hate and judgment. We need to start doing some "translation" work, considering not only what we say, but also what others hear. Catherine Winkworth translated her faith into both words of worship and acts of love. Maybe we can do the same.

We all hear these people speaking in our own languages
about the wonderful things God has done!

ACTS 2:11

PILLOW TALK

Emily Elliott

—————— 1836–97 ——————

You might say she was born to be a writer. Her father, a minister, had written a highly respected study of the end times. (C. S. Spurgeon called it "the standard work on the subject.") Her aunt, Charlotte Elliott, had written a number of hymns, most notably "Just As I Am." With such a pedigree, it's no surprise that Emily went into hymn writing herself and also edited Christian education materials for children.

Though she published several collections of hymns, her best-known work is clearly "Thou Didst Leave Thy Throne."

> *Thou didst leave Thy throne and Thy kingly crown,*
> *When Thou camest to earth for me;*
> *But in Bethlehem's home was there found no room*
> *For Thy holy nativity.*

The song is widely used as a Christmas carol, but the lyrics go on to describe various parts of Jesus' ministry and his ultimate exaltation. The theme is humility—and of course our humble response to the Incarnation.

"Thou Didst Leave Thy Throne" appeared in several of Emily Elliott's hymn collections, including *Under the Pillow*, a large-print hymnal designed especially for invalids. She might have gotten the idea for such a hymnal from her aunt Charlotte, who had published a similar collection (the *Invalid's Hymn Book*), and was herself bedridden for much of her life. Whatever inspired the publication, it was a very appropriate place for this hymn. When people are suffering, they often feel far from the Lord, as if he doesn't know or care how they feel. But as this song strongly says, Jesus left heaven's glory to join in the suffering of humanity. He knows what we're going through.

> *O come to my heart, Lord Jesus,*
> *There is room in my heart for Thee.*

> *You must have the same attitude that Christ Jesus had. Though*
> *he was God, he did not think of equality with God as something*
> *to cling to. Instead, he gave up his divine privileges; he took the*
> *humble position of a slave and was born as a human being.*
>
> PHILIPPIANS 2:5-7

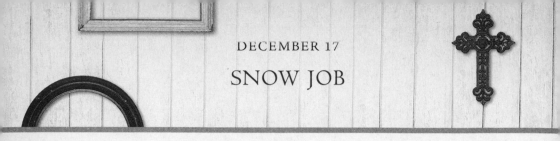

Christina Rossetti

1830–94

Christina came from an artsy family full of intellectual energy. They emigrated from Italy to England and quickly made friends with many of the leaders in London's social, scientific, and literary spheres. Then Christina's father became ill, and the family suddenly had financial troubles. She herself had a nervous breakdown at age fourteen and was plagued with depression for much of her life.

Plenty and poverty, energy and ennui—it all seems like a recipe for the making of a great artist, and so it was. Christina Rossetti came through it all as one of the most renowned poets in England, at least on a par with Elizabeth Barrett Browning. With a background in both the Anglican and Catholic churches, Christina often wrote on biblical themes.

In 1872, after she had already gained fame with a couple of books of poetry, Christina was asked to provide a Christmas poem for an American magazine, *Scribner's Monthly*. She responded with "In the Bleak Midwinter," which was later set to music as a Christmas hymn.

In the bleak midwinter, frosty wind made moan,
Earth stood hard as iron, water like a stone;
Snow had fallen, snow on snow, snow on snow.

Perhaps you've heard some well-meaning fact-checker explain that Jesus was probably born in the spring, not midwinter, and that the chances of snow at the Nativity were pretty close to zero. But please, let's allow the poet to do her work. Jesus certainly came to a "bleak" world. This gifted writer was tapping into spiritual realities, not giving a weather report.

And we might imagine how a depressed soul might feel "hard as iron." Haven't we felt that way sometimes, our true selves buried under frozen layers? To get through to us, God needs to burst out of heaven and enter our world. And that's exactly what he did. Sometimes our own midwinter experiences, even in the celebration of this festive holiday, leave us cold. Coming out of her own emotional numbness, this skilled poet brings us to a place of simple wonder.

He came and preached peace to you who were far
away and peace to those who were near.

EPHESIANS 2:17, NIV

MISSION: IMPOSSIBLE

Elizabeth

LUKE 1:5-25

You may be familiar with the story of the angel Gabriel telling Mary she would give birth to God's child. One of Gabriel's jobs must have been delivering news that humans considered crazy. Six months earlier he had brought baby news about Mary's older cousin, Elizabeth, who, as the Bible says, was "very old."

Elizabeth was married to a priest named Zechariah, and they had no children, though they had been married a long time. Elizabeth was past childbearing years. One day Zechariah was in the Temple offering incense to God when he got quite a scare. There was Gabriel, hanging out by the altar waiting to talk to him.

"Your wife, Elizabeth, will give you a son, and you are to name him John," said Gabriel. Zechariah's reaction wasn't quite, "You're crazy," but he questioned Gabriel enough about his announcement that the angel rendered Zechariah mute until after John was born. Imagine a husband being unable to talk for nine months!

At the baby's circumcision, relatives were pressuring Elizabeth to name the child after Zechariah, who was still mute. Both of them came from a line of priests, and we know how opinionated some religious folks can be. "No!" the new mother insisted. "His name is John!" It seems that no one paid much attention to her. Zechariah had to write it down—"His name is John"—and that's when he got his voice back. Of course, the baby grew up to be John the Baptist, the radical preacher who prepared people for Jesus' ministry.

Much is made of Mary's willingness to be used in God's great plans, and rightly so. But Elizabeth was also a miracle mom whom God used to further the divine design. She, too, was faithful, even though the pregnancy might have taxed the health of a woman her age.

And when Mary wondered how God was doing all these things, the angel referred to her way-too-old cousin Elizabeth, who was also with child. "Nothing is impossible with God," he explained.

Are you convinced that some movement of God is "impossible"? Are you convinced that a broken relationship can't be healed, that a mistake made at work is going to ruin your entire career, that you'll never be able to serve God the way you long to? Don't give in to hopelessness. Nothing is impossible with God.

Your relative Elizabeth has become pregnant in her old age! . . . For nothing is impossible with God.

LUKE 1:36-37

LEAVE THE LIGHT ON

The Innkeeper's Wife

LUKE 2:1-7

The story gets enacted every Christmas Eve. Joseph and a very pregnant Mary arrive at an inn in a very crowded Bethlehem. When they ask the innkeeper and his wife for a room, they're told, "Sorry, there's no room at the inn."

In the play, the innkeeper's wife usually intervenes and convinces her husband to let the couple stay in the stable with the animals. It's better than nothing.

That entire story comes from one line in the Bible: "she . . . laid him in a manger; because there was no room for them in the inn" (Luke 2:7, KJV). Because the manger is a feeding trough for animals, people assume there was a stable. Because it mentions an inn, people assume there was an innkeeper—with a wife. Besides, this couple can create some comic relief in Christmas plays. Since medieval times, church dramas have employed these characters.

And maybe that's exactly how it happened. Or not. The Greek word used for *inn* often refers to the guest room of a home (as in Luke 22:11). In some larger homes, rooms were built over courtyards where animals would be kept at night—with a manger for feeding. So it's a very real possibility that Joseph and Mary didn't go to an inn, but to the home of relatives who had already given all their spare rooms to other family members—but the couple could stay downstairs in the courtyard, with the animals.

Does that ruin the story? Not at all. Jesus was still sleeping in a feed bin. The holy family was still forced out of normal sleeping quarters. The innkeeper's wife might be less of a motel manager and more of a sweet aunt, scrambling to find a creative way to show hospitality. She figured out how to make it work.

Do you ever shy away from showing hospitality because your circumstances are less than ideal? Maybe your place is messy or your old car embarrasses you. It's easy to come up with excuses *not* to welcome others. That would be the way of the *old* innkeeper, if there was one. Let's try to follow the new model, offering even our imperfect resources for the Lord to transform.

She gave birth to her first child, a son. She wrapped him snugly in strips of cloth and laid him in a manger, because there was no lodging available for them.

LUKE 2:7

OUT OF CONTROL

Mary, Betrothed

MATTHEW 1:18-25

W ould you want your parents to pick the person you'd marry? We hear about it happening in other cultures, and we think, *How old fashioned! How unfair!* Yet Mary and Joseph most likely had an arranged marriage.

As our Christmas story begins, the two are "betrothed." Betrothal in ancient Israel was different from our engagements of today. It was generally a contract between families, often with money changing hands. When a couple was betrothed, they were legally bound together, although they did not have sex until after their wedding. If something went wrong, couples couldn't just break off the betrothal. Only divorce or death could end it.

We don't know if Mary knew Joseph well or was happy that he was chosen for her. The choice of her husband was probably beyond her control. After her betrothal, she found another thing she had no control over. She was pregnant by the Holy Spirit, chosen to bear the Son of God.

Joseph could have divorced her. She was pregnant and not by him. That would be legitimate grounds for breaking a betrothal, and he was planning to do so, quietly, respectfully—until the Lord told him what was really going on. Then he willingly entered into the situation, as Mary had. Both of them acknowledged that events were spinning out of their control and they could only trust God for the outcome.

What do you do when things are truly out of your control? When someone is ill and his life is in the hands of the doctors, not yours? When you lose your job because of layoffs? When your child heads off to college, and you aren't in control of where she goes or who she hangs out with anymore?

One option many people choose is worry, but what good is that? Mary gives us an example of courage in the midst of downward-spiraling circumstances. She heard the angel's announcement that her life would change forever, and she said, "Let it be." She trusted that God would be with her through it all. And he was.

Before the marriage took place, while she was still a virgin, she became pregnant through the power of the Holy Spirit. Joseph, her fiancé, was a good man and did not want to disgrace her publicly, so he decided to break the engagement quietly.

MATTHEW 1:18-19

THE RIGHT WOMAN
FOR THE JOB

Mary at the Annunciation

LUKE 1:26-38

What are you capable of? Or maybe the question should be, what does God think you're capable of?

We don't know anything about who Mary was before the angel came to her to tell her she would carry the Son of God. We assume she already had great faith, because the angel tells her that she has found favor with God. Then we see that faith played out.

She didn't say no. But she did ask how.

"But how can this happen?" Mary wondered. "I am a virgin."

Mary figured that she lacked the requirements to be a mother—namely, relations with a man who would be the child's father. She might have worried about other shortcomings as well. Could she handle the physical stress of pregnancy and childbirth? Would she be able to nurture and discipline the child properly—especially if he was the Son of God?

She was willing, but she wasn't sure she was the right person for the job.

Are you familiar with that feeling? In our lives we see many tasks that need doing, but do we really have what it takes to accomplish them? Our spirit is often willing, but we're just terribly aware of the weakness of the flesh.

Fortunately, when God chooses one of us for a job, he's choosing the right person. He doesn't leave us on our own to accomplish whatever it is he wants us to do. The angel explained to Mary that the Holy Spirit of God would make these things happen—and the same Spirit works in us, making up for our failings.

So don't be so quick to say, "I don't have what it takes" when you have an opportunity to do something for God. You have exactly what it takes: the Spirit of the living God working within you. Put aside your self-doubt and gather up your courage. Maybe you, too, can say, with Mary, "I am the Lord's servant. May everything you have said about me come true" (Luke 1:38).

"Don't be afraid, Mary," the angel told her, "for you have found favor with God!"

LUKE 1:30

STORY WITHIN A STORY

Mary's Magnificat

LUKE 1:46-55

The newly pregnant Mary went to visit her relative Elizabeth. It was only a few days since the angel Gabriel had told Mary she would bear the Christ child. Elizabeth was older than Mary—old enough to think she couldn't get pregnant. She was wrong. Gabriel had already announced a miracle pregnancy for Elizabeth. She was in her sixth month.

We don't know what sort of small talk occurred during this meeting or throughout the next three months as Mary stayed with Elizabeth. The Bible hits only the high points. Elizabeth's baby seemed to leap in her womb at Mary's approach; the older woman blessed the younger woman; and Mary responded in song. The song has become known as the Magnificat, from its opening word in Latin.

Throughout her song, Mary praises God over and over. She calls him her Savior, the Mighty One, describing him as holy, merciful, powerful, and a keeper of promises. It is very similar to an Old Testament song of praise sung by Hannah, who thought she was barren but prayed, and then bore Samuel (see 1 Samuel 2). You might expect a very personal reflection from Mary in this moment, but the Magnificat presents a much broader picture. It *is* personal, but the fact that God has chosen this "lowly servant girl" indicates that he is turning the whole world upside down. He deposes princes and exalts the humble. In the birth of this child, God is fulfilling his promises to Abraham. Mary rightly puts her story within the context of God's redeeming work in the world.

We should all sing songs like that. Whether you have musical ability or not, you can cultivate an impulse of praise. As you see God working in your life—in pleasant ways or not-so-pleasant ways—can you praise him for it?

There's nothing wrong with telling God how you feel—the Psalms are full of such offerings—but can you also, as Mary did, connect your story to God's story? Can you thank God, not only for helping you in this situation, but also for demonstrating that he is a God who cares about us?

In this way we "magnify" the Lord, helping ourselves and others see him better.

The Mighty One is holy, and he has done great things for me.

LUKE 1:49

Mary, Traveling

LUKE 2:1-7

As we discovered a few days ago with the innkeeper's wife, there are things we take as fact regarding Jesus' birth that aren't in the Bible. Often during those nativity plays, Joseph and Mary, who is close to giving birth, show up at the inn-that-has-no-room with a donkey. Guess what. There's no donkey in the biblical Christmas story.

In reality, there could have been a donkey. It was a common beast of burden in that place and time. Some three decades later, Jesus would ride into Jerusalem on one. And it's a fair assumption that Joseph would try his best to make sure the nine-months-pregnant Mary wouldn't have to walk across the country.

Yet it's also likely that the couple journeyed in a caravan with other travelers. There would certainly be many others moving from place to place for the census— perhaps even some relatives. In this case, there might have been a wagon or cart for Mary to ride in, at least part of the way. And donkeys.

It was a trip of eighty to one hundred miles, depending on the route taken. There was a good road that followed the mountain range through the center of Israel, but it led through Samaria, which could be dangerous for Jewish travelers. Another route hooked west toward the sea, and another hugged the eastern side of the Jordan River. Able-bodied travelers and caravans routinely went twenty miles a day, so it was a four- or five-day trip. With a pregnant woman, it might have taken a week.

Whatever the details, it's safe to assume that the trip was physically uncomfortable and difficult for Mary. Pregnancy is hard enough when you're sitting still! It's easy to imagine that at times during the trip she thought she wouldn't be able to endure.

How do you deal with pain and discomfort? Have you had times you thought you just couldn't get through—physical illness or injury, or perhaps emotional loss? When you're in the middle of such pain, it's hard to see the light ahead.

Mary had a promise that kept her going. God was alive within her. In a different way, the same could be said of us.

Because Joseph was a descendant of King David, he had to go to Bethlehem in Judea, David's ancient home. He traveled there from the village of Nazareth in Galilee. He took with him Mary, his fiancée, who was now obviously pregnant.

LUKE 2:4-5

ALL THAT SHE COULD BEAR

Mary, Giving Birth

LUKE 2:1-7

Maya Angelou, author of *I Know Why the Caged Bird Sings*, recalled something her grandmother used to say: "If you don't like something, change it. If you can't change it, change your attitude, but don't complain."

That is very good advice, but it's hard to follow at times. You have to wonder what Mary would have done with that advice when it came time to give birth.

Instead of giving birth in the comfort of her own home (as comfortable as a home birth could have been two thousand years ago), Mary had to trek to Bethlehem, a walk of four to seven days. She was very, very pregnant. When she got to Bethlehem, there was no guest room for her, so she had to give birth where the animals were kept.

She probably didn't like that she had to do it that way, but Mary couldn't change it. Imagine telling a woman who is about to give birth in those circumstances, "Change the way you think about it, but don't complain."

Do you think Mary complained? Maybe she did. She's often portrayed as a mild-mannered young woman who always behaved perfectly, but think about it. Wouldn't the person God chose to raise his Son have to have some fire in her?

Before Jesus was born, Mary surely had to fend off the judgment of people who knew she was pregnant before she married Joseph. After Jesus was born, she had to keep him safe from a king who wanted to kill him. It makes more sense to see Mary as someone with some spark. It also makes sense to believe that she, like almost anyone else, might have a complaint or two about the circumstances under which she gave birth.

But remember her response nine months earlier, when the angel showed up and her life changed forever. Not "No way!" Not "Let's negotiate." But "I am the Lord's servant." So let's grant her the moans and groans of discomfort and an occasional fiery barb. But she seemed to understand that there was something huge going on here, something she wouldn't change if she could. Her attitude had already changed. There was no need to complain, especially when the Creator was about to save the world.

While they were there, the time came for her baby to be
born. She gave birth to her first child, a son.

LUKE 2:6-7

PUTTING IT ALL TOGETHER

Mary, Pondering

LUKE 2:8-20

Mary was a ponderer.

It's a great moment in the Christmas story, a quiet moment away from the angels singing and the shepherds scampering to the manger and then away again. Mary was paying attention to everything that went on, and she pondered the events of that night.

The shepherds were running around, telling anyone who would listen about this incredible, amazing child who had been born. The angels had perched in the night sky to tell them. This baby was very good news. This baby was the Messiah. *Of course* they were telling everyone!

But the baby's mother, it seems, was quiet. She wasn't running around saying, "Hey, look what I did! I just gave birth to the Messiah. Isn't that amazing?" Instead, she treasured the information and thought deeply about it.

The Greek word Luke uses in Luke 2:19 for "treasured" or "kept" has the sense of preserving something precious. The word for "pondered" was often used for conversations between people, but here Mary was "conversing" with herself. The root word means "throw" or "place." In this case, Mary was gathering her own experiences and the reports of the shepherds and putting them all together in her mind. (And if you've ever wondered how Luke got this story, this description suggests that Mary gathered the details first, preserved them, and was interviewed years later.)

But look at the contrasting styles in the story. The shepherds are going crazy while Mary quietly ponders. Were the shepherds wrong to spread the news? Not at all. Was Mary wrong to keep quiet? Of course not. She simply needed to deal with all that had happened in a way that was right for her. She needed to take some time, be quiet, treasure what had happened, and do a little pondering.

When something good happens, how do you react to it? Do you run around telling everyone? Do you rush to tweet friends or update your Facebook status? Or do you softly reflect, quietly treasuring the good news? Especially when we're dealing with God's Good News, the first approach tends to erupt in praise, the second in thankfulness. There's nothing wrong with either.

Mary treasured up all these things and pondered them in her heart.

LUKE 2:19, NIV

A PROMISE KEPT

Anna

LUKE 2:36-38

You've heard it said thousands of times: "God always keeps his promises." But does your patience ever wear thin waiting for a promise to be kept? Do you ever start to doubt because you've waited so long, and it doesn't look like God is going to deliver on a promise you believe he made?

Anna was an elderly prophetess who encountered the baby Jesus in the Temple. She had been waiting a very long time to see how God would redeem his people. Then the day came when Mary and Joseph took Jesus to the Temple to be presented before the Lord. (The Jewish custom was to consecrate a male child around forty days after he was born.) On that day, Anna finally knew she was seeing the fulfillment of God's promises.

The story of this female prophet sometimes gets lost behind the story of Simeon, an elderly man who blessed Jesus on the same day. The Holy Spirit had told Simeon years earlier that he would live to see the Messiah, and when he saw the baby Jesus he declared that he could finally die in peace.

Perhaps Anna overhead Simeon's poetic prayer and came over to see what was going on. She was eighty-four years old. We're told that she had been married only seven years before her husband died and had been a widow ever since. Since women married very young, it's safe to assume she had been widowed sixty years or more, worshiping night and day, praying and fasting in the Temple that she never left.

Like Simeon, she recognized that the baby Jesus was the promised Messiah. She immediately launched praises to God and then went around telling others. Centuries earlier, Isaiah, Micah, Zechariah, and other prophets had foretold the coming of God's anointed Redeemer. *Now, here, in this Temple,* the Promised One was giggling and wriggling in the arms of his young mother. God was keeping his promise.

That promise extends to us as well. Jesus redeems us from the power of sin. He restores a relationship with our Creator. He brings meaning to humdrum lives. He brings hope to hurting souls.

Like Anna, we can see that and give praise to God.

She began praising God. She talked about the child to everyone who
had been waiting expectantly for God to rescue Jerusalem.

LUKE 2:38

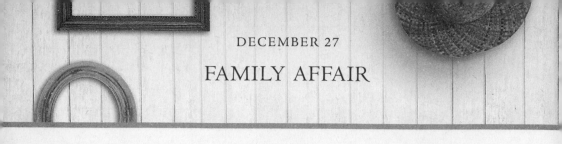

FAMILY AFFAIR

Tamar

GENESIS 38; RUTH 4:12; MATTHEW 1:3

When people start reading the New Testament, they generally skip over the first seventeen verses. That's because Matthew starts with Jesus' family tree—"Abraham begat Isaac" and so on. The Christmas story doesn't really start until verse 18. Or does it?

Matthew considered the genealogical data crucial to an understanding of who Jesus was: a descendant of Abraham, of David, of all the kings of Judah. But it gets very interesting when we look at the four *women* included in the list.

Tamar's appearance is especially surprising. Today she might be labeled a "black widow," a woman who outlives more than one husband. Tamar was a Canaanite who married Judah's oldest son, Er, who soon died. As custom dictated, Tamar then married Er's brother, Onan. It may seem odd today, but if Tamar had a son by Onan, he would be considered Er's heir. (Say that three times fast.) Onan wasn't too happy about that, and so he refused to impregnate Tamar. She was widowed again when Onan died. Her father-in-law, Judah, had one last son, and he promised that the boy would wed Tamar at the proper time, but he reneged.

Widowed and childless, Tamar was now a disgraced woman with few good options. Long story short, she disguised herself as a prostitute and Judah hired her services for his own pleasure. Tamar took his staff, seal, and cord as collateral, and when Judah tried to come back to pay, Tamar had disappeared with his very personal possessions.

When she turned up pregnant, Judah was outraged and said, "Let's burn her." But then she produced Judah's possessions, proving he was the father, and so Judah had to scale back the outrage. Tamar gave birth to twins, Perez and Zerah. Perez is in the genealogical line of Jesus.

This is not your normal Sunday school story. And it raises a question: What's Tamar doing in Jesus' ancestry? Why would our Lord want anything to do with such a disgraced woman?

The Gospels go on to tell us about Jesus' interactions with the Samaritan woman, the demon-possessed Mary Magdalene, a woman caught in adultery, and a few prostitutes—all "disgraced" in some way, until they received the grace of Jesus.

Judah was the father of Perez and Zerah (whose mother was Tamar).

MATTHEW 1:3

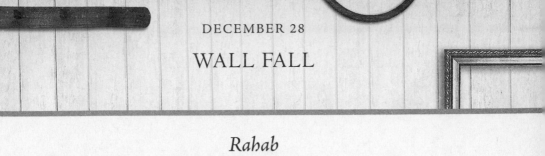

WALL FALL

Rahab

JOSHUA 2; MATTHEW 1:5

Hebrews 11 is the famous "faith chapter," detailing the exploits of a number of Old Testament heroes. A woman named Rahab is in that list. What's her claim to fame?

When the Israelites were about to invade the land of Canaan, they sent two spies into the walled city of Jericho. They found shelter in the home of Rahab, a prostitute. Even when the king of Jericho suspected her of hiding the spies, she continued to conceal them, and she sent the king's men off on a wild goose chase.

Why would she take such a risk to help the Israelites? Because she knew the story of God parting the Red Sea and allowing the Israelites to cross while the Egyptians drowned, as well as other stories of what the God of Israel had done. "The Lord your God is the supreme God of the heavens above and the earth below," she told the spies (Joshua 2:11).

You might remember how the Israelites marched around Jericho once a day for six days, and then seven times on the seventh day—and, as the Sunday school song says, "the walls came tumbling down." Then the army stormed the city, but Rahab and her family were not harmed. Her assistance to the spies was rewarded. At the end of that story, the book of Joshua reports, "She lives among the Israelites to this day" (6:25)—and she apparently married and had a child because she also appears in the genealogy of Jesus.

It's amazing to see the positive attention Rahab receives in Scripture. Not only was she a foreigner, but she was also a prostitute—not the holiest career choice. And yet she acted courageously to help God's people because she trusted in the God of the Israelites. Her faith brought her into the core of the Israelite community despite her past life and nationality.

This was exactly the sort of thing that Matthew, James, and the author of Hebrews wanted to emphasize. Rahab's story indicated that God had always welcomed Gentiles into the community of faith. You didn't need a pure pedigree or a perfect record, just faith in the true God and willingness to act on that faith. That is still true today.

Rahab the prostitute . . . was shown to be right with God by her actions when she hid those messengers and sent them safely away by a different road.

JAMES 2:25

FAITHFUL FOREIGNER

Ruth

THE BOOK OF RUTH; MATTHEW 1:5

Ruth, who is listed in the genealogy of Jesus, is important enough to get her own book in the Bible. In case you don't know her story, here's a quick recap.

An Israelite family—mom, dad, two sons—migrated to the neighboring country of Moab in a time of famine. The two sons grew up and took Moabite brides. One of these was Ruth. In a short time, all three men in the story died, leaving the mom (Naomi) with her two daughters-in-law. Naomi decided to head back to an uncertain future in her hometown of Bethlehem. Only Ruth chose to join her, saying, "Wherever you go, I will go; wherever you live, I will live. Your people will be my people, and your God will be my God" (Ruth 1:16).

Back in Bethlehem, Ruth got work gleaning grain in the fields of a man named Boaz. And she got advice from her mother-in-law on how to attract this well-off landowner. It worked. They wed. They had a son who turned out to be the grandfather of King David.

Like Rahab, Ruth was a foreign woman who got grafted by faith (and by marriage) into Jesus' family tree. Her faith is seen in her commitment to Naomi. She claimed Naomi's God as her own, and this meant a whole new life for her, within the community of Israel.

By including faithful foreigners in the genealogy of Jesus, Matthew was making a powerful statement. The gospel of Jesus was exploding outward into the Gentile world, but Jewish believers didn't need to fear that development. It was really nothing new. Outsiders like Ruth and Rahab had always been included in God's plans because of the faith they displayed.

Too often we try to limit the church to "insiders." We are suspicious of those who didn't grow up in the church, who don't follow all the Christian customs. We make people feel unwelcome if they don't know all the Christian lingo, if they don't seem to be just like us.

But as Ruth demonstrates, people of all backgrounds can learn to put their trust in the Lord, and they can become important parts of God's work in the world.

Ruth fell at his feet and thanked him warmly. "What have I done to deserve such kindness?" she asked. "I am only a foreigner."

RUTH 2:10

PALACE SCANDAL

Bathsheba

2 SAMUEL 11; 1 KINGS 1; MATTHEW 1:6

From the roof of his palace, King David looked out on his city and noticed a beautiful woman bathing—Bathsheba, wife of one of his best soldiers, Uriah. In that moment he wanted her—and he was the king.

Knowing that her husband was off fighting a war, the king sent for Bathsheba and slept with her. She got pregnant. David tried to "fix it" by calling her husband home, thinking Uriah would sleep with Bathsheba. But Uriah refused to enjoy such pleasure while his friends were risking their lives in combat. So David sent Uriah to the front lines with secret orders to the general—*pull back and leave Uriah to die*. And after Bathsheba had a respectable period of mourning, David married her.

The king would have gotten away with it, if not for the pesky prophet Nathan, who announced that God knew all about these sins of adultery and murder. David was deeply—and publicly—repentant. Bathsheba's baby died a week after it was born, but she bore David another son, Solomon, who eventually became Israel's most prosperous king.

Some scholars have suggested that Bathsheba somehow tricked David into these actions, but the biblical text has no hint of that. Bathing was part of the religious purification ritual. From atop his palace, the king saw what he wanted and took it.

Religious groups have been very good at dishing out "scarlet letters" for sexual misconduct, whether deserved or not. Maybe you've seen this in your own church—or in your own life. People can get branded with some big sin or scandal. Some people define *themselves* by some major life error. "How can God forgive me? Just look at what I did!"

Matthew puts Bathsheba in Jesus' ancestry as "widow of Uriah." This phrasing does two things. Since Uriah was a Hittite, it advances Matthew's interest in foreigners. But it also makes us face up to the sordid story of David's adultery. Come to think of it, the other women in Jesus' genealogy are also touched by sexual scandal, whether excusable or not—Tamar seducing her father-in-law, Rahab working as a prostitute, Ruth lying down at the feet of Boaz (which was considered scandalous at the time). Maybe Matthew was subtly responding to charges that Jesus was illegitimate.

By putting together this speckled roster, Matthew might be saying, "Hey, we're *all* stained with sin. That's why we need a Savior like Jesus."

David was the father of Solomon (whose mother was Bathsheba, the widow of Uriah).

MATTHEW 1:6

HA!

Sarah

GENESIS 11–23

"Who me?" "You're crazy." "I could never do that." "I'm not qualified." "I'm too scared." "I'm too young." "I'm too old." You've probably said a combination of those sentences at some point.

In the Bible, Sarah is the ultimate example of someone who had the right to say, "Who me? You're crazy." God had promised he would make her husband into a great nation (see Genesis 12:2). For that to happen, they would need to have children—or at least one—but by her midseventies, Sarah was still childless. She talked Abraham into having a child with one of her servants. That didn't work out so well.

Now she was about ninety, and there were divine messengers telling Abraham that Sarah would have a child within the year. Out of earshot, Sarah laughed to herself because she and Abraham were so worn out and old (see Genesis 18:12).

Of course nothing is ever out of earshot to God, and the messengers asked Abraham, "Why did Sarah laugh? . . . Is anything too hard for the Lord?" (Genesis 18:13-14). And, as most of us would do in that situation, Sarah denied laughing, but God just said, "No, you did laugh" (verse 15).

Can anyone blame Sarah for being skeptical in that situation? Getting pregnant seemed a biological impossibility, but as we see again and again in the Bible, nothing is impossible with God.

We include Sarah in our collection of "women in the Christmas story" because she is an ancestor of Jesus. Matthew did not name her in his genealogy, but he could have. Sarah was not only the genetic mother of all Israelites, but the faith mother of all God's people. "She believed that God would keep his promise," says the book of Hebrews (11:11). Isaac fulfilled that promise in her day. Generations later, it was another babe in arms, Jesus.

And yet Sarah laughed.

As you go into the new year, remember that God can do "impossible" things *through you*. It doesn't matter if you're too old, too young, too fat, too underqualified, or too sinful. He specializes in surprises.

So keep laughing with Sarah all year long as you watch God work in flabbergasting ways.

It was by faith that even Sarah was able to have a child, though she was barren and was too old. She believed that God would keep his promise.

HEBREWS 11:11

NOTES

Works published before 1900 are in the public domain and are not cited here.

April 1: "completely unself-conscious": Dorothy Sayers, "The Human Not-Quite-Human," in On the Contrary: Essays by Men and Women, ed. Martha Rainbolt and Janet Fleetwood (Albany, NY: State University of New York Press, 1984), 13.

May 17: "a joyful end": Translated by Jane Borthwick.

August 23: "chorus came to my mind": Lucy Neeley Adams, "His Name Is Wonderful," www.christianity.com/11562301/.

August 23: "want to express": Andraé Crouch with Nina Ball, Through It All, (Waco, TX: Word Books, 1977), 84.

August 26: "have your way with us": Dan Graves, "Sarah Pollard Didn't Like Her Name," Christianity.com, June 2007, www.christianity.com/church/church-history/timeline/1801-1900/sarah-pollard-didnt-like-her-name-11630530.html.

August 27: "ready to forgive your sins": Mary Ethel Wiess, Singing at Her Work: A Biography of Mrs. C. H. Morris (Kansas City, MO: Lillenas Publishing Company, 1934, 1953), 7.

September 1: "in the South": Richard Wormser, "The Rise and Fall of Jim Crow: Jessie Daniel Ames," PBS, www.pbs.org/wnet/jimcrow/stories_people_ames.html.

September 1: "every person involved": Ibid.

September 2: "urging revolutionary change": Jim Forest, "Servant of God Dorothy Day," The Catholic Worker Movement, www.catholicworker.org/dorothyday/ddbiographytext.cfm?Number=72.

September 4: "nothing to fear": James E. Kiefer, "Gladys Aylward, Missionary to China," Biographical Sketches of Memorable Christians of the Past, http://justus.anglican.org/resources/bio/73.html.

September 5: "and saw Gladys Aylward": Ruth A. Tucker, From Jerusalem to Irian Jaya (Grand Rapids, MI: Zondervan, 1983), 311.

September 7: "no one else can": Miriam Rockness, "About Lilias," Miriam Rockness: Reflections on the Art and Writings of Lilias Trotter, http://ililiastrotter.wordpress.com/about/.

September 7: "and His Righteousness": Miriam Rockness, "About Lilias," Miriam Rockness: Reflections on the Art and Writings of Lilias Trotter, http://ililiastrotter.wordpress.com/about/.

September 7: "hiding the 'best'": Lilias Trotter, Focussed: A Story and a Song, Miriam Rockness: Reflections on the Art and Writings of Lilias Trotter, http://ililiastrotter.wordpress.com/out-of-print-manuscripts/.

September 8: "to help such women": Dan Graves, "Ida Scudder Changed Her Mind," Christianity.com, www.christianity.com/church/church-history/timeline/1801-1900/ida-scudder-changed-her-mind-11630634.html.

September 9: "has to be done": Ibid.

September 10: "you see just love": "The End for Evelyn 'Granny' Brand," Christianity.com, June 27, www.christianity.com/church/church-history/timeline/1901-2000/the-end-for-evelyn-granny-brand-11630839.html.

September 11: "been starving for it": Lisa Beamer, "Ordinary Significance," commencement address, Wheaton College, Illinois, May 8, 2011, video, 15:47, www.wheaton.edu/WETN/All-Media/Graduation?page=3.

September 11: "works in the world": Ibid.

September 11: "by way of your life": Ibid.

September 12: "love without giving": Ann Dunagan, "Inspiring Quotes from Amy Carmichael," *Daring Daughters: Calling Women to World Missions*, April 2, 2013, www.daringdaughters.org/amy-quotes/.

September 17: "and trust the engineer": Skip Heitzig, *The Daily God Book through the Bible: A Bird's-Eye View of the Bible in a Year* (Carol Stream, IL: Tyndale House Publishers, 2010), August 22.

September 19: "my innermost being": Phillip Douglas Chapman, *The Whole Gospel for the Whole World: A History of the Bible School Movement* (Ann Arbor, MI: UMI, 2008), 174.

September 23: "Him as my strength": Rosa Parks, *Quiet Strength: The Faith, the Hope, and the Heart of a Woman Who Changed a Nation* (Grand Rapids, MI: Zondervan, 1994), 54, 16.

September 24: "suffering as I am": William L. Stidger, *The Human Side of Greatness* (New York: Harper & Brothers, 1940), 185.

September 25: "Him in that path": "Daily Catholic Quote from St. Katharine Drexel," *The Integrated Catholic Life*, June 6, 2012, www.integratedcatholiclife.org/tag/st-katharine-drexel/.

September 27: "by what you are": Henrietta C. Mears, *Dream Big: The Henrietta Mears Story* (Ventura, CA: Gospel Light Publications, 1990).

October 1: "for a little love": Mother Teresa, *A Simple Path*, compiled by Lucinda Verdey (New York: Random House, 1995), 79.

October 2: "souls of great silence": Mother Teresa, *In the Heart of the World: Thoughts, Stories & Prayers* (Novato, CA: New World Library, 1997), 19.

October 4: "to that child": Ruth Bell Graham, *Blessings for a Mother's Day: The Treasures of Motherhood* (Nashville, TN: W. Publishing Group, 2001), Encouragement.

October 6: "prove our faith vain": Elisabeth Elliot, *These Strange Ashes* (Grand Rapids, MI: Revell, 1998), 125.

October 10: "how disagreeable it seems": Catherine Marshall, *Christy* (New York: Avon Books, 1967), 116.

November 3: "could not be solved": Ken Dychtwald, "Remembering Maggie Kuhn: Gray Panthers Founder on the 5 Myths of Aging," *HuffPost 50*, May 31, 2012, www.huffingtonpost.com/ken-dychtwald/the-myths-of-aging_b_1556481.html.

November 4: "make the meadows gay": *The Autobiography of Saint Thérèse of Lisieux: The Story of a Soul*, trans. John Beevers (New York: Image Books, 1957), 2.

November 4: "He glances down": Ibid.

November 8: "meaning of forgiveness": Patricia St. John, *Patricia St. John Tells Her Own Story* (Shoals, IN: Kingsley Press, 1993), 68.

November 8: "a bad children's story": C. S. Lewis, "On the Ways of Writing for Children," in *On Stories: And Other Essays on Literature* (New York: Harcourt, Inc., 1982), 33.

November 9: "mentioned with praise": Maria Woodworth-Etter, *Marvels and Miracles* (1922), 19.

November 10: "living in poverty": Eva Burrows, "Why Help the Poor?" *The Salvation Army*, www.salvationist.org/poverty.nsf/vw_sublinks/92987C1D835C28D880256AB90049C235?openDocument.

November 15: "was their witness": Nancy Hardesty, *Great Women of Faith: The Strength and Influence of Christian Women* (Grand Rapids, MI: Baker Book House, 1980), 132.

November 16: "crown at His feet": Arthur T. Pierson, "Seed Thoughts and Gold Nuggets for Public Speakers," in *The Homiletic Review*, vol. 45, ed. I. K. Funk and D. S. Gregory (New York: Funk and Wagnalls, 1903), 533.

November 20: "your peace and welfare": "The Love of John and Mary Newton," Christianity.com, www.christianity.com/church/church-history/timeline/1701-1800/the-love-of-john-and-mary-newton-11630257.html.

November 20: "has preserved our affections": Ibid.

November 21: "of the great need": Ernest Gordon, *A Book of Protestant Saints* (Chicago: Moody Press, 1946), 86.

November 22: "a month before": Anne Galbraith Piggot, *Pen Pictures from India* (London: The Berean Press, 1928), 54.

November 22: "me for something": Ibid., 55.

November 24: "as well as delight": I. D. Stewart, *The History of the Freewill Baptists: For Half a Century* (Dover: Freewill Baptist Printing Establishment, 1862), 338.

November 26: "in our natures": Jon Mertz, "With Gratitude to Sarah Hale, We Have Thanksgiving," *Thin Difference*, November 19, 2012, www.thindifference.com/2012/11/19/with-gratitude -to-sarah-hale-we-have-thanksgiving/.

November 28: "nursing mothers there": Lydia Sexton, *Autobiography of Lydia Sexton* (United Brethren Publishing House, 1882), 201.

November 29: "has left us": Eva Lous, "Karen Jeppe: Denmark's First Peace Philosopher," The Danish Peace Academy, www.fredsakademiet.dk/library/ukjeppe.htm.

November 30: "vain among them": Anna Harriette Leonowens, *The English Governess at the Siamese Court: Being Recollections of Six Years in the Royal Palace at Bankok* (Cambridge: University Press, 1870), 282.

December 2: "undreamed of before": "Annie Armstrong," *Maryland Women's Hall of Fame*, http://msa .maryland.gov/msa/educ/exhibits/womenshall/html/armstrong.html.

December 3: "us for a cross": Joy Davidman, *Out of My Bone: The Letters of Joy Davidman* (Grand Rapids, MI: Eerdmans, 2009), 28.

December 5: "needed her sympathy": Z. K. Matthews, "Mrs. Charlotte M. Maxeke: Defender of Women's Rights," *Imvo Zabantsundu*, September 9, 1961, http://pzacad.pitzer.edu/nam/newafrre /writers/maxeke/maxekeS.htm.

December 5: "but against her sex": A. B. Xuma, *Charlotte Manye (Mrs. Maxeke): "What an Educated African Girl Can Do"* (Women's Parent Mite Missionary Society, 1930).

December 5: "God for Charlotte": Ibid.

December 6: "life of Wales": Jessie Penn-Lewis, "Mini-Bio," *Jessie Penn-Lewis*, www.jessiepenn lewis.com/jessie-penn-louis-collectio/bio-jpl.html.

December 6: "their Master's work": Ibid.

December 6: "I was a woman": Felicity Dale, "Heroines of the Faith: Jessie Penn-Lewis," *Simply Church: A House Church Perspective*, June 3, 2013, http://simplychurch.com/heroines-of-the-faith-jessie-penn -lewis/.

December 7: "fuel there to burn": Mary Peckham, "The Lewis Revival (1950)," Revivals.org, www.revivals.org/docs/article-detail.html?id=41.

December 8: "abiding, deep impression": *Moravian Church, Offices of Worship and Hymns (with Tunes)* (Bethlehem, PA: Moravian Publication Office, 1902), 92.

December 10: "parties, sects and denominations": Almond H. Davis and Junia Smith Mowry, *The Female Preacher, Or Memoir of Salome Lincoln, Afterwards the Wife of Elder Junia S. Mowry* (Boston: A. B. Kidder, 1843), 92.

December 11: "give me grace. Amen": Rachel Hickson, *Eat the Word, Speak the Word: Exercising a Bible- Based Prophetic Ministry* (Oxford: Monarch Books, 2010), 18.

December 12: "since I married you": Jerome Pohlen, *Progressive Nation: A Travel Guide with 400+ Left Turns and Inspiring Landmarks* (Chicago: Chicago Review Press, Inc., 2008), 292.

December 12: "what I could": Fran Grace, *Carry A. Nation: Retelling the Life* (Bloomington, IN: Indiana University Press, 2001), 274.

December 14: "better for its influence": Jone Johnson Lewis, "Dorothea Dix Quotes," About.com Women's History, http://womenshistory.about.com/od/quotes/a/dorothea_dix.htm.

December 16: "on the subject": Dennis M. Swanson, "The Millennial Position of Spurgeon," in *The Master's Perspective on Biblical Prophecy*, ed. Richard Mayhue and Robert L. Thomas (Grand Rapids, MI: Kregel Publications, 2002), 242.

December 16: "Thy holy nativity," "heart for Thee": Emily E. Elliott, "Thou Didst Leave Thy Throne," Cyberhymnal.org, http://cyberhymnal.org/htm/t/h/o/thoudltt.htm.

December 17: "snow on snow": Christina Rossetti, "In the Bleak Midwinter," Cyberhymnal.org, http://cyberhymnal.org/htm/i/n/intbleak.htm.

A NOTE ON THE RESEARCH

This is a devotional book, not an academic study, and so we didn't want to burden you with lots of footnotes. Still, we did careful research on our subjects, pulling dusty tomes from our shelves and scouring the Internet for new sources. Historical accuracy is important to us, and so we've tried to indicate when we've shared legends or theories rather than verifiable fact. Often we have included quotations from the subjects themselves, digging back into their own writings or accounts from their own time. It would be unwieldy to cite every source we used, but here is a sampling of general sources we kept going back to.

BOOKS

Bettenson, Henry, ed. *Documents of the Christian Church*. Oxford UniversityPress, 1963.

Curtis, A. Kenneth, J. Stephen Lang, and Randy Petersen. *The 100 Most Important Events in Christian History*. Revell, 1991.

Deen, Edith. *Great Women of the Christian Faith*. Harper & Row Publishers, 1959.

Douglas, J. D., ed. *Twentieth-Century Dictionary of Christian Biography*. Baker, 1995.

Douglas, J. D. and Philip W. Comfort. *Who's Who in Christian History*. Tyndale House, 1992.

Farmer, David Albert and Edwina Hunter. *And Blessed Is She: Sermons by Women*. Judson Press, 1994.

Foster, Richard J. and Emilie Griffin. *Spiritual Classics: Selected Readings on the Twelve Spiritual Disciplines*. HarperCollins, 2000.

Gordon, Ernest. *A Book of Protestant Saints*. Moody Bible Institute, 1946.

Hardesty, Nancy. *Great Women of Faith*. Baker, 1980.

Jenkins, Philip. *The Lost History of Christianity*. HarperOne, 2008.

Johnson, Jewell. *The Top 100 Women of the Christian Faith*. Barbour Publishing, Inc., 2009.

Kerr, Hugh T. and John M. Mulder. *Conversions*. Eerdmans, 1983.

Kim, Eunjoo Mary. *Women Preaching: Theology and Practice through the Ages*. Pilgrim Press, 2004.

Partner, Daniel. *Quiknotes: Great Women of Faith*. Tyndale House, 2000.

Petersen, William J. and Ardythe Petersen. *The Complete Book of Hymns*. Tyndale House, 2006.

Petersen, William J. and Randy Petersen. *The One Year Great Songs of Faith*. Tyndale House, 1995.

Petersen, William J. and Randy Petersen. *100 Bible Verses that Changed the World*. Revell, 2001.

Petersen, William J. *25 Surprising Marriages: How Great Christians Struggled to Make It Work*. Timothy Press, 1997.

Smith, Jane Stuart and Betty Carlson. *Favorite Women Hymn Writers*. Crossway, 1990.

Thiessen, John Caldwell. *A Survey of World Missions*. Inter-Varsity Press, 1955.

Tucker, Ruth A. and Walter Liefeld. *Daughters of the Church*. Zondervan, 2010.

Wallace, Archer. *Mothers of Famous Men*. Richard R. Smith, Inc., 1931.

PERIODICALS

Christian History Magazine, multiple issues, published by Christian History Institute, Worcester, PA, and Christianity Today, Inc., Carol Stream, IL.

Glimpses, multiple issues, published by Christian History Institute, Worcester, PA.

WEBSITES

www.catholic.org/saints/

vw.christianhistoryinstitute.org

.christianity.com

hristianitytoday.com

ngdaughters.org

www.greatwomen.org

www.librarycompany.org/women/portraits_religion/intro.htm

www.newadvent.org

www.theologyforgirls.com

http://womenofchristianity.com